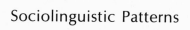

Sociolinguistic Patterns

# Sociolinguistic Patterns

WILLIAM LABOV

University of Pennsylvania Press

Philadelphia

Library of Congress Catalog Card Number 72-80375
ISBN (clothbound edition) 0-8122-7657-4
ISBN (paperbound edition) 0-8122-1040-9
Printed in the United States of America

For Uriel Weinreich

# CONTENTS

# LIST OF FIGURES

# LIST OF TABLES

# INTRODUCTION

I have resisted the term *sociolinguistics* for many years, since it implies that there can be a successful linguistic theory or practice which is not social. When I first published the studies of Martha's Vineyard and New York City that form the basis of the first part of this book, it seemed necessary to make that point again and again. In spite of a considerable amount of sociolinguistic activity, a socially realistic linguistics seemed a remote prospect in the 1960's. The great majority of linguists had resolutely turned to the contemplation of their own idiolects. We have not yet emerged from the shadow of our intuitions, but it no longer seems necessary to argue about what is or is not linguistics. There is a growing realization that the basis of intersubjective knowledge in linguistics must be found in speech—language as it is used in everyday life by members of the social order, that vehicle of communication in which they argue with their wives, joke with their friends, and deceive their enemies.

When I first entered linguistics as a student, in 1961, it was my intention to gather data from the secular world. The early projects that I constructed were "essays in experimental linguistics," carried out in ordinary social settings. My aim was to avoid the inevitable obscurity of texts, the self-consciousness of formal elicitations, and the self-deception of introspection. A decade of work outside the university as an industrial chemist had convinced me that the everyday world was stubborn but consistently so, baffling at the outset but rewarding in the long run for those who held to its rational character. A simple review of the literature might have convinced me that such empirical principles had no place in linguistics: there were many ideological barriers to the study of language in everyday life. First, Saussure had enunciated the principle that structural systems of the present and historical changes of the past had to be studied in isolation (1949:124). That principle had been consistently eroded by Martinet (1955) and others who found structure in past changes, but little progress had been made in locating change in present structures. The second ideological barrier explicitly asserted that sound change could not in principle be directly observed. Bloomfield defended the regularity of sound change against the irregular evidence of the present by declaring (1933:364) that any fluctuations we might observe would only be cases of dialect borrowing. Next Hockett observed that while sound change was too slow to be observed, structural change was too fast (1958:457). The empirical study of linguistic change was thus removed from the program of 20th-century linguistics.

A third restriction was perhaps the most important: free variation could not in principle be constrained. The basic postulate of linguistics (Bloomfield 1933:76) declared that some utterances were the same. Conversely, these were in free variation, and whether or not one or the other occurred at a particular time was taken to be linguistically insignificant. Relations of *more* or *less* were therefore ruled out of linguistic thinking; a form or a rule could only occur always, optionally, or never. The internal structure of variation was therefore removed from linguistic studies and with it, the study of change in progress.

It was also held that feelings about language were inaccessible and outside of the linguist's scope (Bloch and Trager 1942). The social evaluation of linguistic variants was therefore excluded from consideration. This is merely one aspect of the more general claim that the linguist should not use nonlinguistic data to explain linguistic change (see the first section of Ch. 9). Throughout these discussions, we see many references to what the linguist can or cannot do *as a linguist*.

I might indeed have disregarded all these restrictions by the force of my own inclination and resistance to authority. But I was fortunate to encounter at Columbia University a teacher not much older than myself, whose own insight, imagination, and creative force had long since bypassed these restrictions. It is impossible for me to estimate the contribution of Uriel Weinreich to the studies reported here. I learned from him in courses on syntax, semantics, dialectology, and the history of linguistics; he supervised the work on Martha's Vineyard (Ch. 1) which was my Master's essay, and the study of New York City (Chs. 2–6) which was my dissertation; yet in all this he did not put forward his own view or direct suggestion about which way to turn. But with caution, restraint, and example, he helped to direct my own projects into the most profitable channels. Weinreich had an extraordinary sense of direction in linguistics; he rarely made a misstep in his own research projects, and we all profited by his insight. I have recently had the opportunity to read some of Weinreich's unpublished sketches and projects for the study of multilingualism and social variation in the speech community; I found that his thinking had anticipated my own by many years and undoubtedly played a larger part in the results given here than might appear in the overt references. More than anything else, I benefitted from Weinreich's calm conviction that we were moving in the direction that a rational and realistic linguistics must inevitably follow.

In 1966, Weinreich proposed to Marvin Herzog and myself that we write a joint paper on "Empirical Foundations for a Theory of Language Change" for a conference at the University of Texas. As we delivered it, this paper embodied the results of my own work in New York and Martha's Vineyard, Herzog's findings on the dialectology of Yiddish in Northern Poland, and Weinreich's overall insight that created the Language and Culture Atlas of Ashkenazic Jewry. This was set in a larger view of the history of linguistics that was entirely the product of Weinreich's scholarship. In the spring of 1967, when Weinreich realized that he had only a short time to live, he turned to the final revision of this paper with great energy. In the last two weeks of his life, Weinreich recast the introduction to this paper in a way that captures clearly his overall view of the nature of language and its relation to society. It states the major theme of this volume better than any passage of my own:

   The facts of heterogeneity have not so far jibed well with the structural approach to language . . . for the more linguists became impressed with the existence of structure of language, and the more they bolstered this observation with deductive arguments about the functional advantages of structure, the more mysterious became the transition of a language from state to state. After all, if a language has to be structured in order to function efficiently, how do people continue to talk while the language changes, that is, while it passes through periods of lessened systematicity? . . . The solution, we will argue, lies in the direction of breaking down the identification of structuredness with homogeneity. The key to a rational conception of language change—indeed, of language itself—is the possibility of describing orderly differentiation in a language serving a community. We will argue that nativelike command of heterogeneous structures is not a matter of multidialectalism or "mere" performance, but is part of unilingual linguistic competence. One of the corollaries of our approach is that in a language serving a complex (i.e., real) community, it is *absence* of structured heterogeneity that would be dysfunctional. [Weinreich, Labov, and Herzog 1968:100–101]

The first six chapters of this book are reports of particular studies which form part of the evidence for the view which Weinreich expressed and the last three continue the argument in a broader framework. Some chapters have appeared previously, but are here considerably revised. Ch. 3 and 6 have not appeared in print before, although they are based on material reported in part in Labov 1966. Chs. 2–6 cover a large part of the methods and findings of *The Social Stratification of English in New York City* (Labov 1966a); each is organized about a particular problem which was attacked in this work. Chs. 7–9 are synthetic studies which combine these findings with others to project a larger view of the nature of language structure and language change. Chapter 7, "On the mechanism of linguistic change," uses the Martha's Vineyard and New York findings in an overall projection for the course of change which preceded the statement of "Empirical Foundations." Ch. 8, "The study of language in its social context" is a general survey of the problems, findings, and prospects of a socially realistic linguistics. It may be considered a short version of a more general text on "Secular Linguistics," addressed to those who are interested in entering the speech community to find a solid empirical base for linguistic theory. This chapter draws heavily upon research on the black English vernacular which is reported in greater detail in Chs. 1–4 in *Language in the Inner City* (1972) and in the two-volume research report on Cooperative Research Project 3288 (Labov, Cohen, Robins, and Lewis 1968). This work explores more deeply than Chs. 2–6 the variation which is found within a rule schema, and develops the formal treatment of variable rules. Readers who would like to pursue the linguistic issues raised in Ch. 8 will find a more detailed presentation in Chs. 3 and 4 of *Language in the Inner City,* which are concerned, respectively, with contraction and deletion of the copula and negative attraction and concord. Ch. 3 of that book presents the development of variable rules in much greater detail than was possible in Ch. 8, incorporating the revisions of the Cedergren-Sankoff model.

Ch. 9 forms a companion section to Ch. 8, examining the diachronic aspects of the synchronic matters presented there. Both
Chs. 8 and 9 draw heavily upon the findings of other investigators,
and the further developments that proceeded from the work reported in Chs. 1–6 are represented there. Together, Chs. 8 and 9
form a short text in sociolinguistic problems and methods, as well
as the sociolinguistic approach to linguistic theory, and provide a
framework on which sociolinguistic courses have been organized.

I am indebted to many colleagues for help and critical improve-
ments in the work reported here. Michael Kac carried out many of
the Lower East Side interviews which provide the data for Chs. 3–6.
This secondary survey was carried out with the help of the research department of Mobilization for Youth; I am indebted to the
research director, Wyatt Jones, for his assistance at many points.
The survey itself benefited greatly from the instruction and advice
of Herbert Hyman of Columbia University. The work on the black
English vernacular referred to in Ch. 8 was the product of a joint
effort. The analysis and theoretical insights provided by Paul Cohen
made important contributions to the conclusions presented there,
and the field work of Clarence Robins and John Lewis was the
basis of everything that was accomplished.

The general analysis of variation in Ch. 8 has benefitted from
many exchanges with C.-J. Bailey. The formal interpretation of
variable rules included many contributions of Joshua Waletzky; in
the present revised formulation, my indebtedness to Henrietta
Cedergren and David Sankoff is acknowledged at many points. Their
quantitative contribution to the treatment of variable constraints
seems to me a major advance which will strongly influence the
future direction of this field.

At many critical points in this research and analysis, I received
important help from my wife, Teresa, who has deepened my own
understanding of the structure of the social orders that I have encountered.

During the first stages in the preparation of this book, I was the
recipient of a fellowship from the Guggenheim Foundation, whose
help I would like to acknowledge here with thanks.

During the year 1971–72, I served as Research Professor with the
Center for Urban Enthnography, and I am deeply indebted to the
Center for the support which made it possible to assemble this
volume, along with *Language in the Inner City*. The original im-

petus to put these studies together into a single volume and organize them into a single coherent framework came from Erving Goffman, whose help and encouragement is acknowledged with many thanks.

Throughout these pages, it will be obvious that my heaviest indebtedness must be toward the many speakers of English who have invited me into their homes, shared their porches, street corners and park benches with me, and turned aside from other business to talk, transforming their own experience into language for my benefit. Only a small part of what I have learned from them can be found here. But I hope that this work does reflect the infinite variety of every day life, and the great satisfaction of encountering and recording the users of language. Those who have tapped the real resources of the speech community find that field work is a rich pursuit that is never exhausted. I have found that there is no greater pleasure than to travel as a privileged stranger to all parts of the world, to be received with kindness and courtesy by men and women everywhere, and to share their knowledge and experience with them as it reappears in their language. The linguist who enters that world can only conclude that man is the right inheritor of the incredibly complex structure which we are now trying to analyze and understand.

# 1 | The Social Motivation of a Sound Change

THE work which is reported in this chapter concerns the direct observation of a sound change in the context of the community life from which it stems.[1] The change is a shift in the phonetic position of the first elements of the diphthongs /ay/ and /aw/, and the community is the island of Martha's Vineyard, Massachusetts. By studying the frequency and distribution of phonetic variants of /ay/ and /aw/ in the several regions, age levels, occupational and ethnic groups within the island, it will be possible to reconstruct the recent history of this sound change; by correlating the complex linguistic pattern with parallel differences in social structure, it will be possible to isolate the social factors which bear directly upon the linguistic process. It is hoped that the results of this procedure will contribute to our general understanding of the mechanism of linguistic change.

The problem of explaining language change seems to resolve itself into three separate problems: the origin of linguistic variations; the spread and propagation of linguistic changes; and the regularity of linguistic change. The model which underlies this three-way division requires as a starting point a variation in one or several words in the speech of one or two individuals.[2] These variations may be induced by the processes of assimilation or differentiation, by analogy, borrowing, fusion, contamination, random variation, or any number of processes in which the language system interacts with

---

1. First published in Word, 19: 273–309 (1963). An abbreviated version was given at the 37th Annual Meeting of the Linguistic Society of America in New York City on December 29, 1962.
2. See Sturtevant 1947: Ch. 8: "Why are Phonetic Laws Regular?"

the physiological or psychological characteristics of the individual. Most such variations occur only once, and are extinguished as quickly as they arise. However, a few recur, and, in a second stage, they may be imitated more or less widely, and may spread to the point where the new forms are in contrast with the older forms along a wide front. Finally, at some later stage, one or the other of the two forms usually triumphs, and regularity is achieved.

Whereas for the first stage we are often overwhelmed with an excess of possible explanations, we have quite the reverse situation in attempting to account for the propagation and regularity of linguistic changes. A number of earlier theories which proposed general psychological, physiological or even climatic determinants have been discarded for some time.[3] The contribution of internal, structural forces to the effective spread of linguistic changes, as outlined by Martinet (1955),[4] must naturally be of primary concern to any linguist who is investigating these processes of propagation and regularization. However, an account of structural pressures can hardly tell the whole story. Not all changes are highly structured, and no change takes place in a social vacuum. Even the most systematic chain shift occurs with a specificity of time and place that demands an explanation.

Widely divergent ideas appear to exist as to what comprises an explanation of the mechanism of change. The usual diachronic procedure, as followed in palaeontology or geology, is to explore the mechanism of change between states by searching for data on intermediate states. It follows that we come closer and closer to an accurate depiction of the mechanism of change as the interval between the two states we are studying becomes smaller and smaller. This is certainly the method followed by such historical linguists as Jespersen, Kökeritz, and Wyld, and it is the motivation behind their extensive searches for historical detail. On the other hand, a viewpoint which favors the abstract manipulation of data from widely separated states has been propounded by M. Halle (1962); explicit defense of a similar attitude may be found in H. Pilch's (1955)

3. A number of these theories are reviewed in Sommerfelt 1930.
4. The empirical confirmation of many of Martinet's ideas to be found in Moulton's investigation of Swiss German dialects has provided strong motivation for some of the interpretations in the present essay. In particular, see Moulton 1962.

study of the vowel systems of Shakespeare, Noah Webster, and present-day America. Neither Halle nor Pilch distinguish the three aspects of change outlined above.

It would seem that the historical approach is more appropriate to an empirical science concerned with change, even over a narrow time span, as this approach leads to statements which are increasingly subject to confirmation or disconfirmation. At the same time, such a close view of historical change makes us increasingly sceptical of the value of limitations on the kinds of data which may be considered: as, for instance, that the linguist explain linguistic events only by other linguistic events. One would expect that the application of structural linguistics to diachronic problems would lead to the enrichment of the data, rather than the impoverishment of it.[5]

The point of view of the present study is that one cannot understand the development of a language change apart from the social life of the community in which it occurs. Or to put it another way, social pressures are continually operating upon language, not from some remote point in the past, but as an immanent social force acting in the living present.

Sturtevant (1947:74–84) has outlined a concise theory of the spread and consolidation of language changes which consistently views this process in its social dimension. One sentence in particular will serve as an excellent theme for this investigation:

Before a phoneme can spread from word to word . . . it is necessary that one of the two rivals shall acquire some sort of prestige.[6]

It is hoped that the study of the particular case under discussion will lend support to this general view of the role of social interaction in linguistic change.

---

5. For a parallel criticism of restrictions on the data imposed by Bloomfieldian linguistics, see W. Diver's review of W. P. Lehmann's *Historical Linguistics*, in *Word*, 19:100–105 (1963).

6. See also H. Hoenigswald's remarks in "Are There Universals of Linguistic Change?" in Greenberg, ed., 1963, fn. 8: "Sound changes can apparently not be entirely predicted from internal systemic stresses and strains, nor can they be explained as the effect of scatter around a target or norm; they have direction and are in that sense specific, much like other happenings in history."

### The Island of Martha's Vineyard

The island of Martha's Vineyard, Dukes County, Massachusetts, was chosen as a laboratory for an initial investigation of social patterns in linguistic change.[7] Martha's Vineyard has the advantage of being a self-contained unit, separated from the mainland by a good three miles of the Atlantic Ocean. At the same time, the Vineyard has enough social and geographic complexity to provide ample room for differentiation of linguistic behavior. We are also fortunate in having the records of the *Linguistic Atlas of New England* (henceforth abbreviated LANE) as a background for the investigation.[8] It is over thirty years since Guy Lowman visited Martha's Vineyard; his interviews with four members of the old families of the island give us a firm base from which to proceed, and a time depth of one full generation which adds considerably to the solidity of the conclusions which can be drawn.

Fig. 1.1 shows the general outlines of Martha's Vineyard, and Table 1.1 gives the population figures from the 1960 Census. The island is divided into two parts by an informal, but universally used distinction between *up-island* and *down-island*. *Down-island* is the region of the three small towns where almost three-fourths of the permanent population live. *Up-island* is strictly rural, with a few villages, farms, isolated summer homes, salt ponds and marshes, and a large central area of uninhabited pine barrens.

As we travel up-island from Vineyard Haven, we come first to the town of West Tisbury, which contains some of the most beautiful farms and fields of the island, now largely untilled and ungrazed. At Chilmark, the ground rises to a series of rolling hills which look out to the Atlantic on one side, and to Vineyard Sound on the other. Chilmark's salt pond is permanently open to the Sound through a narrow channel, and so serves as a permanent harbor for the dozen fishermen who still operate from the docks of the village of Menemsha in Chilmark. Finally, at the southwest corner of the island,

---

7. For further details on the social and economic background of Martha's Vineyard, see my 1962 Columbia University Master's Essay, "The Social History of a Sound Change on the Island of Martha's Vineyard, Massachusetts," written under the direction of Professor Uriel Weinreich.

8. Kurath et al. 1941. Background information on the informants is to be found in Kurath 1939.

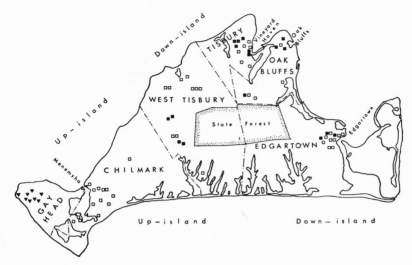

Fig. 1.1. Location of the 69 informants on Martha's Vineyard.
Ethnic origin is indicated as follows: ☐ English, ■ Portuguese,
▼ Indian. Symbols placed side by side indicate members of the
same family.

TABLE 1.1.
POPULATION OF MARTHA'S VINEYARD

| | |
|---|---|
| *Down-island* [*towns*] | 3,846 |
| Edgartown | 1,118 |
| Oak Bluffs | 1,027 |
| Vineyard Haven | 1,701 |
| *Up-island* [*rural*] | 1,717 |
| Edgartown | 256 |
| Oak Bluffs | 292 |
| Tisbury | 468 |
| West Tisbury | 360 |
| Chilmark | 238 |
| Gay Head | 103 |
| Total | 5,563 |

Source: From U.S. Bureau of the Census, *U.S.
Census of Population: 1960. Number of Inhab-
itants. Massachusetts.* Final Report PC(1)—23A
(Washington, D.C.: GPO, 1962), Table 7, p. 23-11.

there is the promontory of Gay Head, and the houses of the 103 Indians who represent the original inhabitants of Martha's Vineyard.

The 6,000 native Vineyarders fall into four ethnic groups which are essentially endogamous. First, there are the descendants of the old families of English stock, who first settled the island in the 17th and 18th centuries: the Mayhews, Nortons, Hancocks, Allens, Tiltons, Vincents, Wests, Pooles—all closely related after ten generations of intermarriage. Secondly, there is a large group of Portuguese descent, immigrants from the Azores, Madeira, and the Cape Verde Islands. There are Portuguese all along the southeastern New England coast, but the Vineyard has the largest percentage of any Massachusetts county. In 1960, 11 percent of the population was of first- or second-generation Portuguese origin; with the third- and fourth-generation Portuguese, the total would probably come close to 20 percent.[9]

The third ethnic group is the Indian remnant at Gay Head. The fourth is the miscellaneous group of various origins: English, French Canadian, Irish, German, Polish. Though the sum total of this residual group is almost 15 percent, it is not a coherent social force, and we will not consider it further in this paper.[10]

Another group which will not be considered directly is the very large number of summer residents, some 42,000, who flood the island in June and July of every year. This tide of *summer people* has had relatively little direct influence on the speech of the Vineyard, although the constant pressure from this direction, and the growing dependence of the island upon a vacation economy, has had powerful indirect effects upon the language changes which we will consider.

The Vineyard is best known to linguists as an important relic area of American English: an island of r-pronouncers in a sea of r-lessness. With a 320-year history of continuous settlement, and a long record of resistance to Boston ways and manners, the island has preserved many archaic traits which were probably typical of southeastern

9. From U.S. Bureau of the Census, *U.S. Census of Population: 1960. General Social and Economic Characteristics. Massachusetts.* Final Report PC(1)—23c (Washington, D.C.: Government Printing Office, 1962), Table 89, p. 23–260.

10. There is a sizeable number of retired mainlanders living on the Vineyard as year-round residents. While they are included in the population total, they do not form a part of the social fabric we are considering, and none of the informants is drawn from this group.

New England before 1800. The most striking feature, still strongly entrenched, is the retention of final and preconsonantal /r/.[11] New England short /o/ is still well represented among the older speakers. Exploratory studies of the Vineyard in 1961 showed that most of the special traits of the island speech shown on the LANE maps may still be found among traditional speakers from 50 to 95 years old.

Lexical survivals of 17th-century English are even clearer indications of the archaic nature of the Vineyard tradition. We find *bannock,* for a fried cake of corn meal, *studdled* for 'dirty, roiled' water, in addition to such items as *tempest* and *buttry* listed in the LANE. Perhaps the most dramatic evidence of the fact that the Vineyard represents an underlying stratum is the presence of *belly-gut,* for a face-down sled ride. In LANE records, this form is shown on the Vineyard and in western New England; in the intervening area, it has been overlaid by three successive layers—*belly-bump, belly-flop,* and currently, no word at all.[12]

As interesting as the structure of Martha's Vineyard English may be, it is not the purpose here to contrast one static system with another. We would like to understand the internal structure of Vineyard English, including the systematic differences which now exist and the changes now taking place within the island. For this purpose, we will select for study a linguistic feature with the widest possible range of variation and the most complex pattern of distribution characteristic of Martha's Vineyard.

### Selection of the Linguistic Variable

It would be appropriate to ask at this point what are the most useful properties of a linguistic variable to serve as the focus for

11. On the LANE maps, we find that Guy Lowman regularly recorded the up-island /r/ as [ɚ] in [wɐlɚ, haɚd, baɚn], and down-island /r/ as [ə] in the same positions. Essentially the same pattern is to be found among the older speakers today, though not with the regularity that Lowman noted. It is possible that this treatment of /r/ was in fact intended as a broad transcription, for the LANE was much more concerned with vowels than consonants.

12. See Kurath 1949, Fig. 162. *Belly-flop* (and the corresponding lexical item in other regions) has generally shifted for the younger generation to denote a flat dive into the water. Coasting is now a less important sport, and its terminology is appropriately impoverished. The lexical data derived from my own study of Martha's Vineyard is analyzed in detail in W. Labov, "The Recent History of Some Dialect Markers in Martha's Vineyard, Massachusetts," in Davis 1972.

the study of a speech community. First, we want an item that is frequent, which occurs so often in the course of undirected natural conversation that its behavior can be charted from unstructured contexts and brief interviews. Secondly, it should be structural: the more the item is integrated into a larger system of functioning units, the greater will be the intrinsic linguistic interest of our study. Third, the distribution of the feature should be highly stratified: that is, our preliminary explorations should suggest an asymmetric distribution over a wide range of age levels or other ordered strata of society.

There are a few contradictory criteria, which pull us in different directions. On the one hand, we would like the feature to be salient, for us as well as for the speaker, in order to study the direct relations of social attitudes and language behavior. But on the other hand, we value immunity from conscious distortion, which greatly simplifies the problem of reliability of the data.[13]

In the exploratory interviews conducted on the Vineyard in 1961, many structural changes were noted that were plainly parallel to changes taking place on the mainland under the influence of the standard Southeast New England pattern. Changes in phonemic inventory were found: New England short /o/ is rapidly disappearing; the two low back vowels, /ɑ/ and /ɔ/ are merging. Important changes in phonemic distribution are occurring: the /or∼ɔr/ distinction is disappearing: initial /hw/ is giving way to /h/.[14] Shifts in structured lexical systems, all in the direction of regional standards, can be traced. Archaic syntactic features are disappearing. Yet as interesting as these changes may be, there is no reason to think that their distribution will follow a pattern peculiar to the Vineyard.

In the case of postvocalic /r/, however, we do have a linguistic variable defined by the geographical limits of the island, which follows a social pattern idiosyncratic to Martha's Vineyard. In some island areas, retroflexion is increasing, and in others, decreasing; as

13. Many ingenious devices are needed to detect and eliminate deceit on the part of metropolitan informants, whether intended or not. On Martha's Vineyard, this is much less of a problem, but the effects of the interview situation are evident in the careful style of some informants.

14. The disappearance of New England short /o/ follows the pattern described in Avis (1961). Exploratory interviews at other points in southeastern New England (Woods Hole, Falmouth, New Bedford, Fall River, Providence, Stonington) indicate that the loss of the /or∼ɔr/ and /hw-∼w-/ distinctions is parallel to that on Martha's Vineyard.

we will note later, the social implications of this fact can not be missed. The variations in /r/ are frequent, salient, and involve far-reaching structural consequences for the entire vowel system.

However, the preliminary exploration of the Vineyard indicated that another variable might be even more interesting: differences in the height of the first element of the diphthongs /ay/ and /aw/. Instead of the common southeast New England standard [aɪ] and [aʊ], one frequently hears on Martha's Vineyard [ɐɪ] and [ɐʊ], or even [əɪ] and [əʊ]. This feature of centralized diphthongs[15] is salient for the linguist, but not for most speakers; it is apparently quite immune to conscious distortion, as the native Vineyarders are not aware of it, nor are they able to control it consciously. As far as structure is concerned, we cannot neglect the structural parallelism of /ay/ and /aw/; on the other hand these diphthongs are marked by great structural freedom in the range of allophones permitted by the system. These are strictly subphonemic differences. Since there are no other up-gliding diphthongs with either low or central first elements in this system, it is not likely that continued raising, or even fronting or backing, would result in confusion with any other phoneme.

The property of this feature of centralization which makes it appear exceptionally attractive, even on first glance, is the indication of a complex and subtle pattern of stratification. This very complexity proves to be rewarding: for when the centralizing tendency is charted in the habits of many speakers, and the influence of the phonetic, prosodic, and stylistic environment is accounted for, there remains a large area of variation. Instead of calling this "free" or "sporadic" variation, and abandoning the field, we will pursue the matter further, using every available clue to discover the pattern which governs the distribution of centralized diphthongs.

The problem becomes all the more significant when it becomes apparent that the present trend on Martha's Vineyard runs counter to the long-range movement of these diphthongs over the past two hundred years. And while this sound change is not likely to become

---

15. The terms centralized diphthongs, centralization, and degree of centralization will be used throughout this study to refer to the various forms of the diphthongs /ay/ and /aw/ with first elements higher than [a]. It is not intended that the terms themselves should imply any process or direction of change, except when used with explicit statements to that effect.

a phonemic change in the foreseeable future, it operates in an area where far-reaching phonemic shifts have taken place in the past. It is, in effect, the unstable residue of the Great Vowel Shift.

### The History of Centralized Diphthongs

It seems generally agreed that the first element of the diphthong /ay/ was a mid-central vowel in 16th- and 17th-century English (Jespersen 1927:234; Kökeritz 1953:216).[16] We may assume that when Thomas Mayhew first took possession of his newly purchased property of Martha's Vineyard in 1642, he brought with him the pronunciation [əɪ] in *right, pride, wine* and *wife.* The later history of this vowel in America indicates that [əɪ] continued to be the favored form well into the 19th century.[17]

When we examine the records of the LANE, we find that centralized /ay/ was a healthy survivor in the speech of the Atlas informants.[18] We find it scattered throughout the rural areas of New England, and strongly entrenched in the Genesee Valley of western New York. It had disappeared completely from the Midland, but was quite regular—before voiceless consonants—in both the Upper and Lower South. This differential effect of voiceless and voiced following consonants was only a directing influence in the North, but stood as a regular phonetic rule in the South. On Martha's Vineyard, as on neighboring Nantucket and Cape Cod, centralized /ay/ was frequently recorded.

The history of /aw/ differs from that of /ay/ more than our general expectations of symmetry would lead us to predict. There is reason to believe that in England the lowering of /aw/ was considerably in advance of /ay/, and it is not likely that the same Thomas Mayhew used [əʊ] in *house* and *out* (Jespersen 1927:235-36; Kökeritz 1953:

---

16. Among recent historical linguists, H. C. Wyld (1920:223-25) is a notable exception in positing a front first element in the transition of M.E.*i:* to Mod. E. /ay/, relying on occasional spellings with *ey* and *ei,* but without considering the many other indications of central position.

17. Abundant evidence is given in Krapp 1925(2):186-91.

18. The best view of the distribution of /ay/ may be had from Maps 26-27 in Kurath and McDavid 1951. Centralized diphthongs are well known as a feature of Canadian English, where the effect of the voiceless–voiced consonant environment is quite regular.

144–49; Wyld 1920:230–31). The American evidence of the late 18th and 19th centuries, as summed up by Krapp (1925 2:192–96), points to [oᴜ] as the conservative, cultured form, giving way to [aᴜ] or [ɑᴜ], with the rural New England form as [æᴜ] or [ɛᴜ]. The Linguistic Atlas records show only a hint of parallelism of /ay/ and /aw/. (Kurath and McDavid 1951: Maps 28–29). We find [əᴜ] mainly in eastern Virginia, before voiceless consonants, with some small representation in upstate New York, but the principal New England form of [aᴜ] stood out against a background of rural and recessive [æᴜ]. Martha's Vineyard shows very little centralization of /aw/ in the LANE maps.

This brief review indicates that the isolated position of /aw/ has facilitated phonetic variation on a truly impressive scale. The first element has ranged from [ɪ] to [ɑ], from [ɛ] to [o] all within the same general structural system. Perhaps one reason why /ay/ has not shown a similar range of variation is the existence of another upgliding diphthong, /ɔy/.[19] In any case, as the stage is set for our present view of Martha's Vineyard diphthongs, /ay/ is well centralized, but /aw/ is not. It may be too strong a statement to say that this represents the phonetic heritage of the seventeenth-century Yankee settlers of the island, but we may venture to say that we have no evidence of any intervening events which disturbed the original pattern.

As we begin the systematic study of this centralization pattern, we will refer to the linguistic variables (ay) and (aw) instead of the phonemes /ay/ and /aw/. Where the subphonemic differences in the position of the nucleus of /ay/ and /aw/ are considered to be in free variation, and linguistically insignificant, the variants of (ay) and (aw) show significant differences in their distribution and carry sociolinguistic information. In this case (but not always), the variables (ay) and (aw) represent the same phonetic substance as the invariant categories /ay/ and /aw/; the parentheses indicate a different approach to the analysis of variation. Whereas // means that internal variation is to be disregarded as insignificant, ( ) indicates that this variation is the prime focus of study.

19. The possibility of phonemic confusion with /ɔy/ apparently became a reality in the 17th and 18th centuries, in both England and America, when both diphthongs had central first elements.

### The Investigation of (ay) and (aw)

The summer visitor to Martha's Vineyard gets only a fleeting impression of the native speech pattern. Seven out of every eight human beings on the island are visitors like himself. But for the Vineyarder, there is no effect of dilution. For him, summer visitors have very little status on the island and their ephemeral nature is convincingly demonstrated in the first week in September of every year, when they disappear even more quickly than the insect population of the summer months. The normal native speech of Martha's Vineyard can then be heard as the dominant sound in public places. A knock on any up-island door will no longer produce a Back Bay stockbroker, but the rightful owner in possession once again. As a rural up-islander he is very likely to use a high degree of centralization of (ay) and (aw); but in the small town areas of down-island one may also hear this feature, particularly in words such as *right, white, twice, life, wife, like,* but not so much in *while, time, line, I, my, try.* Similarly, one may hear in the streets of Vineyard Haven centralized forms in *out, house, doubt,* but not so much in *now, how,* or *around.*

In order to study this feature systematically, it was necessary to devise an interview schedule which would provide many examples of (ay) and (aw) in casual speech, emotionally colored speech, careful speech, and reading style. The first of these diphthongs is more than twice as frequent as the second, but even so, several devices were required to increase the concentration of occurrences of both.

1. A lexical questionnaire, using the regional markers shown as most significant in the maps of the LANE, supplemented with recent observations, and concentrating on the following words containing (ay) and (aw):

| | | | |
|---|---|---|---|
| spider | rareripe | iodine | dying out |
| sliding | swipe | quinine | flattening out |
| | | scrimy | dowdy |
| white bread | nigh | | outhouse |
| white of egg | pie | frying pan | backhouse |
| nightcrawler | sty | fry pan | crouch |
| lightning bug | firefly | | mow |
| Italian | shiretown | | rowen |

2. Questions concerning value judgments, exploring the social orientation of the respondent, were so phrased as to elicit answers containing (ay) and (aw) forms.[20] Answers to such questions often gave a rich harvest of diphthongal forms, with contrasting uses of emotionally stressed and unstressed variants.
3. A special reading, used mainly in the high school, was offered ostensibly as a test of the ability to read a story naturally.[21] Since these readings gave the most exact comparisons between speakers, they were utilized for the spectrographic measurements discussed below.

In addition to the formal interview, observations were made in a great many casual situations: on the streets of Vineyard Haven and Edgartown, in diners, restaurants, bars, stores, docks, and many places where the general sound of public conversation could be noted, if not effectively recorded. But these notations only served as a supplementary check on the tape-recorded interviews. The basic information was gathered in the course of 69 interviews with native island speakers made in three periods: August 1961, late September-October 1961, January 1962. These 69 interviews provide the basis for the discussion to follow.

The 69 speakers, somewhat more than 1 percent of the population, represent a judgment sample of the community of native residents, and the groups which are important in the social life and value systems of the island. The sampling is proportional to area rather than population: 40 are up-islanders, and only 29 are from down-island, though over 70 percent of the people live down-island. The most important occupational groups are represented: 14 in fishing, 8 in farming, 6 in construction, 19 in service trades, 3 professionals,

20. "When we speak of the *right* to *life,* liberty and the pursuit of happiness, what does *right* mean? . . . Is it in *writing?* . . . If a man is successful at a job he doesn't *like,* would you still say he was a successful man?" These questions were generally successful in eliciting the informant's versions of the italicized words.

21. This 200-word reading is constructed as a story told by a teenage Vineyard boy, of the day he found out his father wasn't always right. An excerpt will show the technique involved: "After the high winds last Thursday, we went down to the mooring to see how the boat was making out. . . . My father started to pump out the bottom, and he told me to find out if the outboard would start. I found out all right. I gave her a couple of real hard pulls but it was no dice. 'Let me try her,' my father said. 'Not on your life,' I told him. 'I've got my pride.'"

5 housewives, 14 students. The three main ethnic groups are represented: 42 of English descent, 16 Portuguese, and 9 Indian.

The locations of the 69 informants are shown on Fig. 1.1, coded
by ethnic group. It may be understood that a large proportion of
those engaged in fishing are to be found in Chilmark; the farmers
are well inland, mainly in West Tisbury; the service trades are
heavily concentrated in Edgartown and Vineyard Haven. Of Guy
Lowman's four LANE informants, one was in Chilmark, one in West
Tisbury, and two in Edgartown.

As a result of these 69 interviews, we have about 3,500 instances
of (ay) and 1,500 instances of (aw) as the basic data for this study.

### Scales of Measurement

An important step was to construct a reliable, inter-subjective
index to the degree of centralization. In the original transcriptions
of the tape-recorded interviews a six-point scale of height of the first
element was used, ranging from the standard New England form [aɪ]
to the fully centralized [əɪ].[22] Such a transcription was intended to
push the distinctions noted to the limits of auditory discrimination.
This corresponded to the practice of the LANE, in which the same
number of degrees of height can be symbolized. However, it was
recognized that such fine distinctions could probably only be reproduced consistently by individuals who had attained a high degree
of convergence, and then over a very short time span.

Independent instrumental measurements were used to reduce the
scale by objective criteria, and to give a certain degree of objective
validity to the entire system of transcription.

Acoustic spectrograms were made of 80 instances of (ay) as spoken
and recorded by seven different Vineyarders.[23] A study of the as-

22. The interviews were recorded at $3\frac{3}{4}$ inches per second on a Butoba MT-5, using
a Butoba MD-21 dynamic microphone. A tape recording of the standard reading, "After
the high winds . . ." read by five of the speakers whose formant measurements appear
on Fig. 1.3, and other examples of centralized diphthongs used by Vineyard speakers
in natural conversation, may be obtained from the writer, Department of Linguistics,
University of Pennsylvania, Philadelphia, Pa. 19104.

23. Spectrograms were made on the Kay Sonograph, using both wide and narrow
bands. Seven of these, showing 15 instances of /ai/ and /au/, are reproduced in the
master's essay cited above.

sembled formant patterns indicated that one particular point in time might be best suited for measuring the degree of height of the first element of the diphthong. This is shown in Fig. 1.2, as the point where the first formant reaches a maximum. Measurements of the first and second formant positions at this point seemed to correspond well to the formant measurements for steady state vowels [a] to [ə] in Peterson and Barney's (1952) vowel studies.[24]

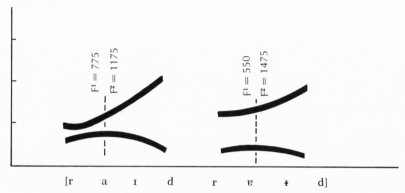

Fig. 1.2. Measurement of typical (ay) diphthongs at first formant maximum.

The 80 measurements were then plotted on a bi-logarithmic scale, with abscissa and ordinate corresponding to first and second formants. The original impressionistic transcriptions were then entered for each measurement, and the result examined for clear separation of impressionistic levels. On the whole, the stratification was good: the impressionistic ratings with more open first elements showed higher first formant and lower second formant readings. However, the separation of grades 2 from 3, and 4 from 5, was not as clear as the others. A reduced four-step scale was then established, and the resulting correlation shown in Fig. 1.3, and the table below.[25]

24. The degree of overlap shown in Fig. 1.3 seems roughly comparable to Peterson and Barney's results.

25. A parallel problem of condensing a finely graded impressionistic scale is discussed in Gauchat et al. 1925: ix. A seven-level transcription of the mid vowels was reduced to five levels, but without the instrumental justification presented here.

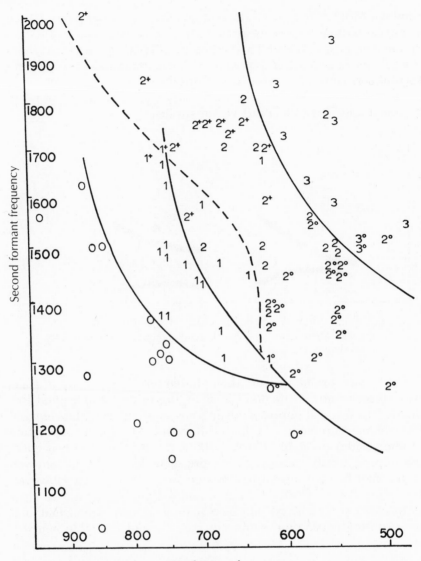

Fig. 1.3.  Correlation of instrumental measurement and impressionistic ratings of centralization. Nos. 0–3: Scale II equivalents
of impressionistic ratings of height of first elements of 86 (ay)
diphthongs, assigned before spectrographic measurement.
Seven different Martha's Vineyard speakers, males aged 14–60,
are represented. ° identifies speaker EP, age 31; ⁺ identifies
speaker GW, age 15.

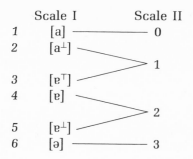

Fig. 1.3 shows the values for Scale II mapped on the bi-logarithmic scale. This is a satisfactory result, with good separation of the four grades of centralization. We have also obtained some justification for the use of the first formant maximum in measuring spectrograms, rather than the second formant minimum. Since the lines separating the four grades parallel the second-formant axis more than the first-formant axis, we have a graphic demonstration that our phonetic impressions are more sensitive to shifts in the first formant than the second.

When this display was originally planned, there was some question as to whether it would be possible to map many different speakers on the same graph. We know that there are significant differences in individual frames of formant reference. Small children, for instance, appear to have vowel triangles organized at considerably higher frequencies than adults. The seven speakers whose readings are displayed in Fig. 1.3 are all male; four are high school students, aged 14 to 15. But the other three are adults, from 30 to 60 years old, with widely different voice qualities.

Ideally, if we were studying the acoustic nature of the (ay) and (aw) diphthongs, we would want a more uniform group of speakers. Secondly, we would ask for better and more uniform recording conditions: one recording was outdoors, two were in living rooms, four in an empty conference room. However, since the object of the testing was to lend objective confirmation to an impressionistic scale of discrimination, it is only realistic to use a range of recordings as varied as the body of material on which the entire study is based. Absence of separation of the four grades in Fig. 1.3 might then have indicated only defects in instrumental technique, but a positive result can hardly be derived from such a bias.

It is interesting to note that measurements from no one speaker are distributed over more than half of Fig. 1.3, and some speakers are sharply limited to a narrow sector—still occupying portions of all the grades of centralization. For instance, the highly centralized speaker EP, aged 31, accounts for all of the readings in the lower right portion marked with a ° sign: 0°, 2°, etc. He shows no readings higher than 650 or 1500 cps. On the other hand, speaker DW, aged 15, also highly centralized, accounts for the upper left portion; his readings, marked with a + sign, are all higher than 625 or 1550 cps. Again, speaker GM, aged 15, is limited to a belt from lower left to upper right, filling the space between the two just mentioned. Despite the differences in vowel placement, these seven speakers utilize the same dimension to produce the effect of centralized or open vowels: widely separated formants for centralized vowels, adjacent formants for open vowels. The opposition, though not distinctive, is clearly seen as ranging from compact to (relatively) noncompact.

This display then indicates for us that the reduced impressionistic scale shows good stratification in terms of physical parameters, and we may proceed to employ such ratings with some confidence in their validity.

### The Linguistic Environment

We can now plot the distribution of centralized forms for each speaker. This is done for each of the 69 interviews on a chart such as is shown in Fig. 1.4. We find that these charts fall into three basic types:

a. uncentralized norms: all words, or almost all, fall into Grade 0, with at most only a few Grade 1's in favored words such as *right* and *out*.
b. centralized norms: most words with Grade 2, and only a few Grade 1's for unfavored forms, such as *time* and *cow*.
c. phonetic conditioning: the influence of the phonetic environment is reflected in a range of values from Grades 0 to 2. Fig. 1.4 is an example of this type.

Such phonetic conditioning is reminiscent of the phonetic regularity found in the southern United States. (Shewmake 1927). But on Martha's Vineyard, the distribution is more complex, and nowhere codified with the precision to be found in the South. Before proceeding to chart the various social factors which influence this

Centralization chart — (ay) and (aw)

| Grade | 0 | 1 | 2 | | 0 | 1 | 2 | |
|---|---|---|---|---|---|---|---|---|
| right | ♦♦ | ♦♦♦♦ | ♦♦♦♦ | | ♦♦♦♦ | ♦♦ | ♦♦♦♦ | out |
|  |  |  | ♦♦ | |  |  |  |  |
| night | ♦♦ | ♦♦ | ♦ | | ♦ | ♦ |  | about |
| white |  |  | ♦ | | ♦ | ♦ |  | trout |
| like |  | ♦♦ |  | |  | ♦ |  | house |
| sight | ♦♦♦ | ♦ |  | |  |  |  |  |
| quite | ♦ |  |  | | ♦♦ | ♦ |  | south |
| striped | ♦♦ |  |  | | ♦ | ♦♦♦ |  | mouth |
| swiped |  | ♦ |  | | ♦ | ♦ |  | couch |
| wife | ♦♦ |  |  | |  |  |  |  |
| life | ♦♦ | ♦♦♦ | ♦ | | ♦♦ |  |  | now |
| knife | ♦ |  | ♦ | | ♦♦ |  |  | how |
| spider |  |  | ♦ | | ♦♦ |  |  | sound |
| side | ♦♦♦♦ | ♦ |  | | ♦♦♦♦ |  |  | down |
|  | ♦♦♦ |  |  | | ♦♦♦♦ |  |  |  |
| tide | ♦♦♦♦♦ | ♦ |  | | ♦♦ |  |  |  |
| applied | ♦ |  |  | | ♦♦♦♦ |  |  | round |
| characterized | ♦ |  |  | | ♦ |  |  | hound |
| Ivory |  |  | ♦ | | ♦ |  |  | ground |
| live | ♦ |  | ♦ | |  |  |  |  |
| five |  | ♦ |  | |  |  |  |  |
| I've |  | ♦ |  | |  |  |  |  |
|  |  |  |  | | (aw)-39 |  |  |  |
| by |  | ♦ |  | |  |  |  |  |
| fly in |  |  | ♦ | |  |  |  |  |
| high | ♦ |  |  | |  |  |  |  |
| fryin | ♦ |  |  | |  |  |  |  |
| why |  | ♦ |  | |  |  |  |  |
| my | ♦♦ |  |  | |  |  |  |  |
| try |  | ♦ |  | |  |  |  |  |
| I'll | ♦ |  |  | |  |  |  |  |
| piles | ♦ |  |  | |  |  |  |  |
| while | ♦♦♦ |  |  | |  |  |  |  |
| mile | ♦ |  |  | |  |  |  |  |
| violence | ♦ |  |  | |  |  |  |  |
| shiners | ♦ |  |  | |  |  |  |  |
| kind | ♦ |  |  | |  |  |  |  |
| iodine |  | ♦ |  | |  |  |  |  |
| quinine | ♦ |  |  | |  |  |  |  |
| time | ♦♦ |  |  | |  |  |  |  |
| line |  | ♦ |  | |  |  |  |  |
| I | ♦ | ♦♦♦♦ | ♦♦♦♦♦ | |  |  |  |  |
|  |  | ♦ | ♦♦♦♦♦ | |  |  |  |  |
| fired | ♦ |  |  | |  |  |  |  |
| tire | ♦ |  |  | |  |  |  |  |
| (ay)-75 |  |  |  | |  |  |  |  |

Fig. 1.4. Phonetic determination of centralization. Centralization chart for North Tisbury fisherman GB.

feature, we should consider the influence of the linguistic environment, and primarily phonetic conditioning.

### Segmental Environment

The influence of the *following consonant* may be indicated by tabulating five general articulatory dimensions:

| Not favoring centralization | | Favoring centralization |
|---|---|---|
| (a)  sonorants | zero final | obstruents |
| (b)  nasals | | orals |
| (c)  voiced | | voiceless |
| (d)  velars | labials | apicals |
| (e)  fricatives | | stops |

If we apply these oppositions in the order given, from (a) to (e), we arrive at a consonant series from most favoring to least favorable to centralization, which seems to conform quite well to the facts:

$$/t, s; p, f; d, v, z; k, \theta, ð: ø: l, r; n; m/^{26}$$

The *preceding consonant* follows a rather different pattern, almost the reverse, and has considerably less effect. The most favoring initial consonants in centralized syllables are /h, l, r, w, m, n/, with the glottal stop allophone of zero heading the list. Thus the most favored words are *right, wife, night, light, nice, life, house, out.*

### Prosodic Factors

Stress regularly increases the degree of centralization for speakers with type (b) and type (c) charts. This is not at all an obvious rule, for the speech of many metropolitan areas shows the opposite tendency: one may note an occasional centralized diphthong in rapid reduced forms, but the same word under full stress is completely uncentralized. This corresponds to the difference between a centralized occurrence and a centralized norm.

A typical case of centralization under stress occurs in this excerpt from a story told by a North Tisbury fisherman:

Why I could do anything with this dog. I used to drop a [naɪf] or my handkerchief or something, and I'd walk pretty near a quarter of a mile,

---

26. (ay) and (aw) are rare before /b, g, ŋ, č, j/; /t/ includes [ʔ]. The non-distinctive [ʔ] variant of zero onset also favors centralization heavily, as in the 1 forms of Fig. 1.3.

and I'd stop and I'd turn to the dog: "You go get that! Where'd I lose that [neɪf]!"

## Stylistic Influence

While we find that most urban speakers have a variety of shifting styles of speech, and that interviews under varying conditions will produce varying counts of phonological features, this is not the case with most Vineyarders. The majority are essentially single-style speakers. Sometimes the conversation will take a livelier tone, or a more formal aspect, but the percentage of centralized forms is not significantly affected. Changes in centralization are apparently aspects of a pattern which develops over longer periods of time.[27]

## Lexical Considerations

A few special words are given greater centralization than their phonetic form or prosodic position would usually account for. An example is *sliding*, meaning coasting with a small sled. It may be that confusion with an alternant form *sledding* is responsible, or that words which originate in childhood, and are seldom spelled, are more prone to centralization.

## Distribution by Age and Time

The overall degree of centralization for each speaker is expressed by the mean of the numerical values of the variants multiplied by 100. Thus for Fig. 1.4, the values are (ay)-75 and (aw)-39. We can then find the values of the variable for any group of persons by averaging the values for the members of the group.

We may first wish to see if centralization varies with the age level of the speaker. Table 1.2 indicates that it does. Centralization of (ay) and (aw) appear to show a regular increase in successive age levels, reaching a peak in the 31 to 45 group. We must now consider the reasons for assessing this pattern as evidence for an historical change in the linguistic development of Martha's Vineyard. Is this an example of sound change, or is it merely evidence for a regular change in speaking patterns which is correlated with age?

At this point it is necessary to consider the general question as to whether sound change can be directly observed. The well-known

27. One small stylistic influence which appeared was in the standard reading. Those with centralized norms, whose charts were of type *b* and *c*, had slightly higher indexes of centralization for reading than for conversation. The opposite effect was noted for those with uncentralized norms.

TABLE 1.2.
CENTRALIZATION OF (ay)
AND (aw) BY AGE LEVEL

| Age | (ay) | (aw) |
| --- | --- | --- |
| 75– | 25 | 22 |
| 61–75 | 35 | 37 |
| 46–60 | 62 | 44 |
| 31–45 | 81 | 88 |
| 14–30 | 37 | 46 |

statement of Bloomfield (1933:347) seems to contradict this possibility:

The process of linguistic change has never been directly observed; we shall see that such observation, with our present facilities, is inconceivable.

When this opinion is viewed in the light of Bloomfield's entire discussion of phonetic change, it appears to be strongly motivated by arguments for the absolute regularity of sound change. Bloomfield wishes to show that such change is quite autonomous, "a gradual favoring of some non-distinctive variants and a disfavoring of others," and quite distinct from the normal fluctuation of non-distinctive forms, "at all times highly variable." Yet since direct observations will always pick up this normal fluctuation, "even the most accurate phonetic record of a language at any one time could not tell us which phonemes were changing" (p. 365). The changes we do observe are likely to be the effects of borrowing and analogic change.

Hockett (1958:439), while recognizing the possibility of divergent views, has further refined the doctrine of imperceptible changes as a basic mechanism of linguistic change. Movements of the center of the normal distribution of random variations are, for all practical purposes, not subject to direct observation, while the cruder forms of change which are observed must be due to minor mechanisms. Weinreich (1959) has pointed out the theoretical limitations of this position;[28] here we may profitably examine the result of applying such neo-grammarian thinking to empirical observations.

The prototype of close studies of sound change in a single com-

28. "It is hard to feel comfortable with a theory which holds that the great changes of the past were of one kind, theoretically mysterious and interesting, whereas everything that is observable today is of another kind, transparent and (by implication) of scant theoretical interest."

munity is Gauchat's (1905) investigation of the patois of Charmey, in French-speaking Switzerland. Gauchat observed and tabulated differences in six phonological features in the speech of three generations: speakers over 60 years old, those between 30 and 60, and those under 30 (see Chs. 7 and 9). Hermann returned to the scene in 1929, one generation later, to investigate four of these features: his results confirmed the interpretation of Gauchat's data as evidence for historical change, since three of the four had advanced considerably in the same direction. Yet Hermann (1929) also showed that real time depth is essential for an accurate view, since the fourth feature had not changed since 1903, and was apparently subject to a number of conflicting influences.

The neo-grammarian viewpoint is that such observable shifts are the results of a series of borrowings, imitations, and random variations.[29] These complicated explanations could be applied without contradiction to the present observations on Martha's Vineyard. But we need not make the gratuitous assumption that sound change is something else again, an ineluctable process of drift which is beyond the scope of empirical studies. Here I would like to suggest that the mixed pattern of uneven phonetic conditioning, shifting frequencies of usage in various age levels, areas, and social groups, as we have observed it on Martha's Vineyard, is the process of linguistic change in the simplest form which deserves the name. Below this level, at the point of individual variation, we have events which are sublinguistic in significance. At the first stage of change, where linguistic changes originate, we may observe many sporadic side-effects of articulatory processes which have no linguistic meaning: no socially determined significance is attached to them, either in the differentiation of morphemes, or in expressive function. Only when social meaning is assigned to such variations will they be imitated and begin to play a role in the language. Regularity is then to be found in the end result of the process, as Sturtevant (1947:78-81) has argued, and not in the beginning.[30]

---

29. Such arguments were indeed advanced in some detail to explain Gauchat's results, by P. G. Goidanich, "Saggio critico sullo studio de L. Gauchat," *Archivio Glottologico Italiano* 20:60–71 (1926) [cited by Sommerfelt 1930]. As implausible as Goidanich's arguments seem, they are quite consistent with Bloomfield's position cited above.

30. See Hoenigswald 1963 for further considerations which support this view.

If we now accept the evidence we have on hand as adequate in quantity, reliable, and valid, we must still decide if this particular case is an example of a change in community habits of speech. Two aspects of the question seem to make a good case for a positive answer.

First, the records of the LANE show only moderate centralization of (ay) for the four informants of 1933, aged 56 to 82. It is impossible to calibrate the Lowman transcription against our present scale, especially since his data put more stress on short utterances with stressed, elicited forms. But if we take the LANE symbol [ɐ] as equivalent to our present [ɐ] of Grade 2, it appears that these speakers had centralized norms for (ay) averaging about 86, as high as the highest point reached in our sample for age level 60 to 90, but only half as high as the highest point for age level 30 to 60. If we weigh their performance against a matched group of present-day speakers, we may conclude that there has been an intervening drop of centralization before the present rise.

Secondly, the question of (aw) is conclusive. The LANE informants had an average rating of 06 for (aw): that is, for all practical purposes, zero. The record shows a steady rise in centralization of (aw)—which we have seen to be a completely new phenomenon in Martha's Vineyard English—reaching values of well over 100 for most old family, up-island speakers, and going as high as 211 in one case. No postulated change in speaking habits with age could account for this rise.

The fact that the amount of centralization for the very old, and the very young speakers, is at a minimum, shows that the effect of age cannot be discounted entirely, and it may indeed be a secondary factor in this distribution over age levels.

### Possible Explanations for a Rise in Centralization

So far, our discussion of centralization, the dependent variable under study, has been merely descriptive. As we turn to the problem of explanation, we are faced with the question of what independent variables to examine. Certainly the structural parallelism of (ay) and (aw) is significant here.[31] Let us assume for the moment that central-

31. We might wish to construct a rule here which would, in essence, convert [+compact] to [−compact], simpler by one feature than a rule which would merely

ization declined to a low point in the late 1930's, and then, after the war, began to rise. At this point we find that a rising first element of (ay) carries the first element of (aw) with it. Such a change in direction would seem to give us a plausible explanation for the parallelism being called into play at this time, rather than the assumption that it suddenly began to operate after a three-hundred-year hiatus.

There remains the prior question, that of explaining (or giving a larger context for) the general rise of centralization on the island. Why should Martha's Vineyard turn its back on the history of the English language? I believe that we can find a specific explanation if we study the detailed configuration of this sound change against the social forces which affect the life of the island most deeply.

If we choose a purely psychological explanation, or one based only on phonological paradigms, we have as much as said that social variables such as occupation, income, education, social aspirations, attitudes, are beside the point. We could only prove such a claim by cross-tabulating the independent social variables, one at a time, with the degree of centralization, and showing that any greater-than-chance correlations are spurious.

However, our first attempts reveal some striking social correlations which are not easily explained away. Table 1.3 shows us the geo-

TABLE 1.3.
GEOGRAPHICAL DISTRIBUTION
OF CENTRALIZATION

|  | (ay) | (aw) |
|---|---|---|
| *Down-island* | 35 | 33 |
| Edgartown | 48 | 55 |
| Oak Bluffs | 33 | 10 |
| Vineyard Haven | 24 | 33 |
| *Up-island* | 61 | 66 |
| Oak Bluffs | 71 | 99 |
| N. Tisbury | 35 | 13 |
| West Tisbury | 51 | 51 |
| Chilmark | 100 | 81 |
| Gay Head | 51 | 81 |

convert [aɪ] to a centralized form. While such a statement is satisfying in its simplicity and neatness, it should be clear from the following discussion that it would explain only a small part of the mechanism of linguistic change.

graphical bias of centralization, favoring rural up-island against
small-town down-island areas. Table 1.4 shows the occupational
biases, with fishermen at the top and farmers at the bottom. If we
add to this the data of Table 1.5, showing the distribution by ethnic

TABLE 1.4.
CENTRALIZATION BY
OCCUPATIONAL GROUPS

|           | (ay) | (aw) |
|-----------|------|------|
| Fishermen | 100  | 79   |
| Farmers   | 32   | 22   |
| Others    | 41   | 57   |

TABLE 1.5.
CENTRALIZATION BY ETHNIC GROUPS

| Age level | English (ay)(aw) | | Portuguese (ay)(aw) | | Indian (ay)(aw) | |
|-----------|------|------|------|------|------|------|
| Over 60   | 36   | 34   | 26   | 26   | 32   | 40   |
| 46 to 60  | 85   | 63   | 37   | 59   | 71   | 100  |
| 31 to 45  | 108  | 109  | 73   | 83   | 80   | 133  |
| Under 30  | 35   | 31   | 34   | 52   | 47   | 88   |
| All ages  | 67   | 60   | 42   | 54   | 56   | 90   |

groups, we find ourselves embarrassed with too many explanations.
Are these social variables connected in any demonstrable way with
the linguistic change? Are they truly independent from one another,
or are some of the correlations spurious, the result of some dependence on a larger factor which is logically prior to these? If such a
larger pattern exists, we must ask how it originated, and in what
way it is connected with the linguistic events. A simple-minded
bookkeeping approach will not answer such questions. We will have
to gain some insight into the social structure of the island, and the
pressures which motivate the social changes of present-day Martha's
Vineyard.

## The Interaction of Linguistic and Social Patterns[32]

To understand Martha's Vineyard, we must first realize that this is a very beautiful place, and a very desirable place to live. But it is not an easy place to earn the kind of living which agrees well with the achievement orientation of modern American society. The 1960 Census shows that it is the poorest of all Massachusetts counties: it has the lowest average income, the highest number of poor people, and the smallest number of rich people.[33] The Vineyard has the highest rate of unemployment: 8.3 percent as against 4.2 percent for the state, and it also has the highest rate of seasonal employment. One might think that life on the island is nevertheless easier: perhaps the cost of living is lower. Nothing could be further from the truth: the high cost of ferrying is carried over to a higher price for most consumer goods. As a result, there are more married women with young children working than in any other county: 27.4 percent as against 17.3 percent for the state as a whole.

The reason for this economic pressure, and the resulting dependence on the tourist trade, is not hard to find. There is no industry on Martha's Vineyard. The island reached its peak in the great days of the whaling industry; for a time, commercial fishing in the local waters buoyed up the economy, but the run of fish is no longer what it used to be. Large-scale fishing is now out of New Bedford on the Grand Banks. Farming and dairying have declined sharply because

32. The information given in the following discussion of social patterns on Martha's Vineyard was derived in part from conversations with the 69 informants. Even more significant, perhaps, was information gained from discussions with community leaders who were in a position to view these patterns as a whole. I am particularly indebted to Mr. Benjamin Morton, head of the Chamber of Commerce, Mr. Henry Beetle Hough, editor of the *Vineyard Gazette,* and Mr. Charles Davis, superintendent of the Martha's Vineyard Regional High School. Among my informants, I am especially grateful to Mr. Donald Poole of Chilmark, Mr. Benjamin Mayhew, selectman of Chilmark, and Mr. Albert Prada, town clerk of Edgartown.

33. Table 36 of the 1960 census report PC(1)—23c, cited above in fn. 9, shows some striking contrasts among Massachusetts counties. The median family income for the Vineyard is $4,745, as against $6,272 for the state as a whole. Barnstable County (Cape Cod) and Nantucket are also dependent on a vacation economy, yet they show median incomes of $5,386 and $5,373. The most agricultural county in Massachusetts, Franklin, shows a median of $5,455. The state as a whole has only 12.4 percent of families with incomes under $3,000; the Vineyard has 23 percent. The state has 17.0 percent with incomes over $10,000; the Vineyard has only 6.6 percent.

of the ferry rate, which raises the cost of fertilizer but lowers the profit on milk.

The 1960 Census shows us that the island's labor force of 2,000 souls is heavily occupied with service trades. Only 4 percent are in manufacturing, one-seventh of the state average. Five percent are in agriculture, 2.5 percent in fishing, and 17 percent in construction; these percentages are five, ten, and three times as high as those for the state as a whole.[34]

These economic pressures must be clearly delineated in order to assess the heavy psychological pressures operating on the Vineyarders of old family stock. Increasing dependence on the summer trade acts as a threat to their personal independence. The more far-seeing Vineyarders can envisage the day when they and their kind will be expropriated as surely as the Indians before them. They understand that the vacation business cannot help but unbalance the economy, which produces far too little for the summer trade, but far too much for the winter. Yet it is very hard for the Vineyarder not to reach for the dollar that is lying on the table, as much as he may disapprove of it. We have already noted that many Vineyarders move out of their own homes to make room for summer people.

Those who feel that they truly own this island, the descendants of the old families, have a hard time holding on. Summer people, who have earned big money in big cities, are buying up the island. As one Chilmarker said, "You can cross the island from one end to the other without stepping on anything but *No Trespassing* signs." The entire northwest shore has fallen to the outsiders. In Edgartown, the entire row of spacious white houses on the waterfront has capitulated to high prices, with only one exception, and the descendants of the whaling captains who built them have retreated to the hills and hollows of the interior.

This gradual transition to dependence on, and outright ownership by the summer people has produced reactions varying from a fiercely defensive contempt for outsiders to enthusiastic plans for furthering the tourist economy. A study of the data shows that high centralization of (ay) and (aw) is closely correlated with expressions of strong resistance to the incursions of the summer people.

The greatest resistance to these outsiders is felt in the rural up-island areas, and especially in Chilmark, the only place where fishing

34. See Table 82 of the 1960 census report, as in fn. 33.

is still a major part of the economy.[35] Chilmarkers are the most different, independent, the most stubborn defenders of their own way of living. In order to assess the changing orientation of island groups towards the old family tradition, I included in my interview a battery of questions dealing with the semantics of the word *Yankee*. One question read: "Where on the island would a typical old Yankee be most apt to live?" By far the most common answer was "Chilmark." Chilmarkers were named most often as examples of "typical old Yankees."

Chilmarkers pride themselves on their differences from mainlanders:

You people who come down here to Martha's Vineyard don't understand the background of the old families of the island . . . strictly a maritime background and tradition . . . and what we're interested in, the rest of America, this part over here across the water that belongs to you and we don't have anything to do with, has forgotten all about. . .

I think perhaps we use entirely different . . . type of English language . . . think differently here on the island . . . it's almost a separate language within the English language.

To a large extent, this last statement is wishful thinking. Much of the language difference depended upon whaling terms which are now obsolete. It is not unnatural, then, to find phonetic differences becoming stronger and stronger as the group fights to maintain its identity. We have mentioned earlier that the degrees of retroflexion in final and preconsonantal /r/ have social significance: at Chilmark, retroflexion is at its strongest, and is steadily increasing among the younger boys.

In Table 1.3, we note that centralization is higher up-island than down-island, and highest of all in Chilmark. In Table 1.4, we note that of all occupational groups, fishermen show the highest centralization. Our total number of cases is too small to allow extensive cross-tabulations, but if we take the group of Chilmark fishermen

35. Despite the low number of Vineyarders listed as fishermen by occupation in the Census, a much larger number of islanders rely upon part-time fishing to supplement their income. In particular, harvesting bay scallops in the salt ponds is a prized source of revenue in the summer months. A great deal of local legislation is designed to protect the professional fishermen from the great number of part-time scallopers taking in too large a share. Much discussion and considerable bitterness develops as a result of this conflict of interest, in which the truly professional Chilmarkers are, psychologically at least, on top.

in the middle age level, from 30 to 60, we find that these five informants have average indexes of 148 for (ay) and 118 for (aw), higher
than any other social group which we might select on the island.
Conversely, let us list the six speakers with the highest degree of
centralization in order of (ay)—that is, the upper 10 percent:

|                               | (ay) | (aw) |
|-------------------------------|------|------|
| Chilmark fisherman, age 60    | 170  | 111  |
| Chilmark fisherman, age 31    | 165  | 211  |
| Chilmark fisherman, age 55    | 150  | 124  |
| Edgartown fisherman, age 61   | 143  | 107  |
| Chilmark fisherman, age 33    | 133  | 79   |
| Edgartown fisherman, age 52   | 131  | 131  |

It should be noted here that the two Edgartown fishermen listed are
brothers, the last descendants of the old families to maintain their
position on the Edgartown waterfront in the face of the incroachment
of summer people.

We have now established within reason that the strong upturn in
centralization began up-island, among Chilmark fishermen, under the
same influence which produced parallel results among the few
Edgartown residents who shared their social orientation.

Table 1.5 shows the developments by age level for each of the three
main ethnic groups. All of the examples we have used so far deal
with the English group of old family descent; in Chilmark, this is
the only group of any size. Let us continue to follow the development
of this group through the succeeding age levels, and examine the
interaction of social and linguistic patterns.

We see that centralization reaches a peak in the age level from
30 to 45, and that centralization of (aw) has reached or surpassed
(ay) at this point. This age group has been under heavier stress than
any other; the men have grown up in a declining economy, after
making a more or less deliberate choice to remain on the island
rather than leave it. Most of them have been in the armed forces
during World War II or in the Korean conflict. Many have been to
college, for the English-descent group has a strong bent towards
higher education. At some point, each of these men elected to make
a smaller living on Martha's Vineyard, while many of their contem-
poraries left to gain more money or more recognition elsewhere.

Severe strains are created in those who are pulled in both directions; the traditional orientation of Martha's Vineyard has long been

inward and possessive, yet the pull of modern achievement-oriented America is even greater for some.

> I think actually it's a very hard thing to make that decision . . . It comes to you later, that you should have made it before. I have another son— Richard—is an aeronautical engineer. He really loves the island. And when he decided to be an aeronautical engineer we discussed it—at length—and I told him at that time: you just can't live on Martha's Vineyard . . . He works at Grumman, but he comes home every chance he gets and stays just as long as he can.

The speaker is a woman of 55, a descendant of the Mayhew family, who left business school in Boston, and returned to the island to become a real estate agent. Her son made the opposite choice; but another family, of long standing in Chilmark, had this to report about their son:

> . . . we had an idea that he'd go away to school, but he really didn't want to go away . . . When he was at Chauncey Hall, they tried to get him to go to M.I.T.; but he said no, he didn't want to go anywhere where he had to learn to do something that he couldn't come back to this island.

We can learn a great deal about centralization by studying such histories of particular families. The two speakers who head the list of centralized speakers on the previous page are father and son. The father, a Chilmark lobsterman, is a thoughtful, well-read man with a passionate concern with the history of the whaling industry; he is perhaps the most eloquent spokesman for the older Vineyard tradition, and the author of the quotation on p. 29. His son is a college graduate who tried city life, didn't care for it, came back to the island and built up several successful commercial enterprises on the Chilmark docks. He shows a high (ay) at 211, considerably more centralized than anyone else I have heard at Chilmark. One evening, as I was having dinner at his parents' house, the conversation turned to speech in general, without any specific reference to (ay) or (aw). His mother remarked, "You know, E. didn't always speak that way . . . it's only since he came back from college. I guess he wanted to be more like the men on the docks . . . "

Here we see a clear case of hypercorrection at work, and from other evidence as well, it is reasonable to assume that this is a very regular force in implementing the phonetic trend we are studying.

When we come to high-school students, we must realize that many of the young people from the old-family group do *not* intend to remain on the island, and this is reflected in the lower average index of Table 1.5. Comparatively few of the sons of the English-descent group will be earning their living on the Vineyard in the next 20 years. In a series of interviews in Martha's Vineyard Regional High School, it was possible to compare speaking habits very closely by means of the standard reading, "After the high winds . . ." A marked contrast was observed between those who plan to leave the island and those who do not. The latter show strong centralization, while the former show little, if any. To highlight this point, we may take four 15-year-old students: the two down-islanders who intend to leave for careers in business and finance show little or no centralization; the two up-islanders who hope to go to college and return to make their living on the island show considerable centralization.[36] The indexes speak for themselves:

| *Down-island, leaving* | *Up-island, staying* |
|:---:|:---:|
| (ay)(aw) | (ay)(aw) |
| 00–40 | 90–100 |
| 00–00 | 113–119 |

One of the down-islanders, from Edgartown, has fallen very much under the influence of the upper-class Bostonian summer visitors. He has lost all constriction in postvocalic /r/, and has a fronted low center vowel as well in such words as [kaː], 'car'.

### Centralization among Other Ethnic Groups

We can now turn to the special position of the Portuguese and Indian ethnic groups, and see if the same approach can account for the distribution of centralized forms among them.

The most common view of the early Portuguese immigration is that the settlers came from an island with a very similar economy, shared the Yankee virtues of thrift and industry, and fitted into the island life almost perfectly. The Azoreans who came first seemed to have a strong inclination for farming and fishing, rather than factory work; in the Vineyard's rather diffuse economy, there was

---

36. On the question of leaving the island, one of these boys said: ". . . I can't see myself off island somewhere . . . I like it a lot here, like my father goes lobstering. That's quite a bit of fun . . . as long as I get enough money to live and enjoy myself. I was figuring on . . . going into oceanography because you'd be outdoors: it wouldn't be office work."

little concentration of the Portuguese into the kinds of industrial pockets we find on the mainland.[37] Even among the tough-minded Chilmarkers, we find a certain grudging acknowledgement of the Yankee-like orientation of the Portuguese:

. . . they worked, that's why they were respected. Nobody ever particularly interfered with 'em. You hear somebody make a remark about the dumb Portagee or something, but actually I think they've been pretty well respected because they mind their own business pretty well. They didn't ask for anything.

It took some time, however, for the Portuguese-descent group to make its way into the main stream of island life. Intermarriage of Portuguese and Yankee stock occurs, but it is rare. Second-generation Portuguese certainly do not feel at home in every situation: as some Vineyarders put it, these Portuguese have "a defensive attitude." A member of the English group will as a rule speak his mind freely, condemning the summer people and his neighbors with equal frankness. But the second-generation Portuguese never criticizes the summer people in the interview situation, and he is extremely wary of criticizing anyone. When the word *Yankee* is introduced, he shifts uneasily in his chair, and refuses to make any comment at all.

While the speech of the Portuguese second generation is free of any detectable Portuguese influence,[38] it is also lacking the special Vineyard flavor. If we examine the Portuguese age groups over 45 in Table 1.5, which contain a large proportion of second-generation speakers, we find little or no centralization.

This is not the case with third- and fourth-generation Portuguese speakers. In this group, we find centralization very much on the increase, particularly with (aw). In Table 1.5, we see that the age group from 31 to 45 has a very high degree of centralization. This age level contains a great many third-generation Portuguese. It is the first Portuguese group which has entered the main stream of island life, occupying positions as merchants, municipal officers, and many other places of secondary leadership. These speakers consider

37. In many ways, the Vineyard seems to be more democratic than the mainland. I have heard on the mainland strong expressions of hostility between Portuguese groups from the Azores and those from the Cape Verde Islands, but never on Martha's Vineyard.

38. On the other hand, I have heard a strong Portuguese accent from a second-generation Portuguese man, about 40 years old, who was raised on a farm near Taunton, Mass.

themselves natives of the island, and in response to the term *Yankee*, they either include themselves, or make fun of the whole idea.

In the youngest age level, the Portuguese-descent group shows a very regular use of centralization, whether second or third or fourth generation, and their average centralization index in the table is, at this point, higher than the English group.

One might think that centralization might be on the way to becoming a marker of the ethnic Portuguese on the island, if such a trend continues. But this possibility runs counter to the strongly democratic nature of present-day Vineyard society. Among high-school students, for example, there appear to be no social barriers between the ethnic groups, in clubs, at dances, and between friends. This situation is especially shocking to some former mainlanders, who would like to draw a color line against some of the children with Cape Verde backgrounds. But despite a few such counter-currents, the unifying, protective nature of Vineyard society shields the island native from the kind of reality which is practised on the outside.[39]

The reason that the youngest Portuguese group shows higher centralization is that a larger percentage identify themselves with the island and the island way of life, than is the case among the English-descent group. Whereas almost all of the English group leave the island to go to college, and few return, almost all of the Portuguese group remain. As a result, they are gradually supplanting the English group in the economic life of the island.

It is fair enough to say that the main problem of the Portuguese group has not been to resist the incursions of the summer people but rather to assert their status as native Vineyarders. Their chief obstacle has not been the outsiders, but rather the resistance to full recognition from the English-descent group. With full participation in native status has come full use of the special characteristics of Martha's Vineyard English, including centralized diphthongs.

The Indian descent group is relatively small and homogeneous. The hundred citizens of Gay Head are united in a few closely related families. One would think that these survivors of the aboriginal

---

39. In several cases, Vineyard youngsters have received rather severe shocks on leaving the island for the armed services or for work in an area where caste restrictions were in force. One boy was put into a black regiment on entering the service, though action from Vineyard leaders had him transferred soon afterwards.

Wampanoag Indians would have had little trouble in asserting their native status. On the contrary, a long tradition of denigration of the Indian has served, for over a hundred years, to rob him of the dignity which should accompany this feat of survival. The issue revolves around the fact that the declining Indian community has necessarily intermarried with outsiders over the past ten generations. The logic of American society dictated that these outsiders should be black. Thus as early as 1764, the Yankee officials of the Vineyard claimed that only one quarter of the Indians were "of pure blood."[40] In 1870, the Governor of Massachusetts took away the reservation status of Gay Head, on the ground that they really weren't Indians at all, and handed them over to the political ministrations of Chilmark.

For many decades, the Indians were literally second-class citizens, and the resentment dating from this period is not entirely gone. On the other hand, we find that a number of Vineyarders, of both English and Portuguese descent, regard the Indians with a mixture of sarcasm and scepticism:

. . . show me a Gay Head Indian and I'll like to see one.

The Indian people are aware of this situation, as shown in this quotation from one of the Indian informants, a woman of 69:

These island folks, they don't want to mix at all, up this end. . . They don't like to give the Indian his name, here on the island. I'll tell you that. They like to be dirty with some of their talk.

Despite the great shift in Vineyard ideology over the past three generations, the Indians still feel blocked, geographically and socially, by the Chilmarkers, "up this end." Their attitude toward the Chilmarkers is ambiguous: on the one hand, they resent the Chilmarkers' possessive attitude toward the island, and the traditional hard-fisted, stiff-necked Yankee line. Their reaction to the word Yankee is sarcastic and hostile.[41] But their main complaint is that they deserve equal status, and whether they will admit it or not, they would like to be just like the Chilmarkers in many ways.

---

40. A very rich vein of information on this score may be tapped from Richard L. Pease's Report of the commissioner appointed to complete the examination . . . of all boundary lines . . . at Gay Head (Boston, 1871). Pease was acting essentially as the hatchet man for the Governor of Massachusetts, to whom he was reporting.

41. "Where they come from—down south somewhere? . . . Lot of 'em come from Jerusalem, you know . . ."

As far as centralization is concerned, Table 1.5 indicates that the Indians follow close behind the Chilmarkers. At the same time, they show a greater relative increase of centralization of (aw), similar to the Portuguese development, especially among the young people. Here there are signs of an additional phonetic feature, shared by both Portuguese and Indians: a backed form of (aw), which may be written [ʌʊ]. It is characteristic of five speakers in the sample, all under 30, all fairly low in socioeconomic status. Whether it represents a general trend cannot be determined at this point.

We may note that there has been a revival of Indian culture in the form of pageants staged for the tourist trade, beadwork, and other Indian crafts, and with these a revived emphasis on tribal organization. The younger Indians acknowledge that this revival was commercially motivated in its beginnings, but they claim that it is now more than that, and that Indian culture would survive if the vacationers disappeared entirely. The Indian language has been dead for several generations, however, and the ritual formulas must be learned from a book. The Indians are truly traditional speakers of English, and their claim to native status must be expressed in that language.

### The Social Meaning of Centralization

From the information we now have at hand, there readily emerges the outline of a unifying pattern which expresses the social significance of the centralized diphthongs.

It is apparent that the immediate meaning of this phonetic feature is 'Vineyarder.' When a man says [rɐɪt] or [hɐʊs], he is unconsciously establishing the fact that he belongs to the island: that he is one of the natives to whom the island really belongs. In this respect, centralization is not different from any of the other subphonemic features of other regions which are noted for their local dialect. The problem is, why did this feature develop in such a complicated pattern on the Vineyard, and why is it becoming stronger in the younger age levels?

The answer appears to be that different groups have had to respond to different challenges to their native status. And in the past two generations, the challenges have become much sharper through severe economic and social pressures.

The old-family group of English descent has been subjected to pressure from the outside: its members are struggling to maintain their independent position in the face of a long-range decline in the economy and the steady encroachment of the summer people. The member of the tradition-oriented community naturally looks to past generations for his values: these past generations form a reference group for him.[42] The great figures of the past are continually referred to, and those who have died only a few years ago have already assumed heroic stature. "If you could only have been here a few years ago and talked to N. He could have told you so many things!"

The sudden increase in centralization began among the Chilmark fishermen, the most close-knit group on the island, the most independent, the group which is most stubbornly opposed to the incursions of the summer people. There is an inherently dramatic character to the fisherman's situation, and a great capacity for self-dramatization in the fisherman himself, which makes him an ideal candidate to initiate new styles in speech. In the early morning, the curtain rises: a solitary figure appears upon the scene. For the course of an entire day, this single actor holds the stage. Then at last, the boat docks; the curtain descends. The play is over, yet the reviews will be read and reread for generations to come.

I can remember as a boy, when I first started going to sea with my father, he said to me: remember two things. Always treat the ocean with respect, and remember you only have to make one mistake, never to come back.

Centralized speech forms are then a part of the dramatized island character which the Chilmarker assumes, in which he imitates a similar but weaker tendency in the older generation.

For younger members of the English-descent group, we can view the mechanism in greater detail. For them, the old-timers and the up-islanders in particular serve as a reference group. They recognize that the Chilmark fishermen are independent, skillful with many kinds of tools and equipment, quick-spoken, courageous, and physically strong. Most importantly, they carry with them the ever-present conviction that the island belongs to them. If someone intends to stay on the island, this model will be ever present to his mind. If he intends to leave, he will adopt a mainland reference group, and the influence of the old-timers will be considerably less. The differ-

42. In the technical sense developed by R. Merton, *Social Theory and Social Structure* (Glencoe, Ill., 1957).

ential effect in the degree of centralization used is a direct result of this opposition of values.

The Portuguese group is not faced with a dilemma of going or staying. The main challenge to which this group has responded is from the English group, which has certainly served as a reference group for the Portuguese until very recent times. As the number of Portuguese in prominent positions grows, it is no longer urgent to minimize the effects of being Portuguese, but rather to assert one's identity as an islander.

The Gay Head developments are dictated by the antinomy of values which reigns there. On the one hand, the Indian group resents any bar to full participation in the island life, and the Indians have plainly adopted many of the same values as the Chilmarkers. But on the other hand, they would like to insist as well on their Indian identity. Unfortunately, they no longer have linguistic resources for this purpose, and whether they like it or not, they will follow the Chilmark lead.

The role of the Chilmarker, or "old-time typical Yankee" has declined as the reference group which governs the meaning of "islander" has shifted away from that which governs "Yankee." Even among the Chilmarkers, the more far-sighted members of the community recognize that the term *Yankee* no longer fits the island. Whereas this word may still be a rallying cry in some parts of New England, it has outlived its usefulness on Martha's Vineyard. In emphasizing descent status rather than native status, *Yankee* summons up invidious distinctions which are no longer good currency on the island.

People don't make so much about it as they used to when I was young. People would make that statement: "I'm a Yankee! I'm a Yankee!" But now you very seldom—mostly, read it in print.[43]

In summary, we can then say that the meaning of centralization, judging from the context in which it occurs, is positive orientation towards Martha's Vineyard. If we now overlook age level, occupation, ethnic group, geography, and study the relationship of centralization to this one independent variable, we can confirm or reject this conclusion. An examination of the total interview for each

---

43. The speaker is one of the Mayhews, a retired Chilmark fisherman, who has as much claim to be a "typical old Yankee" as any person on Martha's Vineyard.

informant allows us to place him in one of three categories: positive—expresses definitely positive feelings towards Martha's Vineyard; neutral—expresses neither positive nor negative feelings towards Martha's Vineyard; negative—indicates desire to live elsewhere. When these three groups are rated for mean centralization indexes, we obtain the striking result of Table 1.6.

TABLE 1.6.
CENTRALIZATION AND ORIENTATION
TOWARDS MARTHA'S VINEYARD

| Persons | | (ay) | (aw) |
|---|---|---|---|
| 40 | Positive | 63 | 62 |
| 19 | Neutral | 32 | 42 |
| 6 | Negative | 09 | 08 |

The fact that this table shows us the sharpest example of stratification we have yet seen, indicates that we have come reasonably close to a valid explanation of the social distribution of centralized diphthongs.

### The Intersection of Social and Linguistic Structures

The following abstract scheme may serve to summarize the argument which has been advanced so far to explain the spread and propagation of this particular linguistic change.

1. A language feature used by a group A is marked by contrast with another standard dialect.
2. Group A is adopted as a reference group by group B, and the feature is adopted and exaggerated as a sign of social identity in response to pressure from outside forces.
3. Hypercorrection under increased pressure, in combination with the force of structural symmetry, leads to a generalization of the feature in other linguistic units of group B.
4. A new norm is established as the process of generalization levels off.
5. The new norm is adopted by neighboring and succeeding groups for whom group B serves as a reference group.

There remains a gap in the logic of the explanation: in what way do social pressures and social attitudes come to bear upon linguistic

structures? So far we have assembled a convincing series of correlations: yet we still need to propose a rational mechanism by which
the deep-seated elements of structure enter such correlations.

It has been noted that centralized diphthongs are not salient in
the consciousness of Vineyard speakers. They can hardly therefore
be the direct objects of social affect. The key to the problem may
lie in the fact that centralization is only one of many phonological
features which show the same general distribution, though none may
be as striking or as well stratified as (ay) and (aw). There are no less
than 14 phonological variables which follow the general rule that
the higher, or more constricted variants are characteristic of the
up-island, "native" speakers, while the lower, more open variants
are characteristic of down-island speakers under mainland influence.[44] We can reasonably assume that this "close-mouthed" articulatory style is the object of social affect. It may well be that social
evaluation interacts with linguistic structures at this point, through
the constriction of several dimensions of phonological space. Particular linguistic variables would then be variously affected by the
overall tendency towards a favored articulatory posture, under the
influence of the social forces which we have been studying. Evidence
for such an hypothesis must come from the study of many comparable developments, in a variety of English dialects and other languages. It is enough to note here that it is a plausible mechanism
for sociolinguistic interaction which is compatible with the evidence
which has been gathered in this investigation.

### Limitations of This Study

We noted earlier that one limitation of this study stems from the
fact that the variable selected is not salient. This limitation, coupled
with the small size of the Vineyard population, made it impractical
to explore thoroughly the subjective response of native speakers to
centralized diphthongs. Other shortcomings of the technique used

---

44. In the following list of the variables in question, the up-island form is given
first. PHONEMIC INVENTORY: /o/~/ou/ in road, toad, boat, whole ... PHONEMIC
DISTRIBUTION: /ɛ/ only before intersyllabic /r/ instead of both /ɛ/ and /æ/; /r/~/ə/
in postvocalic position. PHONEMIC INCIDENCE: /ɪ~ɛ/ in get, forget, when, anyway, can
... ; /ɛ~æ/ in have, had, that; /ʌ~ɑ/ in got. PHONETIC REALIZATION: [ɐɪ~aɪ] and
[ɐu~au]: [r~ɚ]; [ɪr~ər] in work, person ... ; [ə~ʌ] in furrow, hurry ... ; [oɐu~ou]
in go, no ... ; [ii~ɪi] and [uu~ʊu]; [ɪᵊ~ɪ] and [ɛᵊ~ɛ].

on Martha's Vineyard may be seen in the sampling method, which was far from rigorous.[45] The statements made about developments through various age levels among the Portuguese and Indians are based on an inadequate number of cases. The sample is particularly weak in the down-island area, especially in Oak Bluffs, and the picture of down-island trends is correspondingly weaker than up-island developments. Finally, it may be noted that the interviewing technique was not as firmly controlled as it might have been: a number of changes in the interview structure were made as the study progressed.

With these reservations, we can say that the findings give good confirmation of the main theme of the study: the correlation of social patterns with the distributional pattern of one linguistic variable.[46] The reliability of the index used was tested in several cases where the same informant was interviewed twice, with good results.[47] Indexes for reading style did not diverge sharply from other portions of the interview. The validity of the scale of measurement was well established by instrumental methods, and the validity of the whole seems to be reinforced by the unitary nature of the final interpretation.

The techniques developed on Martha's Vineyard were later refined and applied to a much more complex situation in the urban core of New York City. Here multiple-style speakers are the rule, not the exception; instead of three ethnic groups we have a great many; mobility and change are far more rapid; and the population is huge. Here the sampling requirements must be far more rigid; and the techniques used to assess the social meaning of linguistic cues must

45. The problem of sampling technique for linguistic variables is a difficult one at the moment. While we are sure that linguistic behavior is more general than the behavior usually traced by survey methods, we do not know how much more general it is, nor can we estimate easily how far we may relax the sampling requirements, if at all.

46. In addition to the positive correlations discussed above, the explanation given is reinforced by certain negative results of alternate explanations. The educational level of the informants is not correlated significantly with degree of centralization. The distribution of substandard or archaic grammar does not correspond to the distribution of centralized forms.

47. For example, two interviews with Ernest Mayhew, Chilmark fisherman, age 83, showed these results: first interview, (ay)-67, (aw)-58; second interview, (ay)-59, (aw)-40. The count for (aw) is based on about one-third as many items as for (ay).

be more subtle and complex. Yet the basic approach, of isolating the socially significant variables, and correlating them with the patterns of general social forces, was the same as that which was used on Martha's Vineyard. We can expect that these methods will give us further insight into the mechanism of linguistic change.

# 2 | The Social Stratification of (r) in New York City Department Stores

"As this letter is but a jar of the tongue, . . . it is
the most imperfect of all the consonants."
John Walker,
*Principles of English Pronunciation.* 1791

ANYONE who begins to study language in its social context immediately encounters the classic methodological problem: the means used to gather the data interfere with the data to be gathered. The primary means of obtaining a large body of reliable data on the speech of one person is the individual tape-recorded interview. Interview speech is formal speech—not by any absolute measure, but by comparison with the vernacular of everyday life. On the whole, the interview is public speech—monitored and controlled in response to the presence of an outside observer. But even within that definition, the investigator may wonder if the responses in a tape-recorded interview are not a special product of the interaction between the interviewer and the subject. One way of controlling for this is to study the subject in his own natural social context— interacting with his family or peer group (Labov, Cohen, Robins, and Lewis 1968). Another way is to observe the public use of language in everyday life apart from any interview situation—to see how people use language in context when there is no explicit observation. This chapter is an account of the systematic use of rapid and anonymous observations in a study of the sociolinguistic structure of the speech community.[1]

1. This chapter is based upon Chs. 3 and 9 of *The Social Stratification of English in New York City* (1966), revised in the light of further work with rapid and anonymous observations. I am indebted to Frank Anshen and Marvin Maverick Harris for reference to illuminating replications of this study (Allen 1968, Harris 1968).

43

This chapter is the first of a series of six which deal primarily with the sociolinguistic study of New York City. The main base for that study (Labov 1966a) was a secondary random sample of the Lower East Side, and this data will be considered in the following chapters. But before the systematic study was carried out, there was an extensive series of preliminary investigations. These included 70 individual interviews and a great many anonymous observations in public places. These preliminary studies led to the definition of the major phonological variables which were to be studied, including (r): the presence or absence of consonantal [r] in postvocalic position in *car, card, four, fourth,* etc. This particular variable appeared to be extraordinarily sensitive to any measure of social or stylistic stratification. On the basis of the exploratory interviews, it seemed possible to carry out an empirical test of two general notions: first, that the linguistic variable (r) is a social differentiator in all levels of New York City speech, and second, that rapid and anonymous speech events could be used as the basis for a systematic study of language. The study of (r) in New York City department stores which I will report here was conducted in November 1962 as a test of these ideas.

We can hardly consider the social distribution of language in New York City without encountering the pattern of social stratification which pervades the life of the city. This concept is analyzed in some detail in the major study of the Lower East Side; here we may briefly consider the definition given by Bernard Barber: social stratification is the product of social differentiation and social evaluation (1957:1–3). The use of this term does not imply any specific type of class or caste, but simply that the normal workings of society have produced systematic differences between certain institutions or people, and that these differentiated forms have been ranked in status or prestige by general agreement.

We begin with the general hypothesis suggested by exploratory interviews: *if any two subgroups of New York City speakers are ranked in a scale of social stratification, then they will be ranked in the same order by their differential use of* (r).

It would be easy to test this hypothesis by comparing occupational groups, which are among the most important indexes of social stratification. We could, for example, take a group of lawyers, a group of file clerks, and a group of janitors. But this would hardly go beyond the indications of the exploratory interviews, and such an extreme example of differentiation would not provide a very exacting test of the hypothesis. It should be possible to show that the hypothesis is so general, and the differential use of (r) pervades New York City so thoroughly, that fine social differences will be reflected in the index as well as gross ones.

It therefore seemed best to construct a very severe test by finding a subtle case of stratification within a single occupational group: in this case, the sales people of large department stores in Manhattan. If we select three large department stores, from the top, middle, and bottom of the price and fashion scale, we can expect that the customers will be socially stratified. Would we expect the sales people to show a comparable stratification? Such a position would depend upon two correlations: between the status ranking of the stores and the ranking of parallel jobs in the three stores; and between the jobs and the behavior of the persons who hold those jobs. These are not unreasonable assumptions. C. Wright Mills points out that salesgirls in large department stores tend to borrow prestige from their customers, or at least make an effort in that direction.[2] It appears that a person's own occupation is more closely correlated with his linguistic behavior—for those working actively—than any other single social characteristic. The evidence presented here indicates that the stores are objectively differentiated in a fixed order, and that jobs in these stores are evaluated by employees in that order. Since the product of social differentiation and evaluation, no matter how minor, is social stratification of the employees in the three stores, the hypothesis will predict the following result: salespeople in the highest-ranked store will have the highest values of (r); those in the middle-ranked store will have intermediate values of (r); and those in the lowest-ranked store will show the lowest values. If this result holds true, the hypothesis will have received confirmation in proportion to the severity of the test.

The three stores which were selected are Saks Fifth Avenue,

2. C. Wright Mills, *White Collar* (New York: Oxford University Press, 1956), p. 173. See also p. 243: "The tendency of white-collar people to borrow status from higher elements is so strong that it has carried over to all social contacts and features of the work-place. Salespeople in department stores . . . frequently attempt, although often unsuccessfully, to borrow prestige from their contact with customers, and to cash it in among work colleagues as well as friends off the job. In the big city the girl who works on 34th Street cannot successfully claim as much prestige as the one who works on Fifth Avenue or 57th Street."

Macy's, and S. Klein. The differential ranking of these stores may
be illustrated in many ways. Their locations are one important point:

Highest-ranking: Saks Fifth Avenue
    at 50th St. and 5th Ave., near the center of the high fashion shopping
    district, along with other high-prestige stores such as Bonwit Teller, Henri
    Bendel, Lord and Taylor
Middle-ranking: Macy's
    Herald Square, 34th St. and Sixth Ave., near the garment district, along
    with Gimbels and Saks-34th St., other middle-range stores in price and
    prestige.
Lowest-ranking: S. Klein
    Union Square, 14th St. and Broadway, not far from the Lower East Side.

The advertising and price policies of the stores are very clearly
stratified. Perhaps no other element of class behavior is so sharply
differentiated in New York City as that of the newspaper which
people read; many surveys have shown that the *Daily News* is the
paper read first and foremost by working-class people, while the *New
York Times* draws its readership from the middle class.[3] These two
newspapers were examined for the advertising copy in October
24–27, 1962: Saks and Macy's advertised in the *New York Times*,
where Kleins was represented only by a very small item; in the *News*,
however, Saks does not appear at all, while both Macy's and Kleins
are heavy advertisers.

No. of pages of advertising
October 24–27, 1962

|          | NY Times | Daily News |
|----------|----------|------------|
| Saks     | 2        | 0          |
| Macy's   | 6        | 15         |
| S. Klein | $\frac{1}{4}$ | 10     |

We may also consider the prices of the goods advertised during
those four days. Since Saks usually does not list prices, we can only
compare prices for all three stores on one item: women's coats. Saks:
$90.00, Macy's: $79.95, Kleins: $23.00. On four items, we can compare
Kleins and Macy's:

3. This statement is fully confirmed by answers to a question on newspaper readership in the Mobilization for Youth Survey of the Lower East Side. The readership
of the *Daily News* and *Daily Mirror* (now defunct) on the one hand, and the *New
York Times* and *Herald Tribune* (now defunct) on the other hand, is almost complementary in distribution by social class.

|            | *Macy's*     | *S. Klein*    |
|------------|--------------|---------------|
| dresses    | $14.95       | $ 5.00        |
| girls' coats | 16.99      | 12.00         |
| stockings  | 0.89         | 0.45          |
| men's suits | 49.95–64.95 | 26.00–66.00   |

The emphasis on prices is also different. Saks either does not mention prices, or buries the figure in small type at the foot of the page. Macy's features the prices in large type, but often adds the slogan, "You get more than low prices." Kleins, on the other hand, is often content to let the prices speak for themselves. The form of the prices is also different: Saks gives prices in round figures, such as $120; Macy's always shows a few cents off the dollar: $49.95; Kleins usually prices its goods in round numbers, and adds the retail price which is always much higher, and shown in Macy's style: "$23.00, marked down from $49.95."

The physical plant of the stores also serves to differentiate them. Saks is the most spacious, especially on the upper floors, with the least amount of goods displayed. Many of the floors are carpeted, and on some of them, a receptionist is stationed to greet the customers. Kleins, at the other extreme, is a maze of annexes, sloping concrete floors, low ceilings; it has the maximum amount of goods displayed at the least possible expense.

The principal stratifying effect upon the employees is the prestige of the store, and the working conditions. Wages do not stratify the employees in the same order. On the contrary, there is every indication that high-prestige stores such as Saks pay lower wages than Macy's.

Saks is a nonunion store, and the general wage structure is not a matter of public record. However, conversations with a number of men and women who have worked in New York department stores, including Saks and Macy's, show general agreement on the direction of the wage differential.[4] Some of the incidents reflect a

4. Macy's sales employees are represented by a strong labor union, while Saks is not unionized. One former Macy's employee considered it a matter of common knowledge that Saks wages were lower than Macy's, and that the prestige of the store helped to maintain its nonunion position. Bonuses and other increments are said to enter into the picture. It appears that it is more difficult for a young girl to get a job at Saks than at Macy's. Thus Saks has more leeway in hiring policies, and the tendency of the store officials to select girls who speak in a certain way will play a part in the stratification of language, as well as the adjustment made by the employees to their situation. Both influences converge to produce stratification.

willingness of sales people to accept much lower wages from the store with greater prestige. The executives of the prestige stores pay a great deal of attention to employee relations, and take many unusual measures to ensure that the sales people feel that they share in the general prestige of the store.[5] One of the Lower East Side informants who worked at Saks was chiefly impressed with the fact that she could buy Saks clothes at a 25 percent discount. A similar concession from a lower-prestige store would have been of little interest to her.

From the point of view of Macy's employees, a job in Kleins is well below the horizon. Working conditions and wages are generally considered to be worse, and the prestige of Kleins is very low indeed. As we will see, the ethnic composition of the store employees reflects these differences quite accurately.

A socioeconomic index which ranked New Yorkers on occupation would show the employees of the three stores at the same level; an income scale would probably find Macy's employees somewhat higher than the others; education is the only objective scale which might differentiate the groups in the same order as the prestige of the stores, though there is no evidence on this point. However, the working conditions of sales jobs in the three stores stratify them in the order: Saks, Macy's, Kleins; the prestige of the stores leads to a social evaluation of these jobs in the same order. Thus the two aspects of social stratification—differentiation and evaluation—are to be seen in the relations of the three stores and their employees.

The normal approach to a survey of department store employees requires that one enumerate the sales people of each store, draw random samples in each store, make appointments to speak with each employee at home, interview the respondents, then segregate the native New Yorkers, analyze and resample the nonrespondents, and so on. This is an expensive and time-consuming procedure, but for most purposes there is no short cut which will give accurate and reliable results. In this case, a simpler method which relies upon the

5. A former Macy's employee told me of an incident that occurred shortly before Christmas several years ago. As she was shopping in Lord and Taylor's, she saw the president of the company making the rounds of every aisle and shaking hands with every employee. When she told her fellow employees at Macy's about this scene, the most common remark was, "How else do you get someone to work for that kind of money?" One can say that not only do the employees of higher-status stores borrow prestige from their employer—it is also deliberately loaned to them.

extreme generality of the linguistic behavior of the subjects was used to gather a very limited type of data. This method is dependent upon the systematic sampling of casual and anonymous speech events. Applied in a poorly defined environment, such a method is open to many biases and it would be difficult to say what population had been studied. In this case, our population is well defined as the sales people (or more generally, any employee whose speech might be heard by a customer) in three specific stores at a specific time. The result will be a view of the role that speech would play in the overall social imprint of the employees upon the customer. It is surprising that this simple and economical approach achieves results with a high degree of consistency and regularity, and allows us to test the original hypothesis in a number of subtle ways.

### The Method

The application of the study of casual and anonymous speech events to the department-store situation was relatively simple. The interviewer approached the informant in the role of a customer asking for directions to a particular department. The department was one which was located on the fourth floor. When the interviewer asked, "Excuse me, where are the women's shoes?" the answer would normally be, "Fourth floor."

The interviewer then leaned forward and said, "Excuse me?" He would usually then obtain another utterance, *"Fourth floor,"* spoken in careful style under emphatic stress.[6]

The interviewer would then move along the aisle of the store to a point immediately beyond the informant's view, and make a written note of the data. The following independent variables were included:

the store
floor within the store[7]
sex
age (estimated in units of five years)

6. The interviewer in all cases was myself. I was dressed in middle-class style, with jacket, white shirt and tie, and used my normal pronunciation as a college-educated native of New Jersey (r-pronouncing).

7. Notes were also made on the department in which the employee was located, but the numbers for individual departments are not large enough to allow comparison.

occupation (floorwalker, sales, cashier, stockboy)
race
foreign or regional accent, if any

The dependent variable is the use of (r) in four occurrences:

casual: fou_rth floo_r
emphatic: *fou_rth floo_r*

Thus we have preconsonantal and final position, in both casual and emphatic styles of speech. In addition, all other uses of (r) by the informant were noted, from remarks overheard or contained in the interview. For each plainly constricted value of the variable, (r-1) was entered; for unconstricted schwa, lengthened vowel, or no representation, (r-0) was entered. Doubtful cases or partial construction were symbolized *d* and were not used in the final tabulation.

Also noted were instances of affricates or stops used in the word *fourth* for the final consonant, and any other examples of nonstandard (th) variants used by the speaker.

This method of interviewing was applied in each aisle on the floor as many times as possible before the spacing of the informants became so close that it was noticed that the same question had been asked before. Each floor of the store was investigated in the same way. On the fourth floor, the form of the question was necessarily different:

"Excuse me, what floor is this?"

Following this method, 68 interviews were obtained in Saks, 125 in Macy's, and 71 in Kleins. Total interviewing time for the 264 subjects was approximately 6.5 hours.

At this point, we might consider the nature of these 264 interviews in more general terms. They were speech events which had entirely different social significance for the two participants. As far as the informant was concerned, the exchange was a normal salesman-customer interaction, almost below the level of conscious attention, in which relations of the speakers were so casual and anonymous that they may hardly have been said to have met. This tenuous relationship was the minimum intrusion upon the behavior of the subject; language and the use of language never appeared at all.

From the point of view of the interviewer, the exchange was a systematic elicitation of the exact forms required, in the desired context, the desired order, and with the desired contrast of style.

## Overall Stratification of (r)

The results of the study showed clear and consistent stratification of (r) in the three stores. In Fig. 2.1, the use of (r) by employees of Saks, Macy's and Kleins is compared by means of a bar graph. Since

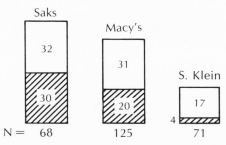

Fig. 2.1. Overall stratification of (r) by store. Shaded area = % all (r-1); unshaded area = % some (r-1); % no (r-1) not shown. N = total number of cases.

the data for most informants consist of only four items, we will not use a continuous numerical index for (r), but rather divide all informants into three categories.

all (r-1): those whose records show only (r-1) and no (r-0)
some (r-1): those whose records show at least one (r-1) and one (r-0)
no (r-1): those whose records show only (r-0)

From Fig. 2.1 we see that a total of 62 percent of Saks employees, 51 percent of Macy's, and 20 percent of Kleins used all or some (r-1). The stratification is even sharper for the percentages of all (r-1). As the hypothesis predicted, the groups are ranked by their differential use of (r-1) in the same order as their stratification by extralinguistic factors.

Next, we may wish to examine the distribution of (r) in each of the four standard positions. Fig. 2.2 shows this type of display, where once again, the stores are differentiated in the same order, and for each position. There is a considerable difference between Macy's and Kleins at each position, but the difference between Macy's and Saks varies. In emphatic pronunciation of the final (r), Macy's employees come very close to the mark set by Saks. It would seem that r-pronunciation is the norm at which a majority of Macy employees aim,

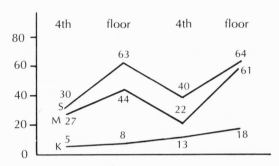

Fig. 2.2  Percentage of all (r-1) by store for four positions. (S = Saks, M = Macy's, K = Kleins.)

yet not the one they use most often. In Saks, we see a shift between casual and emphatic pronunciation, but it is much less marked. In other words, Saks employees have more *security* in a linguistic sense.[8]

The fact that the figures for (r-1) at Kleins are low should not obscure the fact that Kleins employees also participate in the same pattern of stylistic variation of (r) as the other stores. The percentage of r-pronunciation rises at Kleins from 5 to 18 percent as the context becomes more emphatic: a much greater rise in percentage than in the other stores, and a more regular increase as well. It will be important to bear in mind that this attitude—that (r-1) is the most appropriate pronunciation for emphatic speech—is shared by at least some speakers in all three stores.

Table 2.1 shows the data in detail, with the number of instances obtained for each of the four positions of (r), for each store. It may be noted that the number of occurrences in the second pronunciation of *four* is considerably reduced, primarily as a result of some speakers' tendency to answer a second time, "Fourth."

8. The extreme style shifting of the second-highest status group appears throughout the New York City pattern, and is associated with an extreme sensitivity to the norms of an exterior reference group (see Ch. 5 in this volume). In Table 5.1 on p. 133 the data on the Index of Linguistic Insecurity is given, which is the number of items in which a speaker distinguishes between his own pronunciation of a word and the correct pronunciation. The second-highest group has the highest scores on this index. We find parallel phenomena in Shuy, Wolfram, and Riley 1967, Wolfram 1969, and Levine and Crockett 1966, who found in their study of Hillsboro, North Carolina that the second-highest group on the basis of education showed the most extreme stylistic shift of (r).

TABLE 2.1.
DETAILED DISTRIBUTION OF (r) BY STORE AND WORD POSITION

| (r) | Saks | | | | Macy's | | | | S. Klein | | | |
|---|---|---|---|---|---|---|---|---|---|---|---|---|
| | Casual 4th floor | | Emphatic 4th floor | | Casual 4th floor | | Emphatic 4th floor | | Casual 4th floor | | Emphatic 4th floor | |
| (r-1) | 17 | 31 | 16 | 21 | 33 | 48 | 13 | 31 | 3 | 5 | 6 | 7 |
| (r-0) | 39 | 18 | 24 | 12 | 81 | 62 | 48 | 20 | 63 | 59 | 40 | 33 |
| d | 4 | 5 | 4 | 4 | 0 | 3 | 1 | 0 | 1 | 1 | 3 | 3 |
| No data* | 8 | 14 | 24 | 31 | 11 | 12 | 63 | 74 | 4 | 6 | 22 | 28 |
| Total no. | 68 | 68 | 68 | 68 | 125 | 125 | 125 | 125 | 71 | 71 | 71 | 71 |

*The "no data" category for Macy's shows relatively high values under the emphatic category. This discrepancy is due to the fact that the procedure for requesting repetition was not standardized in the investigation of the ground floor at Macy's, and values for emphatic response were not regularly obtained. The effects of this loss are checked in Table 2.2, where only complete responses are compared.

Since the numbers in the fourth position are somewhat smaller than the second, it might be suspected that those who use [r] in Saks and Macy's tend to give fuller responses, thus giving rise to a spurious impression of increase in (r) values in those positions. We can check this point by comparing only those who gave a complete response. Their responses can be symbolized by a four-digit number, representing the pronunciation in each of the four positions respectively (see Table 2.2).

Thus we see that the pattern of differential ranking in the use of

TABLE 2.2.
DISTRIBUTION OF (r) FOR COMPLETE RESPONSES

| (r) | % of total responses in | | |
|---|---|---|---|
| | Saks | Macy's | S. Klein |
| All (r-1)   1 1 1 1 | 24 | 22 | 6 |
| Some (r-1) 0 1 1 1 | 46 | 37 | 12 |
|             0 0 1 1 | | | |
|             0 1 0 1 etc. | | | |
| No (r-1)    0 0 0 0 | 30 | 41 | 82 |
| | 100 | 100 | 100 |
| N = | 33 | 48 | 34 |

(r) is preserved in this subgroup of complete responses, and omission of the final "floor" by some respondents was not a factor in this pattern.

### The Effect of Other Independent Variables

Other factors, besides the stratification of the stores, may explain the regular pattern of r-pronunciation seen above, or this effect may be the contribution of a particular group in the population, rather than the behavior of the sales people as a whole. The other independent variables recorded in the interviews enable us to check such possibilities.

*Race*

There are many more black employees in the Kleins sample than in Macy's, and more in Macy's than in Saks. Table 2.3 shows the percentages of black informants and their responses. When we compare these figures with those of Fig. 2.1, for the entire population, it is evident that the presence of many black informants will contribute to a lower use of (r-1). The black subjects at Macy's used less (r-1) than the white informants, though only to a slight extent; the black subjects at Kleins were considerably more biased in the r-less direction.

The higher percentage of black sales people in the lower-ranking stores is consistent with the general pattern of social stratification, since in general, black workers have been assigned less desirable jobs. Therefore the contribution of black speakers to the overall pattern is consistent with the hypothesis.

TABLE 2.3.
DISTRIBUTION OF (r) FOR BLACK EMPLOYEES

|  | % of responses in | | |
|---|---|---|---|
| (r) | Saks | Macy's | S. Klein |
| All (r-1) | 50 | 12 | 0 |
| Some (r-1) | 0 | 35 | 6 |
| No (r-1) | 50 | 53 | 94 |
|  | 100 | 100 | 100 |
| N = | 2 | 17 | 18 |
| % of black informants: | 03 | 14 | 25 |

*Occupation*

There are other differences in the populations of the stores. The types of occupations among the employees who are accessible to customers are quite different. In Macy's, the employees who were interviewed could be identified as floorwalkers (by red and white carnations), sales people, cashiers, stockboys, and elevator operators. In Saks, the cashiers are not accessible to the customer, working behind the sales counters, and stockboys are not seen. The working operation of the store goes on behind the scenes, and does not intrude upon the customer's notice. On the other hand, at Kleins, all of the employees seem to be operating on the same level: it is difficult to tell the difference between sales people, managers, and stockboys.

Here again, the extralinguistic stratification of the stores is reinforced by objective observations in the course of the interview. We can question if these differences are not responsible for at least a part of the stratification of (r). For the strongest possible result, it would be desirable to show that the stratification of (r) is a property of the most homogeneous subgroup in the three stores: native New York, white sales women. Setting aside the male employees, all occupations besides selling itself, the black and Puerto Rican employees, and all those with a foreign accent,[9] there are still a total of 141 informants to study.

Fig. 2.3 shows the percentages of (r-1) used by the native white sales women of the three stores, with the same type of graph as in Fig. 2.1. The stratification is essentially the same in direction and outline, though somewhat smaller in magnitude. The greatly reduced Kleins sample still shows by far the lowest use of (r-1), and Saks is ahead of Macy's in this respect. We can therefore conclude that the stratification of (r) is a process which affects every section of the sample.

9. In the sample as a whole, 17 informants with distinct foreign accents were found, and one with regional characteristics which were clearly not of New York City origin. The foreign language speakers in Saks had French, or other western European accents, while those in Kleins had Jewish and other eastern European accents. There were three Puerto Rican employees in the Kleins sample, one in Macy's, none in Saks. There were 70 men and 194 women. Men showed the following small differences from women in percentages of (r-1) usage:

|            | men | women |
|------------|-----|-------|
| all (r-1)  | 22  | 30    |
| some (r-1) | 22  | 17    |
| no (r-1)   | 57  | 54    |

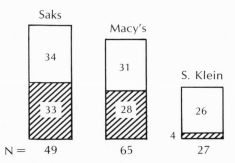

Fig. 2.3. Stratification of (r) by store for native New York white sales women. Shaded area = % all (r-1); unshaded area = % some (r-1); % no (r-1) not shown. N = total number of cases.

We can now turn the heterogeneous nature of the Macy's sample to advantage. Fig. 2.4 shows the stratification of (r) according to occupational groups in Macy's: in line with our initial hypothesis, this is much sharper than the stratification of the employees in general. The total percentage of those who use all or some (r-1) is almost the same for the floorwalkers and the sales people but a much higher percentage of floorwalkers consistently use (r-1).

Another interesting comparison may be made at Saks, where there is a great discrepancy between the ground floor and the upper floors. The ground floor of Saks looks very much like Macy's: many crowded counters, salesgirls leaning over the counters, almost elbow to elbow, and a great deal of merchandise displayed. But the upper floors of Saks are far more spacious; there are long vistas of empty carpeting, and on the floors devoted to high fashion, there are models who display the individual garments to the customers. Receptionists

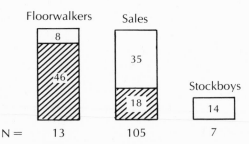

Fig. 2.4. Stratification of (r) by occupational groups in Macy's. Shaded area = % all (r-1); unshaded area = % some (r-1); % no (r-1) not shown. N = total number of cases.

are stationed at strategic points to screen out the casual spectators from the serious buyers.

It would seem logical then, to compare the ground floor of Saks with the upper floors. By the hypothesis, we should find a differential use of (r-1). Table 2.4 shows that this is the case.

TABLE 2.4.
DISTRIBUTION OF (r) BY FLOOR IN SAKS

| (r) | Ground floor | Upper floors |
|---|---|---|
| % all (r-1) | 23 | 34 |
| % some (r-1) | 23 | 40 |
| % no (r-1) | 54 | 26 |
|  | 100 | 100 |
| N = | 30 | 38 |

In the course of the interview, information was also collected on the (th) variable, particularly as it occurred in the word *fourth*. This is one of the major variables used in the study of social stratification in New York (Labov 1966a) and elsewhere (Wolfram 1969; Anshen 1969). The most strongly stigmatized variant is the use of the stop [t] in *fourth, through, think,* etc. The percentage of speakers who used stops in this position was fully in accord with the other measures of social stratification which we have seen:

Saks      00%
Macy's    04
S. Klein  15

Thus the hypothesis has received a number of semi-independent confirmations. Considering the economy with which the information was obtained, the survey appears to yield rich results. It is true that we do not know a great deal about the informants that we would like to know: their birthplace, language history, education, participation in New York culture, and so on. Nevertheless, the regularities of the underlying pattern are strong enough to overcome this lack of precision in the selection and identification of informants.

### Differentiation by Age of the Informants

The age of the informants was estimated within five-year intervals, and these figures cannot be considered reliable for any but the simplest kind of comparison. However, it should be possible to break down the age groups into three units, and detect any overall direction of change.

If, as we have indicated, (r-1) is one of the chief characteristics of a new prestige pattern which is being superimposed upon the native New York City pattern, we would expect to see a rise in r-pronunciation among the younger sales people. The overall distribution by age shows no evidence of change, however in Table 2.5:

TABLE 2.5.
DISTRIBUTION OF (r) BY ESTIMATED AGE

| (r) | Age groups | | |
| | 15–30 | 35–50 | 55–70 |
| --- | --- | --- | --- |
| % all (r-1) | 24 | 20 | 20 |
| % some (r-1) | 21 | 28 | 22 |
| % no (r-1) | 55 | 52 | 58 |

This lack of direction is surprising, in the light of other evidence that the use of (r-1) as a prestige variant is increasing among younger people in New York City. There is clearcut evidence for the absence of (r-1) in New York City in the 1930's (Kurath and McDavid 1951) and a subsequent increase in the records of Hubbell (1950) and Bronstein (1962). When we examine the distributions for the individual stores, we find that the even distribution through age levels disappears. Fig. 2.5 shows that the expected inverse correlation with age appears in Saks, but not in Macy's or Kleins. Instead, Macy's shows the reverse direction at a lower level, with older subjects using more (r-1), and Kleins no particular correlation with age. This complex pattern is even more puzzling, and one is tempted to dismiss it as the absence of any pattern. But although the numbers of the subgroups may appear to be small, they are larger than many of the subgroups used in the discussions of previous pages, and as we will see, it is not possible to discount the results.

The conundrum represented by Fig. 2.5 is one of the most significant results of the procedures that have been followed to this point. Where all other findings confirm the original hypothesis, a single result which does not fit the expected pattern may turn our attention in new and profitable directions. From the data in the department store survey alone, it was not possible to account for

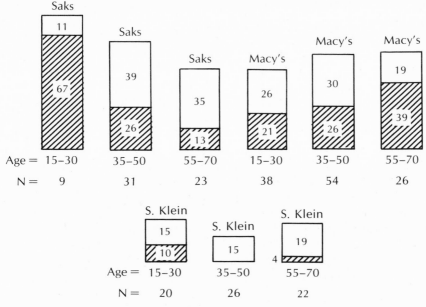

Fig. 2.5. Stratification of (r) by store and age level. Shaded area = % all (r-1); unshaded area = % some (r-1); % no (r-1) not shown. N = total number of cases.

Fig. 2.5 except in speculative terms. In the original report on the department store survey, written shortly after the work was completed, we commented:

How can we account for the differences between Saks and Macy's? I think we can say this: the shift from the influence of the New England prestige pattern (r-less) to the Midwestern prestige pattern (r-ful) is felt most completely at Saks. The younger people at Saks are under the influence of the r-pronouncing pattern, and the older ones are not. At Macy's, there is less sensitivity to the effect among a large number of younger speakers who are completely immersed in the New York City linguistic tradition. The stockboys, the young salesgirls, are not as yet fully aware of the prestige attached to r-pronunciation. On the other hand, the older people at Macy's tend to adopt this pronunciation: very few of them rely upon the older pattern of prestige pronunciation which supports the r-less tendency of older Saks sales people. This is a rather complicated argument, which would certainly have to be tested very thoroughly by longer interviews in both stores before it could be accepted.

The complex pattern of Fig. 2.5 offered a considerable challenge for interpretation and explanation, but one possibility that always had to be considered was that it was the product of the many sources of error inherent in rapid and anonymous surveys. To confirm and explain the results of the department store survey it will be necessary to look ahead to the results of the systematic interviewing program discussed in Chs. 3-7. When the results of the major study of the Lower East Side were analyzed, it became clear that Fig. 2.5 was not an artifact of the method but reflected real social patterns (Labov 1966a:342 ff). The Lower East Side data most comparable to the department store study are the distribution of (r) by age and class in Style B—the relatively careful speech which is the main bulk of the individual interview (see Ch. 3 for the definition of styles). To Saks, Macy's, Kleins, we can compare upper middle class, lower middle class, and working class as a whole. The age ranges which are most comparable to the department store ranges are 20-29, 30-39, and 40-. (Since the department store estimates are quite rough, there would be no gain in trying to match the figures exactly.) Fig. 2.6 is

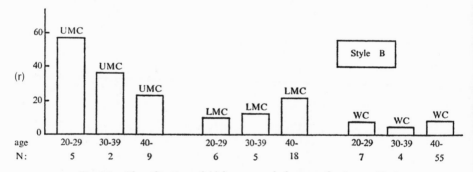

Fig. 2.6.  Classification of (r) by age and class on the Lower East
Side: in style B, careful speech.

then the age and class display for the Lower East Side use of (r) most comparable to Fig. 2.5. Again, we see that the highest status group shows the inverse correlation of (r-1) with age: younger speakers use more (r-1); the second-highest status group shows (r) at a lower level and the reverse correlation with age; and the working-class groups at a still lower level with no particular correlation with age.

This is a very striking confirmation, since the two studies have quite complementary sources of error. The Lower East Side survey was a secondary random sample, based on a Mobilization for Youth survey, with complete demographic information on each informant. The interviews were tape-recorded, and a great deal of data on (r) was obtained from each speaker in a wide variety of styles. On the other hand, the department-store study involved a much greater likelihood of error on a number of counts: the small amount of data per informant, the method of notation, the absence of tape recording and reliance on short-term memory, the method of sampling, the estimation of age of the informant, and the lack of background data on the informants. Most of these sources of error are inherent in the method. To compensate for them, we had the uniformity of the interview procedure, the location of the informants in their primary role as employees, the larger number of cases within a single cell, the simplicity of the data, and above all the absence of the biasing effect of the formal linguistic interview. The Lower East Side survey was weak in just those areas where the department-store study was strong, and strong where it was weak. The methodological differences are summed up in the table below.

|  | Lower East Side survey | Department-store study |
| --- | --- | --- |
| LES > DS |  |  |
| sampling | random | informants available at specific locations |
| recording of data | tape-recorded | short term memory and notes |
| demographic data | complete | minimal: by inspection and inference |
| amount of data | large | small |
| stylistic range | wide | narrow |
| DS > LES |  |  |
| size of sample | moderate | large |
| location | home, alone | at work, with others |
| social context | interview | request for information |
| effect of observation | maximal | minimal |
| total time per subject (location and interview) | 4–8 hours | 5 minutes |

   The convergence of the Lower East Side survey and the department-store survey therefore represents the ideal solution to the Observer's Paradox (Ch. 8): that our goal is to observe the way people use language when they are not being observed. All of our methods involve an approximation to this goal: when we approach from two different directions, and get the same result, we can feel confident that we have reached past the Observer's Paradox to the structure that exists independently of the analyst.

Given the pattern of Fig. 2.5 as a social fact, how can we explain it? The suggestions advanced in our preliminary note seem to be moving in the right direction, but at that time we had not isolated the hypercorrect pattern of the lower middle class nor identified the crossover pattern characteristic of change in progress. We must draw more material from the later research to solve this problem.

Figs. 2.5 and 2.6 are truncated views of the three-dimensional distribution of the new r-pronouncing norm by age, style, and social class. Fig. 2.7 shows two of the stylistic cross sections from the more

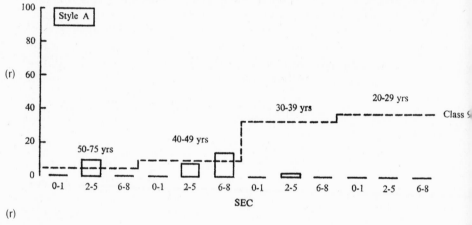

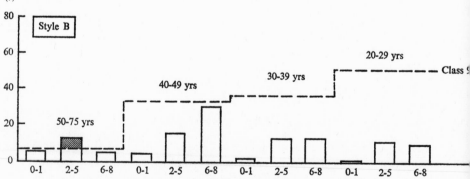

Fig. 2.7. Development of class stratification of (r) for casual speech (Style A) and careful speech (Style B) in apparent time. SEC = socioeconomic class scale.

detailed study of the Lower East Side population, with four sub-
divisions by age. The dotted line shows us how the highest status
group (Class 9) introduces the new r-pronouncing norm in casual
speech. In Style A only upper-middle-class speakers under 40 show
any sizeable amount of (r-1). None of the younger speakers in the
other social groups show any response to this norm in Style A,
though some effect can be seen in the middle-aged subjects, especially in the second-highest status group (Class 6–8, lower middle
class). In Style B, this imitative effect is exaggerated, with the middle-aged lower-middle-class group coming very close to the upper-
middle-class norm. In more formal styles, not shown here, this
subgroup shows an even sharper increase in r-pronunciation, going
beyond the upper-middle-class norm in the "hypercorrect" pattern
that has appeared for this group in other studies (see Ch. 5 in this
volume; Levine and Crockett 1966; Shuy, Wolfram, and Riley 1967).
Fig. 2.7 is not a case of the reversal of the age distribution of (r-1);
rather it is a one-generation lag in the peak of response to the new
norm. The second-highest status group responds to the new norm
with a weaker form of imitation in connected speech, with middle-
aged speakers adopting the new norm of the younger high-status
speakers; Fig. 2.8 shows this schematically. Our studies do not give
the exact profile of the use of (r) among younger upper-middle-class
speakers, since we did not focus on that age range. In later observations, I have met some upper-middle-class youth who use 100 percent (r-1), but in most families, (r-1) is still a superposed pronunciation in adolescence and Fig. 2.8 reflects this. If we wish to express
the (r-1) distribution in a single function, we can say that it is in-

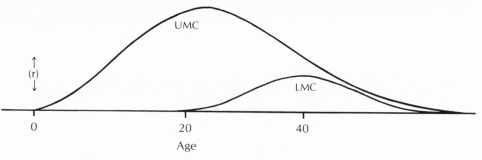

Fig. 2.8.  Hypothetical distribution of (r) as an incoming prestige
    feature.

versely correlated with distance from the highest-status group (taking Class 9 as 1, Classes 6–8 as 2, Classes 2–5 as 3, and Classes 0–1 as 4). It is also directly correlated with the formality of style and the amount of attention paid to speech (taking casual speech, style A, as 0, careful speech, style B, as 1, etc.). The slope of style shifting is modified by a function which may be called the "Index of Linguistic Insecurity" (ILI), which is maximized for the second-highest status group (see Table 5.1, p. 133 for the quantitative index). The age distribution must be shown as greatest for the upper middle class at age 20 and at age 40 for the lower middle class. We can formalize these observations by writing

$$(r\text{-}1) = -a\,(\text{Class}) + b\,(\text{Style})(\text{ILI}) - c|(\text{Class}) \cdot 20 - (\text{Age})| + d$$

The third term is minimized for the upper middle class at age 20, for the lower middle class at age 40, the working class at age 60, etc. Fig. 2.7 supports this semiquantitative expression of a wave effect, which still has a number of unspecified constants.

There is a considerable difference between the behavior of the highest-status group and the others. The upper middle class develops the use of (r-1) early in life—as a variable expression of relative formality to be found at all stylistic levels. For the other groups in New York City, there is no solid basis for (r-1) in the vernacular style of casual speech; for them, (r-1) is a form which requires some attention paid to speech if it is realized at all. As in so many other formal marks of style-shifting, the lower middle class overdoes the process of correction. This is a process learned late in life. When speakers who are now 40–50 were growing up, the prestige norm was not (r-1) but (r-0). Before World War II, the New York City schools were dominated by an Anglophile tradition which taught that (r-1) was a provincial feature, an incorrect inversion of the consonant, and that the correct pronunciation of orthographic r in car was (r-0), [kɑ · ], in accordance with "international English".[10]

_____

10. See for example *Voice and Speech Problems*, a text written for New York City schools in 1940 by Raubicheck, Davis, and Carll (1940:336):

There are many people who feel that an effort should be made to make the pronunciation conform to the spelling, and for some strange reason, they are particularly concerned with r. We all pronounce *calm, psalm, almond, know, eight, night,* and *there* without worrying . . . Yet people who would not dream of saying kni: or psai'kɒlədʒi insist on attempting to sound the r in words like pɑ·k or faðə just because an r marks the spot where our ancestors used a trill

No adjustment in the pronunciation of this consonant was then necessary for New Yorkers who were trying to use the prestige norm—it was only vowel quality which had to be corrected. This r-less norm can be seen in the formal speech of upper-middle-class speakers, over 40, and lower-middle-class speakers over 50. It also appears in subjective-reaction tests (Ch. 6) for older speakers. The lower-middle-class speakers who now shift to (r-1) in formal styles have abandoned their prestige norm and are responding to the form used by the younger high-status speakers that they come into contact with. On the other hand, many upper-middle-class speakers adhere to their original norm, in defiance of the prevailing trend. The pattern which we have observed in the department-store survey is therefore a reflection of the linguistic insecurity of the lower middle class, which has led the older generation to adopt the most recent norm of (r-1) in preference to the older norm. The process of linguistic socialization is slower for lower-middle-class groups who do not go to college than for upper-middle-class speakers, who begin adjusting to the new norm in the upper class tracks of the academic high schools. For those who do not follow this path, it takes 10 or 20 years to reach maximum sensitivity to the hierarchical organization of formal language in their community.

## Some Methodological Directions

The most important conclusion of the department-store study is that rapid and anonymous studies can be a valuable source of information on the sociolinguistic structure of a speech community. There are a number of directions in which we can extend and improve such methods. While some sources of error are inherent in the method, others can be eliminated with sufficient attention.

---

. . . More often than not, people do not really say a third sound in a word like pɑ·k but merely say the vowel ɑ: with the tongue tip curled back toward the throat. This type of vowel production is known as "Inversion."

Letitia Raubicheck was the head of the speech program in the New York City schools for many years and exerted a powerful influence on the teaching of English there. The norm of "international English" was maintained by William Tilly of Columbia and followed by Raubicheck and many others in the 1930's and 1940's. As far as I know, this norm has lost entirely its dominant position in the school system: a detailed study of its disappearance from the radio networks and the school system in the 1940's would tell us a great deal about the mechanism of such shifts in the prestige form.

In the department-store survey, the approach to sampling might have been more systematic. It would have been preferable to select every *nth* sales person, or to use some other method that would avoid the bias of selecting the most available subject in a given area. As long as such a method does not interfere with the unobtrusive character of the speech event, it would reduce sampling bias without decreasing efficiency. Another limitation is that the data were not tape-recorded. The transcriber, myself, knew what the object of the test was, and it is always possible that an unconscious bias in transcription would lead to some doubtful cases being recorded as (r-1) in Saks, and as (r-0) in Kleins.[11] A third limitation is in the method used to elicit emphatic speech. Fig. 2.2 indicates that the effect of stylistic variation may be slight as compared to the internal phonological constraint of preconsonantal vs. final position. The total percentages for all three stores bear this out.

*% of all (r-1) for each position*

| Casual | | Emphatic | |
|--------|--------|--------|--------|
| *fourth* | *floor* | *fourth* | *floor* |
| 23 | 39 | 24 | 48 |

A simple request for repetition has only a limited effect in inducing more formal speech. The use of reading passages, word lists, and minimal pairs in the Lower East Side study gave a wider range of styles. It might be possible to enlarge the stylistic range in rapid and anonymous studies by emphasizing the difficulty in hearing by one technique or another.

The sources of error in the department-store study are offset by the comparability of the three subsections, the size of the sample, and the availability of the population for rechecking. Though the individual speakers cannot be relocated, the representative population can easily be reexamined for longitudinal studies of change in progress. There are limitations of such a "pseudopanel" as compared to a true panel study of the same individuals; but the advantages in cost and efficiency are overwhelming.

---

11. When the phonetic transcriptions were first made, doubtful cases were marked as *d* and were not included in the tabulations made later. There is however room for interviewer bias in the decision between (r-0) and *d* and between *d* and (r-1).

With such promising results in hand, it should be possible to refine and improve the methods used, and apply them in a wider range of contexts. In large cities it is reasonable to select single large institutions like department stores, but there is no reason to limit rapid and anonymous surveys to sales people or to institutions of this character. We can turn to any large body of individuals located at fixed "social addresses" and accessible to interaction with the public: policemen, postal clerks, secretaries, ushers, guides, bus drivers, taxi drivers, street peddlers and demonstrators, beggars, construction workers, etc. The public groups which are most clearly identified tend to be concentrated towards the lower end of the social scale, with sales people at the upper end. But we can reach a more general public by considering shoppers, spectators at sports events, parades or construction sites, amateur gardeners, park strollers, and passersby in general; here the general character of the residential area can serve the same differentiating function as the three department stores mentioned above. Many professionals of relatively high social standing are available for public interaction: particularly teachers, doctors, and lawyers. Such public events as courtroom trials and public hearings allow us to monitor the speech of a wide range of socially located and highly differentiated individuals.[12]

There is in all such methods a bias towards those populations that are available to public interaction, and against those which are so located as to insure privacy: business and social leaders, or those engaged in aesthetic, scholarly, scientific, or illegal activities. Any of these groups can be studied with sufficient ingenuity: sociolinguistic research should certainly rise to the challenge to develop rapid and anonymous studies that will escape the limitations of convenience. But it should be emphasized that since those who are

12. Hearings of the New York City Board of Education were recorded during the study of New York City, and preliminary analysis of the data shows that the pattern of social and stylistic stratification of (r) can easily be recovered from the wide variety of speakers who appear in these hearings. Courtroom proceedings at the New York Court of General Sessions are a natural focus for such studies, but speakers often lower their voices to the point that spectators cannot hear them clearly. Only a small beginning has been made on the systematic study of passersby. Plakins (1969) approached a wide variety of pedestrians in a Connecticut town with requests for directions to an incomprehensible place, phrased at three levels of politeness. She found systematic differences in mode of response according to dress (as an index of socioeconomic position) and mode of inquiry; there were no "rude" responses [huh?] to polite inquiries.

most available to public interaction may have the most direct effect
upon linguistic change and the sociolinguistic system, the bias
through missing the more extreme and obscure ends of the social
spectrum is not as great as it may first appear.

Since the department-store survey was carried out in Manhattan,
several parallel studies have been made. In Suffolk County, Long
Island, rapid and anonymous observations of the use of (r) were
made by Patricia Allen (1968). In three stratified stores, 156 employees were observed. In the highest-status store (Macy's), only 27
percent of the subjects used no (r-1); in the intermediate store (Grant
City), 40 percent; and in the low-status store (Floyd's), 60 percent.
We see that the general New York City pattern has moved outward
from the city, producing a comparable stratification of (r) in three
stores of a somewhat narrower range than those studied in Manhattan. Our own analysis of the New York City situation shows that
rapid and anonymous surveys of this kind cannot be interpreted fully
without detailed knowledge of the dialect history of the area, and
a more systematic study of the distribution of linguistic variables
and subjective norms.[13] In this case, rapid and anonymous surveys
should be considered a supplement or preliminary to other methods,
not substitutions for them. Yet there are cases where rapid methods
can give solutions to problems that have never been circumnavigated

---

13. Allen's tables resemble the New York City patterns but with one major difference; the number of speakers who use all (r-1) is roughly constant in all three stores:
27 percent in Floyd's, 27 percent in Grant City, 32 percent in Macy's. Examination
of the distribution in apparent time showed that this phenomenon was due to the
presence of a bimodal split in the lower-store adults (over 30 years old). Eighty percent
used no (r-1) and 20 percent used a consistent all (r-1): there were none who varied.
On the other hand, 50 percent of the adults were showing variable (r) in the two other
stores. This points to the presence of an older r-pronouncing vernacular which is now
dominated by the r-less New York City pattern (Kurath and McDavid 1961), but
survives among working-class speakers. The disengagement of such bimodal patterns
is a challenging problem (Levine and Crockett 1966), and certainly requires a more
systematic survey. Similar complexity is suggested in the results of rapid and anonymous survey of stores in Austin, Texas by M. M. Harris (1969). In this basically
r-pronouncing area, the prestige norms among whites appear to be a weak constricted
[r], with a strongly retroflex consonant gaining ground among younger speakers. But
for the few blacks and Mexican-Americans encountered, this strong [r] seems to be
the norm aimed at in careful articulation. Although these results are only suggestive,
they are the kind of preliminary work which is required to orient a more systematic
investigation towards the crucial variables of the sociolinguistic structure of that
community.

by conventional techniques. We have used observations of the speech of telephone operators to construct a national map of the merger of the low back vowels in *hock* and *hawk,* and the merger of *i* and *e* before nasals in *pin* and *pen.* In our recent study of the Puerto Rican speech community in New York City, we utilized such natural experimentation to find out what percentage of those heard speaking Spanish on the street were raised in the United States, and what percentage were born in Puerto Rico (Labov and Pedraza 1971).

Future studies of language in its social context should rely more heavily on rapid and anonymous studies, as part of a general program of utilizing unobtrusive measures to control the interactive effect of the observer (Webb et al. 1966). But our rapid and anonymous studies are not passive indices of social use, like observations of wear and tear in public places. They represent a form of nonreactive experimentation in which we avoid the bias of the experimental context and the irregular interference of prestige norms but still control the behavior of subjects. We are just beginning to study speech events like *asking for directions,* isolating the invariant rules which govern them, and on this basis develop the ability to control a large body of socially located public speech in a natural setting. We see rapid and anonymous observations as the most important experimental method in a linguistic program which takes as its primary object the language used by ordinary people in their everyday affairs.

# 3 | The Isolation of Contextual Styles

THE investigation of sound change on Martha's Vineyard can be seen as the first step in a program for the study of language in its social context. The second was an attack on a much larger problem: to find some system or order in the extensive variation of English in New York City.[1] Previous reports had registered a chaotic proliferation of free variation in almost every part of the vowel system (Labov 1966a:2). Those who identify structure with homogeneity will find very little structure in New York City. In addition to a great range of social variation, there was also reported widespread stylistic variation, giving the general impression that anyone could say anything. Typical was Hubbell's report on (r):

The speaker heard both types of pronunciation about him all the time, both seem almost equally natural to him, and it is a matter of pure chance which one comes to his lips. (1950:48)

Linguists have never been unconscious of the problems of stylistic variation. The normal practice is to set such variants aside—not because they are considered unimportant, but because the techniques of linguistics are thought to be unsuitable or inadequate to handle them. Structural analysis is normally the abstraction of those unvarying, functional units of language whose occurrence can be

1. This paper is adapted from Ch. 4 of *The Social Stratification of English in New York City* (1966), and represents the techniques for isolating casual speech and other styles which were developed in the 1963–64 study of the Lower East Side of New York City. These methods are still basic to any series of individual interviews, and are now utilized regularly in studies of sound change in progress in a wide variety of English, Spanish, and French dialects. For later techniques utilizing group interaction, see Labov et al. 1968:1.

predicted by rule. Since the influence of stylistic conditioning on linguistic behavior is said to be merely statistical, it leads to statements of probability rather than rule and is therefore uninteresting to many linguists.

For the present purposes, I would rather say that stylistic variation has not been treated by techniques accurate enough to measure the extent of regularity which does prevail. The combination of many stylistic factors imposed upon other influences may lead to seemingly erratic behavior; but this apparent irregularity is comparable to the inconsistencies which seemed to govern the historical development of vowels and consonants until some of the more subtle conditioning factors were perceived.

In the last chapter, we considered one approach to discovering the system within this variation. The department-store survey showed some stylistic variation as well as vertical stratification. But the major attack on the New York City system requires much richer data: long interviews with individuals whose social position and geographic history is known; here the problem of stylistic variation becomes paramount.

The New York City study began with 70 exploratory interviews which examined in detail the phonological variation of a wide range of speakers. They were concentrated in the Lower East Side, where the population had been enumerated and a sociological survey carried out by the research branch of Mobilization for Youth, a job training agency. It seemed possible to do a secondary survey of the Lower East Side, using the sample already constructed by MFY.

These exploratory interviews showed five phonological variables that seemed to exhibit regular variation in different styles and contexts. The five variables will form the main substance for Chs. 3-6, and will enter into the more general discussions of Chs. 7-9. We may therefore consider them in some detail at the outset. To define a linguistic variable, we must (a) state the total range of linguistic contexts in which it occurs, (b) define as many phonetic variants as we can reasonably distinguish, (c) set up a quantitative index for measuring values of the variables. These steps have already been illustrated in the discussion of centralization in Martha's Vineyard; we will follow them now for the five New York City variables, (r), (eh), (oh), (th), and (dh).

The notational conventions used in the discussion of the variables and throughout this volume are given below, pp. 72-78. As pointed out in Ch. 1, the variable indicates a focus on significant distributions within the unit, constraining what would otherwise be considered free and unconstrained variation. The variables (ay) and (aw) were isomorphic with the phonemes /ay/ and /aw/; but the variable (r) corresponds to the presence or absence of /r/; and the variable (eh) includes in its range the phonemes /æh/, /eh/, and /ih/.

Particular variants or values of the variables will be indicated by a number within the parentheses, as (r-1) or (eh-4). Index scores derived from mean values of the variants will be indicated by numbers outside the parentheses, as (r)-21 or (eh)-28. Brackets will continue to indicate phonetic notation, showing impressionistic representations of the speech sounds heard; slashes will indicate here autonomous phonemes as /eh/ or /r/: the system of contrastive units independent of grammatical alternations. The more abstract morphophonemic units or systematic phonemes will be indicated by italicized forms as *r* or short *a* which are often close to the orthographic representation. Since we are dealing with low-level phonological rules, we will not normally be concerned with this higher-level representation, but it will be helpful to note at various stages the occurrence of merger of the autonomous level. This is particularly useful in establishing discrete index values in a continuous range of phonetic forms.

The correct analysis of the linguistic variable is the most important step in sociolinguistic investigation. We want to isolate the largest homogeneous class in which all subclasses vary in the same way. If we fail to do this, and throw together invariant subclasses, high-frequency, and low-frequency subclasses, our view of the sociolinguistic structures will be blurred. The regular pattern of the variable may be submerged by a large number of irregular cases—or even elements varying in a reverse direction. Once we have established this linguistic definition of the variable, we are in a position to follow the important *principle of accountability*: we will report values for every case where the variable element occurs in the relevant environments as we have defined them.

### The Five Phonological Variables

(r): the presence or absence of consonantal constriction for postvocalic, word-final and preconsonantal /r/. This includes *beer, beard, bare, bared, moor, moored, bore, board, fire, fired, flower, flowered*, where the /r/ is usually represented by a vocalic inglide [ə]; unstressed syllables in *Saturday, November*, where we have only a schwa [ə]; and *bar, barred*, where /r/ is usually represented by a lengthened vowel. However, we can get long monophthongs with high vowels, as in *beer* [bɨː], and there is sometimes an inglide heard with *bar*.

Specifically excluded from the variable are the cases where /r/ follows a mid-central vowel, as in *her* and *bird*. These two subclasses have different histories and behavior in New York City as in most r-less dialects (Labov 1966a:10). In stressed *her* we have an alternation of [hʌ∼hʌr∼hɜ∼hɜː] and with *bird*, the stigmatized palatal upglide [bɜᶦd] which is replaced with a constricted /r/ [bɝd] more often than the main subclasses. We can account for this by representing *bird* and *her* in the dictionary as /hr/ and /brd/ (see Bloomfield 1933); the term "postvocalic" in our definition thus eliminates this class, and the phonetic vowel is inserted by a later rule (see Ch. 5 in Labov 1972a).

We also exclude word-final /r/ where the next word begins with a vowel, as in *four o'clock*. This forms a separate subcase in New York City, with a much higher percentage of constricted /r/.

The two basic variants of (r) are thus

(r-1)   [r, ɚ, ə]   i.e., presence of weak or strong consonantal constriction
(r-0)   [ə, ə, ː]   i.e., absence of constriction

Borderline cases are recorded in parentheses and excluded from the count. There are relatively few of these. The (r) index is then the mean value of the variants recorded multiplied by 100: i.e., the percentage of constricted forms.

(eh): the height of the nucleus of the vowel in tensed short *a* or /æh/. This phoneme is established in New York City by a complex tensing rule which selects certain phonological subclasses; the lengthened, fronted [æˤ:] is then affected by a raising rule which carried the vowel to [ɛˤ:ə], [eˤ:ə] and [ɪˤ:ə].

The tensing rule selects short *a* before front nasal consonants /m/ and /n/, voiceless fricatives, and /f, θ, s, ʃ/, voiced stops /b, d, ž, g/. The rule is variable (by types and tokens) for voiced fricatives /v,z/ so that *razz, jazz, rasberry* are unpredictable. The consonants mentioned must be followed by a word boundary ## or inflectional boundary # or an obstruent; if a vowel or a liquid /r,l/ follows

directly, the tensing rule does not apply. Thus NYC opposes tense
*waggin', draggin', stabbin',* to lax *wagon, dragon, cabin.* In general,
the rule does not recognize a derivational boundary +, giving lax
*passage, Lassie,* etc., though there is some variation after sibilants
as in *fashion, fascinate,* etc. The rule does not apply to weak words—
that is, function words which can have schwa as their only vowel:
*am, an, can*(Aux), *has, had, as,* etc. There are lexical exceptions like
tense *avenue,* and variably tense *wagon, magic,* etc. The most regular
aspect of the rule takes the form:

$$\begin{bmatrix} +\text{low} \\ -\text{back} \end{bmatrix} \rightarrow [+\text{tense}] \overline{[-\text{Wk}]} \left\{ \begin{bmatrix} \begin{bmatrix} +\text{nas} \\ -\text{back} \end{bmatrix} \\ \begin{bmatrix} \alpha\text{tense} \\ \alpha\text{cont} \end{bmatrix} \end{bmatrix} \left\{ \begin{matrix} \# \\ [+\text{obstr}] \end{matrix} \right\} \right\}$$

For further details on the New York City tensing rule see Trager 1942
and Cohen 1970. It is plain here that there is a great deal of variation
in polysyllables and derivational forms. Learned words like *lass* and
*mastodon* are also quite variable. Since we are interested primarily
in the raising of tense (eh), we can best focus on the invariant core
of the tense class: monosyllables before front nasals, voiced stops,
and voiceless fricatives. Among monosyllables, this invariant tense
class can be opposed to a class of invariant lax and variably tense
forms:

(a) always lax    *cap, bat, batch, bat, pal, can* (Aux),
                  *had, has*
(b) variable      *jazz, salve*
                  *bang*
(c) tense         *cab, bad, badge, bag*
                  *half, pass, cash, bath,*
                  *ham, dance*

The third word class is uniformly affected in the New York City
vernacular by a lower-level raising rule. This can best be shown as
a variable rule which variably decreases the openness of the vowel:

$$\begin{bmatrix} +\text{tense} \\ -\text{back} \end{bmatrix} \rightarrow \langle x - \delta \text{ open} \rangle$$

In this form, the rule progressively affects all front vowels as the
scope of x is increased to include the most open (low) vowels, and

less open (mid) vowels. The quantity δ is a function of age, sex, style, and social class and ethnic group as we will see.

For the purposes of our study, it is necessary to establish discrete phonetic variants for the (eh) variable. Though the height of the vowel is a continuous variable, we can establish such discrete coding points with the help of other word classes that are relatively fixed.

*Scale for (eh) Index*

| No. | Approximate phonetic quality | Level with the vowel of |
|-----|------------------------------|--------------------------|
| (eh-1) | [ɪˁ :ᵊ] | NYC *beer, beard* |
| (eh-2) | [eˁ :ᵊ] | NYC *bear, bared* |
|        | [ɛˁ :ᵊ] | |
| (eh-3) | [æˆ:] | |
| (eh-4) | [æ:] | NYC *bat, batch* |
| (eh-5) | [a:] | E. New England *pass, aunt* |

The last point on the scale occurs only in hypercorrection or imitation of the older prestige norm of New England broad *a*.

The index score for (eh) is determined by coding each occurrence of a member of word class (c) above as one of the six variants, taking an average of the numerical values and multiplying by 10. Thus (eh)-25 would be the index value for a person who pronounced half of the (eh) words with (eh-3) and half with (eh-2). A person who always used a tense vowel, level with the nucleus of *bat*, will be assigned (eh)-40.

We have examined the raising of (eh) in much greater detail by spectrographic means in recent work on sound change in progress. Our instrumental studies confirm most of the impressionistic ratings assigned by the above scale, and show the emergence of a sharp differentiation between lax and tense vowels as well. Vowels affected by social correction are often lowered to first formant positions equal to *bat*, but with higher second formant positions—that is, with more extreme fronting. For further details, see Labov 1970b, and Labov, Yaeger, and Steiner (1972). Fig. 3.1 shows spectrographic measurements of the vowel system of one informant from the New York City study: the subject is Jacob S., an older man, who shows a moderate degree of raising of (eh) but a clear differentiation of the tense and lax class. Within the tense class, there are further differentiations of the three subclasses with short *a* before front nasals showing the most advanced positions.

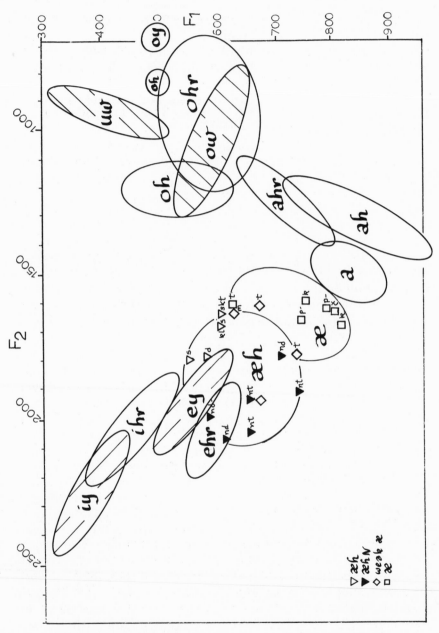

Fig. 3.1.  Vowel system of Jacob S., 57, New York City (from
Labov, Yaeger and Steiner 1972).

(*oh*): The corresponding back vowel (oh) is also raised variably in New York City: vowels in the class of *off, lost, more, talk, caught, wash*, etc., are raised progressively to mid and high position. There is no need for a tensing rule: common short *o* words before voiceless fricatives /f, θ, s/ and back nasals/ŋ/ were raised at an earlier period and are now included in the New York City class of long open *o* words: *off, lost, cloth, long, song, wrong*. These are added to the miscellaneous class of words which have coalesced into long open *o* and form the basis for the variable (oh), along with *o* before /r/.

The raising rule for (oh) is a generalization of the raising rule for (eh). It is only necessary to remove the feature [-back] from the left hand side of the rule. The variable constraint <-back> will then appear in the environment for different social classes and ethnic groups, as we will see in Ch. 5 below.

A six-point linear scale parallel to that for (eh) is used to measure the height of this vowel: the great number of diacritics needed in the phonetic quality is matched by the miscellaneous collection of reference points. The difficulty of the phonetic description of this vowel is so great that none of these methods are satisfactory, and the following discussion may be of some help.

### Scale for (oh) Index

| No. | Approximate Phonetic quality | Level with the vowel of |
|-----|------------------------------|-------------------------|
| (oh-1) | [ʊːᵊ] | NYC *sure* |
| (oh-2) | [oˁːᵊ] | |
| (oh-3) | [ɔˆːᵊ] | General American *for, nor* |
| (oh-4) | [ɔː] | IPA cardinal /ɔ/ |
| (oh-5) | [ɒ] | E. New England *hot, dog* |
| (oh-6) | [ɑ] | NYC *dock, doll* |

(oh-4) is the vowel height level with the fixed position for cardinal [ɔ]. It is heard frequently in the speech of upstate New York residents, and in many other parts of the country, but never with enough consistency for the speech of a particular region to serve as a firm reference point. (oh-3) is somewhat higher, and may be identified fairly accurately as the sound preceding [r] in *for, or, nor*, in almost any region of the United States where [r] is pronounced in those words.

(oh-2) is higher than (oh-3), more forward, and more rounded. The centering glide which follows is often more marked than with (oh-3), but a glide does not necessarily follow. (oh-1) is raised and centered beyond (oh-2), level with most pronunciations of *sure*, and is rounded with what appears to be considerable tension. The rounding is quite different from that observed in British tense [ɔ:]: it is actually a pursing of the lips, in women; in men, a similar but distinct phonetic quality is imparted by what seems to be a hollowing of the tongue.

The impressionistic transcription of (oh) has been confirmed and checked by spectrographic measurement in our studies of sound change in progress. On Fig. 3.1 we can see the raising of (oh) for Jacob S., with a fairly advanced state of the variable.

(*th*) and (*dh*). These two variables are the initial consonants of *thing* and *then*; they are well known throughout most of the United States as the stereotype *dese*, *dem*, and *dose*. These consonants do not of course show any close relation to the vowel system; they are incorporated in this study as a pair of correlated variables which are not involved in any of the processes of structural change which affect the first three variables.

|   |                          | (th)   | (dh)   |
|---|--------------------------|--------|--------|
| 1 | an interdental fricative | [θ]    | [ð]    |
| 2 | an affricate             | [tθ]   | [dð]   |
| 3 | a lenis dental stop      | [t]    | [d]    |

The prestige form in this scale is the fricative, and the stop with its [t]-like or [d]-like effect is everywhere considered to have less prestige. This stop consonant may be formed in a number of different ways, but its essential quality is that no turbulent, fricative, or scraping sound is heard as it is articulated. The affricate is a rapid succession of the two forms—or more precisely, it is heard as the fricative with a sudden onset, instead of a gradual beginning.

The stop that is formed is usually dental. The [t] is usually not aspirated as fully as the phoneme /t/ and the [d] is usually not voiced as fully as /d/. Under stress, these phones can merge with /t/ and /d/, yielding an intersection of the phonemes /θ,t/, and /ð,d/. Nevertheless, native speakers keep the two word classes quite separate; we hear no hypercorrection in formal style such as /ða°nðɛ:r/ for *down there*.

The zero variant in *'at, 'ere*, etc. is rated as (dh-2), with the same value as the affricate.

## Contextual Styles

The initial exploration of the use of English in New York City suggested regular variation in different styles and contexts for these five phonological variables. The problem is to control the context, and define the styles of speech which occur within each context, so that this hypothesis of regular variation can be tested.

For accurate information on speech behavior, we will eventually need to compare the performance of large numbers of speakers. Furthermore, we will want to study a sample which is representative of a much larger group, and possibly of the New York speech community as a whole. This cannot be done without random sampling. Yet to complete random sampling, and to make the data for many speakers comparable, we need structured, formal interviews. But the formal interview itself defines a speech context in which only one speaking style normally occurs, that which we may call *careful speech*. The bulk of the informant's speech production at other times may be quite different. He may use careful speech in many other contexts, but on most occasions he will be paying much less attention to his own speech, and employ a more relaxed style which we may call *casual speech*. We can hear this casual speech on the streets of New York, in bars, on the subway, at the beach, or whenever we visit friends in the city. Yet anonymous observations in these contexts will also be biased. Our friends are a very special group, and so too are those New Yorkers who frequent bars, play stickball in the streets, visit public beaches, or talk loud enough in restaurants to be overheard. Only through a painstaking random sampling of the entire population can we avoid serious bias. The problem is now to see what can be accomplished within the bounds of the interview. We will begin with the dominant situation of the face-to-face interview, which we will designate *Context B*, reserving *Context A* for those situations which escape the social constraints of the interview situation.

### Context B. The Interview Situation

The simplest style to define is the one we have called *careful speech*. In our investigation, this is the type of speech that normally occurs when the subject is answering questions which are formally recognized as "part of the interview." Generally speaking, an interview which has as its professed object the language of the speaker will rate higher on the scale of formality than most conversation.[2] It is not as formal a situation as a public address, and less formal than the speech which would be used in a first interview for a job, but it is certainly more formal than casual conversation among friends or family members. The term "consultative," introduced by Joos (1960), seems very apt for this stylistic level. The degree of spontaneity or warmth in the replies of individuals may vary greatly, but the relation of their careful speech to the speech of less formal contexts is generally constant. Careful speech will then be defined as that speech which occurs in Context B, and will be designated *Style B*.

It is a relatively simple matter to shift the context from Context B in a more formal direction, though there are a number of ways of refining this procedure. In the following discussion, we will pursue the definition and control of more formal styles to its ultimate conclusion, before attempting to move in the opposite direction.

### Context C. Reading Style

After the main body of the interview, which might last anywhere from half an hour to an hour, the informant is asked to read two standard texts. One of these is designed to concentrate the main phonological variables in successive paragraphs, and the other to juxtapose minimal pairs in a text. Both are written in a colloquial style, to get as smooth a flow of language as possible, and to involve the reader as much as possible in the story line. This involvement gives us a maximum spread between Style C and the more formal inquiries to follow, without any danger of reducing the distance between B and C: the most formal conversational style will still be sharply differentiated from reading style in the phonological variables. Secondly, the involvement in the story insures that there will be a continuous flow of speech, with appropriate sandhi rules. It

2. The formal interviews on the Lower East Side were conducted as research of the "American Language Survey," which provided a framework for the study of reading, of word lists, of attitudes towards language, and subjective reaction tests. Our more recent studies do not take language as the overt topic of the research, but a broader subject which includes language—such as "common-sense learning." However, the stylistic constraints are roughly the same; the basic situation is that questions are being asked by one person and answered by another. The more casual or vernacular style is used primarily with those who share the most knowledge together, where the minimum amount of attention is paid to speech.

might have been possible to standardize in a different direction, by urging the subject to read carefully and slowly, but very slow reading is accompanied by special phonetic characteristics which would make it difficult to compare conversation and reading style. For example, the variable (r # #v)—final (r) followed by another word beginning with a vowel, as in *four o'clock*—may become hard to code if the tempo is very slow. In normal speech, a pronunciation in which no consonant occurs between *four* and *o'clock* would be entered as a violation of the rule followed by most New Yorkers which preserves [r] in this position. But such a rule begins to break down if speech is slow enough. Then too, at a very slow tempo of reading the minimal pairs are more likely to be noticed by the reader. Therefore the overall design of the two texts is to encourage a reasonably fast reading style.

The instructions given to the reader are designed to establish a set towards the colloquial end of the reading style; but the effect is slight, since people have little conscious control over their use of the variables in reading style. The actual content of the test is more influential. It has been found in the construction of a number of such readings that a text which is written as a narrative of a teenage boy seems to lend itself to the least artificial performance of most people. In such a framework, it was possible to incorporate such phrases as, "He was a funny kid, all right." Elderly women might balk at such a phrase if it were placed in the mouth of an adult, but as the utterance of a teenage boy, it made natural reading for them.

The content of the readings carries this point further by focusing on two main themes: the teenager's traditional protest against the restrictions of the adult world, and his exasperation at the foibles and inconsistencies of the girls he dates. In this context, adult readers find it easy to handle colloquial phrases like "got her finger in the pie," which they might not use in their own speech.

The first reading, "When I was nine or ten . . . " consists of five paragraphs in which the chief variables are successively concentrated (Labov 1966a:597). The first paragraph is a zero section, in which none of the variables being studied are to be found. The second paragraph concentrates (oh), beginning "We *a*lways had *cho*colate milk and *cof*fee cake around *four* o'clock." (Occurrences of the variable are italicized here, but not in the actual text used.) The third is concerned with (eh), as in "One m*a*n is IT: you run p*a*st him as f*a*st as you can, and you kick a tin c*a*n so he c*a*n't t*a*g you."

The fourth concentrates on (r), as in "He darted out about four feet before a car, and he got hit hard." The last paragraph has a high concentration of (th) and (dh), e.g. "There's something strange about that—how I can remember everything he did—this thing, that thing, and the other thing." The text has a double purpose. First, it allows us to measure in Context C the speaker's use of all five variables as efficiently as possible. The close juxtaposition of many examples gives us a fatigue factor not present in word lists, which differentiates the speaker's use of a recently learned "superposed" form from the vernacular forms produced without effort. Secondly, this reading contains the sentences that are used in the Subjective Reaction Test (the full text is given in Ch. 6). The subjects who have read the text themselves will be clear when they hear others read them that they are judging the form of speech rather than the content.

The second reading, "Last Saturday night I took Mary Parker to the Paramount Theatre . . . ," is designed to juxtapose a number of words that form minimal pairs, including those involving the phonological variables studied in "When I was nine or ten . . . " The pairs are italicized in the text given below, but not, of course, as the informant reads them.

Last Saturday night I took Mary Parker to the Paramount Theatre. I would rather have gone to see the Jazz *Singer* myself, but Mary got her *finger* in the pie. She hates jazz, because she can't *carry* a tune, and besides, she never misses a new film with *Cary* Grant. Well, we were waiting on line about half an hour, when some farmer from Kansas or somewhere asked us how to get to Palisades Amusement Park.

Naturally, I told him to take a bus at the Port Authority Garage on 8th Avenue, but *Mary* right away said no, he should take the I.R.T. to 125th St., and go down the escalator. She actually thought the ferry was still running.

"You're certainly in the *dark*," I told her. "They tore down that *dock ten* years ago, when you were in diapers."

"And what's the *source* of your information, Joseph?" She used her sweet-and-sour tone of *voice*, like ketchup mixed with tomato *sauce*. "Are they running submarines to the Jersey *shore*?"

When *Mary* starts to sound humorous, that's *bad: merry* hell is *sure* to break loose. I remembered the *verse* from the Bible about a good woman being worth more than rubies, and I *bared* my teeth in some kind of a smile. "Don't tell this man any *fairy* tales about a *ferry*. He can't go that way."

"Oh yes he *can!*" she said. Just then a little old lady, as *thin* as my grandmother, came up shaking a *tin can,* and this farmer asked <u>her</u> the same question. She told him to ask a subway *guard*. My *god!* I thought, that's one sure way to get lost in New York City.

Well, I managed to sleep through the worst part of the picture, and the stage show wasn't too hard to *bear*. Then I wanted to go and have a bottle of *beer*, but she had to have a *chocolate* milk at *Chock* Full O'Nuts. *Chalk* this up as a total loss, I told myself. I bet that farmer is still wandering around looking for the 125th St. Ferry.

In this reading, the minimal contrasts are brought as close together as possible, under comparable stress, so the analyst can compare their pronunciation without editing, but naturally enough so that the reader is not aware of making the contrast overtly. The examples with (r) illustrate the technique. In "You're certainly in the dark! They tore down that dock" we can determine if the contrast of *dock* and *dark* is by length alone [ɑ~ɑː] or by length and backing [ɑ~ɒː]. In "she told him to ask a subway guard. My god! I thought" we have close to the optimum juxtaposition of *guard* to *god*, which can be identical, or differ in any of the three ways shown above. Less elegant is the collocation of "source of your information" with "tomato sauce". Here /ohr/ in *source* is compared to /oh/ in *sauce;* unless the /r/ is realized, these two words are generally reported as homonyms.[3] In these three cases, we have an opportunity to observe the careful but unreflecting use of /r/ to differentiate words which otherwise can be homonyms, and we make a direct comparison with the same contrast in minimal pairs (see below). This reading also gives us potential contrasts of /ŋ~ŋg/ in *Singer~finger,* /ehrV~erV~ærV/ in *Mary~merry* and *Cary~carry,* and *fairy~ferry,* /ehr~ihr/ in *bear~beer,* /en~in/ in *ten~tin,* /oy~əhr/ in *voice~verse,* /θ~t/ in *thin~tin,* /æh~ehr/ in *bad~bared,* /ohr~uhr/ in *shore~sure,* /æ~æh/ in *can[N]~ can[AUX]*, and /a~oh/ in *chock~chalk~chocolate.*

The style used in reading under Context C will be designated *Style C.*

---

3. Our recent spectrographic studies of this data show that *source* and *sauce* are usually not homonyms, even though the speaker thinks so and reports them as "the same." The second formant of the nucleus of the vowel in *source* is usually lower, (further back in terms of the normal articulatory correlate), and in connected speech the first formant may also be lower (that is, the vowel is higher). During the minimal pair test, the vowels are brought closer together, but second formant differences persist. The phonetic differentiation of these nuclei is the same as that normally found in r-pronouncing dialects.

*Context D. Word Lists*

A further step in the direction of a more formal context is to consider the subject's pronunciation of words in isolation. There are three types of word lists which are used for the investigation of the variables (r), (eh), and (oh). One is a list which the subject knows by heart: the days of the week and the months of the year. A second type is a printed list of words with the same or similar segment. One of these contains the (eh) variable, alternating lax with tense. A reading pattern which followed the basic vernacular for this word list would show:

| *Lax* | *Tense* | *Lax* | *Tense* |
|------|--------|------|--------|
| bat   |         |        | can      |
|       | bad     |        | half     |
| back  |         |        | past     |
|       | bag     |        | ask      |
| batch |         |        | dance    |
|       | badge   | have   |          |
|       | bath    | has    |          |
| bang  |         | razz   ~ razz |   |
| pat   |         | jazz   ~ jazz |   |
|       | pad     | hammer |          |
|       | pass    |        | hamster  |
| pal   |         |        | fashion  |
|       | cash    |        | national |
|       |         | family ~ family |   |

This list therefore gives us, first, the height of the vowel in formal pronunciation of the tense forms, and second, any disturbance through social correction of the New York City vernacular form of the tensing rule.[4] The (oh) list has no such complexity, since the raising rule affects all members of the /oh/ and /ohr/ class. One member of the /a/ class—*chock*—is included in that list: *Paul, all, ball, awful, coffee, office, chalk, chocolate, chock, talk, taught, dog, forty-four.*

The third type of word list continues the phonemic investigation begun in the "Last Saturday night I took Mary Parker . . ." reading.

4. For a detailed study of this rule, see Cohen 1970. The Lower East Side study was concerned with the extent of raising of the tense vowel, and not the selection of environments by the tensing rule. Variation in the latter seems to be immune from social correction, and shows geographic and idiolectal variation of a very complex nature, controlled to a degree by the implicational ordering of the environments.

The subject is shown a list of words containing most of the minimal pairs which occurred in that reading, and a few more:

| | |
|---|---|
| dock | dark |
| pin | pen |
| guard | god |
| "I *can*" | tin *can* |
| . . . | . . . |

The subject is asked to read each pair of words aloud, and then say whether they sound the same as or different from the way he usually pronounces them. Thus in addition to the unreflecting contrasts of Style C, we have the subject's considered performance in Style D, and his subjective reaction to that performance. Eventually, all of this data is to be used for a structural analysis of the system; here the mean values of the variables in the word lists (except (r) in minimal pairs—see below) give us the index values for *Style D.*

*Context D'. Minimal Pairs*

For the variable (r), it is useful to extend the spectrum of formality one stage further. In the word lists of Context D, (r) occurs in two situations. In one, the pronunciation of (r) is seemingly incidental, as in the reading of *hammer* and *hamster* in the (eh) list, or the names of the months ending in -*er*, or with such minimal pairs as *finger* and *singer*, *mirror* and *nearer*. Here (r) is pronounced in the formal context of a word list, but it does not receive the full attention of the reader. But in minimal pairs such as *dock* and *dark*, *guard* and *god, source* and *sauce, bared* and *bad*, (r) is the sole differentiating element, and it therefore receives maximum attention. We will therefore single out this subgroup of Style D for (r) as *Style D'.*

## The Problem of Casual Speech

Up to this point, we have been discussing techniques for extending the formal range of the interview by methods which fall naturally into the framework of a discussion about language. But even within the interview, we must go beyond the interview situation if we can. We must somehow become witnesses to the everyday speech which the informant will use as soon as the door is closed behind us: the style in which he argues with his wife, scolds his children, or passes the time of day with his friends. The difficulty of the problem is considerable; yet the rewards for its solution are great, both in furthering our present goal, and in the general theory of stylistic variation.

First, it is important to determine whether we have any means of knowing when we have succeeded in eliciting casual speech. Against what standard can we measure success? In the course of the present study of New York City speech, there are several other approaches to casual speech that have been used. In the exploratory interviews, I recorded a great deal of language which is literally the language of the streets. This material included the unrestrained and jubilant activity of a great many small children, and also some recordings of street games among young men, 18 to 25 years old, where I was an anonymous bystander. It may be that none of the conversation within the interview will be as spontaneous and free as this material. But if the informants show a sudden and marked shift of style in this direction, we will be justified in calling this behavior casual speech.

Another check is random and anonymous observation such as the department-store survey discussed in Ch. 2, in which the bias of the linguist's presence disappears completely. Here we can judge whether the type of alternation which is found within the interview gives us a range of behavior comparable to that which is found under casual conditions in everyday life.

The immediate problem, then, is to construct interview situations in which casual speech will find a place, or which will permit spontaneous speech to emerge, and then set up a formal method for defining the occurrence of these styles. By *casual speech*, in a narrow sense, we mean the everyday speech used in informal situations, where no attention is directed to language. *Spontaneous speech* refers to a pattern used in excited, emotionally charged speech when the constraints of a formal situation are overridden. Schematically:

> Context:     Informal     Formal
> Style:       Casual       Careful/Spontaneous

We do not normally think of "spontaneous" speech as occurring in formal contexts: yet, as we will show, this frequently happens in the course of the interview. Spontaneous speech is defined here as the counterpart of casual speech which does occur in formal contexts, not in response to the formal situation, but in spite of it.

While there is no *a priori* reason to assume that the values of the variables will be the same in spontaneous as in casual speech, the results of this investigation show that they can be studied together. At a later point, as we examine more deeply the mechanism of stylistic variation, it will be possible to suggest an underlying basis for this identification. For the moment, either term will be used according to the nature of the context, but they will both be measured under the heading of *Style A,* or casual speech in general.

The formal definition of casual speech within the interview requires that at least one of five contextual situations prevail, and also at least one of five nonphonological cues. We will first discuss the contextual situations, which will be identified as Context $A_1$ through $A_5$.

### Context $A_1$. Speech Outside the Formal Interview

There are three occasions within the larger context of the interview situation which do not fall within the bounds of the formal interview proper, and in these contexts, casual speech is apt to occur.

Before the interview proper begins, the subject may often address casual remarks to someone else in the household, his wife or his children, or he may make a few good-natured remarks to the interviewer. Although this is not the most common context for a good view of casual speech, the interviewer will not hurry to begin formal proceedings if there seems to be any opportunity for such an exchange. In several cases, where a housewife took time to wash the dishes, or a family to finish dinner, the interviewer overheard casual speech in some quantity.

After the interview begins, there may be interruptions, when someone else enters the room, or when the informant offers a glass of beer or a cup of coffee. In the following example, the three paragraphs represent, 1, speech in the formal interview directly before the break, 2, speech used while opening a can of beer for the interviewer, and 3, the first sentences spoken on the resumption of the formal interview.

1      If you're not careful, you will call a lot of them the same. There are a couple of them which are very similar; for instance, *width* and *with.* [What about *guard* and *god*?] That's another one you could very well pronounce the same, unless you give thought to it.

2              . . . these things here—y'gotta do it the right way—otherwise
               [laughter] you'll need a pair of pliers with it . . . You see, what
               actually happened was, I pulled it over to there, and well . . . I
               don't really know *what* happened . . . Did it break off or get stuck
               or sump'm?
               . . . just the same as when you put one of these keys into a can of
               sardines or sump'm—and you're turning it, and you turn it lop-
               sided, and in the end you break it off and you use the old fashioned
               opener . . . but I always have a spoon or a fork or a screw driver
               handy to wedge into the key to help you turn it . . . [laughter] I
               always have these things handy to make sure.

3              [How do you make up your mind about how to rate these people?]
               Some people—I suppose perhaps it's the result of their training and
               the kind of job that they have—they just talk in any slipshod
               manner. Others talk in a manner which has real finesse to it, but
               that would be the executive type. He cannot [sic] talk in a slipshod
               manner to a board of directors meeting.

The shift in style from 1 to 2 and back to 3 is quite evident even
in conventional orthography. The prosodic channel cues, and the
phonological variables point in the same direction as the shifts in
lexicon, syntax, and content.

The interviewer may make every use of this opportunity by moving away from his chair and tape recorder, and supporting the
emergence of casual conversation. One great advantage of such a
break is that it occurs in close juxtaposition with very careful speech,
and the contrast is very sharp, as in this example given above. The
sudden occurrence of radically different values of the variables is
particularly marked in this example. The word *otherwise* in extract
2 has (dh) in medial position; this is rarely [d] in the careful speech
of this subject, but [d] does occur here and makes a sharp impression
on the listener.

The most frequent place for casual speech to emerge in Context
$A_1$ is at the end of the interview. It is perhaps most common when
the interviewer has packed away his equipment, and is standing with
one hand on the door knob.[5]

5. The interviewer is not a passive agent in any of these circumstances. By his
participation in the developing informality, he can help casual speech to emerge. At
the termination of the interview, he can also terminate his role as interviewer, and
behave like any other tired, hot, or sleepy employee who has now finished his job
and is free to be himself.

*Context A₂. Speech with a Third Person*

At any point in the interview, the subject may address remarks to a third person and casual speech may emerge. One of the most striking examples occurred in an interview with a black woman, 35, raised in the Bronx, and then living on the Lower East Side in poor circumstances as a widow with six children. The following three sections illustrate the sharp alternations between the careful, quiet, controlled style used in talking to the interviewer, and the louder, higher-pitched style used with her children. Again, the grammatical and stylistic differences shown in conventional orthography illustrate the shift of style.

1            . . . Their father went back to Santo Domingo when they had the uprising about two years ago that June or July . . . he got killed in the uprising . . . I believe that those that want to go and give up their life for their country, let them go. For my part, his place was here with the children to help raise them and give them a good education . . . that's from my point of view.

2            Get out of the refrigerator, Darlene! Tiny or Teena, or whatever your name is! . . . Close the refrigerator, Darlene! . . . What pocketbook? I don't have no pocketbook—if he lookin' for money from me, dear heart, I have no money!

3            I thought the time I was in the hospital for three weeks, I had peace and quiet, and I was crying to get back home to the children, and I didn't know what I was coming back home to.

Interruptions of the interview by telephone calls sometimes provide unusually good opportunities to study casual speech. In one interview, the telephone interrupted the proceedings at the very middle. The informant, Dolly R., had just returned from a summer spent in North Carolina, and one of her cousins was anxious for news of the family. I left the room with her nephew, and continued to talk to him quietly in another room; for twenty minutes, the informant discussed the latest events in a very informal style, and we thus obtained an excellent recording of the most spontaneous kind of speech. The contrast is so sharp that most listeners cannot believe it is the same person talking. The style that Dolly R. used with me was friendly, relaxed, seemingly informal and casual: in talking about common sense she said:

> Smart? Well, I mean, when you use the word *intelligent* an' *smart*
> I mean—you use it in the same sense? . . . (Laughs) So some
> people are pretty witty—I mean—yet they're not so intelligent!

Although the laughter and informality of this passage would seem
to place it in a "casual" category, no absolute judgment can be made
without contrasting it with other styles. And the values of the linguistic variables are suspiciously remote from the vernacular—(r)
is almost consistently [r], and there is only one nonstandard (dh),
in *they're*. Here on the other hand is a passage from the telephone
conversation:

5           Huh? . . . Yeah, go down 'e(r)e to stay. This is. So you know what
            Carol Ann say? Listen at what Carol Ann say. Carol Ann say,
            "An' then when papa die, we can come back" [belly laugh] . . .
            Ain't these chillun sump'm [falsetto]? . . . An' when papa die,
            can we come back? . . . [laughs].

The laughter of this passage is very different from 4: it is a full-bodied
performance that begins low and ends high, shaking from somewhere
down deep. Listening to it, we realize that the laughter of 4 is forced
by comparison—a "Ha ha ha" drawn from a white repertoire. The
voice quality and personality of 5 are also very different, and the
intonation contours are dramatically opposed.[6] The phonological and
grammatical variables are altogether different. The contrast is so
dramatic in the case of Dolly R. that we are forced to recognize the
limitations of our other methods of eliciting the vernacular: for some
speakers, at least, our best techniques within the interview situation
will shift the speaker part of the way toward the vernacular but there
is no guarantee that we have covered the major part of the distance.
We have defined a direction but not the destination.

### Context $A_3$. Speech Not in Direct Response to Questions

In some types of interview schedules, it is necessary to cut off long,
rambling replies, or sudden outbursts or rhetoric, in order to get

6. We used these two passages cited here in a Family Background test in our
interviews with adults in south-central Harlem (Labov et al. 1968 2:4.7). Many of the
subjects were acutely embarrassed by 5; they shifted in their chairs as they listened.
They assumed, naturally, that it was a performance done to order for the tape recorder,
and for anyone to use this intimate family style in such a public situation is clearly
playing "Uncle Tom." They could not know, of course, that Dolly R. did not realize
at the time that she was being recorded, and that she assumed that the conversation
she heard from the other room was the interview proper.

through with the work. In this interview program, the opposite policy prevailed. Whenever a subject showed signs of wanting to talk, no obstacle was interposed: the longer he digressed, the better chance we had of studying his natural speech pattern. Some older speakers, in particular, pay little attention to the questions as they are asked. They may have certain favorite points of view which they want to express, and they have a great deal of experience in making a rapid transition from the topic to the subject that is closest to their hearts.

Context $A_3$ forms a transition from those contexts in which casual speech is formally appropriate, to those contexts in which the emotional state or attitude of the speaker overrides any formal restrictions, and spontaneous speech emerges.

## Context $A_4$. Childhood Rhymes and Customs

This is one of the two topics within the interview itself which is designed to provide the context in which spontaneous speech is likely to emerge. The atmosphere or tone required for such a shift is provided by a series of questions which lead gradually to the topic of jump-rope rhymes, counting-out rhymes, the rules of fighting, and similar aspects of language drawn from the preadolescent period when the youngster participates in a culture distinct from that of adult society. Rhymes, for example, cannot be recited correctly in Style B of careful conversation. Both the rhyme itself, and the tempo, would be wrong if Style B were used in

> Cinderella,
> Dressed in yella
> Went downtown to buy some mustard,
> On the way her girdle busted,
> How many people were disgusted?
>    10, 20, 30 . . .

The following song, which is popular in New York City schools, does not permit the r-pronunciation which would creep into Style B:

> Glory, glory, Hallelujah,
> The teacher hit me with the ruler,
> The ruler turned red,
> And the teacher dropped dead,
> No more school for me.

Equally r-less pronunciation is implied in the traditional

> Strawberry short cake, cream on top
> Tell me the name of your sweetheart . . .[7]

If the compulsion of these rhymes demanded a return to a childhood pronunciation which was no longer normal, their use as evidence would be wrong. However, the pattern which is used in Context $A_4$ is quite comparable to that which is used in the four other contexts which are utilized. There is no necessity for the following rhyme to assume any particular value of (oh), yet (oh-1) is very common:

> I won't go to Macy's any more, more, more
> There's a big fat policeman at the door, door, door,
> He pulls you by the collar
> And makes you pay a dollar,
> I won't go to Macy's any more, more, more.

The nine examples of (oh) in this rhyme provide an efficient means of studying that variable.

Even in counting-out rhymes, where meter and rhyme are less compelling for the informant, we find that Style B is inadequate for

> My mother and your mother were hanging out the clothes,
> My mother punched your mother right in the nose.
> What color blood came out?
> [Green.] G-R-E-E-N spells green and you are not IT.

or for the much simpler

> Doggie, doggie, step right out.

Men as well as women will be able to repeat counting-out rhymes such as "Eeny meeny miny moe," or "Engine, engine, number nine." Lacking this, spontaneous speech is often obtained from men in the rules for playing marbles, the complex New York City game of skelley, punchball, or stickball.

*Context $A_5$. The Danger of Death*

Another series of questions in a later section of the interview leads to the following:

---

7. The acceptable half-rhyme used here implies a pronunciation of *-heart* as [hat], with a fairly short vowel. Such shortenings are not rare in the city, especially in polysyllables.

> Have you ever been in a situation where you thought
> you were in serious danger of being killed—where
> you thought to yourself, "This is it?"

If the informant answers yes, the interviewer pauses for one or two seconds, and then asks, "What happened?" As the informant begins to reply, he is under some compulsion to show that there was a very real danger of his being killed; he stands in a very poor light if it appears that there was no actual danger. Often he becomes involved in the narration to the extent that he seems to be reliving the critical moment, and signs of emotional tension appear. One such example occurred in an interview with six brothers, from 10 to 19 years old, from a lower-class Irish-Italian household. While most of the boys had spoken freely and spontaneously in many contexts, the oldest brother, Eddie, had been quite reserved and careful in his replies. He had given no examples of casual or spontaneous speech until this topic was reached. Within a few short sentences, a sudden and dramatic shift in his style took place. At the beginning of Eddie's account, he followed his usual careful style:

6        [What happened to you?] The school I go to is Food and Mari-
         time—that's maritime training—and I was up in the masthead,
         and the wind started blowing. I had a rope secured around me
         to keep me from falling—but the rope parted, and I was just
         hanging there by my fingernails.

At this point, the speaker's breathing became very heavy and irregular; his voice began to shake, and sweat appeared on his forehead. Small traces of nervous laughter appeared in his speech.

7        I never prayed to God so fast and so hard in my life . . . [What
         happened?] Well, I came out all right . . . Well, the guys came
         up and they got me. [How long were you up there?] About ten
         minutes. [I can see you're still sweating, thinking about it.] Yeh,
         I came down, I couldn't hold a pencil in my hand, I couldn't
         touch nuttin'. I was shakin' like a leaf. Sometimes I get scared
         thinkin' about it . . . but . . uh . . well, it's training.

All of the phonological variables in 7 shift towards the forms most typical of casual speech, including (th), (dh), and (ing). At the very end, Eddie returns to his careful style with an effort: "Well, it's training!" The effect of probing for the subject's feelings at the moment of crisis can be effective even with speakers who are quite used to holding the center of the stage. One of the most gifted story tellers and naturally expressive speakers in the sample was Mrs. Rose B. She was raised on the Lower East Side, of Italian parents; now in her late 30's, she recently returned to work as a sewing machine operator. The many examples of spontaneous narrations which she provided show a remarkable command of pitch, volume and tempo for expressive purposes.

8          . . . And another time—that was three times, and I hope it never happens to me again—I was a little girl, we all went to my aunt's farm right near by, where Five Points is . . . and we were thirteen to a car. And at that time, if you remember, about 20 or 25 years ago, there wasn't roads like this to go to Jersey—there was all dirt roads. Well, anyway, I don't know how far are—I don't remember what part we were—one of the wheels of the car came off—and the whole car turned, and they took us all out. They hadda break the door off. And they took us out one by one. And I got a scar on my leg here . . . 'ats the on'y thing . . . [When the car turned over, what did you think?]

          . . . it was upside dow—you know what happened, do you know how I felt? I don't remember anything. This is really the truth—till today, I could tell that to anybody, 'n' they don't believe me, they think I'm kiddin' 'em. All I remember is—I thought I fell asleep, and I was in a dream . . . I actually saw stars . . . you know, stars in the sky—y'know, when you look up there . . . and I was seein' stars. And then after a while, I felt somebody pushing and pulling—you know, they were all on top of each other—and they were pulling us out from the bottom of the car, and I was goin' "Ooooh."

          And when I came—you know—to, I says to myself, "Ooooh, we're in a car accident,"—and that's all I remember—as clear as day—I don't remember the car turning or anything. All I know is I thought I went to sleep. I actually felt I went to sleep.

### Channel Cues for Casual Speech

The five contexts just described are only the first part of the formal criteria for the identification of Style A in the interview. It is of course not enough to set a particular context in order to observe casual speech. We also look for some evidence in the type of linguistic production that the speaker is using a speech style that contrasts with Style B. To use phonological variables would involve a circular argument, because the values of these variables in Styles A and B are exactly what we are trying to determine by the isolation of styles. The best cues are channel cues: modulations of the voice production which affect speech as a whole.[8] Our use of this evidence must follow the general procedure of linguistic analysis: the absolute values of tempo, pitch, volume, and breathing may be irrelevant, but contrasting values of these characteristics are cues to a differentiation of Style A and Style B. A *change* in tempo, a *change* in pitch range, a *change* in volume or rate of breathing, form socially significant signs of shift towards a more spontaneous or more casual style of speech.

Whenever one of these four channel cues is present in an appropriate context, the utterance which contains them is marked and measured under Style A. The fifth channel cue is another modulation of voice production: laughter. This may accompany the most casual kind of speech, like the nervous laughter in the example from Eddie D., and is frequently heard in the description of the most dramatic and critical moments in the danger-of-death narration. Since laughter involves a more rapid expulsion of breath than in normal speech, it is always accompanied by a sudden intake of breath in the following pause. Though this intake is not always obvious to the listener in the interview situation, the recording techniques being used in this study detect such effects quite readily; it is therefore possible to regard laughter as a variant type of changes in breathing, the fourth channel cue.[9]

The question now arises, what if a very marked constellation of channel cues occurs in some Context B? Intuition may tell us that this is spontaneous speech, but the formal rules of this procedure instruct us to consider it Style B. This is a necessary consequence of a formal definition. The situation may be schematized in this way:

8. These would be considered modifications of the Message Form rather than the Channel in the terminology used by Dell Hymes (1962). In the framework suggested by Hymes, the more formal styles of reading would represent a shift in the channel; the elicitation of casual speech would be encouraged by shifts in the Setting and Topic, and the phonological variables appear as variations in the Code.

9. The case of Dolly R., noted above, shows that we may also have to take laughter as a contrastive cue—a change in the form of laughter is more important than laughter itself.

| intuitive observations | Careful speech | Casual speech |
|---|---|---|
| formal definition and measurement | Style B | Style A |

As this diagram indicates, Style B formally defined overlaps casual speech intuitively observed. Some examples of casual speech will occur outside the five contexts given, conditioned by some less prominent context we have not considered, and these will be lost by the formal definition. However, since the body of careful speech bulks much larger than casual speech, this small amount of comparatively casual speech now included under Context B and Style B will not seriously distort the values for careful speech. If, on the other hand, there should be overlap in the other direction, with a definition which specified the contexts of careful speech, the resulting admixture in the smaller bulk of casual speech would be a source of serious distortion. By leaving careful speech as the unmarked category, we are protected from such distortion.

What are the actual proportions in our material of casual and careful speech as defined? We can obtain a good estimate from the records which show the total occurrences of (r) and (dh) in the styles as defined above, since these very frequent variables give us a measure of the total volume of speech. Ten percent of the adult interviews from the Lower East Side survey were randomly selected, and the relative volume of speech in each style was measured by a combined index of the total incidence of (r) and (dh).[10] The average percentages for this sample are, for Style A, casual speech: 29 percent; and for Style B, careful Speech: 71 percent.

An alternative approach to identifying casual speech would have been to rely only upon channel cues, without reference to the context. This would have been far less reliable, for in many contexts, the channel cues vary continuously, and to determine where contrast

10. The use of (dh) or (r) alone would have produced serious bias. For some speakers, primarily lower-class white and black speakers, (r) is not a variable, and is not recorded as such on the transcription forms. For others, primarily middle-class speakers, (dh) is always a fricative, and is not tabulated. There are no speakers in the sample for whom neither of these features is a variable. It is interesting to note that the (dh) variable gives a somewhat higher percentage for casual speech: 33 percent as against 26 percent for (r). This is probably a reflection of the greater spontaneity and more casual approach of many working-class speakers.

occurred and where it did not would have often been very difficult. The interview as now constructed provides for sudden shifts of contexts which have sharp boundaries. These shifts thus enable us to observe sudden contrasts in the channel cues. Another alternative would be to adopt certain sections of the interview as casual speech, without regard to channel cues or any other measure. Obviously this would weaken our approach to the vernacular, since there is no technique which is certain to relax the constraints of the interview situation for everyone.[11] It is not contended that Style A and Style B are natural units of stylistic variation: rather they are formal divisions of the continuum set up for the purposes of this study, which has the purpose of measuring phonological variation along the stylistic axis. The discovery of natural breaks in the range of stylistic phenomena would have to follow a very different procedure. It is not unlikely that results of the present work, yielding sensitive indexes to linguistic variation, may eventually be applied to this end.

The validity of this method may be tested by a comparison with other means of recording casual speech. A number of anonymous observations in public places were made on the Lower East Side which match quite closely the characteristics of casual speech as obtained in the interview (see Appendix B in Labov 1966a for the Punch Ball Game and the Lunch Counter). We can also approach validation and explanation from the experimental direction. Mahl has conducted a series of studies on the effect of removing subjects' ability to monitor speech (1972). This was done by feeding random noise through earphones at a volume high enough to prevent the subject from hearing his own speech. In addition, the subject was sometimes facing away from the interviewer so that he could not see the interviewer's face. The speech of each subject was then studied during three interviews under four conditions: with white noise, facing or not facing; and without white noise, facing or not facing. In many cases the loss of audio-monitoring produced sharp changes in pitch, volume, intonation, and in the length of responses; in several cases, there were changes in speech patterns which seemed to Mahl to resemble differences in social dialects. In cooperation with Mahl, I examined some of these recordings to see if the style shifting

11. This is in fact the approach taken by Trudgill (1971). Whatever weaknesses this technique may have, it did not prevent Trudgill from showing a regular differentiation between Casual and Careful speech.

could be measured objectively by linguistic variables. An exploratory study of other New Haven speakers developed a list of socially
significant variables: the most important of these for the style shifting
of Mahl's subjects was (dh). Fig. 3.2 shows the percentage of the
standard fricative form [ð] in the speech of one subject whose style
shifting was most striking. The horizontal axis shows the series of
three interviews, with the four different conditions in the order that
they were administered. There is an overall familiarization effect,
in which the percentage of standard forms drops steadily. The four
conditions are also clearly differentiated: both the loss of audio-
monitoring and the loss of visual monitoring of the addressee interfered with the subject's control over the (dh) variable. We can
infer that a consistent production of fricative forms is part of a
superposed dialect not characteristic of this speaker's early vernacular pattern, and requires a certain amount of attention paid to
speech which is facilitated by audio-monitoring of the self and
stimulated by visual monitoring of the other.

The parallel with style shifting of (dh) in our interviews is quite
striking. We note another phenomenon in our interviews which

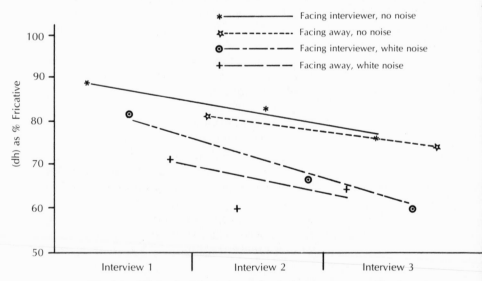

Fig. 3.2.   Effect of white noise and orientation on one subject's
use of (dh).

points in this direction. We ask subjects to start to say *ten* and tell us where the tip of their tongue is. Even though this occurs in the formal context of the discussion of speech, the forms used in this reply are shifted strongly towards casual speech. Attention directed to the location of the tongue seems to interfere with attention to articulation in the answer that follows.

We can therefore put forward the hypothesis that the various styles of speech we are considering are all ranged along a single dimension of attention paid to speech, with casual speech at one end of the continuum and minimal pairs at the other. If future research succeeds in confirming this hypothesis, and quantifying attention paid to speech, we will then have a firmer foundation for the study of style shifting, and more precise relations can be established in the study of sociolinguistic structures as a whole.

### The Array of Stylistic Variation

Given the techniques for isolating styles outlined above, we can now ask how this stylistic dimension correlates with our dependent variables. For this purpose we can lay out the following array of the five main phonological variables:

| Variable | Casual A | | Careful B | | Reading C | | Word lists D | | Minimal pairs D′ |
|---|---|---|---|---|---|---|---|---|---|
| (r) | x | > | x | > | x | > | x | > | x |
| (eh) | x | > | x | > | x | > | x | > | |
| (oh) | x | > | x | > | x | > | x | | |
| (th) | x | < | x | < | x | | | | |
| (dh) | x | < | x | < | x | | | | |

A separate style D′ for minimal pairs is shown only for (r). The (th) and (dh) variables are not studied in word lists, but only in reading style. We then have altogether 19 points where the mean values of the variables can be placed in a stylistic array. If their use is correlated with the stylistic continuum as we expect, we should find that the first three are at a maximum for Style A, and decline steadily for B, D, C, and D′; and the last two are at a minimum for A and rise regularly for B and C.

The first native New Yorker to whom this method was applied

was Miss Josephine P., 35, who lived with her Italian-born mother in the same Lower East Side tenement apartment where she was born. Miss P. attended high school on the Lower East Side, and completed almost four years of college. At the time of the interview, she worked as a receptionist at Saks 5th Avenue. Josephine P.'s style of speech is lively and rapid; she seems to be an outgoing person who has no difficulty in making friendly contact with strangers. Her careful conversation, in Context B, seems at first to be equivalent to the casual conversation of most speakers. Two short samples of casual speech were recorded, which contrasted with her speech in Context B. We thus have the complete array of average values of the variables for this speaker.

STYLISTIC ARRAY FOR JOSEPHINE P.

| Variable | A | B | C | D | D' |
|----------|-----|-----|-----|-----|-----|
| (r) | 00 | 03 | 23 | 53 | 50 |
| (eh) | 25 | 28 | 27 | 37 | |
| (oh) | 21 | 23 | 26 | 37 | |
| (th) | 40 | 14 | 05 | | |
| (dh) | 34 | 09 | 09 | | |

The (r) values for Josephine P. rise from 00 to 50 as we would expect; (eh) and (oh) also rise, though B and C are essentially the same for (eh). There is a sharp upturn in Style D which is generally characteristic of lower-middle-class speakers (see Ch. 5 in this volume). The (th) and (dh) variables are at a low level in Style A, and fall to a very low point in more formal styles, as we would expect from a speaker of her background.

The two sections of casual speech which were recorded in contrast to Style B occurred in Context $A_1$, extra-interview. In one section, Josephine P. talked with some emotion about her dead father, as she remembered him from her childhood, and about the dolls he brought her from the factory where he worked. The associated channel cues were laughter, increase in tempo, and a change in the rate of breathing. The second section was a burst of irritation at the behavior of other tenants in the building, with increased pitch and volume. Both of these were recorded after the interview, as I sat having coffee with Josephine P. and her mother.

In the course of a normal dialectological interview, the whole conversation of Josephine P. would have been accepted as free and spontaneous; but since the present procedure assumes that the speech of Context B cannot be truly casual, all of the contexts relevant to Style A were examined. The emergence of a very different speech pattern in the measurements of the five variables under Style A especially—for (th) and (dh)—confirms our expectation. Without the sections of casual speech, we would have to report that Josephine P. rarely used affricates or stops for these variables.

In the overall pattern, there are two departures from the expected array, both less than 5 percent in magnitude. This is remarkable when we consider the irregular fluctuations of the variables that seem to mark the individual sections of speech. For example, here are the occurrences of (th) in casual speech, in the order that they occurred: 1221221111; and here a continuous series in careful speech: 221111111111112121. There seems to be no pattern or system within this sequence—yet it fits into the larger pattern shown in the array of styles. The total number of items upon which the array of Josephine P. was based is not large; a relatively small number of occurrences establish the progressions, despite the variations within each style. The number of instances in each cell are given in the frequency array.

FREQUENCY ARRAY FOR JOSEPHINE P.

| Variable | A | B | C | D | D' |
|----------|-----|-----|-----|-----|-----|
| (r) | 18 | 66 | 44 | 15 | 4 |
| (eh) | 4 | 4 | 28 | 13 | |
| (oh) | 10 | 11 | 19 | 11 | |
| (th) | 10 | 29 | 20 | | |
| (dh) | 26 | 65 | 35 | | |

This array of frequencies shows three weak points, at (r) D', and at (eh) A and B, where there were only four occurrences of the variable in each cell. This limitation of the data allows errors in perception and transcription to affect the final result significantly, as well as the inherent variation of the individual. If this array is now compared with the table of the average values of the variables given on Josephine P. above, it appears that the low points of frequency coincide exactly with the points where small deviations from the overall pattern were found. The implication of this finding is that if more occurrences of (eh) A and B and (r) D' were introduced, the behavior of the subject might be seen as perfectly regular.

The next New Yorker who was interviewed by this procedure was Abraham G., 47, a high-school graduate, native of the Lower East Side, of Polish-Jewish parents. He lived in a public housing project, and drove a taxi for his regular income. In contrast to Josephine P., this informant was immediately and obviously a multiple-style speaker. In Context B, he used a fluent but self-conscious style, which reflected his experience in many committee meetings as head of his American Legion chapter. His Style B, which employed such phrases as *the armed forces* for 'army' and *fair and equitable* for 'fair', was obviously not his casual style. He even managed to tell several long and exciting stories of near-hold-ups, in the danger-of-death section, without losing the elevated manner of Style B. However, midway through the interview, he stopped to offer me a can of beer, and delivered the humorous monologue quoted on page 88, which is the main basis for the Style A column in his array. The blank spot in this array, at (th) A, is the point where the single occurrence of (th), as a stop, could not be used for a rating. The only apparent irregularity is the change of direction at (oh) D: as further studies showed, this is not uncommon.

STYLISTIC ARRAY FOR ABRAHAM G.

| Variable | A | B | C | D | D' | N | | | | |
|----------|----|----|----|-----|-----|----|----|----|----|---|
| (r) | 12 | 15 | 46 | 100 | 100 | 8 | 60 | 39 | 7 | 5 |
| (eh) | 35 | 36 | 39 | 40 | | 6 | 22 | 18 | 13 | |
| (oh) | 10 | 18 | 29 | 20 | | 3 | 11 | 16 | 11 | |
| (th) | | 17 | 00 | | | 1 | 20 | 20 | | |
| (dh) | 72 | 33 | 05 | | | 18 | 78 | 35 | | |

In most cases, the interview procedure isolates Style A in more than one context. The case of Mrs. Doris H., 39, is typical. She is black, raised on Staten Island, a high-school graduate; her husband is a New York City policeman. Mrs. H. showed a wide range of stylistic behavior, from the careful, well-reasoned, highly organized replies in Context B, to sudden outbursts of spontaneous humor that marked her as a person of considerable wit and charm. Her chart shows spontaneous speech in Context $A_2$ (speech to a third person) as she rallied her 13-year-old son on his tendency to show off; in Context $A_3$ (not in direct response) as a long account of the tactless behavior of some of her friends, with direct quotations; in four cases within Context $A_4$ (childhood rhymes) and in Context $A_5$ (danger of death). In these seven sections of Style A, the most prominent channel cues are sudden increase in volume, and laughter; occasionally there was an increase in tempo and in rate of breathing. The resulting array of the variables is quite regular in its left to right progression except for (eh). Part of the reason for the irregularity of (eh) is that Style A is represented only by three vowels. We do find that small numbers of (r) in Style D' are usually quite regular, even when there are only four instances. The overriding effect of the formality of the context seems to provide quite uniform results. But in all other contexts, three or four items seem to be insufficient to provide values that fit into a regular array. This problem disappears as we begin to sum the arrays of individuals to obtain values for social groups. The other deviation at (eh) D, is based on sufficient evidence, and indicates again that a reversal at (eh) D and (oh) D is more common than a reversal in the pattern anywhere else. The great range in (r-1) pronunciation which is seen here, from 00 to 100, is a frequent characteristic of the linguistic class of speakers to which Mrs. H. belongs—the lower middle class (see Ch. 5 in this volume).

STYLISTIC ARRAY FOR DORIS H.

| Variable | A | B | C | D | D' | N | | | | |
|---|---|---|---|---|---|---|---|---|---|---|
| (r) | 00 | 31 | 44 | 69 | 100 | 29 | 64 | 55 | 19 | 4 |
| (eh) | 30 | 26 | 32 | 29 | | 3 | 10 | 25 | 13 | |
| (oh) | 18 | 21 | 23 | 25 | | 16 | 21 | 18 | 11 | |
| (th) | 80 | 24 | 12 | | | 5 | 29 | 24 | | |
| (dh) | 50 | 22 | 16 | | | 28 | 85 | 42 | | |

The three New Yorkers considered so far are typical of the speech community in their concern with language and their overt rejection of the New York vernacular. But the pattern of style shifting is not directly governed by overt values; even when the explicit norms expressed by the individual are reversed, the pattern is the same. The case of Steve K. will illustrate this crucial point. He was a very intense young man of 25, a copyreader's assistant, living in a fifth-floor walk-up on the East Side. He had come to the Lower East Side only three years before from Brooklyn, where he was raised, a third-generation New Yorker. His grandparents were Jewish immigrants from Eastern Europe.

Steve K. might be considered a deviant case in many ways. He studied philosophy for four years at Brooklyn College, but left without graduating; he had turned away from the academic point of view, and as an intense student of Wilhelm Reich, sought self-fulfillment in awareness of himself as a sexual person.[12] His attitude towards language was much more explicit than that of most people. He was unique among the informants in being aware of all five of the chief variables, and believed that he was able to control or at least influence his own usage. He had consciously tried to reverse his college-trained tendency towards formal speech, and to reinstate the natural speech pattern of his earlier years. In other words, he deliberately rejected the pattern of values reflected in the array of numbers shown in the preceding examples; in his own words, he wanted to "go back to Brooklyn."

Steve K.'s self-awareness and his set of values might prepare us to find a radically different pattern in the array of the variables—if we believed that the linguistic and social forces operating here are subject to conscious manipulation. But as a matter of record they are not. Except for the fact that the (th) and (dh) patterns operate at a low level, his array is quite similar to that of Abraham G. The only deviation from a regular progression is that at (eh) D.

STYLISTIC ARRAY FOR STEVE K.

| Variable | A | B | C | D | D' | N |
|----------|-----|-----|-----|-----|------|-----------------|
| (r) | 00 | 06 | 08 | 38 | 100 | |
| (eh) | 28 | 33 | 34 | 30 | | 37  70  49  16  3 |
| (oh) | 22 | 23 | 25 | 30 | | 6  16  25  13 |
| (th) | 09 | 00 | 00 | | | 5  27  18  11 |
| (dh) | 15 | 06 | 05 | | | 11  12  24 |
| | | | | | | 34  55  42 |

For New Yorkers of Steve K.'s age, all of these variables will remain variables in normal speech, no matter what conscious adjustments are attempted. Not one speaker in the sample who was raised in New York City was able to use 100 percent (r-1) in conversation, and this includes a great many speakers who were consciously aiming in that direction after (r) had been discussed. For example, Steve K. claimed that his present performance was a deliberate step backward from his college days, when he had pronounced all or most (r) as (r-1). I then asked him to reread the r paragraph from "When I was nine or ten," and pronounce all (r) as (r-1).

12. Steve K.'s definition of a *successful man* puts his point of view very concisely: "a man who is fully aware of himself . . . of his own sexuality and of his emotions . . . who always knows what he feels towards each person he meets."

His first attempt was a complete failure, and his second no better. I asked him to read a little more slowly. He continued and produced an (r) index of 33. A third try produced a step upward to 45. A fourth attempt gave 61, and in a fifth trial, he seemed to level off at 69. He then confessed that he probably could not have pronounced that much (r-1) when he was in college.

Steve K.'s inability to deal with a few sentences containing only thirteen (r)'s suggests that the original reading score of 38 is probably very close to the pattern which was solidified in his college days. Despite his profound shift in ideology, the speech pattern dictated by equally profound forces remains constant. It is not likely that he could, by his own efforts, return to zero or reach much higher than 38 in extended reading style.

Many similar tests could be cited. The most consistent and highly controlled speaker in the survey was Warren M., 27, a social worker and graduate student. At college he had been intensively trained in speaking technique, had done a great deal of acting, and was justly proud of the control he could exert over his voice. His original reading of the r paragraph was at an index of 68. After a thorough discussion of (r), he read again to produce a perfectly consistent version. A very slow reading gave 90; fast, 56; more careful, 80; a repeat, 80; again, concentrating on voice quality 63; he then recited Jabberwocky at 88.[13]

Merwin M., a less sophisticated speaker of the same age, was able to improve his performance from (r)-28 to (r)-50. There is reason to think that older speakers would have less ability to shift, and that only very young ones, just emerging from their preadolescent years, would be able to make radical changes in their pattern by conscious attention.

Martha S., a very careful, Jewish middle-class speaker of 45, was asked to read several paragraphs after discussion.

| Variable | Original reading | Conscious effort |
|----------|-----------------|------------------|
| (r) | 45 | 47 |
| (eh) | 40 | 40 |
| (oh) | 28 | 29 |

13. It appears here, as indicated in fn. 5, that a high concentration of (r) words makes more difficulties than a long text with the (r)'s dispersed. A similar effect was noted in the (th) paragraph; some speakers saw the phrase *this thing, that thing, and the other thing,* some even took a breath before attempting it, but by the time they reached the fifth or sixth item, fatigue set in, and with it, (dh-3).

The (eh) index was already at the point preferred by the speaker, but the (oh) items still fluctuated considerably, and the small increases in both (r) and (oh) show her inability to attain the desired result. On the other hand, her daughter, Susan S., 13, was able to read with an (r) index of 50, and after discussion, reach as high as 75. Her normal (oh) index of 15 was shifted to 28 as she imitated her mother.

An even more dramatic case was that of Bonnie R., 10 years old. Whereas her parents used no more than 5 or 10 percent (r-1) in reading, she was able to go from an (r) index of 14 to (r)-64 after this variable was discussed in the family interview.

The compelling nature of the pattern of stylistic alternation appears to operate at the extremes of the social scale, as well as in the center. Below, we may compare the record of two New Yorkers of radically different education and social status. On the left is the performance of Bennie N., 40, a truck driver who finished only the first term of high school. On the right is the record of Miriam L., 35, who graduated from Hunter College and St. John's Law School, and is now practicing law on the Lower East Side (heading for styles and variables as before).

| STYLISTIC ARRAY FOR BENNIE N. | | | | | STYLISTIC ARRAY FOR MIRIAM L. | | | | |
|---|---|---|---|---|---|---|---|---|---|
| 00 | 00 | 13 | 33 | 33 | 32 | 47 | 39 | 56 | 100 |
| 19 | 21 | 26 | 22 | | 28 | 38 | 40 | 39 | |
| 15 | 20 | 24 | 20 | | 20 | 26 | 30 | 30 | |
| 168 | 81 | 58 | | | 00 | 00 | 00 | | |
| 153 | 96 | 38 | | | 25 | 04 | 02 | | |

The absolute values of these variables are as totally opposed as any pair of speakers we might choose. But the structure of stylistic variation is essentially the same. In this comparison, one can find a statement of the theme which will dominate this study of social stratification of language: that New York City is a speech community, united by a common evaluation of the same variables which serve to differentiate the speakers. The structures seen above are concrete manifestation of that evaluation.

The differences between the speakers are, of course, very real. Bennie N. uses no (r-1) in conversation; at her most casual, Miriam L. uses large numbers of (r-1) variants. The (eh) sound for Bennie N. is normally that of *where*; Miriam L. aims for the sound of *that* and *bat* and usually reaches it. For Bennie N., stops are practically normal forms of (th) and (dh); Miriam L. never uses anything but the prestige form for (th), and only a few affricates for (dh) except in the most casual style. At this point, one might ask whether the difference may be in large part that Miriam L. recognizes the formal situation of the interview, and never uses her casual style in this interview, while Bennie N. doesn't care that much about making a good impression. Perhaps Miriam L.'s true casual style, outside of the interview, is not so different, after all.

The record of the survey in general shows that this is not the case. In this particular case, I can resolve a part of the doubt since I spent fifteen minutes waiting in Miss L.'s office while she discussed business affairs with a client. The client seemed to be an old friend, and in any case, Miss L. did not know who I was, and language had not entered the picture. We may compare the record of this conversation with the Style A and Style B of the interview: the former appears to lie somewhere in between Style A and Style B, perhaps closer to B. In any case, the casual style elicited by the interview is considerably less formal than that which Miss L. uses in the daily execution of her business affairs.

|        | With Client | Style A | Style B |
|--------|-------------|---------|---------|
| (r)    | 40          | 32      | 47      |
| (eh)   | 30          | 28      | 38      |
| (oh)   | 27          | 20      | 26      |
| (th)   | 00          | 00      | 00      |
| (dh)   | 00          | 25      | 04      |

### The Structure of Stylistic Variation

In the study of the Lower East Side, we proposed to reduce the irregularity in the linguistic behavior of New York speakers by going beyond the idiolect—the speech of one person in a single context. We first isolated the most important variables which interfered with the establishment of a coherent structure for these idiolects. After defining and isolating a wide range of styles in highly comparable interview situations, we were able to discover a regular pattern of behavior governing the occurrence of these variables in the speech of many individuals.

The term *structure* has been used so often in linguistic discussion that it sometimes slips away from us, or becomes fixed in denoting a particular kind of unit which was originally analyzed by structural considerations. Thus a list of phonemes may be taken as a structural statement, though no structure uniting the list is given, other than the fact that each unit is different. The excellent definition of Webster's New International Dictionary (2nd Edition): "*structure,* the interrelationship of parts as dominated by the general character of the whole" describes the pattern of stylistic variation which has been shown in the foregoing pages. But in addition to this description, 20th-century linguistics has added the requirement that linguistic structures be composed of discrete units, which alternate in an all-or-none relationship.[14]

The dimensions of stylistic variation that have been illustrated cannot satisfy this requirement—at least, not by the evidence that has been presented. The sharp contrasts among Styles A through D' are in part artifacts of the procedure. If this dimension is thought of as a continuum, then the method of dividing that continuum used here is perfectly adequate; if one suspects that natural breaks in the continuum exist so that in natural situations one does not pass evenly and continuously from careful to increasingly casual speech, this must be demonstrated by other methods.

If contrast exists between casual and careful styles, and the variables which we are using play a significant role in that contrast, they do not seem to operate as all-or-none signals. The use of a single variant—even a highly stigmatized one such as a centralized diphthong in "boid" for *bird*—does not usually produce a strong social reaction; it may only set up an expectation that such forms might recur, so that the listener does begin to perceive a socially significant pattern. Every speaker occasionally begins a (dh) word with a sharp onset, which can be interpreted as an affricate, [dð]. However, in the prestige form of speech, these forms recur so seldom that they are negligible. Any pattern of expectation set up by them dies out before the next is heard. It is the frequency with which Bennie N. uses such forms that has social significance, and it is essentially one level of frequency which contrasts with another level in the structures outlined above.

Are there breaks in the continuum of possible frequencies? This varies from one variable to another, as the overall study of strati-

---

14. Thus the phonological structure is built with discrete units, phonemes that are themselves the products of the natural economy of the language. The structural units of the vowel systems are not artifacts of the analytical procedure; the categorizing procedure which breaks the continuum into highly discrete units can be tested and observed.

fication in New York City showed. However, the very clearcut type of all-or-none reaction which is characteristic of phonemic units will be found not in performance so much as in evaluation (see Ch. 6). But whether or not we consider stylistic variation to be a continuum of expressive behavior, or a subtle type of discrete alternation, it is clear that it must be approached through quantitative methods. We are in no position to predict exactly when a given speaker will produce a fricative, or when he will produce a stop. A complex of many factors operates to obscure stylistic regularities at the level of the individual instance. The remarkable fact is that the basic unit of stylistic contrast is a frequency set up by as few as ten occurrences of a particular variable.

The methods developed here for the isolation of contextual styles were preliminary to the general analysis of social and stylistic strati-fication in New York City. But they are quite general in their scope and have since been successfully used in many other contexts. The techniques for extending the formal end of the stylistic range have been used more widely than the techniques for isolating casual speech but both directions have been followed (see Shuy, Wolfram and Riley 1967; Wolfram 1969; Cook 1969; Sankoff and Cedergren 1971; Trudgill 1971). The methods for bypassing the constraints of the interview situation are of course only one way of obtaining a view of casual speech, and not necessarily the most definitive. In more recent work we have relied more upon group sessions, in which the interaction of members overrides the effect of observation, and gives us a more direct view of the vernacular with less influence of the observer (Cf. Gumperz 1964; Labov et al. 1968; Legum et al. 1971). However, individual face-to-face interviews will always be needed for the large body of accurately recorded speech that we need for a detailed study of the speech of a given individual. Individual interviews were used for a random sample of 100 adult speakers in south-central Harlem, and the techniques developed here were used to isolate casual speech (Labov et al. 1968). In recent instrumental studies of sound change in progress, individual interviews were required to produce the large body of continuous speech needed to chart the vowel system of each individual in full. In a series of exploratory interviews in various regions of the United States and England, we have been developing further the techniques for elicit-ing the vernacular in face-to-face situations. It therefore seems likely that the principles behind the methods outlined here will provide a foundation for future sociolinguistic studies.

# 4 | The Reflection of Social Processes in Linguistic Structures

IN the last chapter, we presented five phonological variables of the New York City system and showed how a wide range of styles could be isolated within the individual interview. When styles are organized along a single dimension according to the amount of attention paid to speech, it can be seen that most speakers follow a regular pattern of style shifting in the same direction. We will now examine a second dimension of linguistic variation: the differentiation of speakers by their social status.[1] Our debt to sociology and survey methodology is very great: the main findings are based on a secondary survey of the Lower East Side, utilizing the careful and exhaustive enumeration of the population by the Mobilization for Youth research staff and their construction of a random sample; the clarity of the results depends upon a sophisticated index of socioeconomic status, itself the product of a long line of sociological development. This chapter is therefore addressed directly to sociologists and those who are interested in the more systematic, quantitative aspects of class stratification. But we will also consider other aspects of social differentiation of language which emerged from the Lower East Side survey. Our focus will be frankly and directly sociolinguistic, and the conclusion will consider more generally the ways in which the study of language and the study of society may interact.

The procedures of descriptive linguistics are based upon the conception of language as a structured set of social norms. It has

1. This chapter first appeared in Joshua Fishman, ed., *Readings in the Sociology of Language* (The Hague: Mouton, 1968), pp. 240–51. It has been revised for publication here.

been useful in the past to consider these norms as invariants, shared by all members of the speech community. However, closer studies of the social context in which language is used show that many elements of linguistic structure are involved in systematic variation which reflects both temporal change and extralinguistic social processes.

As a form of social behavior, language is naturally of interest to the sociologist. But language may have a special utility for the sociologist as a sensitive index of many other social processes. Variation in linguistic behavior does not in itself exert a powerful influence on social development, nor does it affect drastically the life chances of the individual; on the contrary, the shape of linguistic behavior changes rapidly as the speaker's social position changes. This malleability of language underlies its great utility as an indicator of social change.

Phonological indexes—based upon the elements of the sound system of a language—are particularly useful in this respect. They give us a large body of quantitative data from relatively small samples of speech: 50–200 occurrences of a single item in a half-hour conversation. To a large extent, the variation on which these indexes are based is independent of conscious control of the subject. Finally, phonological systems show the highest degree of internal structure of all linguistic systems, and thus provide the investigator with an extensive series of parallel and convergent results.

The five phonological variables described in Ch. 3 were studied in a population drawn from a linguistic survey of the Lower East Side. This survey was based upon a primary survey of social attitudes of Lower East Side residents, carried out by Mobilization for Youth in 1961. The original sample of the population of 100,000 consisted of 988 adult subjects. Our target sample was 195 of these respondents, representing about 33,000 native English speakers who had not moved within the previous two years. Through the assistance of Mobilization for Youth, and the Columbia School of Social Work, we had available a large body of information on the social characteristics of the informants, and we were able to concentrate entirely on their linguistic behavior in this secondary survey. Eighty-one percent of the target sample was reached in the investigation of language on the Lower East Side.

New York City presents some exceptionally difficult problems for the study of linguistic systems. As we have seen in Ch. 3, New

Yorkers show a remarkable range of stylistic variation, as well as social variation, to such an extent that earlier investigators failed to find any pattern, and attributed many variables to pure chance. To study social variation, it was first necessary to define and isolate a range of contextual styles within the linguistic interview (see Ch. 3). Since the context of the formal interview does not ordinarily elicit casual or spontaneous speech, the methods which were developed to overcome this limitation were crucial to the success of the investigation. Our success in defining and eliciting casual conversation is evident in the convergence of these results with other studies which utilized anonymous observations (Ch. 2), and also in the consistency of the patterns of stylistic variation which were found.

Although there is a great range in the absolute values of these variables as used by New Yorkers, there is great agreement in the *pattern* of stylistic variation. Almost 80 percent of the respondents showed patterns of stylistic variation consistent with the status of (r-1) as a prestige marker, and stops and affricates for (th) as stigmatized forms.

This pattern of stylistic variation is primarily of concern to linguists and to students of the ethnography of speaking. However, it is closely associated with the pattern of social stratification which pervades many aspects of urban society. The pattern of stylistic variation and the pattern of social variation enter into the complex and regular structure which we see in Fig. 4.1.

Fig. 4.1 is a class stratification diagram for (th), derived from the behavior of 81 adult respondents, raised in New York City (Labov 1966a, Ch. 7). This is the first of the sociolinguistic patterns which are the main focus of this and the following two chapters. The vertical axis is the scale of average (th) index scores. The horizontal axis represents the four contextual styles, A-D, established in Ch. 3. The horizontal lines connecting the values show the progression of average index scores for socioeconomic class groups. These groups are defined as divisions of the ten-point socioeconomic scale constructed by Mobilization for Youth on the basis of their data in the original survey. The socioeconomic index is based on three equally weighted indicators of productive status: occupation (of the breadwinner), education (of the respondent), and income (of the family).[2]

---

2. The original socioeconomic index, as developed by Mobilization for Youth, utilized the education of the breadwinner rather than of the respondent. The net result of both approaches in the study of social stratification is the same.

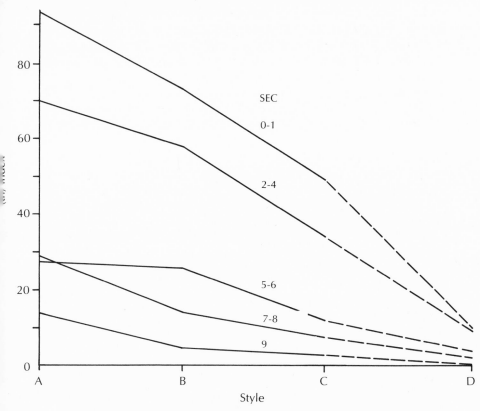

Fig. 4.1. Class stratification of a linguistic variable with stable social significance: (th) in *thing, through,* etc. Socioeconomic class scale: 0–1, lower class; 2–4, working class; 5–6, 7–8, lower middle class; 9, upper middle class. A, casual speech; B, careful speech; C, reading style; D, word lists.

Informally, we may describe these class groups as follows: group 0–1, lower class; 2–4, working class; 5–8, lower middle class; 9, upper middle class. Classes 2 and 5 are marginal groups, which sometimes show the linguistic behavior of the next lower group, and sometimes that of the next higher group.

Fig. 4.1 is an example of what we may call sharp stratification. The five strata of the population are grouped into two larger strata with widely different use of the variable. The parallel variable (dh) shows the same kind of sharp stratification (Labov 1966a:253). Fig. 4.2 is a class stratification diagram which shows a somewhat different

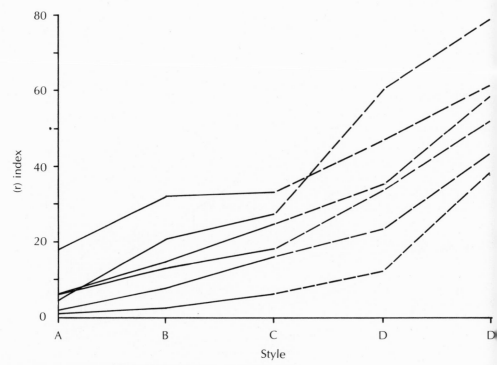

Fig. 4.2.  Class stratification of a linguistic variable in process of
change: (r) in *guard, car, beer, beard, board,* etc. SEC (Socioeconomic class) scale: 0–1, lower class; 2–4, working class; 5–6,
7–8, lower middle class; 9, upper middle class. A, casual speech;
B, careful speech; C, reading style; D, word lists; D′, minimal
pairs.

type of stratification. The vertical axis is the phonological index for
(r), in which 100 represents a consistent *r*-pronouncing dialect, and
00 a consistent *r*-less dialect. The horizontal axis shows five, not four,
stylistic contexts, including, at D′, the reading of word pairs in which
(r) is the sole focus of attention: *guard* vs. *god, dock* vs. *dark.* This
structure is an example of what we may call fine stratification: a
great many divisions of the socioeconomic continuum in which
stratification is preserved at each stylistic level. Other investigations
carried out in New York City, including the department-store survey,
support the general hypothesis on the fine stratification of (r) advanced in Ch. 2: any groups of New Yorkers that are ranked in a

hierarchical scale by nonlinguistic criteria will be ranked in the same order by their differential use of (r).

The status of (r-1) as a prestige marker is indicated by the general upward direction of all horizontal lines as we go from informal to formal contexts. At the level of casual, everyday speech, only the upper middle class (9) shows a significant degree of r-pronunciation. But in more formal styles, the amount of r-pronunciation for other groups rises rapidly. The lower middle class, in particular, shows an extremely rapid increase, surpassing the upper-middle-class level in the two most formal styles. This crossover pattern appears at first sight to be a deviation from the regular structure shown in Fig. 4.1. It is a pattern which appears in other diagrams: a similar crossover of the lower middle class appears for two other phonological indexes—in fact, for all those linguistic variables which are involved in a process of linguistic change under social pressure. On the other hand, the social and stylistic patterns for (th) have remained stable for at least 75 years, and show no sign of a crossover pattern. Thus the hypercorrect behavior of the lower middle class is seen as a synchronic indicator of linguistic change in progress. We will consider this hypercorrect pattern in much greater detail in the next chapter, and its significance for the study of change in progress will be examined in Ch. 9.

The linear nature of the ten-point scale of socioeconomic status is confirmed by the fact that it yields regular stratification for many linguistic variables, grammatical as well as phonological. The linguistic variables have been correlated with the individual social indicators of productive status—occupation, education and income—and it appears that no single indicator is as closely correlated with linguistic behavior as the combined index. However, an index which combines occupation and education—neglecting income— gives more regular stratification for the (th) variable. For education, there is one sharp break in linguistic behavior for this variable: the completion of the first year of high school. For occupation, there are sharp differences between blue-collar workers, white-collar workers, and professionals. If we combine these two indicators, we obtain four classes which divide the population almost equally, and stratify (th) usage regularly. This classification seems to be superior to the socioeconomic scale for analysis of variables such as (th) which reflect linguistic habits formed relatively early in life (Labov 1966a). However, the combined socioeconomic index, utilizing income, does show more regular stratification for a variable such as (r). Since (r-1) is a recently introduced prestige marker in New York City speech, it seems consistent—almost predictable—that it should be closely correlated with a socioeconomic scale which includes current income, and thus represents most closely the current social status of the subject.

Fig. 4.3 shows the distribution of (r) by age levels, a distribution

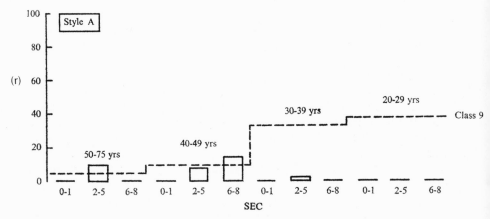

Fig. 4.3.  Development of class stratification of (r) for casual speech (Style A) in apparent time. SEC = socioeconomic class scale.

in apparent time which indicates a sudden increase in real time of the social stratification of (r) in everyday, casual speech. For the two oldest age levels, there is little indication of social significance of (r-1). But beginning with those under 40 years old, there is a radically different situation, with (r-1) acting as a prestige marker of upper-middle-class usage only. This sudden change in the status of (r) seems to have coincided with the events of World War II.

So far, we have been considering only one aspect of social stratification: the differentiation of objective behavior. In our studies of New York City, the complementary aspect of social stratification was also examined: social evaluation. A subjective reaction test was developed to isolate unconscious social responses to the values of individual phonological variables. In these tests, the subject rated a number of short excerpts from the speech of other New Yorkers on a scale of occupational suitability (see Fig. 6.1), and cross com-

parison of these ratings enabled us to isolate the unconscious subjective reactions of respondents to single phonological variables. This
subjective dimension will be examined in detail in Ch. 6: most
striking is the uniformity of New Yorkers under 40 years old. All
subjects between 18 and 39 agreed in their positive evaluation of
(r-1) (Fig. 6.2) despite the fact (as shown in Fig. 4.3) that the great
majority of these subjects do not use any (r-1) in their everyday
speech. Thus sharp diversification of (r) in objective performance
is accompanied by uniform subjective evaluation of the social significance of this feature. On the other hand, the subjects over 40 years
old, who show no differential pattern in their use of (r), show a very
mixed pattern in their social evaluation of this variable.

This result is typical of many other empirical findings which
confirm the view of New York City as a single speech community,
united by a uniform evaluation of linguistic features, yet diversified
by increasing stratification in objective performance.

The special role of the lower middle class in linguistic change has
been illustrated here in only one example, the crossover pattern of
Fig. 4.2. We can look ahead to the more detailed discussion of the
next chapter and consider other evidence for the special behavior
of this group. When Fig. 4.3 is replicated for increasingly formal
styles, we see that in each age level, the lower middle class shows
the greatest tendency towards the introduction of r-pronunciation,
and in the most formal styles, goes far beyond the upper-middle-class
level in this respect. A great deal of evidence shows that lower-
middle-class speakers have the greatest tendency towards linguistic
insecurity, and therefore tend to adopt, even in middle age, the
prestige forms used by the youngest members of the highest-ranking
class. This linguistic insecurity is shown by the very wide range of
stylistic variation used by lower-middle-class speakers; by their great
fluctuation within a given stylistic context; by their conscious striving for correctness; and by their strongly negative attitudes towards
their native speech pattern.

A simple yet accurate measure of linguistic insecurity was obtained by an independent approach, based on lexical behavior. The
subjects were presented with 18 words which have socially significant variants in pronunciation: *vase, aunt, escalator,* etc., and were
asked to select the form they thought was correct: [veɪz - vɑːz], [æ · nt
- ɑ · nt], [ɛskəleɪtɚ - ɛskjʊleɪtɚ], etc. They were then asked to indicate
which form they usually used themselves. The total number of cases

in which these two choices differed was taken as the Index of Linguistic Insecurity (ILI). By this measure, the lower middle class showed much the greatest degree of linguistic insecurity (see Table 5.1).

Social stratification and its consequences are only one type of social process which is reflected in linguistic structures. The interaction of ethnic groups in New York City—Jews, Italians, blacks, and Puerto Ricans—is also reflected in these and other linguistic variables. For some variables, New York City blacks participate in the same structure of social and stylistic variation as white New Yorkers. For other variables, there is an absolute differentiation of white and black which reflects the process of social segregation characteristic of the city. For example, there is a southern phonological characteristic which merges the vowels /i/ and /e/ before nasals: *pin* and *pen, since* and *sense,* are homonyms: "I asked for a straight [pɪn] and he gave me a writing [pɪn]." In New York City, this phonological trait has been generalized throughout the black community, so that the younger speakers, whether or not they show other southern characteristics in their speech, regularly show this merger. Thus this linguistic characteristic acts as an absolute differentiator of the black group, reflecting the social processes which identify the racial group as a whole. Similar phonological characteristics can be found marking the Puerto Rican group.[3]

Segregation of black and white may be seen in aspects of linguistic behavior quite distinct from the phonological system. Our investigation of New York City speech includes a number of semantic studies: one of the most fruitful of these concerns the semantic structures which revolve about the term *common sense.* This term lies at the center of one of the most important areas of intellectual activity for most Americans. It is a term frequently used, with considerable effect; its meaning is often debated, and questions about common sense evoke substantial intellectual effort from most of our subjects. Blacks use the term *common sense,* but also an equivalent

3. Most New Yorkers differentiate the vowels of *can* as in "tin can" from those of *can* in "I can." None of the Puerto Rican subjects interviewed showed a consistent use of this phonemic distinction. Puerto Rican speakers also show patterns of consonant cluster simplification which are different from those of both black and white New Yorkers. Clusters ending in *-rd* are simplified, and preconsonantal r is treated as a consonant: *a good car' game.* This does not fall within the range of variations open to other New Yorkers, who treat -r- as a vowel tactically, quite different from -l- in *good ol' Mike.*

term which is not a part of the native vocabulary of any white speakers. This term is *mother-wit,* or *mother-with* [mʌðɚwɪθ]. For a few white speakers, *mother-wit* is identified as an archaic, learned term: but for blacks, it is a native term used frequently by older members of the household, referring to a complex of emotions and concepts that is quite important to them. Yet blacks have no idea that white people do not use *mother-wit,* and whites have no inkling of the black use of this term. Contrast this complete lack of communication in an important area of intellectual activity, with the smooth and regular transmission of slang terms from black musicians to the white population as a whole.

The process of social segregation springs from causes and mechanisms which have been studied in detail. However, the opposing process of social integration is less obvious, and on the plane of linguistic structure, it is not at all clear how it takes place. Consider the semantic structure of *common sense.* When we analyze the semantic components of this term, its position in a hierarchical taxonomy, and its relation to coordinate terms in a semantic paradigm, we see great differences in the semantic structures used by various speakers.

I can best illustrate this diversity by contrasting two types of responses to our questions on common sense, responses which usually fall into two consistent sets. Respondent A may think of *common sense* as just 'sensible talk.' If he understands the cognitive content of an utterance, that to him is common sense. Respondent B considers common sense to be the highest form of rational activity, the application of knowledge to solve the most difficult problems. Do most people have common sense? A says yes, B says no. Who has a great deal of common sense? A thinks that doctors, lawyers, professors have the most. B thinks that uneducated people are more apt to have common sense, and immediately calls to mind some highly educated people with no common sense at all. If we say "two and two make four," is that an example of common sense? A says yes, B says no. Can we say that a person is intelligent, yet has no common sense? A says no, because intelligence is the same as common sense. B says yes, common sense and intelligence are quite different. A believes that if someone can be called *smart,* he would also have common sense; B sees no connection between smartness and common sense. Can one have *wisdom,* and yet no common sense? A says yes, B says no.

The extreme differences between types A and B, which are not

independent of social stratification, lead us to question the possibility
of semantic integration. Can such individuals, who have radically
opposed semantic structures for *common sense,* be said to understand one another? Can the term *common sense* be used to communicate meaning between these speakers? Some writers (particularly
the followers of General Semantics) feel that native speakers of
English usually do *not* understand one another, that such opposing
structures inevitably lead to misunderstanding. My own results lead
me to infer the opposite. People do understand one another: semantic
integration seems to take place through a central set of relations of
equivalence and attribution upon which all English speakers agree.
With only a few exceptions, all subjects agree that *common sense*
falls under the superordinate *judgment:* it is 'good judgment'. Equally
high agreement is found in the collocation of *practical,* or *everyday,*
with *common sense.* We have no simple term to describe the quality
of 'not being learned from books', yet there is also a very high degree
of agreement in this attribute of *common sense.*

If semantic integration takes place, it must be by a social process
in which extreme variants are suppressed in group interaction at the
expense of central, or core values. Further studies are required to
determine if such a mechanism does in fact operate.

This discussion has presented a number of aspects of language
behavior in which linguistic structures are seen to reflect social
processes. In the overall view, there is a wide range of benefits which
may be drawn from the interaction of sociological and linguistic
investigations. These may be considered under three headings, in
order of increasing generality:

1. Linguistic indexes provide a large body of quantitative data which
   reflect the influence of many independent variables. It does not
   seem impractical for tape-recorded data of this type to be collected and analyzed by social scientists who are not primarily
   linguists. Once the social significance of a given linguistic variant
   has been determined, by methods such as those outlined above,
   this variable may then serve as an index to measure other forms
   of social behavior: upward social aspirations, social mobility and
   insecurity, changes in social stratification and segregation.
2. Many of the fundamental concepts of sociology are exemplified
   in the results of these studies of linguistic variation. The speech
   community is not defined by any marked agreement in the use

of language elements, so much as by participation in a set of shared norms; these norms may be observed in overt types of evaluative behavior, and by the uniformity of abstract patterns of variation which are invariant in respect to particular levels of usage. Similarly, through observations of linguistic behavior it is possible to make detailed studies of the structure of class stratification in a given community. We find that there are some linguistic variables which are correlated with an abstract measure of class position, derived from a combination of several non-isomorphic indicators, where no single, less abstract measure will yield equally good correlations.

3. If we consider seriously the concept of language as a form of social behavior, it is evident that any theoretical advance in the analysis of the mechanism of linguistic evolution will contribute directly to the general theory of social evolution. In this respect, it is necessary for linguists to refine and extend their methods of structural analysis to the use of language in complex urban societies. For this purpose, linguistics may now draw upon the techniques of survey methodology; more importantly, many of the theoretical approaches of linguistics may be reinterpreted in the light of more general concepts of social behavior developed by other social sciences. Thus the main achievements of linguistic science, which may formerly have appeared remote and irrelevant to many sociologists, may eventually be seen as consistent with the present direction of sociology, and valuable for the understanding of social function and social change.

# 5 | Hypercorrection by the Lower Middle Class as a Factor in Linguistic Change

A LARGE part of our approach to language concerns the isolation of invariant functional units, and the invariant structures which relate these units to each other.[1] Considerable progress has been made through this approach to the analysis of language, but in many areas we have reached a point where a different approach is required, in which the variable features of language become the primary focus of attention, rather than the constant features. The empirical study of linguistic variants shows us that linguistic structure is not confined to the invariant, functional units such as phonemes, morphemes, or tagmemes; rather, there is a level of variant structure which relates entire systems of functional units, and which governs the distribution of subfunctional variants within each functional unit. This type of variant structure thus becomes a new type of invariant at a more refined level of observation.

The study of social variation in language is simply one of many aspects of the study of variant linguistic structures. One motivation for the linguist to study such structures is that they provide empirical evidence to resolve alternate structural analyses at the functional level, providing empirical solutions to problems which are otherwise meaningless. Secondly, variant structures are defined by quantitative methods which allow the detailed studies of linguistic changes in progress. The central theoretical problem with which the present report is concerned is the mechanism of linguistic change, in which the dynamics of social interaction appear to play an important part.

1. This chapter is based on a paper first given at a conference on Sociolinguistics held at the University of California, Los Angeles, in 1964, and first published in William Bright, ed., *Sociolinguistics* (The Hague: Mouton, 1966).

The process of linguistic change may be considered as having three stages (cf. Sturtevant 1947:Ch. 8). In the *origin* of a change, it is one of innumerable variations confined to the use of a few people. In the *propagation* of the change, it is adopted by such large numbers of speakers that it stands in contrast to the older form along a broad front of social interaction. In the *completion* of the change, it attains regularity by the elimination of competing variants. In this discussion, the second stage will be of primary concern: at this stage, it appears that social significance is inevitably associated with the variant and with its opposition to the older form.

Social forces exerted upon linguistic forms are of two distinct types, which we may call *pressures from above,* and *pressures from below.* By *below* is meant "below the level of conscious awareness." Pressures from below operate upon entire linguistic systems, in response to social motivations which are relatively obscure and yet have the greatest significance for the general evolution of language. In this presentation, we will be concerned primarily with social pressures from above, which represent the overt process of social correction applied to individual linguistic forms. In this process the special role of the lower middle class, or more generally, the role of the second-ranking status group, will be the principal focus of attention.

The role of hypercorrection in the propagation of linguistic change was indicated in the Martha's Vineyard study (Ch. 1). Here we will examine the hypercorrect behavior of a single class group in the speech community of New York City, and the consequences of this behavior for the process of linguistic change.

Most of the evidence to be presented is based upon the quantitative measurement of phonological indexes, although lexical and grammatical behavior is also considered. The methods of selecting, defining, and measuring phonological variables, and of defining and isolating contextual styles, have been presented in Ch. 3. These methods were applied in a survey of the Lower East Side of New York City, an area with a population of 100,000, using informants from the Mobilization for Youth survey discussed in Ch. 4. A total of 207 adults and children were interviewed; most of the data to be presented here is based on the speech of 81 adults raised in New York City, whose speech was studied in the greatest detail, but information from several other subgroups will be utilized as well.

The methods of quantitative analysis were applied to the problem of describing the phonological structure of the community as a whole, as opposed to the speech of individuals. Indeed, it was found that the speech of most individuals did not form a coherent and rational system, but was marked by numerous oscillations, contradictions and alternations which were inexplicable in terms of a single idiolect. For this reason, previous investigators had described large parts of the linguistic behavior of New Yorkers as being a product of pure chance, "thoroughly haphazard" (Hubbell 1950:48; cf. Bronstein 1962:24). But when the speech of any one person in any given context was charted against the overall pattern of social and stylistic variation of the community, his linguistic behavior was seen to be highly determined and highly structured.

Such a structure of social and stylistic variation was seen in Fig. 4.1, (p. 113) showing the stratification of (th). Let us return to the extraordinarily regular properties of this pattern (for convenience, Figs. 4.1 and 4.2 are repeated here).

Figure 4.1 shows a complex pattern of regular relations. Each value for a given class, in a given style, is lower than the value for the next most informal style, and higher than the next most formal style; it is also lower than the value for the next lower status group, and higher than the next higher status group (with one exception). From this figure, it is plain that the fricative form of (th) is the prestige form in New York City (as it is throughout the United States), and the stops and affricates are stigmatized forms. All class groups agree in their gradual reduction of the use of stops and affricates in more formal styles, and in each style there is a clearcut stratification of the variable. In other words, we have a structure consisting of two invariant sets of relations.

### Hypercorrect Behavior of the Lower Middle Class

By contrast, Fig. 4.2 of Ch. 4 shows a different type of structure. At one extreme we see that only one class group shows any degree of r-pronunciation in casual speech; that is, in everyday life, (r-1) functions as a prestige marker of the highest-ranking status group. The lower middle class, 6-8, shows only the same negligible amount of r-pronunciation as the working class and lower class. But as one follows the progression toward more formal styles, the lower middle class shows a rapid increase in the values of (r), until at Styles D and D', it surpasses the usage of the upper middle class. (See Ch.

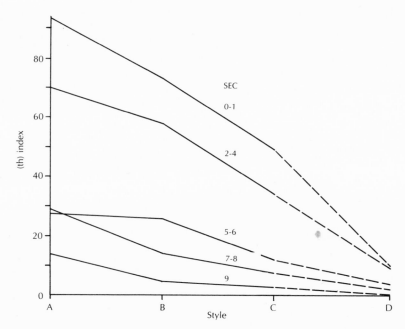

Fig. 4.1.  Class stratification of (th) (see p. 113).

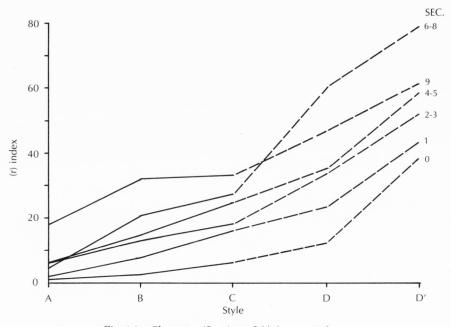

Fig. 4.2.  Class stratification of (r) (see p. 114).

3 for definitions of the contextual styles of A-D'). The crossover pattern appears to be a deviation from the regularity of the behavior shown by the other classes and Fig. 4.2 thus departs from the regularity of Fig. 4.1. To describe this phenomenon, the term *hypercorrection* will be used, since the lower-middle-class speakers go beyond the highest-status group in their tendency to use the forms considered correct and appropriate for formal styles. (This is of course an extension of the usual use of the term to indicate an irregular misapplication of an imperfectly learned rule, as in the hypercorrect case marking of *whom did you say is calling?*) If the deviation shown in Fig. 4.2 were found only in one case, it would be difficult to interpret—an irregularity in the method or in linguistic behavior. However, we find a similar crossover pattern in several other structures. Fig. 5.1, for example, is the class stratification diagram for (eh), the height of the vowel in *bad, ask, dance,* etc. as defined in Ch. 3.

The class stratification shows four class groups, with the lower middle class crossing over the value for the upper middle class in the most formal style. That is, in reading a word list such as *bat, bad, back, bag, batch, badge,* the lower-middle-class speakers show the greatest tendency to say [bæt, bæːd, bæk, bæːg . . . ], although in everyday speech, they are more likely to say [bɛːᵊd], homonymous with *bared:* "I had a [bɛːᵊd] cut; I [bɛːᵊd] my arm."

We find a similar hypercorrect pattern for the socially significant variable (oh). Fig. 5.2 is a style stratification diagram for this variable. The vertical axis in Fig. 5.2 represents the phonological index, formed from ratings which are parallel to those for (eh) (see page 76). For each socioeconomic class, the value of the index in each contextual style is plotted on Fig. 5.2, and the values for the same style are connected along horizontal lines. This diagram preserves all of the information present in the original data, and allows us to follow the differentiation of stylistic behavior in great detail. For the lower class, 0-2, the variable (oh) has no social or stylistic significance, as shown by the chaotic distribution of values in the four contextual styles. There is an intimate connection between stylistic and social variation, and as we see here, deviations from one axis of variation are usually accompanied by deviations from the other. The lower class shows no trace of the stratified pattern of the three higher-ranking classes.

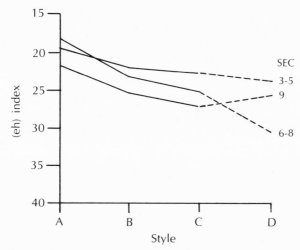

Fig. 5.1 Class stratification for (eh). SEC = socioeconomic class scale. A, casual speech; B, careful speech; C, reading style; D, word lists.

The upper section of the working class begins to show the high values of (oh-1)—[u:ᵊf]—in casual speech, values which are characteristic of the lower middle class as well. However, the social significance for the working class is not exactly the same as for the lower middle class, since the working-class speakers show only a slight tendency towards correction of this vowel to more open values in formal style. The lower middle class, on the other hand, shows an extreme tendency towards correction, reading a list of words such as *Paul, all, ball, awful, office,* with a determined, though inconsistent effort towards (oh-5):[pɔ:⊥l, ɒl, ɒfəl, bɔ:⊥l, ɒfɪs, dʊ:ᵊg . . . ]. The highest-ranking group, the upper middle class, shows a more moderate tendency in both casual and formal styles; as a result, we see the familiar crossover pattern in Fig. 5.3, which is the class stratification diagram for the variable (oh), without the lower class.

If we now compare Figs. 4.2, 5.1, and 5.3, it is evident that the same hypercorrect behavior of the lower middle class is displayed. This deviation from regular structure is not, in fact, a deviation, but rather a recurrent aspect of a regular structure quite distinct from that of Fig. 4.1. Fig. 4.1 represents the structure typical of variables not involved in the process of linguistic change. A similar pattern may

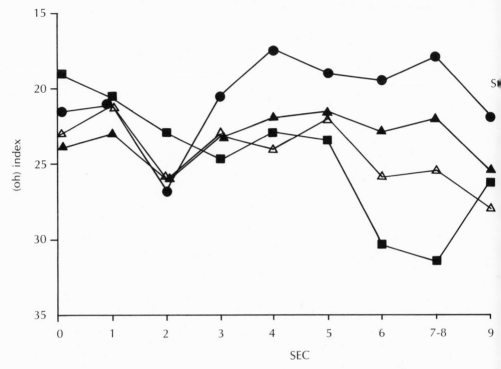

Fig. 5.2.   Style stratification of (oh). SEC = socioeconomic class
scale. A, casual speech; B, careful speech; C, reading style; D,
word lists.

be found in the parallel case of (dh), the initial consonant of *this*,
*that,* etc., or the morphological variable of the suffix *-ing.* On the
other hand, the pattern of (r), (eh), (oh) is that of phonological variables involved in the process of linguistic change, as we shall see.
The special role of the lower middle class in this pattern is apparent
in the sensitivity of this group to social pressures from above. We
may gain further understanding of the behavior of this class by
studying other types of evidence which go beyond the tabulation
of objective performance.

<h3 style="text-align:center">Hypersensitivity of the Lower Middle Class<br>in Subjective Reactions</h3>

In the study of the social stratification of language, we need not be
confined to the evidence of objective differentiation of behavior.

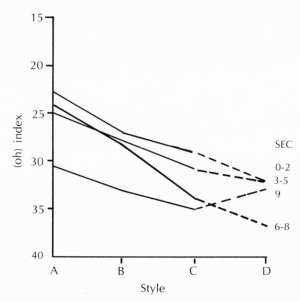

Fig. 5.3. Class stratification for (oh). SEC = socioeconomic class scale; A, casual speech; B, careful speech; C, reading style; D, word lists.

Social stratification has two aspects: differentiation, on the one hand, and social evaluation, on the other. In the survey of the Lower East Side, methods were devised to measure unconscious subjective reactions to individual values of the phonological variables. These subjective reaction tests are the principal subject of Ch. 6; here we will draw from them just the information relevant to the hypercorrect pattern of the lower middle class.

In the subjective reaction test (SR test), a tape-recording of 22 sentences is played for respondents, who are asked to rate the speech heard in each sentence on a scale of occupational suitability. Only five different speakers are represented, all reading the same standard text, in which the values of the main phonological variables are successively concentrated. Since the respondent cannot know exactly how he has marked any given speaker in earlier sentences in the series, each rating is effectively independent. It is therefore possible to compare the rating given to a speaker for a given treatment of a phonological variable with that given in a "zero section" which contains none of the variables. The effects of voice quality,

reading style, etc., are cancelled out, and the unconscious reactions
to values of a single variable are isolated.

In the test for subjective reactions to (oh), the respondents heard
three different speakers use high vowels in the sentences, "We
[oːˤ we·z] had [tʃoˤ :klɪt] milk and [kʊːᵊfi] cake around four o'clock."
If the respondent's ratings of all three speakers are equal or lower
to ratings given by him to the same speakers in the zero section, his
response is termed (oh)-negative. The percentage of respondents who
show (oh)-negative response for each class group is as follows:

| | | |
|---|---|---|
| Lower class | 0–2 | 24% |
| Working class | 3–5 | 61 |
| Lower middle class | 6–8 | 79 |
| Upper middle class | 9 | 59 |

In this table, we see the subjective correlate of a number of objective
patterns discussed before. The lower class, which does not participate in a pattern of social or stylistic variation for (oh), shows no
sensitivity to (oh) in the SR test. Secondly, there is here evidence
of a very general principle that pervades all of the results of the SR
test: those who show the greatest use of a stigmatized feature in
casual speech show the greatest sensitivity to this feature in subjective reactions. Thus, for example, Italian working-class men, who
show the highest use of stops for (th), also show the greatest sensitivity to this stigmatized feature in the speech of others. Here, the
working class, and particularly the lower middle class, who show
high (oh) vowels in casual speech, show the most negative reactions
to high (oh) in the SR test. Finally, we see that the lower middle
class shows hypersensitivity, in that it goes beyond the reaction of
the upper middle class in its negative response to high (oh).

A similar pattern emerges from subjective reactions to (eh), differ-
ing from that of (oh) only in that we see a higher level of sensitivity
on the part of the two lower classes: the following percentages of
(eh)-negative response were shown by the four class groups:

| | | |
|---|---|---|
| Lower class | 0–2 | 63% |
| Working class | 3–5 | 81 |
| Lower middle class | 6–8 | 86 |
| Upper middle class | 9 | 67 |

Here again we see the hypersensitive behavior of the lower middle class, which reacts more sharply to high (eh) vowels than the high-est-status class (and is joined here by the working class).

In the case of (r), the lower middle class shows a level of sensitivity to this variable which goes beyond the reaction of the upper middle class, even though the behavior of the upper middle class in everyday speech is closer to the norm. The test for subjective reactions to (r) is described in detail in the next chapter: essentially, it measures the degree to which a respondent's reactions are consistent with the status of (r-1) as a prestige marker. The percentages of (r)-positive response for the various class groups again show the hypersensitive pattern of the lower middle class:

| | | |
|---|---|---|
| Lower class | 0–1 | 50% |
| Working class | 2–5 | 53 |
| Lower middle class | 6–8 | 86 |
| Upper middle class | 9 | 75 |

If this hypersensitive behavior is indeed associated with linguistic change in progress, and consistent with the findings on objective performance, then we should find that the lower middle class does *not* exceed the upper middle class in reaction to the variable (th) (see Ch. 6). The percentage of (th)-sensitive responses for the several class groups show that this is indeed the case, as there is no evidence here for a hypersensitive response of the lower middle class:

| | | |
|---|---|---|
| Lower class | 0–2 | 58% |
| Working class | 3–5 | 76 |
| Lower middle class | 6–8 | 81 |
| Upper middle class | 9 | 92 |

So far, we have been considering evaluation of the speech of others. In another section of the linguistic interview, we explored the re-spondent's evaluation of his own usage of the variables. He was asked to choose which of four alternate pronunciations of a given word (*cards, chocolate, pass,* etc.) was closest to the way he usually pronounced the word himself. This self-evaluation test shows quite clearly that the extraordinary agreement in subjective response to the speech of others is not matched by an accurate perception of the respondents' own speech production. On the contrary, the re-spondents identified their own speech with those subjective norms which governed the direction of stylistic variation. For example, most respondents reported themselves as using variants of (eh) and (oh) which were lower than their own speech production, even in the most formal style.

It appears from this and other evidence that the New York speaker perceives his own phonic intention, rather than the actual sounds he produces; in this sense, the pattern which governs the direction of stylistic variation is determined by a structured set of social norms. It is phonemic, in the broadest sense.

The behavior of the lower middle class in this test is consistent with the hypercorrect pattern already shown. Lower-middle-class speakers show the greatest tendency to report very low values of (eh)—that is, they reported that they said [pæ:s] instead of [pɛ:ᵊs]— and by far the greatest tendency to report low (oh) vowels—claiming that they said [tšʊklɪt] when they actually said [tʃɔ:⊥klɪt]. On the other hand, the lower middle class showed no hypercorrect tendency towards inaccurate reporting in the self-evaluation of (th).

### Linguistic Insecurity of the Lower Middle Class

The great fluctuation in stylistic variation shown by the lower middle class, their hypersensitivity to stigmatized features which they themselves use, and the inaccurate perception of their own speech, all point to a high degree of linguistic insecurity for these speakers. Linguistic insecurity may be measured directly by several methods which are independent of the phonological indexes. In Ch. 4, we discussed the Index of Linguistic Insecurity (ILI) which contrasts "own use" and "correctness" for 18 lexical items. Table 5.1 shows the percentage distribution of scores for the four class groups, for four levels of the ILI. The lower middle class shows a much higher concentration at the highest levels of the index than any other group—a conclusion reinforced by the attitude of respondents in this class to the language of New York City.

In general, New Yorkers show a strong dislike for the sound of New York City speech. Most have tried to change their speech in one way or another, and would be sincerely complimented to be told that they do not sound like New Yorkers. Nevertheless, most of the respondents have been identified by their speech as New Yorkers whenever they set foot outside of the metropolitan area. They firmly believe that outsiders do not like New York City speech, for one reason or another. Most New Yorkers show a strong belief in correctness of speech, and they strive consciously to achieve such correctness in their careful conversation.

TABLE 5.1
DISTRIBUTION OF INDEX OF LINGUISTIC
INSECURITY SCORES BY SOCIOECONOMIC CLASS

| ILI scores | Socioeconomic class | | | |
|---|---|---|---|---|
| | 0–2 | 3–5 | 6–8 | 9 |
| 0 | 44% | 50% | 16% | 20% |
| 1–2 | 25 | 21 | 16 | 70 |
| 3–7 | 12 | 25 | 58 | 10 |
| 8–13 | 19 | 04 | 10 | — |
| | 100 | 100 | 100 | 100 |
| N= | 16 | 28 | 19 | 10 |

In all these respects, lower-middle-class speakers exceed all other New Yorkers.[2] The profound linguistic insecurity of the New York City speech community is most clearly exemplified in the conscious statements of the lower-middle-class respondents, as well as their unconscious behavior.

**The Role of the Lower Middle Class in Linguistic Change**

We can now approach the question of linguistic change, particularly as it affects the phonological variables. In this discussion, the principal approach to change will be through internal evidence, in the distribution of linguistic behavior through the various age levels of the population. This distribution forms a dimension which we may call apparent time, as opposed to real time. In the complete report of the New York City survey, the relations of apparent time and real time have been analyzed in detail, and the following cases considered (Labov 1966a, Ch. 9):

1. A stigmatized feature  A. not in process of change
   B. in process of change
2. A prestige marker  A. not in process of change
   B. in process of change
3. Change from below  A. early stage
   B. later stage, with correction from above

2. With the exception that a number of lower-middle-class respondents stated that they had been identified by outsiders as not coming from New York City.

We can find empirical data for examples of each of these types, which in general confirm the analysis provided. In particular, the variable (th) corresponds to the case of a stigmatized feature not involved in change; (oh) to an early stage of change from below; and (eh) to a later stage of change from below, with correction from above. The latter cases are complicated by the fact that the principal dynamic does not lie in the area of class stratification, but rather in the contrastive behavior of ethnic groups. In the remainder of this discussion, we will consider the case of (r), a prestige marker recently introduced into New York City speech. This variable is of course more than a simple phonemic alternation: to the extent that (r-1) is introduced, a whole series of shifts occur which reverse the main line of evolution of the New York City vowel system.

To begin with, we must consider the relations of real time to apparent time for a prestige marker in the process of change. For the highest-ranking group, which shows the greatest linguistic security, these two dimensions match most closely. The oldest members of the upper middle class would tend to preserve their older prestige forms, as solidified relatively early in their development, and the younger members would show the adoption of the newer prestige form. When we consider the next highest ranking group, usually the lower middle class, the reverse situation prevails. The great linguistic insecurity of these speakers would lead to fluctuation in their norms for formal contexts, and even in middle age they tend to adopt the latest prestige markers of the younger upper-middle-class speakers. In this respect, they would surpass the younger members of their own group, who would not have had as wide an exposure to the structure of social stratification, and its consequences.

The working-class respondents might be expected to follow the same general lines of behavior as the lower middle class, but to a less pronounced degree. Only the lower class would be largely immune from the tendency to follow the latest prestige norms. On the basis of these general considerations, we would expect the following scheme of relations between younger and older sections of the four class groups, as far as their use of the prestige feature is concerned:

|           | Lower class | Working class | Lower middle class | Upper middle class |
|-----------|-------------|---------------|--------------------|--------------------|
| Younger   | low         | [lower]       | lower              | high               |
| Older     | low         | [higher]      | higher             | low                |

We can now consider the empirical data which corresponds to this diagram. Fig. 4.3 (p. 116) showed the distribution of (r) values for casual speech. For the two older age groups, there is no indication of a social significance of (r); but for all those under 40 years old, there is sharp stratification, in which (r-1) has become the mark of the highest-status group only. This sudden break corresponds exactly with a change in the social evaluation of (r), as shown in Table 6.1 (see p. 149). While those over 40 years old show a very mixed pattern in their subjective response to (r), those from 18 to 39 show a complete unanimity in their positive evaluation of this prestige feature. Note that in the older group, the lower middle class shows the highest degree of (r)-positive response.

Table 6.1 has important implications for our general view of society as well as the development of language within society. We see the New York City speech community moving towards an increased diversification of speech performance (in Fig. 4.3); but at the same time, in Table 6.1, there has developed complete agreement in subjective evaluation. This sudden change may precede and outrun the parallel development in overt behavior.

The data for successively more formal styles of speech appear in Fig. 5.4. Beginning with Style B, careful speech, there is an increasing tendency for all class and age groups to use more (r-1). However, it is the middle-aged members of the lower-middle-class group who show the greatest tendency to increase their use of (r-1) in formal styles, until in Styles D and D', they far surpass the level of the upper middle class. The hatched areas in Fig. 5.4 represent the degree by which a given index score exceeds the level of the upper middle class.

Fig. 5.4 is a complex structure, relating four variables. From top to bottom, there is a regular increase in (r-1) with increase of formality of contextual style; from left to right, there is a pattern of class behavior, repeated many times, in which the lower middle class leads the working class and lower class in the use of (r-1). Finally, the larger left-to-right pattern shows a complex relationship of age level to (r), in which the younger class 9 speakers show more and more (r-1), while the reverse pattern holds for the correlation of age and (r-1) in the three lower classes.

With the background of all of the data presented in this discussion, the complex structure of Fig. 5.4 seems comprehensible, and indeed, almost predictable. This data made it possible to account for earlier results that seemed puzzling—the unexpected configurations that emerged from the study of three New York department stores (in Ch. 2). In Fig. 2.5 we saw that the highest-ranking store, Saks, showed the expected increase of (r-1) with decreasing age. However, the middle-ranking store, Macy's, showed the reverse relation, at a lower level. The lowest-ranking store, Kleins, showed no clearcut pattern. When we rearranged Fig. 5.4 in the form of Fig. 2.5, we obtained Fig. 2.6, Style B (p. 60). Point by point, feature by feature, the two diagrams matched. This convergence is the strongest possible verification of the findings of both surveys, for they approached the data by completely opposite methods. The possible sources of error are complementary: in each area where the department-store survey is liable to error, the Lower East Side survey is most reliable, and vice-versa.

The convergence of the two surveys establishes the validity of the analysis given above of the relations of apparent time and real time for a prestige marker which has recently been introduced into the linguistic structure of a community.

### The Role of Hypercorrection in the
### Mechanism of Linguistic Change

There is sufficient evidence to support the view that the introduction of (r-1) into New York City is indeed a relatively recent process, which showed a sharp qualitative increase in the years immediately following World War II. Traces of a similar development may be found in other r-less areas, but nowhere is the tendency so great as in New York City, and nowhere has it penetrated so deeply throughout the structure of the community. We can, of course, look to the influence of the broadcast media, where r-less patterns have all but disappeared, but this is a factor which affects all sections of the United States. In order to account for the special development of New York City, it is necessary to look to social and linguistic mechanisms which are peculiar to the metropolitan area.

New York City, as a speech community, may be regarded as a sink of negative prestige. This is not a recent pattern: the prestige dialect seems to have been a borrowed one for as long as we can trace it, and the process we are witnessing here is primarily one of substituting a northern-midwestern r-pronouncing dialect for the older r-less prestige dialect borrowed from eastern New England. Yet the

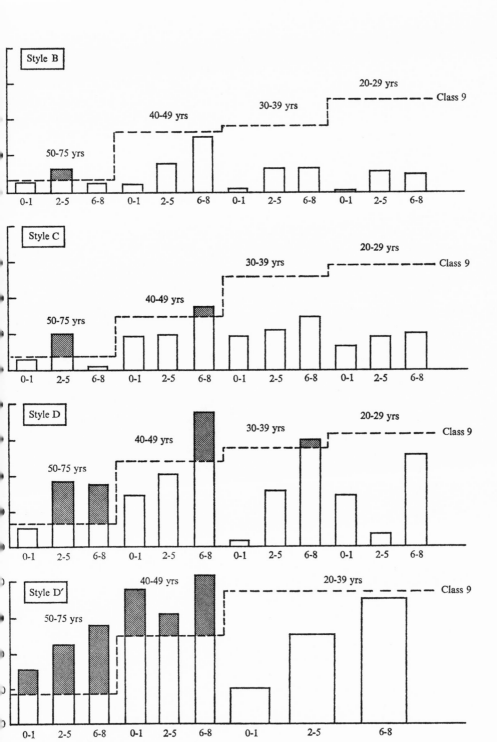

Fig. 5.4. Class stratification of (r) in apparent time for Styles B–D′.
B, careful speech; C, reading style; D, word lists; D′, minimal
pairs. Nos. 0–9 indicate socioeconomic class scale.

differences between the newer and the older forms are profound from the point of view of phonological structure. All of the New York City respondents had grown up speaking an r-less dialect: since they had acquired r-pronunciation long after their primary speech pattern had been established, it was not possible for them to achieve consistency in the use of (r-1), even in the most formal context.

The evidence of this study as a whole indicates the following sequence of events in the genetic development of the complex linguistic structures that have been displayed here. The child's first experience in the use of English, at 2 to 3 years old, is usually dominated by the example of his parents. But from about 4 to 13 years old, his speech pattern is dominated and regulated by that of the preadolescent group with which he plays. These are the peers who are able, by their sanctions, to eliminate any deviations from the dialect pattern of the group. It appears that this preadolescent period is the age when automatic patterns of motor production are set: as a rule, any habits acquired after this period are maintained by audio-monitoring in addition to motor-controlled patterns.

It is in the first year of high school that the speaker begins to acquire the set of evaluative norms which have been displayed in this presentation. He becomes sensitive to the social significance of his own form of speech, and other forms; complete familiarity with the norms of the community seems to be attained at the age of 17 or 18. On the other hand, the ability to use prestige forms of speech, such as r-pronunciation, is not acquired until relatively late: the youngster seems to begin this process at 16 or 17. A working-class or lower-middle-class youth never attains the security in the use of this prestige form which the youngster from an upper-middle-class family does: as we have seen, even at the age of 30 or 40, the lower-middle-class speaker may be intent on changing his careful style, shifting his concept of the prestige norm to meet the most recent standards. In contrast, the college graduate has attained a certain degree of security in his use of English, partly through extensive contact with prestige speakers, and partly through the approval of his fellow students. Despite the fact that he may thus depend upon an acquired secondary prestige pronunciation, his use of this form may remain relatively constant from that time forth.

From the Lower East Side study we can derive systematic evidence to show the gradual acquisition of these sociolinguistic norms, and the differential rate of acquisition of different class groups. Fig. 5.5

is a composite chart of all the forms of linguistic behavior which reveal the recognition of such norms. In regard to any given variable, a subject can show a regular pattern of style shifting towards the prestige norm, self-report biased towards the norm, subjective reaction tests sensitive to the norm, and overt recognition of the socio-linguistic feature as a stereotype. The vertical axis is the total score for the acquisition of sociolinguistic norms, and the horizontal axis is the age of the subject. All the subjects shown in Fig. 5.5 are children of the main subjects of the Lower East Side survey. Horizontal lines connect brothers and sisters, so that the upward direction of these lines shows the rate of acquisition of the norms by age. When we examine the socioeconomic status of each family, it immediately becomes apparent that there is sharp differentiation by social class. Children of upper-middle-class families start higher on the scale and show a more complete response to sociolinguistic norms than lower-middle-class children, and so on down the line. While every family is moving in the same general direction, lower-class youth are still located at a relatively low point on the scale at the age of 18 or 19. It follows that by the time they acquire a good knowledge of sociolinguistic norms, they are no longer able to modify their basic vernacular to achieve consistent productive control.

The problem which must be faced now is: how can such a mechanism lead to the solidification of r-pronunciation as a native speech pattern, for careful or casual speech? The period when primary speech patterns are solidified is separated by a gap of at least four or five years from the period when secondary prestige forms are learned. The preadolescent may be influenced in his speech pattern by those who are one or two years older, but it is hard to imagine that he would be in close contact with those who are four or five years older. It would then seem that this mechanism can lead only to permanent stratification, and that r-pronunciation would never penetrate to the preadolescent period.

Yet one must consider that the original solidification of New York City as an r-less area must have followed the same pattern as that we are now witnessing, but in reverse. R-less speech was originally a prestige form, modeled on the fashion of Southern British speech, and the present configuration of r-less areas, surrounding Boston, New York, Richmond, and Charleston must represent the successful introduction of a prestige form into the primary native speech pattern. If the process was completed once, it can be completed again.

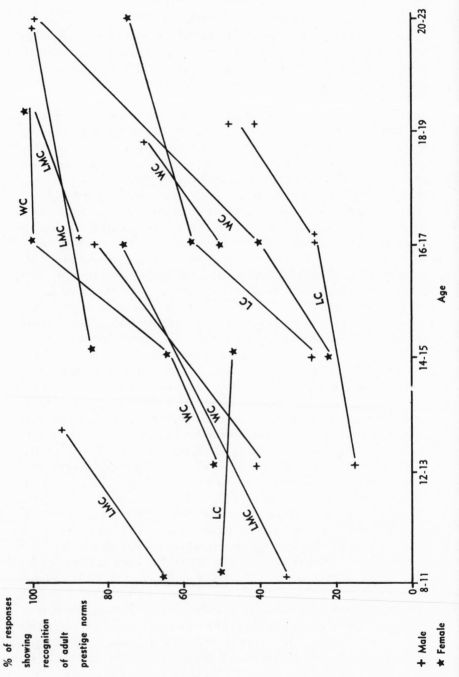

Fig. 5.5. Acquisition of prestige norms in families with two or more children. Reprinted by permission of the National Council of Teachers of English.

The key to this puzzle may lie in the hypercorrection of the lower middle class. We have seen that middle-aged, lower-middle-class speakers tend to adopt the formal speech pattern of the younger, upper-middle-class speakers. This tendency provides a feed-back mechanism which is potentially capable of accelerating the introduction of any prestige feature. Instead of a gradual, generation-by-generation spread of a feature from the highest-ranking group to the lowest-ranking group, we have here a means by which the process can be brought to an entirely different tempo. The lower-middle-class youth (and to a lesser extent the working-class youth) is in contact with the new prestige pronunciation on two fronts. On the one hand, he is familiar with the speech of those who are going to college, whether or not he belongs to this group. On the other hand, his parents (and his teachers) also use this prestige pattern in the most formal circumstances. Normally, the dialect used by his parents has little obvious effect upon his own native dialect form: it makes no difference whether they come from Maine or Brooklyn, as far as his own speech is concerned. However, it is not impossible that repeated use of (r-1) by the parents in the earliest stage of language learning may lay the groundwork for automatic and consistent r-pronunciation. Such an effect is not strong in New York City today, except perhaps in some upper-middle-class homes. But it may well be that in another half-generation or so, the use of r-pronunciation in formal styles on the part of adults may have increased to the point that children will acquire this pattern among their earliest, motor-controlled habits. One might think that parents would use only casual speech patterns in speaking to their young children; but on the contrary, I have heard respondents using the most careful, r-pronouncing forms when scolding their children. Since r-pronunciation has been adopted as the norm for the most careful type of communication, it has perhaps become appropriate for many types of interaction between parent and child. Hypercorrectness is certainly strongest in women—and it may be that the lower-middle-class mother, and the grade-school teacher, are prime agents in the acceleration of this type of linguistic change.

The existence of the hypercorrect pattern in New York City has been established beyond any reasonable doubt. The suggested role of hypercorrection in the acceleration of linguistic change has been put forward with the expectation that further empirical studies may confirm or refute this possibility. Similar investigations may profitably be carried out in other cities, perhaps in those which do not show as great a range of stylistic variation in the speech community. Furthermore, it is necessary to explore more deeply the social motivation which underlies the more systematic and obscure process of change from below. All of these investigations will help in the illumination of the important problem of establishing the mechanism of linguistic change.

# 6 | Subjective Dimensions of a Linguistic Change in Progress

TRADITIONAL studies of regional dialects in the United States have shown that isolation leads to linguistic diversity, while the mixing of populations leads to linguistic uniformity. Yet as we turn to the study of language differences in metropolitan centers, a new and different situation appears.[1] Instead of horizontal, spatial differentiation, we have a vertical cross-section which does not presuppose isolation of the linguistic strata. On the contrary, groups living in close contact may participate in rapid linguistic changes which lead to increased diversity, rather than uniformity.

Studies of the social stratification of language in New York City show two overall directions of change in the phonological system contributing to such diversity. One direction is the further development of the traditional New York City pattern, continuing the lines of its earlier evolution, with new phonemic mergers and chain shifts comparable to the Great Vowel Shift itself. The other large-scale change is the superposition of a new prestige pattern, almost directly opposed to the traditional dialect in most of its variable elements.

This chapter will deal with one variable of the new prestige pattern: (r), the presence or absence of consonantal [r] in final and preconsonant position in *beer, beard, car, card*, etc. We have already dealt with this variable in many ways. Its use in everyday interaction was examined in the rapid and anonymous survey of department stores in Ch. 2; the pattern of style shifting of (r) was delineated in Ch. 3; the pattern of social and stylistic stratification of (r) was

---

1. This is a revised version of a paper originally given before the Linguistic Society of America's Winter Meeting in Chicago, Illinois, in December, 1963. It incorporates some of the more detailed treatment of the subject in Chapter 11 of *The Social Stratification of English in New York City* (1966).

outlined in Ch. 4; and it was seen as one element of the hypercorrect
pattern of the lower middle class in Ch. 5. At various points we have
considered results of the tests which trace the subjective dimension
of this variable: in this chapter, subjective reactions will be our
primary focus. We will trace a sudden change in the subjective
evaluation of the new prestige pattern by native New Yorkers: the
development of a uniform attitude toward (r), a norm which tran-
scends class differences, in sharp contrast to the increasing differentiation of the objective performance of speakers.

Many patterns of linguistic variation that we find in New York
run parallel to the dominant and increasingly rigid pattern of social
stratification. Techniques for studying linguistic differentiation by
quantitative indexes first developed in the study of Martha's Vineyard (Ch. 1) were applied in the Lower East Side study to construct
indexes for five phonological variables. But the other side of the
problem, measuring subjective evaluation to particular variables, had
to be solved for the first time in New York City. Reactions to phonological variables are inarticulate responses, below the level of
conscious awareness, and occur only as a part of an overall reaction
to many variables. There is no vocabulary of socially meaningful
terms with which our informants can evaluate speech for us. Tests
for reactions to social dialects as a whole have been developed by
Lambert and his associates for discussion of the principles involved
(see below and Ch. 8). For our linguistic purposes, we need to elicit
a kind of evaluative behavior that is sensitive enough to register the
effect of a particular linguistic feature—and a way of presenting a
stimulus which concentrates that feature. The method developed in
this survey appears to answer such a requirement; it will be discussed here in its application to the social evaluation of (r).

This r-pronunciation is the chief manifestation of the new prestige
pattern which prevails in New York City. The introduction of /r/
into this previously r-less dialect is not a mere phonetic change,
substituting (r-1) for (r-0). It has widespread phonemic consequences.
With (r-1), a speaker differentiates *guard* and *god*, *source* and *sauce*,
*bared* and *bad*, which are homonyms[2] in traditional New York City

2. As indicated here, *God* and *guard* can be differentiated by the quality of the
vowel, with a back raised [ɒː] being used where an underlying /r/ follows. However,
the most recent developments in the New York City system show /a/ before a voiced
final shifting to the class of *guard*, so that *got* with [ɑ] is now opposed to *God*, *gart-*
and *guard* with [ɒː]. The classes of *source* and *sauce* are also reported to be homonyms

speech: [gɑːd] and [gɑːd], [sɔːs] and [sɔːs], [bɛ⁹d] and [bɛ⁹d]. Along
with the use of (r-1) we have the reversal of chain shifts in the low
and mid vowels: as for example, the movement of *farmer* [fɑːmə]
to [fɑːʸmə] and then to [fɒːmə] is reversed with the introduction
of (r-1).

The evidence presented in Chs. 3 and 4 for the social differentiation
of this feature is conclusive. The evidence for change in the use of
(r) is also quite definite. We know that New York City was an
r-pronouncing region in the 18th century, and became completely
r-less in the 19th. This change seemed to follow the influence of
London speech, where the r-less pattern was overtly observed by
Walker in 1791. New York followed the example of Boston, Charleston, Savannah, and other Eastern seaboard cities, so the model may
have been simultaneously that of the prestige pattern of New England and London. It seems to be one of our best examples of a
"change from above"—originating in the highest social group—which
eventually spread to the entire speech community and became the
vernacular form. Our first documented evidence for r-less pronunciation in New York City dates to the middle of the 19th century;
Richard Norman has observed that the New York poet Frederick
Cozzens rhymed *shore* and *pshaw* in 1856.[3] Babbitt's study of 1896
was the first linguistic report, and it showed that the r-less speech
was the regular vernacular pattern of the city. Babbitt's report as
well as Linguistic Atlas interviews of the 1930's show a completely
r-less dialect for the 21 speakers of the city proper (Frank 1948).
Hubbell's study (1950) and Bronstein's observations (1962) both
mention an increasing use of (r-1) by college students. Fig. 4.2 (p.
00) showed that (r) has now become for most New Yorkers a function
of both the formality of the context and the social status of the
speaker. Our question now is: what is the subjective correlate of this
social differentiation?

The "matched guise" technique developed by Lambert (1967) is
the basic tool now widely utilized for the study of subjective reactions towards language. The essential principle which emerges from

---

by most New Yorkers. But recent spectrographic work shows that this is not the case
for most speakers. Even when they do not pronounce /r/, the nucleus of *source* is
higher and/or further back than *sauce*, although it appears to be "the same" to native
speakers (Labov 1970, Labov, Yaeger, and Steiner 1972).

3. Richard Norman, "An ear to New York," unpublished manuscript.

Lambert's work is that there exists a uniform set of attitudes towards language which are shared by almost all members of the speech community, whether they use a stigmatized or a prestige form of that language. These attitudes do not emerge in a systematic form if the subject is questioned directly about dialects; but if he makes two sets of personality judgments about the same speaker using two different forms of language, *and does not realize that it is the same speaker,* his subjective evaluations of language will emerge as the differences in the two ratings.

Thus, we find that the first step is to expose each informant to utterances with contrasting values of the variable in which all other variables would be held constant. This might be done with synthetic speech, or with utterances of a trained phonetician. But then we would have to prove that the phonetic detail of the variant was equivalent to that of the natural variants, and also, that the artificiality of the utterance did not itself introduce a new variable that disturbed subjective reactions. It seems preferable to approach the problem from above, by using natural utterances of native speakers. In casting the net a little wider, we may dredge up some extraneous variables, but we will be certain of our main object, the natural occurrences of (r).

On Martha's Vineyard we could not follow this procedure, because in such a small community there were no anonymous native voices (see Ch. 1). In New York, this was no problem, and we began with 40 versions of a standard reading, "when I was nine or ten . . .", collected in exploratory interviews on the East Side. The full text is given in Appendix A to this chapter; the first paragraph is the "zero" level for calibration of the speaker's voice and reading style, with none of the five phonological variables used. In each succeeding paragraph, the five variables are successively concentrated; (eh), (oh), (eh), (r), and the two *th* variables together, (th), and (dh). We will be concerned here with the fourth paragraph, beginning, "I remember where he was run over, not far from our corner . . . " Each occurrence of (r) is underlined in the text. From five readings of this paragraph by women speakers, I chose 22 sentences and assembled them on a test tape in which each was heard twice in succession. The first five sentences are from the zero paragraph; then sentences are taken from successive paragraphs in the reading, with speakers occurring in mixed order.

This tape was played to the subjects near the end of the interview, when only the direct discussion of speech remained. The subject had already read the text himself; now he was asked to register his feelings about the speech of these other native New Yorkers on a scale of occupational suitability, shown as Fig. 6.1. He was asked to place himself in the position of a personnel manager, and use this

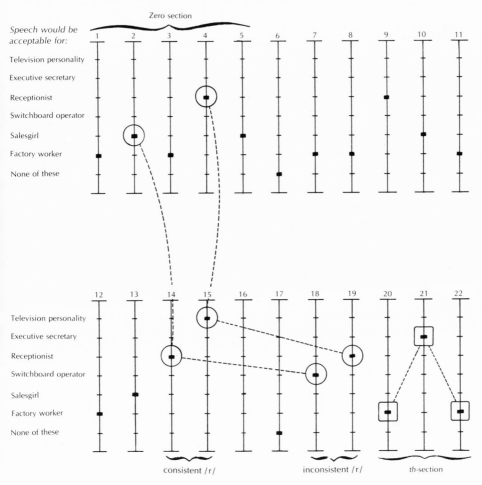

Fig. 6.1.  Subjective evaluation form and patterns for (r) and (th).

scale to rate the speakers as if they were candidates for jobs. A mark across the line meant that the speaker could hold that job, and all below, but did not speak well enough to hold any of the jobs above. The marks on this chart represent the median performance of younger middle-class speakers.

Altogether, 200 tests were completed. Some subjects realized that voices were recurring in the test, but no one could know exactly how he had ranked the speaker in earlier occurrences. Each rating is therefore effectively independent. As a result, we can compare ratings given to a speaker as she was first heard in the zero paragraph, with ratings given to her in other sentences marked by many occurrences of a particular variable. We then use this difference as a measure of the subject's evaluation of that particular value of that variable. Voice quality, reading style, intonation, contribute the same effect to each rating, and their influence may then be cancelled out. Fig. 6.1 also shows the structure of the test in regard to (r). The speaker who is first heard as No. 2 in the zero section is later heard as No. 14 pronouncing all (r) as (r-1)—usually a weakly constricted [ɚ], but indicated here more broadly as [r]:

> He [dɑrtɪd] out about [fɔɚ] feet [bifɔɚ] a [kɑr], and he got hit [hɑrd].

But in No. 18, she is heard repeating the same sentence with one (r-0) at the end:

> He [dɑrtɪd] out about [fɔɚ] feet [bifɔɚ] a [kɑr] and he got hit [hɑʼ:d].

The same alternation is shown by the speaker who is first heard as No. 4. In No. 15 she reads the sentence "He darted out . . ." with a precise articulation of all (r) as (r-1), but then in No. 19 is heard saying

> We didn't have the [hɑrt] to play ball [ɔr] [kɑʼ:dẓ] all [mɔrnɪŋ].

We thus have two consistent examples of (r-1) in Nos. 14 and 15, followed at a short distance by two inconsistent versions in Nos. 18 and 19. Those who are sensitive to (r-1) as a mark of prestige pronunciation show a remarkably fine ability to discriminate between these two pairs, rating 18 a rank or two lower than 14, and 19 one or two ranks below 15. Only a few especially knowledgeable subjects are aware of this inconsistent (r): most people cannot explain why they lower the ratings for 18 and 19, though they are quite firm in their opinion.

How shall we reduce these ratings to a single index? Let us consider that there are two possible responses consistent with the recognition of (r-1) as a prestige marker: rating 18 and 19 lower than 14 and 15 respectively, or in view of the fact that they are after all the same speakers, rating 18 as the same as 14, 19 the same as 15. Either of these reactions, or a combination, we will treat as (r)-*positive*. If in either case, the subject followed a contrary direction, rating 18 higher than 14 or 15 higher than 19, we will call his reaction (r)-*negative*.

Table 6.1 shows the percentages of (r)-positive response to the two-choice test for four age levels, and five divisions of the socioeconomic scale (the same divisions used for the original class stratification of (r) in Ch. 4). In this table, our attention is immediately

TABLE 6.1
(r)-POSITIVE RESPONSE TO THE
TWO-CHOICE TEST BY SOCIOECONOMIC
CLASS AND AGE

| Age | 0-1 | 2-3 | 4-5 | 6-8 | 9 | Total | N | | | | |
|---|---|---|---|---|---|---|---|---|---|---|---|
| 8-17 | 16% | 57% | 67% | 89% | (50)% | 61% | 6 | 14 | 12 | 9 | 2 |
| 18-19 | 100 | — | 100 | 100 | 100 | 100 | 2 | — | 2 | 1 | 3 |
| 20-39 | 100 | 100 | 100 | 100 | 100 | 100 | 3 | 6 | 7 | 11 | 5 |
| 40- | 63 | 67 | 50 | 70 | 57 | 62 | 8 | 18 | 8 | 10 | 7 |

taken by a regularity more absolute than any that has been encountered so far. One hundred percent of the speakers from age 20 to 39 showed (r)-positive reactions to the two-choice test, but only 62 percent of those over 40. Furthermore, this regularity is extended to the respondents 18 and 19 years old. A simple four-cell table shows a remarkable distribution of respondents who show (r)-positive and (r)-negative response for two age levels:

| Age | (r)-*positive* | (r)-*negative* |
|---|---|---|
| 18-39 | 40 | 0 |
| 40- | 31 | 20 |

This is a startling result. It establishes beyond a doubt that there is a great difference in the behavior of these two age groups, and it implies that the recognition of (r-1) as a prestige marker has reached the stage of absolute regularity which we associate with completed linguistic changes.

In Table 6.1, class differences have largely disappeared, and only differences in age level stand out. This is a particularly striking fact, since in Chs. 2 and 4, (r) showed the finest and most regular class stratification of all of the variables in the Lower East Side Study. We now find that this uniform stratification of (r) in performance is accompanied by a uniform evaluation of the prestige norm by younger speakers of all classes. There has been no overall increase in the use of (r-1) in the vernacular of everyday speech; but there has been a sudden increase in the stratification of (r). Fig. 6.2a shows the social stratification of (r) in Style A—casual speech—for those under 40 and those over 40 years old in the Lower East Side sample. In the older age level there is no particular difference in the use of the four socioeconomic groups. But for younger speakers, there is a sharp differentiation between the highest group—the upper middle class—and the rest. The total amount of (r-1) used may actually have decreased—what has increased is the differentiation of social class. We can compare this development with the subjective evaluations, shown in Fig. 6.2b. Here we shift from more or less random response for the older level to a uniform positive evaluation for the younger. Fig. 6.2 thus demonstrates the general principle that social stratification in the use of a variable is correlated with a uniform subjective evaluation of it.

A more difficult test may now be constructed to include the two original sentences 2 and 4. Consistent recognition of (r-1) as a prestige marker should lead to the rating of sentences 14 and 15 equal or higher than the zero level of speakers 2 and 4. Instead of a two-choice test, a *four-choice test* will be used to establish an (r)-positive response. For an (r)-positive rating the subject must rate the consistent use of (r-1) equal or higher than the zero level, and the inconsistent use equal or lower than the consistent use. A reversal in any one of these four choices will give the subject an (r)-negative rating. Table 6.2 shows the data for the four-choice test which corresponds to Table 6.1 for the two-choice test.

The more difficult four-choice test reduces the overall percentages slightly, but preserves the relationships intact. The results of the

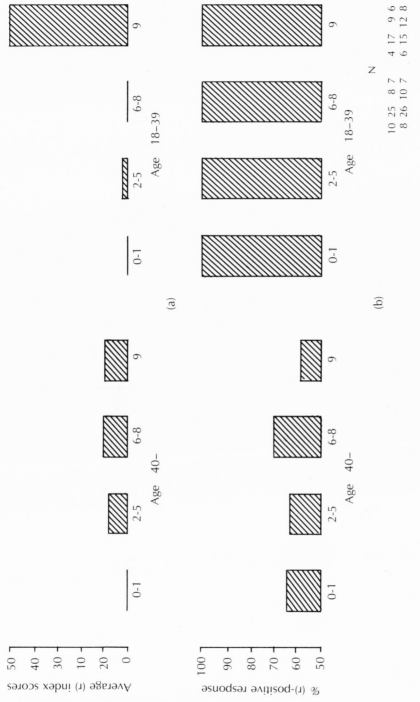

Fig. 6.2.  (a) Class stratification of (r) by age in casual speech
(b) Subjective evaluation of (r) by age and class groups.
Nos. 0–9 indicate socioeconomic class scale.

TABLE 6.2
(r)-POSITIVE RESPONSE TO THE
FOUR-CHOICE TEST BY SOCIOECONOMIC
CLASSIFICATION AND AGE

| Age | Socioeconomic class | | | | | Total | | $N$ | | | |
|-----|------|------|------|------|------|-------|---|---|----|----|----|
|     | 0-1  | 2-3  | 4-5  | 6-8  | 9    |       |   |   |    |    |    |
| 8-17  | 00% | 36% | 33%  | 67%  | (50)% | 37  | 6 | 14 | 12 | 9  | 2 |
| 18-19 | 50  | —   | 100  | 100  | 100  | 88   | 2 | —  | 2  | 1  | 3 |
| 20-39 | 75  | 84  | 86   | 100  | 100  | 87   | 3 | 6  | 7  | 11 | 5 |
| 40-   | 38  | 44  | 25   | 70   | 57   | 48   | 8 | 18 | 8  | 10 | 7 |

four-choice test are more impressive in several ways. If we take the total number of choices which the respondents had to make, for sentences 14, 15, 18, and 19, the following contrast between age groups appears:

| Age | Choices consistent with recognition of prestige marker | No differences from zero level | Choices inconsistent with recognition of prestige marker |
|-----|-----|-----|-----|
| 18-39 | 128 | 35 | 5 |
| 40-   | 108 | 48 | 48 |

The consistency of the younger group is the more remarkable when one considers that sentences 14 and 15 are widely separated from sentences 2 and 4 in the course of the SR test. Only five deviations from the pattern of (r)-positive responses appear for younger speakers. Furthermore, these deviations were all in class 4 and below, so that it is evident that minor differences in sensitivity to (r) still exist among the several class groups.[4]

4. Differences exist in the fineness of reaction to sentences 18 and 19. For all of the variables, the average values of the absolute differences in ratings of the same speakers are correlated with class. In the present case, the higher-ranking classes seem to hear the difference between sentences 14 and 18, 15 and 19, as slight differences; the ratings of the speakers drop one or two ranks only. Lower-ranking respondents react as a rule in an exaggerated fashion, and penalize the inconsistent utterances by rating them much lower than sentences 14 and 15. If we sum the absolute differences between 14 and 18, 15 and 19, for all respondents between 18 and 39, we obtain the following progression:

| Working class and lower class 0-5 | Lower middle class 6-8 | Upper middle class 9 |
|-----|-----|-----|
| 3.9 | 3.5 | 3.1 |
| N = 20 | 12 | 8 |

From Tables 6.1 and 6.2, there can be no doubt that the age differences in (r)-positive response are well established. There is little room for differences of sex or ethnic group, or even socioeconomic class, in the face of such a general change in apparent time. We see that socioeconomic differentiation, obscured in the two-choice test, reappears to some extent in the four-choice test. The differences in age groups are repeated in every class, however, they are larger in magnitude than any difference between classes.

The break is actually sharper than it appears in Tables 6.1 and 6.2. Fig. 6.3 shows the percentages of (r)-positive response for nine age groups. The break seems to come exactly with those who were born in 1923 as far as our sample is concerned. No particular direction for those over 40 is shown in this figure, while at the other end of the scale, it seems to be just about at the age of 18 that young people learn to recognize the social significance of this feature.

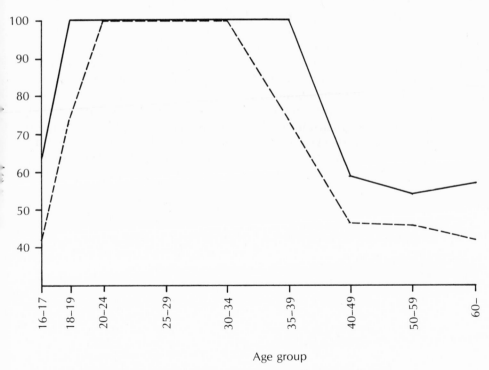

Fig. 6.3. Development of social evaluation of (r) in two subjective reaction tests. Solid line, two-choice test; dotted line, four-choice test.

These results are clear, but there are still doubts to resolve. First, the consistent response may not be governed by variation in (r), but some other variables instead; second, the difference in response between age groups may be spurious if the younger and older groups differ in other respects besides age.

It is true that there is a class bias in the age groups. The younger group has more education, and better prospects, as a natural product of the upward movement of succeeding generations on the Lower East Side. And the higher classes show somewhat better response in the recognition of (r-1). Let us then divide both age groups down the middle, into two overall groups: upper middle combined with lower middle on the one hand, working class combined with lower class on the other. We find that the difference in age groups applies to both upper and lower halves equally. For the four-choice test, in terms of percentage of (r)-positive response:

|          | Upper half | Lower half |
|----------|------------|------------|
| over 40  | 63         | 39         |
| 18–39    | 95         | 79         |

If now we see that the difference in age levels is preserved in both class groups, it is still possible that it is due to the fact that the younger group hears better, or has more interest in the test, or shows less fatigue. We can check this question by correlation with another variable: the perception of the initial consonants of *thing* and *then*. Figure 6.1 also shows the structure of the test in regard to (th) and (dh) in sentences 20, 21, 22. In 20, the speaker of 3 is heard with a typical mixture of fricative and stop and affricate forms for (th) and (dh).

20.         [ð]ere's some[θ]ing strange about [d]at—how I can re-
            member every[θ]ing he did: [ð]is [tθ]ing, [ð]at [θ]ing, and
            [d]e o[d]er [θ]ing.

In sentence 21, the speaker of sentence 4 is heard pronouncing the same sentence with all fricative forms: [θ] and [ð]. And finally, the speaker of 3 and 20 is heard again in sentence 22 with

I suppose it's [ð]e same [t]ing wi[t] most of us.

Any pattern in which the middle sentence, 21, is rated higher than both 20 and 22, is consistent with the recognition of the fricatives in [θɪŋ] and [ðɛn] as higher in prestige than the affricates in [tθɪŋ]

and [dð̣ɛn] or the lenis stops in [tɪŋ] and [dɛn]. As far as we know, the status of these variables is not changing, and usage is divided on class lines alone. There is evidence for the stigmatization of the stop form in America going back to as early as 1783.[5] Since these sounds are harder to hear than most, and occur at the end of the test, we can say that those who do respond positively with a low-high-low pattern are roughly comparable in hearing, span of attention, and sensitivity to prestige forms of speech.

For the subgroup of respondents who showed (th)-sensitive response, the factors of fatigue, loss of hearing, or lack of interest should be considerably less than for the (th)-insensitive group. If there is a connection between these factors and (r)-response, the difference between age levels in (r)-response will appear significantly reduced for respondents who were uniformly (th)-sensitive (see Table 6.3).

TABLE 6.3
(r)-POSITIVE RESPONSE TO THE FOUR-CHOICE TEST
BY AGE AND (th)-SENSITIVITY

| Age | All respondents | (th)-sensitive respondents | (th)-insensitive respondents | N | | |
|---|---|---|---|---|---|---|
| 20–39 | 87% | 92% | 80% | 34 | 29 | 5 |
| 40– | 48 | 46 | 50 | 51 | 35 | 16 |

It appears that (r)-positive response is independent of (th)-sensitivity. The pattern of (r)-positive response by age levels is repeated for the (th)-insensitive group as well as the (th)-sensitive group. Only 5 younger respondents showed (th)-insensitive ratings: 4 of them were (r)-positive on the four-choice test. Sixteen older respondents were (th)-insensitive: 8 of these were (r)-positive, and 8 (r)-negative.

We may conclude that the (r)-positive response which was measured is a function of age, and that the factors of hearing loss, fatigue, or lack of interest in the test are not likely to have played a part in this result.

We may now consider the possibility that other variables associ-

5. As Richard Norman points out, Noah Webster marked the use of stops for (th) and (dh) as nonstandard in the late 18th century. The earliest documents we have stigmatizing this feature in New York date from the middle of the 19th century— travelers' accounts and plays about the Bowery Boys—but we can assume that the social stereotype arose earlier.

ated with sentences 14 and 15, 18 and 19 were responsible in whole or in part for the differential reaction of the age levels to the pairs of sentences.

When a speaker shows an inconsistency in (r), she is likely to show other pronunciation features which are less typical of careful speech. For example, in sentence 19, speaker 4 hesitated after the word *ball* [trouble with her eyesight]; her consonants were not formed or released as forcefully in 19 as in 15: she did not, for example, pronounce the final /t/ in sentence 19, and one or two respondents noticed this.

Sentence 18 was taken from a first reading of the text by speaker 2, and in this reading she was a little further away from the microphone than in the second reading, from which sentence 14 is taken. Such differences as these may account for a part of the reaction which placed sentences 14 and 15 higher than sentences 2 and 4, 18 and 19. However, if this is true, there is no reason to suspect that out-of-town speakers would react any differently from native New Yorkers to the text. They should be able to hear such differences as preciseness of articulation, speed of reading, or distance from the microphone, just as well as New Yorkers. We may therefore turn to the 32 speakers in our survey who came to New York after they were 13 years old, to check this point.

Table 6.4 shows the out-of-town percentages of (r)-positive response to the four-choice test. The older out-of-town speakers show about the same response as New Yorkers did, but the younger speakers, instead of showing *more* (r)-positive response, actually show *less*. This relationship is exactly what we would expect if the test does measure the special New York response to (r-1) as a new prestige marker. The older out-of-town respondents have had about as much exposure to the new prestige form in New York City as the native New York respondents. But the younger out-of-town subjects were raised outside of New York, away from this influence,

TABLE 6.4
(r)-POSITIVE RESPONSE TO THE
FOUR-CHOICE TEST FOR NEW YORK
AND OUT-OF-TOWN RESPONDENTS

| Age | New Yorkers | Out-of-town | $N$ | |
|-----|-------------|-------------|-----|-----|
| 20–39 | 87% | 40% | 14 | 10 |
| 40– | 48 | 50 | 51 | 22 |

and have had only a brief exposure to it. The distribution of (r)-positive response among out-of-town speakers therefore confirms the fact that it is the variable (r) which is the focus of subjective reactions.[6]

We can use the out-of-town speakers to check this question in another way. If (r) is indeed the variable which is being measured in the SR test, then speakers who come from an r-pronouncing region should have more tendency to show (r)-positive response than those who come from an r-less region, where an r-less dialect has prestige. This is indeed the case. For the four-choice test, out-of-town respondents show very different results depending on whether they come from an r-less or an r-pronouncing region.[7]

| | Out-of-town Respondents | |
| | --- | --- |
| | *From r-pronouncing region* | *From r-less region* |
| (r)-positive | 10 | 5 |
| (r)-negative | 7 | 10 |

The evidence that we have presented shows that the reactions to sentences 14 and 15, 18 and 19, are indeed reactions to the use of (r). The evidence for a sudden change in the norms of r-pronunciation cannot be explained by the presence of associated variables. The original presentation of subjective reactions to (r) in this chapter showed a sudden increase in (r)-positive response in apparent time, and this increase points to a corresponding change in the structure of the New York City speech community in real time. As we have

6. A majority of the out-of-town respondents were black. This group is therefore not comparable to the New York respondents, and it is possible that the special (r) response of black subjects was responsible for the difference. However, when we compare only black out-of-town subjects with only black New York subjects, the difference in (r) response holds. The younger New York black respondents showed even more consistent (r)-positive response than the younger New York white respondents.

7. In this case, we do not expect to find that the low use of (r-1) among younger speakers is associated with high sensitivity to this prestige feature. The younger out-of-town subjects who were raised in an area where the prestige norm was an r-less dialect would have no reason to stigmatize sentences 18 and 19, or award high ratings to 14 and 15 on the basis of consistent (r-1) pronunciation—except in so far as they have absorbed the New York City standard. It seems natural that they could apply this standard less accurately than those who had been born and raised in the city.

noted before, the change seems to be closely associated with the period of World War II: all those in the sample who were raised during and after the war show a uniform (r)-positive response in the test.

These results support other evidence that bears on the definition of a speech community. As Fig. 6.2 shows, a speech community cannot be conceived as a group of speakers who all use the same forms; it is best defined as a group who share the same norms in regard to language. In this sense, older and younger speakers in New York City belong to slightly different speech communities, with a fairly distinct discontinuity for those speakers born in the mid 1920's.

Our conclusion should be sufficient to prove that we have indeed found a means of measuring subjective reactions to a single phonological feature, despite the co-occurrence of other socially meaningful variables. This measurement has shown us an astonishing regularity in the evaluation of (r) by younger speakers—the same speakers who are sharply divided along class lines in their use of (r) in everyday speech. Thus we see a society moving towards greater linguistic diversity among subgroups that are in close contact, and indeed share a common set of linguistic norms. This may be a characteristic intermediate stage as a language change moves towards completion. Or we may witness a hardening of the situation into a permanent stratification of language. Since we are now in a position to observe further developments along two dimensions rather than one, we can expect that the resolution of this question will add considerably to our understanding of linguistic evolution. In the next chapter we apply some of these findings to the general problem of elucidating the mechanism of linguistic change.

## Appendix A

*Standard Reading for Five Phonological*
*Variables of New York City Speech*

zero

When I was nine or ten, I had a lot of friends who used to come over to my house to play. I remember a kid named Henry who had very big feet, and I remember a boy named Billy who had no neck, or at least none to look at. He was a funny kid, all right.

/ɔ/

We always had chocolate milk and coffee cake around four o'clock. My dog used to give us an awful lot of trouble. He jumped all over us when he saw the coffee cake. We called him Hungry Sam.

/æ/

We used to play Kick-the-can. One man is "IT": you run past him as fast as you can, and you kick a tin can so he can't tag you. Sammy used to grab the can and dash down the street. We'd chase him with a baseball bat, and yell, "Bad boy! Bad! Bad!" But he was too fast. Only my aunt could catch him. She had him do tricks, too: she even made him ask for a glass of milk, and jump into a paper bag.

/r/

I remember where he was run over, not far from our corner. He darted out about four feet before a car, and he got hit hard. We didn't have the heart to play ball or cards all morning. We didn't know we cared so much for him until he was hurt.

*th*

There's something strange about that—how I can remember everything he did: this thing, that thing, and the other thing. He used to carry three newspapers in his mouth at the same time. I suppose it's the same thing with most of us: your first dog is like your first girl. She's more trouble than she's worth, but you can't seem to forget her.

# 7 | On the Mechanism of Linguistic Change

IN our studies of Martha's Vineyard and the New York City speech community, regular relations have been found where previous reports showed chaotic oscillation or massive free variation. These findings have enabled us to state a number of sociolinguistic principles concerning the relations of stylistic variation, class stratification, and subjective evaluation. In other studies, such data have been applied to general problems of linguistic structure: particularly, the characterization of linguistic rules (see Ch. 8). The most general issues that have been raised so far concern the explanation of linguistic change, and in this chapter we will attempt to focus the data assembled so far on the mechanism of linguistic change, specifically, sound change.

## The Problems of Linguistic Evolution

Despite the achievements of 19th-century historical linguistics, many avenues to the study of linguistic change remain unexplored. In 1905, Meillet (1921:16) noted that all of the laws of linguistic history that had been discovered were merely possibilities:

. . . it remains for us to discover the variables which permit or incite the possibilities thus recognized.

The problem as we face it today is precisely that which Meillet outlined over 60 years ago, for little progress has been made in ascertaining the empirical factors which condition historical change. The chief problems of linguistic evolution might be summarized as five questions:

1. Is there an overall direction of linguistic evolution?

160

2. What are the universal constraints upon linguistic change?
3. What are the causes of the continual origination of new linguistic changes?
4. By what mechanism do changes proceed?
5. Is there an adaptive function to linguistic evolution?[1]

One approach to linguistic evolution is to study changes completed in the past. This has of course been the major strategy of historical linguistics, and it is the only possible approach to the first two questions—the direction of linguistic evolution, and the universal constraints upon change. On the other hand, the questions of the mechanism of change, the inciting causes of change, and the adaptive functions of change are best analyzed by studying in detail linguistic changes in progress. The mechanism of linguistic change will be the chief topic of the discussion to follow; however, many of the conclusions will plainly be relevant to the questions of inciting causes and adaptive functions of change, and it will be apparent that more complete answers to these questions will require methods similar to those used here.

An essential presupposition of this line of research is a uniformitarian doctrine: that is, the claim that the same mechanisms which operated to produce the large-scale changes of the past may be observed operating in the current changes taking place around us.

### A Strategy for the Study of Linguistic Changes in Progress

Although answers to the five questions given above are the ultimate goals of our current research, they do not represent the actual strategy used. For the empirical study of changes in progress, the task can be subdivided into three separate problems which jointly serve to answer the questions raised above.

1. The *transition* problem is to find the route by which one stage of a linguistic change has evolved from an earlier stage. We wish to trace enough of the intervening stages so that we can eliminate all but one of the major alternatives. Thus questions of the regu-

1. This question is all the more puzzling when we contrast linguistic with biological evolution. It is difficult to discuss the evolution of the plant and animal kingdoms without some reference to adaptation to various environments. But what conceivable adaptive function is served by the efflorescence of the Indo-European family? On this topic, see Hymes 1961 and Ch. 9.

larity of sound change, of grammatical influence on sound change, of "push chains" versus "pull chains," of steady movement versus sudden and discontinuous shifts, are all aspects of the transition problem.

2. The *embedding* problem is to find the continuous matrix of social and linguistic behavior in which the linguistic change is carried. The principal route to the solution is through the discovery of correlations between elements of the linguistic system, and between those elements and the nonlinguistic system of social behavior. The correlations are established by strong proof of concomitant variation: that is, by showing that a small change in the independent variable is regularly accompanied by a change of the linguistic variable in a predictable direction.[2]

3. The *evaluation* problem is to find the subjective (or latent) correlates of the objective (or manifest) changes which have been observed. The indirect approach to this problem correlates the general attitudes and aspirations of the informants with their linguistic behavior. The more direct approach is to measure the unconscious subjective reactions of the informants to values of the linguistic variable itself.

With tentative solutions to these problems in hand, it would be possible to provide an explanation of a linguistic change which answers the three questions of inciting cause, mechanism, and adaptive function.[3] As in any other investigation, the value of an explanation rises in relation to its generality, but only to the extent that it rests upon a foundation of reliable and reproducible evidence.

2. The concept of the linguistic variable is that developed in Labov 1966a and reflected in Ch. 2. It is further developed in the notion of variable constraints on variable rules (Ch. 8). The definition of such a variable amounts to an empirical assertion of covariation, within or without the linguistic system. It appears that the fundamental difference between an explanation of a linguistic change, and a description, is that a description makes no such assertion. In terms of a description of change, such as that provided by Halle 1962 there is no greater probability of the change taking place in the observed direction, as in the reverse direction. Note that the embedding problem is presented here as a single problem, despite the fact that there are two distinct aspects: correlations within the linguistic system, and with elements outside the system. The main body of this chapter provides justification for this decision.

3. To these three problems we can add the *constraints* problem and the *actuation* problem as developed in Weinreich, Labov, and Herzog 1968. The search for general

### The Observation of Sound Change

The simplest data that will establish the existence of a linguistic change is a set of observations of two successive generations of speakers—generations of comparable social characteristics which represent stages in the evolution of the same speech community. Hermann (1929) obtained such data at Charmey in 1929, by developing Gauchat's (1905) original observations of 1899. We have such data for Martha's Vineyard, adding the 1961 observations to the 1933 data of the Linguistic Atlas (Kurath et al. 1941). For New York City, we add the current data of 1963 to the Linguistic Atlas data of 1940; in addition, we have many other reports, including the excellent observations of Babbitt in 1896 to add further time depth to our analysis (Frank 1948; Kurath and McDavid 1951; Hubbell 1950; Babbitt 1896).

Solutions to the transition problem proposed here will depend upon close analysis of the distribution of linguistic forms in *apparent time*—that is, along the dimension formed by the age groups of the present population. Such an analysis is possible only because the original simple description of change in *real time* enables us to distinguish age-grading in the present population from the effects of linguistic change (Hockett 1950).

The evidence obtained in the research reported here indicates that the regular process of sound change can be isolated and recorded by observations across two generations. This process is characterized by a rapid development of some units of a phonetic subsystem, while other units remain relatively constant. It affects word classes as a whole, rather than individual words: yet these classes may be defined by a variety of conditions, morphophonemic and grammatical as well as phonetic. It is regular, but more in the outcome than in its inception or its development. Furthermore, it appears that the process of sound change is not an autonomous movement within the confines of a linguistic system, but rather a complex response to many aspects of human behavior.

Some comment is required on the possibility of observing regular sound change, since arguments inherited from the neo-grammarian

---

constraints on sound change is one theme in our current work on sound change in progress (Labov, Yaeger, and Steiner 1972). Some progress on the actuation riddle is suggested by the conclusion of this chapter.

controversy have impeded the progress of empirical research in this area. The inheritors of the neo-grammarian tradition, who should be most interested in the empirical study of regular change in progress, have abandoned the arena of meaningful research in favor of abstract and speculative arguments. Indeed, Bloomfield (1933:347, 365) and Hockett (1958:439,444) have maintained that phonetic change cannot in principle be observed by any of the techniques currently available.[4] Hockett has proceeded to identify sound change with a level of random fluctuations in the action of the articulatory apparatus, without any inherent direction, a drift of the articulatory target which has no cognitive, expressive or social significance.[5] All of the empirical observations of change in progress which have been reported are explained as the results of a complex process of borrowing, and are relegated to a type of linguistic behavior known as the fluctuation or conflict of forms. No claims are made for the regularity of this process, and so the basic tenet of the regularity of sound change has been deprived of all empirical significance. Furthermore, the changes which actually are observed are regarded as unsystematic phenomena, to be discussed with anecdotal evidence, subject to forces "quite outside the linguist's reach," factors which "elude our grasp," fluctuations "beyond our powers" to record (Bloomfield 1933:343–68).

The evidence of current research suggests that this retreat was premature, that the regular process of sound change can be observed by empirical methods. The refinements in methodology called for are not the mechanical elaborations suggested by the writers cited above; for the mere multiplication of data only confounds analysis

4. Hockett writes: "No one has yet observed sound change: we have only been able to detect it via its consequences. We shall see later that a more nearly direct observation would be theoretically possible, if impractical, but any ostensible report of such an observation so far must be discredited." His theoretical proposal is that "over a period of fifty years we made, each month, a thousand accurate acoustic records . . . all from the members of a tight-knit community." The suggestion to multiply the data in this way is not necessarily helpful, as the experience of sociological survey analysts has shown: for relatively small numbers are needed to measure change in a population if the bias of selection is eliminated or minimized. Otherwise, we merely multiply the errors of measurement.

5. According to Hockett, the variables responsible for sound change include "the amount of moisture in the throat, nose and mouth of the speaker, random currents in his central nervous system, muscular tics . . . the condition of the hearer's outer ear [presence of wax or dirt] . . ." (1958:443–444).

and perpetuates the bias of selection. It is rigor in the analysis of a population and in the selection of informants which is required. Furthermore, we need ingenuity in the resolution of stylistic variation, to go beyond the sterile method of endless dissection into idiolects. With such techniques, we find that regularity emerges where only confusion was seen before. Random fluctuations in articulation can certainly be found: indeed, this is the level of "noise" which prevents us from predicting the form of every utterance which our informants will make. But it would be an error to ascribe a major role to such fluctuations in the economy of linguistic change. The forces which direct the observed changes appear to be of an entirely different order of magnitude, and the changes take place much more rapidly than any process of random drift could account for.[6]

A single example of a sound change observed will be used to illustrate the general approach to solving the transition, embedding and evaluation problems. This example is one of the simplest cases—that of the centralization of (aw) on Martha's Vineyard, discussed in Ch. 1. In the development of this case, some new evidence will be presented on the mechanism of sound changes.

### The Centralization of (aw) on Martha's Vineyard

We begin with a clearcut case for the existence of a linguistic change from observations in real time. In 1933, Guy Lowman found no more than the barest trace of centralization of /aw/; the significant variation observed was the fronting of /aw/ from [aʊ] to [æʊ]. In 1961, a comparable set of older eighth-generation descendants of Yankee settlers from the same villages showed a very pronounced centralization of /aw/—now clearly the variable (aw).

The *transition* problem is studied through a detailed examination of the distribution of forms through apparent time—that is, through the various age levels in the present population. The first step in the analysis is to construct a quantitative index for discrete values of the variable:

6. Thus the following table contrasts the two points of view:

| Neo-grammarian: | sound change | fluctuation of forms | ultimate regularity |
|---|---|---|---|
| Present discussion: | sublinguistic fluctuations | sound change | ultimate regularity |

aw-0    [aʊ]
aw-1    [aˆʊ]
aw-2    [ɐʊ]
aw-3    [əʊ]

The index of centralization was constructed from this scale by averaging the numerical values assigned to each variant. Thus (aw)-00 would mean no centralization at all, while (aw)-300 would mean consistent centralization at the level of [əʊ]. This index was applied to interviews with 69 informants by rating each of the words in which (aw) occurred. The first approach to the transition problem can then be made by correlating average (aw) index scores for these interviews with the age level of the speakers. The first three columns of Table 7.1 (a rearranged version of Table 1.2) show a regular correlation, in which the centralization index rises regularly for four successive age levels.

The overall tendency of Table 7.1 represents an amalgamation of many different types of speakers and many different trends in the use of (aw). Fig. 7.1 presents a more detailed analysis of the transition problem for a critical subgroup. Here are displayed the percentage distribution of lexical items for eight individuals from 92 to 31 years of age. The horizontal axes show the four coded levels of the variable (aw). The vertical axes are the percentages of lexical items used with each variant. The vocabulary is broken into two sections that are tabulated separately: the solid line represents words in which (aw) is followed by a voiceless obstruent, as in *out, house, about, mouth;* the broken line represents all other words (and principally those ending in a nasal, as in *town, found,* or with no consonant final, as in *now, how,* etc.)[7]

The first diagram in Fig. 7.1 is not that of an individual, but shows the composite results for the four Linguistic Atlas informants interviewed in 1933. They show only the barest trace of centralization. The second diagram, *b,* is that of the oldest informant of 1961, a man

7. The phonetic conditioning of (aw) was actually more complex than this: both following and preceding consonants are involved. We have returned to the phonetic mechanism of the change in our recent studies of sound change in progress. Spectrographic studies confirm the gradual development of phonetic conditioning, the gradual rise in importance of a following voiceless obstruent, and the final development of discrete allophonic conditioning (Labov 1972c). The spectrographic displays suggest that there may not be a retrograde movement of the voiced environments, but rather that they are heard as the raising in voiceless environments reaches mid position.

TABLE 7.1
CENTRALIZATION INDEXES BY AGE LEVEL

| Generation | Age | (aw) | (ay) |
|---|---|---|---|
| Ia | over 75 | 22 | 25 |
| Ib | 61–75 | 37 | 35 |
| IIa | 46–60 | 44 | 62 |
| IIb | 31–45 | 88 | 81 |

92 years old. The average age of the Atlas informants was 65 years; Mr. H. H. Sr. would have been 64 years old in 1933, and so he is of the same age group. His centralization profile is quite similar to that of the Atlas informants in a. In c, we have an 87-year-old woman who shows only a slight increase in centralization. Fig. d, Mr. E. M., 83 years old, indicates a small but distinct increase in the occurrence of variant (aw-2). Mr. H. H. Jr., in e, is considerably younger; he is 61 years old, the first representative of the next generation, since he is the son of Mr. H. H. Sr. Here we have a marked increase in centralization, with both classes of words centered about a norm of (aw-1). In f, Mr. D. P., 57 years old, shows a distinct difference between words ending in voiceless obstruents and all others; the first are now centered upon a norm of (aw-2), while the second group is concentrated at (aw-1). This process is carried further in the speech of Mr. P. N., 52 years old, who shows perfect complementary distribution. Before voiceless obstruents, /aw/ has an allophone which is almost always (aw-2), while before other terminals it is usually uncentralized. And at this point, there is no overlap in the distribution. Finally, in h, the most extreme case of centralization, we see an even sharper separation: this is Mr. E. P., 31 years old, the son of Mr. D. P. in f.

On the right hand side of Fig. 7.1 are the figures for the actual numbers of lexical items observed, and the composite index scores for each of the eight cases. It may be noted that (aw) is only one-third as frequent as (ay), and the regularity which appears here does not require a vast corpus of observations. The regularity emerges through the controlled selection of informants, methods of elicitation, and of recording the data.

The eight diagrams of Fig. 7.1 represent the most homogeneous type of population. All of the speakers are Yankee descendants of the original settlers of the island, all are interrelated, many from the

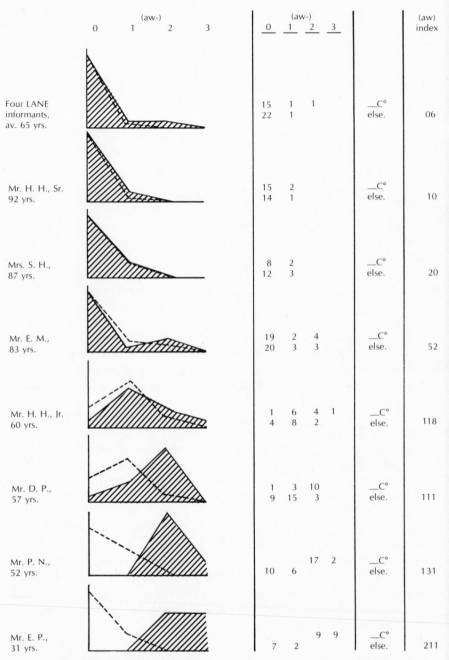

Fig. 7.1. Stages in the centralization of (aw) on Martha's Vineyard, Mass. Solid line: (aw) followed by voiceless obstruent; broken line: all other words.

same families, with similar attitudes towards the island. All had rural upbringing, and worked as carpenters or fishermen, with one exception. Thus the continuous development of centralization represents the very model of a neo-grammarian sound change, accomplished within two generations.

The *embedding* problem was first approached by correlating the centralization of the obviously related variables (ay) and (aw)—that is, the change of (aw) was embedded in the system of upgliding diphthongs. The Atlas records indicate a moderate degree of centralization in the 1930's, so that we know that the centralized forms of (ay) preceded the rise of (aw). The fourth column of Table 7.1 shows a close correlation of the two variables, with (ay) slightly in the lead at first, but (aw) becoming more dominant at the end. This pattern was repeated when the variables were correlated with a number of independent extralinguistic factors: the occupation, education, and geographic location of the speaker, and most importantly, the ethnic group to which he belonged. The significant differences in the transition rates of these various subgroups allowed the following statement of a solution to the embedding problem:

The centralization of (aw) was part of a more general change which began with the centralization of (ay). This initial change proceeded from a moderate level of (ay) centralization which was probably a regional and recessive trait inherited from the original settlers of the island. The increase of centralization of (ay) began in a rural community of Yankee fishermen descended directly from these original settlers. From there, it spread outward to speakers of the same ethnic group in other occupations and in other communities. The structurally symmetrical variable (aw) began to show similar tendencies early in this process. The change was also adopted by the neighboring Indian group at Gay Head, and a generation later, spread to the large Portuguese group in the more settled sections of the island. In these two ethnic groups, centralization of (aw) overtook and surpassed centralization of (ay).

Fig. 7.1 would lead us to believe that the phonetic environment of (aw) was a powerful factor in the initiation of the sound change. Moreover, we can observe that the centralization of (ay) also showed a strong tendency towards phonetic conditioning in Generation Ib, similar to that displayed for (aw) in Generation IIb.[8] However, pho-

8. This phonetic conditioning is more in the nature of a continuum than that for (aw). Fig. 1.4, p. 19 gives the complete data for a speaker of the same age and background as Mr. H. H. Jr. of Fig. 7.1.

netic restriction on (ay) was overridden in the following generation, so that Generation II shows a uniform norm for (ay) in all phonetic environments. This development would support the view that phonetic conditioning does not play a significant role as an inciting cause of the centralization of (aw), but acts rather as a conditioning factor which may be eliminated by further change.

On Martha's Vineyard, the *evaluation problem* was approached by analyzing a number of clues to the subjective attitudes towards island life which appeared in the course of the interviews. Attitudes towards summer tourists, towards unemployment insurance, towards work on the mainland, towards other occupational and ethnic groups, were correlated with data obtained from community leaders and historical records, and then with the linguistic variables. It appeared that the rise of (aw) was correlated with the successive entry into the main stream of island life of groups that had previously been partially excluded. It was concluded that a social value had been, more or less arbitrarily, associated with the centralization of (ay) and (aw): to the extent that an individual felt able to claim and maintain status as a native Vineyarder, he adopted increasing centralization of (ay) and (aw). Sons who had tried to earn a living on the mainland, and afterwards returned to the island, developed an even higher degree of centralization than their fathers had used. But to the extent that a Vineyarder abandoned his claim to stay on the island and earn his living there, he also abandoned centralization and returned to the standard uncentralized forms.

The solution to the evaluation problem is a statement of the social significance of the changed form—that is, the function which is the direct equivalent on the noncognitive level of the meaning of the form on the cognitive level. In the developments described here, the cognitive function of /ay/ and /aw/ has remained constant. It is plain that the noncognitive functions which are carried by these phonological elements are the essential factors in the mechanism of the change. This conclusion can be generalized to many other instances of more complex changes, in which the net result is a radical change of cognitive function. The sound change observed on Martha's Vineyard did not produce phonemic change, in which units defined by cognitive function were merged or split. But many of the changes in progress that have been observed in New York City did produce such mergers and splits on the level of the bi-unique phoneme. One such change is the raising of (oh), the vowel of *law, talk, off, more,* etc., which will serve to illustrate many aspects of the mechanism of linguistic change not relevant to the simpler example on Martha's Vineyard.

### The Raising of (oh) in New York City

It was not possible to make a direct attack upon the transition problem in New York City. Although the records of the Linguistic Atlas showed sporadic raising of (oh) at a fairly low level, the Atlas informants in New York City were not selected systematically enough so that we could construct a comparable sample in 1963.[9] Furthermore, an overall comparison of the usage of this variable by older and younger speakers did not show the clearcut and regular progression which we saw for (aw) on Martha's Vineyard. It was suspected that the reason for this difficulty was the greater tendency towards stylistic variation among New Yorkers, and the heterogeneity of the population in terms of socioeconomic class and ethnic membership. Therefore it was necessary to attack the embedding problem first, before the transition problem.

The variable (oh), as we have defined it in Ch. 3, is a part of the system of long and ingliding vowels in the *r*-less vernacular of New York City.-Thus we will code the six variants of (oh) in *law, lore, talk, stork, broad, board, all,* etc. (p. 76).

Ch. 3 describes the methods used for isolating a range of well-defined contextual styles in the speech of individual informants. Average index scores were determined for each style, and a systematic sampling of a large urban population undertaken. The embedding problem was then attacked by correlating the five chief linguistic variables each with each other, and with other elements of the linguistic system, with the level of stylistic variation in which they were recorded, and with the independent variables of socioeconomic class (occupation, education, and income) sex, ethnic group, and age level.

In our studies of hypercorrection in Ch. 5, we presented (p. 128) a style stratification diagram for (oh) in which the transitional state

9. Convenience was apparently a greater factor in the selection of Atlas informants in New York than on Martha's Vineyard. The great bulk of the New York population was poorly represented in the sample, including the working class and lower middle class. The old-family stock used for Atlas interviews represents only a very small fraction of the ethnic composition of the city, at most 1 or 2 percent.

of this variable is seen in synchronic section. Fig. 5.2 thus indicates that the change has not yet affected all social classes: (oh) is not a significant variable for lower-class speakers, who do not use particularly high values of this vowel and show no stylistic stratification at all. Working-class speakers show a recent stage in the raising of (oh): very high vowels in casual speech, but otherwise very little stratification in the more formal styles, and little tendency towards the extreme, hypercorrect (oh-4) and (oh-5). But lower-middle-class speakers show the most developed state of the sound change, with high values in casual speech, and extreme stylistic stratification. Finally, the upper-middle-class group is more moderate in all respects than the lower middle class, still retaining the pattern of stylistic stratification.

The ethnic group membership of New York City speakers is even more relevant to their use of (oh) than socioeconomic class. Fig. 7.2 shows the differences between speakers of Jewish and Italian background in the treatment of (oh) in casual speech. For all but the upper middle class, the Jewish group uses higher levels of (oh).[10] Table 7.2

10. The black group does not show any significant response to the variable (oh), and shows a constant index of performance at a low level. As noted above, the lower class in general is similarly indifferent to (oh). Table 7.2 shows Jewish and Italian ethnic groups only, with the lower class excluded.

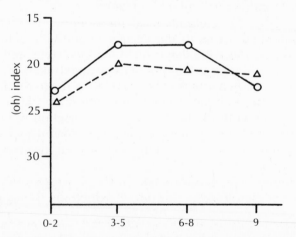

Fig. 7.2.   Class stratification for (oh) by ethnic group in casual speech. Solid line, Jews; broken line, Italians. SEC: 0–2, lower class; 3–5, working class; 6–8, lower middle class; 9, upper middle class.

TABLE 7.2
AVERAGE (oh) INDEXES BY AGE LEVEL
AND ETHNIC GROUP IN CASUAL SPEECH

| Age | Jews | Italians |
|------|------|----------|
| 8–19 | 17 | 18 |
| 20–35 | 18 | 18 |
| 36–49 | 17 | 20 |
| 50–59 | 15 | 20 |
| 60– | 25 | 30 |

shows that both Jewish and Italian speakers have participated in the raising of (oh) but the increase seems to have reached its maximum early for the Jewish group, and later for the Italian group. A separate solution for the transition problem is therefore required for each ethnic group.

The *transition problem* for the Italian group can be seen analyzed in Fig. 7.3. The procession of values is not absolutely regular, since

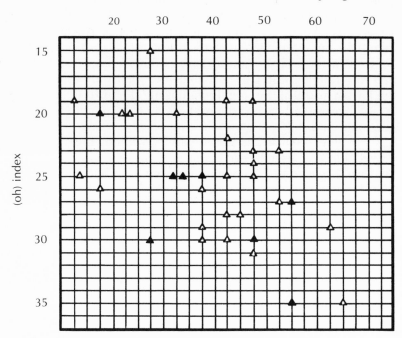

Fig. 7.3.  Distribution of (oh) index scores for Italian subjects by age. △ women; ▲ men.

socioeconomic membership, sex, and other factors affect the values; nevertheless, there is a steady upward movement from the oldest speakers on the right to the youngest speakers on the left. Within the present sample of New York City speakers, this is the finest resolution of the transition problem which can be obtained.[11]

The *embedding problem* for (oh) requires an intricate set of correlations with other elements in the linguistic system, in addition to the extralinguistic correlations exemplified above. We find that (oh) is firmly embedded within the subsystem of long and ingliding vowels, and also related structurally to other vowel subsystems. Quantitative studies of these relations fall into five sets:

1. There is a strong correlation between the height of (oh) and the height of the corresponding front ingliding vowel (eh) in the word class of *bad, ask, dance,* etc. This variable originated as a raising of /æh/, but early in the evolution of New York City speech it merged with /eh/, the word class of *bare, bared, where,* etc. The relation between (eh) and (oh) is strikingly parallel to that of (ay) and (aw) on Martha's Vineyard. The front vowel was raised first, as early as the 1890's in New York, and the back vowel followed. Like (aw) on Martha's Vineyard, the variable (oh) became specialized in the usage of a particular ethnic group: to the extent that the Italian group shows higher use of (eh) in casual speech, the Jewish group shows higher values of (oh), until the difference is largely resolved in the youngest age level by merger of (eh) and /ih/, (oh) and /uh/.

2. The variable (oh) also has close relations with the higher ingliding vowel /uh/. As we observe higher and higher variants of (oh) in the casual speech of the younger informants, it becomes apparent that a merger of (oh) and /uh/ is imminent. This merger has undoubtedly occurred in the youngest speakers in our sample from the working class and lower middle class. In fact, we have many informants who show the merger even in the most formal styles, in the reading of isolated word lists, and we can conclude *a fortiori* that the merger exists in casual speech. Close study of the variants of their casual speech shows the merger as an accomplished fact: though most listeners who are not conscious of

11. Fig. 7.3 includes Italian informants who refused the original interview, and whose speech patterns were sampled by the television interview, as described in Appendix D of Labov 1966a.

the overlap will hear *sure* as higher than *shore*, it is in fact in-
distinguishable out of context.

3. There is also a close correlation between (oh) and /ah/, the long
   tense vowel heard in *guard, father, car,* etc. The variable (ah)
   represents the choice of back or center options for the subclasses
   of *hot, heart, hod,* and *hard.* High values of (oh) are correlated
   with low back positions of *heart, hod,* and *hard* (with the last
   two generally homonymous); lower values of (oh) are correlated
   with low center positions of the vowels in these word classes. This
   correlation is independent of socioeconomic class or ethnic group.
   Whereas (oh) is firmly embedded in the sociolinguistic structure
   of the speech community, /ah/ is not. As a linguistic variable,
   (ah) seems to be a function only of the height of (oh): a purely
   internal variable.[12]

4. (oh) is also related to the variable height of the vowel in *boy, coil,*
   etc., (oy) in the front upgliding system. The height of the vowels
   in *coil* and *call* seem to vary directly together in casual speech,
   but only (oh) is corrected to lower values in more formal styles.
   (oh) carries the major burden of social significance, and is the
   focus of nonsystematic pressure from above.

5. Finally, we find that (oh) and (oy) are jointly correlated with the
   variable (ay), which represents the backing or fronting of the first
   element of the diphthong in *my, why, side,* etc. High values of
   (oh) and (oy) are correlated with back values of (ay), and low
   values of (oh) and (oy) with low center values of (ay).

Beyond these immediate correlations, there are more indirect,
diffuse relations with such variables as (aw) and /ih/, through which
(oh) is connected with all of the other vowels in the vernacular
system of New York City speech. This is not the place to pursue the
full details of this intricate set of structural correlations within the
linguistic system: however, it should be apparent that a full solution
to the embedding problem will reveal the ways in which the internal
relations of linguistic elements determine the direction of sound
change. We can summarize the most important relations that center
about (oh) in the following notation, which defines the structural
units on the left hand side of the equations as linguistic variables:

---

12. The quantitative correlations are given in Labov 1966a: Ch. 12. The relationship
of (oh) and (ah) held even within a single ethnic group. For a spectrographic display
of all these correlations, see Labov, Yaeger, and Steiner 1972.

$$(oh) = f_1(St, C, E, A, Sx, (eh)) \qquad St = style$$
$$(ah) = f_2((oh)) \qquad\qquad\qquad C = socio\text{-}economic\ class$$
$$(oy) = f_3((oh)) \qquad\qquad\qquad E = ethnic\ group$$
$$(ay) = f_4((ah)) = f_4(f_2((oh))) \qquad A = age\ level$$
$$(ay) = f_5((oy)) = f_5(f_3((oh))) \qquad Sx = sex$$

In New York City, the *evaluation problem* was approached more directly than on Martha's Vineyard. The unconscious subjective reactions of the informants to each of the variables were determined. The details of this method have been presented in Ch. 6; in general, we can say that the reliability of the tests can be measured by the high degree of uniformity showed by New Yorkers in contrast to the scattered results from those raised outside of New York City.

The subjective reaction responses to (oh) give us a clear view of the social significance of the variable, as shown in Table 7.3. The majority of informants responded to the test in a way consistent with the stigmatized status of high (oh).[13] Just as the solution to the embedding problem showed no significant stylistic response to (oh) for lower-class speakers, here we find that lower-class speakers showed no significant (oh)-negative response. The other groups showed (oh)-negative response in proportion to the average height of (oh) used in their own casual speech, and to the degree of stylistic stratification in their speech patterns. This result illustrates the principle which holds quite generally in New York City: that those who used the highest percentage of a stigmatized form in casual speech were the most sensitive in stigmatizing it in the speech of others. Thus the lower-middle-class speakers between the ages of

TABLE 7.3
(oh)-NEGATIVE RESPONSE BY
SOCIOECONOMIC CLASS AND AGE LEVEL

| Age | Socioeconomic class | | | | *N* | | | |
|-----|------|------|------|------|------|------|------|------|
|     | 0-2  | 3-4  | 5-8  | 9    |      |      |      |      |
| 20-39 | 25% | 80% | 100% | 60% | 4 | 10 | 11 | 5 |
| 40-59 | 18  | 60  | 62   | 57  | 11 | 15 | 13 | 7 |
| 60-   | 33  | [00] | —   | —   | 6 | 1 | — | — |

13. The (oh)-negative response shown here consisted of rating three speakers lower on a scale of job suitability when they pronounced sentences with high, close (oh) vowels, as compared to sentences with no significant variables. Those making the ratings were unaware that they were rating the same speakers.

20 and 39, who use the highest values of (oh) in their own casual speech, show 100 percent (oh)-negative response. Similarly, we find that the percentage of (oh)-negative response among Jewish and Italian speakers is proportionate to the height of (oh) in casual speech.

This solution to the evaluation problem can hardly be called satisfactory. It is not clear why a group of speakers should adopt more and more extreme forms of a speech sound which they themselves stigmatize as bad speech.[14] Some further explanation must be given.

First of all, it has become clear that very few speakers realize that they use the stigmatized forms themselves. They hear themselves as using the prestige forms which occur sporadically in their careful speech and in their reading of isolated word lists. Secondly, the subjective responses tapped by our test are only the overt values— those which conform to the value systems of the dominant middle-class group. There are surely other values, at a deeper level of consciousness, which reinforce the vernacular speech forms of New York City. Our early evidence for this conclusion was anecdotal. But more recent studies of the black English vernacular in New York City have demonstrated the existence of such covert norms through alternate scales on subjective reaction tests (see Ch. 8).

In the case of the alternate preference of Jewish and Italian ethnic groups for (oh) and (eh), we can put forward a reasonable suggestion based upon the mechanism of hypercorrection.[15] The influence of the Yiddish substratum leads to a loss of the distinction between low back rounded and unrounded vowels in first-generation Jewish speakers of English, so that *cup* and *coffee* have the same vowel. In second-generation speakers of Jewish descent, the reaction against this tendency leads to a hypercorrect exaggeration of the distinction, so that (oh) becomes raised, tense and over-rounded. A parallel argument applies to Italian speakers. This suggestion is all the more plausible since hypercorrection has been demonstrated to be an important mechanism of linguistic change in a variety of circumstances.[16]

14. Many subjects reacted to the test with violent and unrealistic ratings; as, for example, marking a person who used high vowels for *coffee* and *chocolate* as not even speaking well enough to hold a factory job.

15. I am indebted to Marvin Herzog for this suggestion.

16. As noted in Ch. 5, *hypercorrection* is used here not to indicate the sporadic and irregular treatment of a word class, but the movement of an entire word class

### The Mechanism of Sound Change

Solutions to the transition, embedding, and evaluation problems have been illustrated by two examples, drawn from Martha's Vineyard and New York City. It is possible to apply the results of our work with these and other variables to a provisional answer to the question: what is the mechanism by which sound change proceeds? The following outline is based upon analysis of twelve sound changes: three on rural Martha's Vineyard, and nine in urban New York City.[17]

1. The sound changes usually originated with a restricted subgroup of the speech community, at a time when the separate identity of this group had been weakened by internal or external pressures. The linguistic form which began to shift was often a marker of regional status with an irregular distribution within the community. At this stage, the form is an undefined linguistic variable.
2. The changes began as generalizations of the linguistic form to all members of the subgroup; we may refer to this stage as *change from below,* that is, below the level of social awareness. The variable shows no pattern of stylistic variation in the speech of those who use it, affecting all items in a given word class. The linguistic variable is an *indicator,* defined as a function of group membership.
3. Succeeding generations of speakers within the same subgroup, responding to the same social pressures, carried the linguistic variable further along the process of change, beyond the model set by their parents. We may refer to this stage as *hypercorrection from below.* The variable is now defined as a function of group membership and age level.
4. To the extent that the values of the original subgroup were adopted by other groups in the speech community, the sound change with its associated value of group membership spread to these adopting groups. The function of group membership is now redefined in successive stages.

---

beyond the target point set by the prestige model. This mechanism is evident on Martha's Vineyard, as well as New York.

17. The stages suggested here are necessarily ordered in approximately the manner listed, but there are some rearrangements and permutations in the data observed.

5. The limits of the spread of the sound change were the limits of the speech community, defined as a group with a common set of normative values in regard to language.

6. As the sound change with its associated values reached the limits of its expansion, the linguistic variable became one of the norms which defined the speech community, and all members of the speech community reacted in a uniform manner to its use (without necessarily being aware of it). The variable is now a *marker*, and begins to show stylistic variation.

7. The movement of the linguistic variable within the linguistic system always led to readjustments in the distribution of other elements within phonological space.

8. The structural readjustments led to further sound changes which were associated with the original change. However, other subgroups which entered the speech community in the interim adopted the older sound change as a part of the community norms, and treated the newer sound change as stage 1. This *recycling* stage appears to be the primary source for the continual origination of new changes. In the following development, the second sound change may be carried by the new group beyond the level of the first change.

   [Stages 1–8 dealt with *change from below;* stages 9–13 concern *change from above.*]

9. If the group in which the change originated was not the highest-status group in the speech community, members of the highest-status group eventually stigmatized the changed form through their control of various institutions of the communication network.

10. This stigmatization initiated *change from above,* a sporadic and irregular correction of the changed forms towards the model of the highest status group—that is, the *prestige model.* This prestige model is now the pattern which speakers hear themselves using: it governs the audio-monitoring of the speech signal. The linguistic variable now shows regular stylistic stratification as well as social stratification, as the motor-controlled model of casual speech competes with the audio-monitored model of more careful styles.

11. If the prestige model of the highest-status group does not correspond to a form used by the other groups in some word class, the other groups will show a second type of *hypercorrection:*

shifting their careful speech to a form further from the changed form than the target set by the prestige group. We may call this stage *hypercorrection from above.*

12. Under extreme stigmatization, a form may become the overt topic of social comment, and may eventually disappear. It is thus a *stereotype,* which may become increasingly divorced from the forms which are actually used in speech.

13. If the change originated in the highest-status group of the community, it became a prestige model for all members of the speech community. The changed form was then adopted in more careful forms of speech by all other groups in proportion to their contact with users of the prestige model, and to a lesser extent, in casual speech.[18]

Many of the stages in the mechanism of sound change outlined here are exemplified in the two detailed examples given above. The centralization of (aw) on Martha's Vineyard appears to be a stage 4 change from below. It may indeed have reached stages 5 and 6, but the techniques used on Martha's Vineyard did not provide the evidence to decide this question. There is no doubt, however, that the centralization of (aw) is a secondary change, produced by the recycling process when the centralization of (ay) reached stage 8.

To place the raising of (oh) in this outline, it is necessary to consider briefly the evolution of the New York City vowel system as a whole. The first step in the historical record is the raising of (eh). We have reason to believe that the merger of /æh/ with /eh/ began in the last quarter of the 19th century (Babbitt 1896). The upward movement of the linguistic variable (eh) continued beyond this merger, leading to the current cumulative merger of /eh/ with /ih/ among most younger New Yorkers. For the entire community, (eh) is subject to the full force of correction from above: the change has reached stage 11 so that the linguistic variable is defined by covariation with social class, ethnic membership, age level, and contextual style. The raising of (oh) was the first recycling process which began when (eh) reached stage 8. The major burden of the raising of (oh) has been carried by the Jewish ethnic group; the extreme upward social mobility of this group has led to a special sensitivity to (oh)

18. We find some support in these observations for the idea that people do not borrow much from broadcast media or from other remote sources, but rather from those who are at the most one or two removes from them in age or social distance.

in the lower middle class. Thus the merger of /oh/ and /uh/ has gone quite quickly, and (oh) has reached stage 11 for the lower middle class; yet it has hardly touched stage 1 for the lower class.

The third stage in the recycling process occurred when (oh) reached stage 8. The structural readjustments which took place were complex: (oy) and (ah) were closely associated with (oh), and were defined as linguistic variables only by their covariation with (oh). Thus the raising of (oy) and the backing of (ah) were determined by internal, structural factors. Change from above is exerted upon (oh), but not upon (oy). In careful speech, a New Yorker might say [ɪts ɒːl tɪn fuː-ɪ], *It's all tin foil*. But the shift of (ah) and (oy) have in turn led to a shift of (ay), and this process has apparently begun a third recycling. Indeed, the backing of (ay) has reached stage 8 itself, and produced an associated fourth recycling, the fronting of (aw). There are indications that (ay) has evolved to stage 9, with the beginning of overt correction from above, although (aw) has reached only stage 4 or 5 (Labov 1966a:Ch. 12).

It is evident that the type of structural readjustments that has been considered here requires a linguistic theory which preserves the geometry of phonological space. The structural relations found here are strikingly parallel to those established by Moulton (1962) in his study of covariation of mid and low vowels in Swiss German dialects. The techniques, the area, the societies studied are quite different, and the coincidence of results provides strong empirical evidence for the functional view of phonological structure advanced by Martinet (1955). Nevertheless, the purely internal equilibria projected by Martinet do not provide a coherent theory of the mechanism of sound change. In the scheme that has been outlined here, they are only part of a more comprehensive process, embedded in the sociolinguistic structure of the community.

## Conclusion

This discussion has focused on the theme that internal, structural pressures and sociolinguistic pressures act in systematic alternation in the mechanism of linguistic change. It can no longer be seriously argued that the linguist must limit his explanations of change to the mutual influences of linguistic elements defined by cognitive function. Nor can it be argued that a changing linguistic system is autonomous in any serious sense. Here I have attempted to carry the argument beyond the mere cataloguing of possibilities by introducing a large body of evidence on sound changes observed in progress. On the basis of this evidence, we can make the stronger claim that it is not possible to complete an analysis of structural relations within a linguistic system, and then turn to external relations. The recycling process outlined here suggests the kind of answer we can make to the basic questions of the inciting causes of linguistic change, and the adaptive functions of change, as well as the mechanism by which change proceeds. We can expect that further investigations will modify the outline given here, but that data from the speech community will continue to form an essential part in the analysis of linguistic change.

# 8 The Study of Language in Its Social Context

THE first seven chapters of this volume have documented an approach to linguistic research which focuses upon language in use within the speech community, aiming at a linguistic theory adequate to account for these data. This type of research has sometimes been labelled as "sociolinguistics," although it is a somewhat misleading use of an oddly redundant term. Language is a form of social behavior: statements to this effect can be found in any introductory text. Children raised in isolation do not use language; it is used by human beings in a social context, communicating their needs, ideas, and emotions to one another. The egocentric monologues of children appear to be secondary developments derived from the social use of language (Vygotsky 1962:19) and very few people spend much time talking to themselves. It is questionable whether sentences that communicate nothing to anyone are a part of language. In what way, then, can "sociolinguistics" be considered as something apart from "linguistics"?

One area of research which has been included in "sociolinguistics" is perhaps more accurately labelled "the sociology of language." It deals with large-scale social factors, and their mutual interaction with languages and dialects. There are many open questions, and many practical problems associated with the decay and assimilation of minority languages, the development of stable bilingualism, the standardization of languages and the planning of language development in newly emerging nations. The linguistic input for such studies is primarily that a given person or group uses language X in a social context or domain Y. A number of recent reviews have discussed work in this area (Fishman 1969) and I will not attempt to deal with these questions and this research here.

There is another area of study sometimes included in "sociolinguistics" that is more concerned with the details of language in actual use—the field which Hymes has named "the ethnography of speaking" (1962). There is a great deal to be done in describing and analyzing the patterns of use of languages and dialects within a specific culture: the forms of "speech events"; the rules for appropriate selection of speakers; the interrelations of speaker, addressee, audience, topic, channel, and setting; and the ways in which the speakers draw upon the resources of their language to perform certain functions. This functional study is conceived as complementary with the study of linguistic structure. Current research and the aims of the field have been well reviewed by Hymes (1966); in our discussion of methodology, some of the material of this descriptive study will be involved, but this review will not attempt to cover the ethnography of speaking as a whole. A number of readers and reviews of this larger field of "sociolinguistics" have appeared recently; and the reader will find a number of excellent and penetrating studies in Bright 1966; Gumperz and Hymes 1966; Lieberson 1966; Fishman 1968; Ervin-Tripp 1968; and Grimshaw 1968.

This chapter will deal with the study of language structure and evolution within the social context of the speech community. The linguistic topics to be considered here cover the area usually named "general linguistics," dealing with phonology, morphology, syntax, and semantics.[1] The theoretical questions to be raised will also fall into the category of general linguistics. We will be concerned with the forms of linguistic rules, their combination into systems, the coexistence of several systems, and the evolution of these rules and systems with time. If there were no need to contrast this work with the study of language out of its social context, I would prefer to say that this was simply *linguistics*. It is therefore relevant to ask why there should be any need for a new approach to linguistics with a broader social base. It seems natural enough that the basic data for any form of general linguistics would be language as it is used by native speakers communicating with each other in everyday life. Before proceeding, it will be helpful to see just why this has not been the case.

---

1. We have also extended these studies into the area of discourse analysis, which has not been considered a part of general linguistics or seriously investigated in the past. Sect. 4 of this chapter gives a brief indication of the nature of this work.

## The Saussurian Approach to "Langue"

The basic orientation to the structural analysis of language as most linguists pursue it today departs from the point of view first expressed by Ferdinand de Saussure at the beginning of this century. Linguists often begin theoretical discussions with reference to Saussure's concept of *langue,* to be distinguished from *parole* or 'speech' on the one hand, and *langage* or 'language as a whole' on the other. According to Saussure, *langue* "est la partie sociale du langage . . . elle n'existe qu'en vertu d'une sorte de contrat passé entre les membres de la communauté" (1962:321). For this reason, Saussure's Geneva school is often referred to as the "social" school of linguistics. Saussure conceived of linguistics as one part of "une science qui étudie la vie des signes au sein de la vie sociale." Yet curiously enough, the linguists who work within the Saussurian tradition (and this includes the great majority) do not deal with social life at all: they work with one or two informants in their offices, or examine their own knowledge of *langue.* Furthermore, they insist that explanations of linguistic facts be drawn from other linguistic facts, not from any "external" data on social behavior.[2]

This development depends on a curious paradox. If everyone possesses a knowledge of language structure, if *langue* is "un système grammatical existant virtuellement dans chaque cerveau" (p. 30), one should be able to obtain the data from the testimony of any one person—even oneself.[3] On the other hand, data on *parole,* or speech,

2. Saussure's contemporary Meillet thought that the 20th century would see the development of historical explanation based on the examination of language change embedded in social change (1921). But students of Saussure such as Martinet (1964) actively repudiated this notion, and urged that linguistic explanation be confined to the interrelations of internal, structural factors. In so doing, they were certainly following the spirit of Saussure's doctrine: for closer study of his writings suggests that for him, "social" meant no more than "multi-individual," with no suggestion of the broader implications of social interaction.

3. Saussure himself was a bit hesitant on this point. For after the quotation just given, he adds "ou plus exactement dans les cerveaux d'un ensemble d'individus: car la langue n'est complète dans aucun, elle n'existe parfaitement que dans la masse". But *virtuellement* became equivalent to *for all practical purposes.* Saussure himself did not engage in any detailed synchronic studies, but linguists who did so discarded his reservation completely. Thus Bloomfield presents a structural analysis of "standard English, as spoken in Chicago" without further identification (1933:90–92); we assume that he is speaking of his own system, though he does not reach a level of detail where this would become an issue. Benjamin L. Whorf wrote a paper on the "Phonemic analysis of the English of Eastern Massachusetts" (1943) which was again a report based on his own way of speaking.

can only be obtained by examining the behavior of individuals as they use the language. Thus we have the *Saussurian Paradox:* the social aspect of language is studied by observing any one individual, but the individual aspect only by observing language in its social context. The science of *parole* never developed, but this approach to the science of *langue* has been extremely successful over the past half-century.

The study of this abstract "language"—the knowledge available to every native speaker—has received new impetus from Chomsky, who has re-emphasized the Saussurian dichotomy, opposing *competence,* or the abstract knowledge of the rules of language, to *performance,* or the selection and execution of these rules (1965).[4] For Chomsky, linguistics is properly the study of competence, and he makes explicit the practice which followed from the Saussurian paradox: that the proper object of linguistic study is an abstract, homogeneous speech community in which everyone speaks alike and learns the language instantly (1965:3). Furthermore, Chomsky insists that the data of linguistics is not the utterance by the individual to be studied, but his intuitions about language—primarily his judgments as to which sentences are grammatical and which are not—and also judgments on the relatedness of sentences—which sentences mean "the same." Theories of language are to be constructed to explain these intuitions.

This theoretical development is based upon two more or less explicit assumptions:

1. That linguistic structure is closely associated with homogeneity. (Weinreich, Labov, and Herzog 1968.) Saussure says that "tandis que le langage est hétérogène, la langue ainsi délimitée est de nature homogène" (1962:32).[5] The general view then, is that lin-

---

4. Although Chomsky criticized Saussure's conception of *langue* as somewhat limited (1964:59–60), he sees no difference between Saussure's *langue/parole* dichotomy and his own *competence/performance* terminology. "The generative grammar internalized by someone who has acquired a language defines what in Saussurian terms we may call *langue* . . . Clearly the description of intrinsic competence provided by the grammar is not to be confused with an account of actual performance, as de Saussure emphasized with such lucidity" (1964:52).

5. In an introductory textbook by John Lyons, representing a viewpoint somewhat independent of generative grammar, we find: "When we say that two people speak the same language we are of necessity abstracting from all sorts of differences in their speech . . . For simplicity of exposition, we shall assume that the language we are describing is uniform (by 'uniform' is meant 'dialectally and stylistically' undifferenti-

guistic theories can be fully developed on the basis of that portion of language behavior which is uniform and homogeneous; though language variation may be important from a practical or applied viewpoint, such data are not required for linguistic theory—and in fact will be best understood when the theory of competence is fully developed.

2. Speakers of the language have access to their intuitions about *langue* or competence, and can report them.

Linguistics has thus been defined in such a way as to exclude the study of social behavior or the study of speech. The definition has been convenient for the formulators, who by disposition preferred to work from their own knowledge, with individual informants, or with secondary materials. But it has also been a successful strategy in our attack on linguistic structure. There is no a priori reason why one *must* enter the speech community to search for data. The large expenditure of time and effort needed would have to be justified, and the success of abstract linguistic analysis in the past five decades has plainly precluded such a development. Indeed, the limiting of our field of inquiry has certainly been helpful in the development of generative grammar—the working out of abstract models based upon our intuitive judgments of sentences. We cannot afford any backward steps: anyone who would go further in the study of language must certainly be able to work at this level of abstraction. At the same time, it is difficult to avoid the common-sense conclusion that the object of linguistics must ultimately be the instrument of communication used by the speech community; and if we are not talking about *that* language, there is something trivial in our proceeding. For a number of reasons, this kind of language has been the most difficult object for linguistics to focus on. Some of the reasons for this difficulty will be outlined below.

## Problems in Dealing with Speech

Despite the general orientation of the field towards the study of language in isolation, there have been many situations where linguists have hoped to obtain confirmation from the study of speech.

---

ated: this is, of course, an 'idealization' of the facts . . . ) and that all native speakers will agree whether an utterance is acceptable or not." (1968:140–141). It should be noted that Lyons' textbook is an introduction to "Theoretical Linguistics" and this idealization does not represent a response to any practical problems.

There are four distinct difficulties that have been cited, and which have had profound effects upon linguistic practice.

## 1. The Ungrammaticality of Speech

At one time, linguists of the Bloomfieldian school asserted that native speakers never made mistakes. But the opposite point of view prevails today: that speech is full of ungrammatical forms, since the difficulties of performance stand in the way of the full display of the speaker's competence.[6] It is generally believed that a corpus drawn from spoken language does not form good evidence, since it will contain many examples of badly formed sentences which the speakers themselves condemn and change when their attention is drawn to them.

## 2. Variation in Speech and in the Speech Community

It is common for a language to have many alternate ways of saying "the same" thing. Some words like *car* and *automobile* seem to have the same referents; others have two pronunciations, like *working* and *workin'*. There are syntactic options such as *Who is he talking to?* vs. *To whom is he talking?* or *It's easy for him to talk* vs. *For him to talk is easy*.[7] In each of these cases, we have the problem of deciding the place of this variation in linguistic structure. Current formal analysis provides us with only two clear options: (1) the variants are said to belong to different systems, and the alternation is an example of "dialect mixture" or "code-switching"; (2) the variants are said to be in "free variation" within the same system, and the selection lies below the level of linguistic structure. Both approaches place the variation outside of the system being studied. There are of course many cases which fall appropriately under one or the other of these labels. But to demonstrate that we have a true case of code-switching, it is necessary to show that the speaker moves

6. Chomsky has asserted that the "degenerate" character of the everyday speech which the child hears is a strong argument in support of the nativist position: the child must have an inborn theory of language, since he could not induce rules from the ungrammatical speech with which he is surrounded (1965:58).

7. It is customary to say that these expressions have the same *meaning*, which we define narrowly by some criterion such as 'having the same truth value'. The end result of our studies of syntactic variation will be to assign a certain meaning or *significance* to a transformation, a type of functional load which we may want to distinguish sharply from representational meaning.

from one consistent set of co-occurring rules to another; to demonstrate "free variation" one has to show that he has not moved at all.
It is rare for either of these claims to be established empirically. Most
cases are not easily described under either heading; consider for
example an actual example of language in use.[8]

An' den like IF YOU MISS ONESIES, de OTHuh person shoot to skelly;
ef he miss, den you go again. An' IF YOU GET IN, YOU SHOOT TO
TWOSIES. An' IF YOU GET IN TWOSIES, YOU GO TO tthreesies. An'
IF YOU MISS tthreesies, THEN THE PERSON THa' miss skelly shoot THE
SKELLIES an' shoot in THE ONESIES: an' IF HE MISS, YOU GO f'om
tthreesies to foursies.

   In this extract, a 12-year-old black boy is explaining the game of
Skelly. We can treat his variations as examples of code-switching;
each time he uses a marked variant, he moves into the "system"
containing that variant. Lower case would then indicate the "Black
English Vernacular" [BEV] and upper case "Standard English" [SE].
But it is an unconvincing effort: there is no obvious motivation for
him to switch 18 times in the course of this short passage. Furthermore, the great majority of the forms are shared by both systems
and are assigned to one or the other code by the accidents of sequencing. In line 2, *you go again* is assigned to BEV only because
it happens to follow *den,* and YOU GET IN is assigned to SE only
because it follows the marked form IF. But on the other hand, can
we treat the difference between *de* and *THE* as "free variation"? Such
a decision would make no sense to either the speaker or the analyst,
who both know that *de* is a stigmatized form. Without any clear way
of categorizing this behavior, we are forced to speak of "stylistic
variants," and we are then left with no fixed relation at all to our
notion of linguistic structure. What is a style if not a separate sub-
code, and when do we have two of them? We normally think of
language as a means of translating meaning into linear form. Where
and how do stylistic meanings enter into this process? We speak of
the need for communicating meaning as a controlling factor in
linguistic evolution. What kind of control if any is exerted by the
need to communicate "stylistic" messages?
   An even more puzzling problem arises when we consider a varia-

---

8. This quotation is from an interview with "Boot," the verbal leader of a preadolescent group of black children in south-central Harlem, New York City (Labov
et al. 1968).

ble phenomenon such as consonant cluster simplification in BEV—a process which lies on the intersection of grammar and phonology. A word such as *bold* is often simplified to *bol'*, but not always. This is also the case with *rolled*. We immediately want to know if past tense clusters CVC + D can be treated in the same way as simple CVCC forms, without danger of losing the past tense information. Careful investigation shows us that the distinction is never lost—the past tense forms are simplified *less* often by everyone. But our theory has no way of registering this fact formally: both *bold* and *rolled* fall under the same "optional" rule, and our observations have no theoretical status in the rules of *langue*.

### 3. Difficulties of Hearing and Recording

Records of speech observed in actual use are often very poor in quality. Acoustic phoneticians gather their data in soundproof rooms, under the best possible conditions. In the field, we find that room noise, street noise, and other interference reduces the phonetic value of our data. If the informant is brought to record under ideal conditions, then his speech has the properties of formal, elicited speech we tried to avoid.[9] The fundamental problem is that most linguistic signals are supported by a great many redundant signals, and it is rare that any one of them carries a heavy burden of meaning; it is not essential to the overall message that listeners receive any one signal. Yet to record this item in full form, the linguist would like to hear it at its clearest, *as if* it were the only means of signaling that message. It would therefore follow that the elicited forms given in the laboratory give the clearest indication of the underlying system.

### 4. The Rarity of Syntactic Forms

The data based on what speakers actually say may be adequate for the most common phonological and syntactic forms. For any deep analysis of the sound pattern of a language, it will be necessary to elicit such rare words as *adz* (the only English morpheme ending in a cluster of voiced obstruents). In the study of syntax, the inadequacy of the average corpus is even plainer. Any attempt to specify

9. This situation is not so damaging for phonological analysis as for grammatical research. In phonology, we can wait for the clear, stressed forms to emerge from the background noise. But many grammatical particles are reduced to minimal consonants or even features of tenseness or voicing which are difficult to hear in less than the best conditions, and many are so rare that we cannot afford to let one escape us.

syntactic rules inevitably involves forms which one could not expect to hear in any limited investigation. For example, an analysis of the *got* passive may depend upon whether it is possible to say such sentences as "He got kicked out of the army by playing the trumpet", where we are looking for such rare forms as X *got Verb* + *ed* . . . *by* $\phi$ *Verb* + *ing* − Z.

These difficulties make clear the basic motivation for the concentration on *langue* or "competence" to the exclusion of other data. Given the fact that considerable progress has been made in the abstract study of *langue,* and given these difficulties of work in a natural setting, it should not be surprising that linguistics has turned firmly away from the speech community. But there are also disadvantages to the abstract study of language. Some of its limitations have recently become painfully prominent; the difficulties of developing linguistic theory with this limited data base are perhaps even greater than those outlined above for the study of the speech community.

### Problems in the Study of Intuitions

When Chomsky first made the explicit proposal that the subject matter of linguistics be confined to the intuitive judgments of native speakers, he hoped that the great majority of these would be clear judgments (1957:14). It was expected that the marginal cases, which were doubtful in the mind of the theorist and/or the native speaker, would be few in number and their grammatical status would be decided by rules formed from the clear cases. The situation has not worked out in this way, for it is difficult to find doubtful cases which have *not* remained problematical for the theory. It is not the number of doubtful cases which is at issue here: it is their locations at points which are crucial in arguing questions of grammatical theory. One can see examples of this problem at any linguistic meeting, where paper after paper will cite crucial data as acceptable or unacceptable without obtaining agreement from the audience. This is not due to carelessness or lack of linguistic ability on the part of the authors: in their earnest intent to explore linguistic theory on the basis of their intuitions, they inevitably reach a point where their data take this form. The two assumptions of the homogeneity and accessibility of *langue* which led to this situation are seriously brought into question by this development.

When challenges to data arise on the floor of a linguistic meeting, the author usually defends himself by stating that there are many "dialects" and that the systematic argument he was presenting held good for his own "dialect." This is an odd use of the term, and it raises the question as to what the object of linguistic description can or should be.

### The Object of Linguistic Description: "Dialect" and "Idiolect"

The use of the term "dialect" in the discussions of the variability of judgments is difficult to justify. No evidence is given of differences in two systematic sets of rules used by two groups of speakers; what we observe are individual differences of opinion on isolated points. As we will see, individuals are not at all consistent from one judgment to the next. The question arises, what is being described? In the search for a homogeneous object to conform to the needs and assumptions of the Saussurian model, linguists have gradually contracted their focus to smaller and smaller segments of language. Thus Bloch introduced the term "idiolect" to represent the speech of one person talking on one subject to the same person for a short period of time (1948). Although this term has been widely adopted, it is doubtful if anyone has found within such an "idiolect" the homogeneous data which Bloch hoped for. But it must be noted that the very existence of the concept "idiolect" as a proper object of linguistic description represents a defeat of the Saussurian notion of *langue* as an object of uniform social understanding.

It was hoped that, by concentrating upon the judgments of the native speaker rather than his actual speech, much of this variation could be bypassed. In some ways, this hope is justified: members of a speech community do share a common set of normative patterns even when we find highly stratified variation in actual speech (Labov 1966a:4–35ff.) But such uniformity in intuitive judgments is characteristic only of well-developed sociolinguistic variables which have received overt social correction. Most linguistic rules are well below the level of social correction, and have no overt social norms associated with them.

In an earlier version of this chapter I reported difficulties in reproducing the syntactic dialects which Postal (1971) reported for crossover phenomena and pronominalization constraints. More recently we have begun to explore systematically the internal consistency of "idiolectal" syntactic dialects: that is, syntactic dialects reported on the basis of intuitive responses to isolated sentences randomly distributed among subjects without any geographic or social differentiation.

One such area of syntactic variation concerns the quantifier dialects isolated by Carden (1970). Carden has been one of the few careful investigators of syntactic dialects, emphasizing the importance of individual interviews over group questionnaires, controlled technique, and checks for reliability over a period of time. His basic datum is differential response to the sentences

1       All the boys didn't leave.
2       All the boys didn't leave until six.
3       All the boys didn't leave, did they?

The interpretation of 1 as 'Not all the boys left' is said to be characteristic of the NEG-Q dialect, and is consistent with finding 3 acceptable and 2 unacceptable since the negative is then the highest predicate, dictating a positive tag in 3 but stranding *until* in a lower level positive sentence in 2. The interpretation of 1 as 'None of the boys left' is said to be characteristic of the NEG-V dialect and is consistent with finding 2 acceptable and 3 unacceptable, since the negative is then a lower predicate, dominated by a higher predicate with the qualifier *all;* this permits *until* in 2 but demands a negative tag in 3.

My own interest in the matter has proceeded from the generalization of the study of negative attraction to the quantifier *any* (see Sect. 2 below). Together with Mark Baltin, I have developed a number of instruments to approach such intuitions on quantifier dialects and contrast these intuitions with the unreflecting use of the linguistic rules involved. Ten different studies have been carried out with samples of 15 to 40 subjects, using various techniques to sharpen intuitive judgments. Subjects were drawn from middle-class and working-class backgrounds, largely favoring the former, in tests carried out in Philadelphia, New York, Providence, and Kansas City. In general, we find that three-quarters or more of any sample will give initial NEG-Q responses to 1, with a small percentage of NEG-V and some equally balanced ambiguous speakers. For this isolated sentence, we find that only about one-quarter of the subjects are consistently and determinately NEG-Q in responses to 1–3 and refuse to admit NEG-V possibilities; and we rarely find such consistent NEG-V responses. However, we do not find consistent responses to the NEG-Q or NEG-V pattern. In one study of 17 informants, we tested the most consistent kind of response: a preference for sentence A over sentence B, e.g., 2 over 3. The first test pair opposed 3 and 2. The second pair was

4          a. All the guys won't start work until the whistle blows.
           b. All the guys haven't started work, have they?

We also used two pairs showing semantic disambiguation:

5          a. Since the plant's locked, all of them haven't started work yet.
           b. All the guys haven't started work yet; some are still on their lunch hour.
6          a. All the guys don't like John; some of them can't stand him.
           b. All the guys don't like John; none of them has anything good to say about him.

If the speaker indeed has a NEG-Q dialect, he will prefer 3 to 2, 4b to 4a, 5b to 5a and 6a to 6b. Sentence 5a gives the context which most strongly favors the NEG-V interpretation.

If the NEG-Q and NEG-V dialects were characteristic of the grammars of our 17 subjects, we should have obtained a number greater than chance who gave consistent answers to these four pairs. But only 8 out of 17 gave consistent responses to the two pairs showing syntactic disambiguation; only 9 out of 17 gave consistent responses to the two pairs showing semantic disambiguation; and only 3 out of 17 gave consistent responses to both. Furthermore, only 1 of these 3 gave the *same* consistent response to both sets—that is, was consistently NEG-Q or NEG-V throughout.

This result is consistent with other data which show that almost all subjects will in fact respond either NEG-Q or NEG-V when we control the context effectively. That is, all are ambiguous. We constructed a test which looks "through" the grammar to extralinguistic states of affairs. We show the subjects pairs of diagrams such as Figs. 8.1a and 8.1b and ask which one is designated by

7          All the circles don't have dots in them.

Faced with this problem, most subjects now switch to NEG-V interpretations and select 8.1b. In our first approach, we submitted Fig. 8.1 before any sentence tests such as 1–3 and we obtained 100 percent

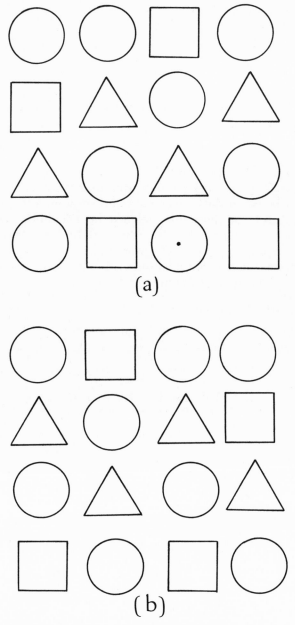

(a)

(b)

Fig. 8.1.  "All the circles don't have dots in them."

NEG-V. When we placed the diagram after the sentence tests, the majority still switched to NEG-V from NEG-Q. In one recent series, 39 of 58 subjects responded NEG-V to the diagrams, and of these only 17 could be led to see NEG-Q as an alternate possibility. Furthermore, we were able to control this response by using variant forms of Fig. 8.1a with one out of eight circles having dots, seven out of eight, or four out of eight. Table 8.1 shows how responses shift systematically from the most favoring situation (1 out of 8) to the least (4 out of 8). When there is only one dot as in Fig. 8.1a, the great majority see only the NEG-V meaning of 7 referring to 8.1b. When the first diagram has four dotted circles about half the subjects now see both NEG-Q and NEG-V interpretations. Moreover, there is no correlation between these responses and responses to isolated sentences. Table 8.1 also shows for each test the distribution by response to sentences 1–3. In this, as in other tests we find that there are *more* subjects who switch responses from sentences to diagrams than those who maintain a consistent position. Table 8.2 shows an even more dramatic inconsistency in another series using a test sentence

8          Everybody doesn't know how to play bridge.

Interpretations of sentence 8 in isolation favor NEG-Q less heavily than sentence 7. In Table 8.2 we see that only 3 out of 19 subjects

TABLE 8.1
EFFECT OF VARIANT FORMS OF FIG. 8.1
ON NEG-V AND NEG-Q RESPONSES

| Reaction to Fig. 8.1 | $\frac{1}{8}$ | | $\frac{4}{8}$ | | $\frac{7}{8}$ | |
|---|---|---|---|---|---|---|
| | Q* | V | Q | V | Q | V |
| V only | 5 | 7 | 1 | 3 | 2 | 5 |
| V > Q | 1 | — | 1 | 1 | 1 | 1 |
| V = Q | 1 | — | 3 | 3 | 1 | — |
| Q > V | — | — | 1 | — | 3 | 1 |
| Q only | — | — | 1 | — | — | — |
| | 7 | 7 | 7 | 7 | 7 | 7 |

NEG-Q sentence: All the guys didn't leave, but some did.
NEG-V sentence: All the girls didn't arrive until eight, so the room was empty at seven thirty.
*Subject's preference for NEG-Q or NEG-V sentences.

TABLE 8.2
INCONSISTENT NEG-Q AND NEG-V RESPONSES
TO DIAGRAMS AND SENTENCES

| Reactions to Fig. 8.1 (1 dot) | Interpretations of sentence 8 | | | |
|---|---|---|---|---|
| | Q only | Q > V | V > Q | V only |
| Q only | — | 1 | 3 | 4 |
| Q > V | — | — | — | — |
| V > Q | 1 | — | — | — |
| V only | 4 | 3 | 1 | 1 |

were consistent between sentence and diagram responses—a result that matches closely the internal consistency pattern for sentences 2–6 noted above. We can obtain an even heavier NEG-V reaction by adding a restrictive modifier to 1, producing

9          All of us here don't play bridge.

The quantifier *all* is now seen by the great majority of speakers as applying to the entire quantity *we who are here,* and this is interpreted as 'None of us here plays bridge.' In test after test, 90 to 95 percent of the subjects select NEG-V interpretations of 9, and the great majority do not accept NEG-Q readings.

To illustrate the force of this shift in construction, we note that in a recent test, 21 of 26 subjects gave a NEG-Q response to 1. When this was followed immediately with sentence 9, the majority switched to NEG-V and only eleven remained NEG-Q.

These responses indicate that the eliciting context can be controlled to produce NEG-Q and NEG-V "dialects" at will. Even more convincing evidence can be derived by observing the use of language in everyday life. When I first introduced Fig. 8.1 to my family, there was a heated argument. My wife gave most determined NEG-Q answers; after thirty minutes of argument between my children and her, she still maintained that the NEG-V interpretation was so remote that it could not be seriously considered. As I was lying in bed the next morning, I heard my wife calling to my son from the hallway:

10          Simon, get up! Everybody's not helping!

The "Quantifier dialects" have played an important role in recent linguistic theory. Dialect differences have been claimed for interpretations of sentences 11a and 11b.

11          a. Half of the people in this room speak two languages.
            b. Two languages are spoken by half of the people in this
               room.

These sentences bear crucially on the problem of whether or not
transformations preserve referential meaning. A linguist who finds
that others disagree with him about whether or not 11a means the
same as 11b will defend his own reaction as "my dialect," and claim
that the theory must account at least for the "facts" of his dialect.

   Grinder and Postal (1971) developed some important arguments
on identity of sense anaphora which they hoped would decide the
conflict between generative semantics and interpretative theory.
Most of the sentence types put forward produce a mixed response;
those who favor generative semantics generally view the data as the
authors do, rejecting such sentences as

12          *Max wasn't imprisoned but Joe was imprisoned and he
            is still there.
13          *Max is off his rocker and so is his mother.

But those who do not favor their position usually do not reject 12
and 13. In their conclusion, Grinder and Postal run into a head-on
conflict with Chomsky in the interpretation of sentences such as

14          John hasn't been here for a month, but Bill has.

The issue here is that generative semantics will expand the ellipsis
to an underlying form

14′         John hasn't been here for a month, but Bill has been here
            for a month.

which allows only a durative interpretation; thus a generative semantic position rules out a punctual interpretation for 14. But
Chomsky allows a punctual reading by an interpretive rule, since
he does not derive 14 from a deep structure with 14′. Postal and
Grinder call Chomsky's argument "misleading and distorting" since
they find that 9 out of 10 subjects they asked agreed with *them*. A
student from the University of California, Los Angeles, has written
to me that the great majority of linguistic students there agree with
Chomsky's intuitions. It should be noted that the linguistics department at U.C.L.A. favors interpretive theory. Postal and Grinder argue
that the best theory is one which can account for the facts of dialect

variation; but these dialects seem to be artifacts of a theoretical position. As linguists become more deeply involved in such theoretical issues, it is likely that their intuitions will drift further and further from those of ordinary people and the reality of language as it is used in everyday life.[10] We return to the painfully obvious conclusion—obvious at least to those outside linguistics—that linguists cannot continue to produce theory and data at the same time.

Again, one must pay tribute to the difficulty and subtlety of the questions posed. Obviously techniques for investigation must be developed further. Yet there is no evidence that consistent and homogeneous judgments can be obtained from native speakers on such crucial matters. Variation in syntactic judgments can be studied with profit and the implicational series within them analyzed to decide the form of the rules (Elliott, Legum, and Thomson 1969). But it is now evident that the search for homogeneity in intuitive judgments is a failure. Once this result is accepted, the strongest motivation for confining linguistic analysis to such judgments disappears. In many ways, intuition is less regular and more difficult to interpret than speech. If we are to make good use of speakers' statements about language, we must interpret them in the light of unconscious, unreflecting productions. Without such control, one is left with very dubious data indeed—with no clear relation to the communicative process we recognize as language itself.

## Problems in the Relation of Theory to Data

The procedures of generative grammar, working with intuitions about language, have enabled us to elaborate elegant and insightful models of linguistic structure. We have unearthed a great fund of problems which had never been touched on or discussed before. It

10. A drift of linguists' intuitions away from the general understanding was indicated in recent unpublished research of N. Spencer of Pennsylvania State University. She took 150 sentences from generative papers of some importance to generative theory by Perlmutter, C. Smith, Postal, Ross, Rosenbaum, and R. Lakoff. These were submitted for judgments of acceptability to 60 subjects: 20 graduate students in linguistics, 20 graduate students not in linguistics, and 20 subjects outside the university. There was more than a little disagreement with the original judgment: in 44 of the 150 cases the authors failed to get a majority of the subjects to agree with them, whether the judges were naive or not. But when there was disagreement among the judges, the non-linguist graduate students regularly sided with the naive judges from town, and the linguistic students were left by themselves.

is now commonplace to assert that generative grammar is the best discovery procedure we have. The study of intuitive judgments focuses our attention on important relations between sentences and the deeper structures which underlie them. But as a theory of language this approach is seriously defective, since it offers us no means of discovering whether our model is right or wrong. Originally, the generative grammar was constructed to produce all the acceptable sentences of the language and none of the unacceptable ones. But if we now compare the model with what speakers say, we cannot draw any decisive conclusions from the way it matches or fails to match the data.

1. If someone uses a sentence structure that is not generated by the grammar, there is nothing to prevent us from setting it aside as a mistake or a dialect difference.
2. If no one ever uses a sentence structure which is predicted by the grammar, this fact can be discounted because most complex syntactic forms are known to be very rare—the occasion simply has not arisen.

This second situation can be extremely embarrassing when the syntactic forms concerned are at the very center of the theoretical argument. Chomsky's original argument against finite state grammars (1957) depended on the existence of self-embedded structures in natural language. Everyone seems to accept such sentences as

15          The man (that) the girl (that) I used to go with married
            just got drafted.

as grammatical (in competence) though a bit difficult to follow (in performance). But now that Peter Reich has challenged the grammatical status of this pattern and reasserted the finiteness of natural language (1969) one looks in vain for empirical evidence of the use of such doubly embedded forms.[11] In the interviews and conversations we have recorded, no such example from unreflecting, natural speech has yet emerged. Current explorations with sociolinguistic techniques of enriching the data suggest that we can establish the grammaticality of 15, but until we have strong evidence of its use or comprehension in natural conversation, the basic argument for

11. A finite state grammar may produce single embeddings such as "The girl I used to go with just got married." The problem only arises when the grammar must be in a state to "remember" that it has two subjects stored for which it must produce predicates.

hierarchical phrase structure will not rest on a solid foundation.

The problems we as linguists face in dealing directly with the data of language are not peculiar to our discipline. This is a general problem for all the social sciences. Garfinckel (1967) has demonstrated that there exists in every field of research an inevitable gap between the raw data as it occurs and the protocols in which the data are recorded as input to the theoretical pursuit. In the sociolinguistic literature cited, we find many kinds of data used to provide information about language in actual use: census data; questionnaires; extracts from plays and novels; psychological tests; ethnographic reports of community norms. No matter how insightful or productive these studies may be, they do not bring us much closer to the fundamental data of language in use than we were before. There are many open questions we simply cannot answer. What is the relation between the novelist's stereotype and the language behavior of the people in question? what is the connection between word association tests and the semantics of natural language? how do we discover when a speaker uses *tu* when all we have is his self-report, or discover when he speaks French by asking him when he does so? what is the relation between the norms which the anthropologist reports and the practice of members in conforming to those norms? There are many acts of perceiving, remembering, selecting, interpreting, and translating that lie between the data and the linguist's report, and these are almost all implicit in such papers. As Garfinckel has pointed out, every coding and reporting procedure that transforms the data will show an ineradicable residue of common-sense operation which cannot be reduced to rule. To come to grips with *language,* we must look as closely and directly at the data of everyday speech as possible, and characterize its relationship to our grammatical theories as accurately as we can, amending and adjusting the theory so that it fits the object in view. We can then turn again and re-examine the methods we have used, an inquiry which will greatly increase our understanding of the object we are studying.

### The Direct Study of the Linguistic Data

The critique of the conventional linguistic methods just given must not be taken as a suggestion that they be abandoned. The formal elicitation of paradigms, the exploration of intuitive judgments, the study of literary texts, experimentation in the laboratory, and questionnaires on linguistic usage are all important and valuable modes of investigation. The first two procedures must be mastered by anyone who hopes to do significant linguistic analysis. The techniques to be discussed below for the direct observation of language in use presuppose that the outlines of the grammar have been sketched in—that the main possibilities are known. Thus the phonetic transcription of an unknown language (or even unknown words) is quite beyond our capacity. The ear is a very poor instrument for judging the absolute quality of isolated sounds. But given an understanding of the syntax and the morphemes intended, the ear is a superb instrument for judging which of several possibilities are realized.[12] In syntax, our first analyses of a given form are relatively superficial; but when many relationships with other sentence forms are noted, a rich field of possible underlying structures begins to emerge. There is a second *Cumulative Paradox* involved here: *the more that is known about a language, the more we can find out about it.*

The limitations placed upon the input data by Chomsky have led him to the conviction that the *theory is underdetermined by the data* (1966)—that there will always be many possible analyses for each body of data, and we will need internal evaluation measures to choose among them. We take the opposite view. Through the direct study of language in its social context, the amount of available data expands enormously, and offers us ways and means for deciding which of the many possible analyses is right. In our preliminary operations upon the initial data, considerations of simplicity will always find a place; but given the correct line of attack,[13] it is possible to prove whether the simple hypothesis constructed is the correct one. The studies of covariation and change in progress discussed below will provide considerable support for this claim.

12. Our own work in tracing sound changes in progress through spectrographic measurements confirms the remarkable accuracy of impressionistic phonetics used to compare two sounds. See Chs. 1 and 2.

13. Watson's discovery of the structure of DNA is one of the most striking cases of the role of simplicity in scientific research. Watson was convinced that the solution must be a simple one, and this conviction motivated his persistent attempts at model-building (1969). But simplicity merely suggested the best approach: the validity of his model was established by the convergence of many quantitative measures. Hafner and Presswood (1965) cite another case in the theory of weak interactions where considerations of simplicity led to a new theoretical attack; but again, as in all other cases I know, the acceptance of the theory as correct depended upon new quantitative data.

### Resolution of Problems in the Study of Everyday Language

Among the motivations discussed for the restriction of linguistic data to intuitions were difficulties in working with everyday speech. Fortunately for our studies, many of these problems turned out to be illusory, or greatly exaggerated.

1. *The ungrammaticality of everyday speech* appears to be a myth with no basis in actual fact. In the various empirical studies that we have conducted, the great majority of utterances—about 75 percent—are well-formed sentences by any criterion. When rules of ellipsis are applied, and certain universal editing rules to take care of stammering and false starts, the proportion of truly un- grammatical and ill-formed sentences falls to less than two per- cent (Labov 1966b). When nonacademic speakers are talking about subjects they know well—narratives of personal experience—the proportion of sentences that need any editing at all in order to be well-formed drops to about ten percent. I have received con- firmation of this general view from a great many other linguists who have worked with ordinary conversation. The myth of the ungrammaticality of spoken language seems to have two sources: data taken from transcripts of learned conferences, where highly educated speakers are trying to express complex ideas for the first time; and the usual tendency to accept ideas that fit into our frame of reference without noticing the data with which we are sur- rounded.

2. The existence of *variation and heterogeneous structures* in the speech communities investigated is certainly well-established in fact. It is the existence of any other type of speech community that may be placed in doubt. There is a kind of folk-myth deeply embedded among linguists that before they themselves arrived on the scene there existed a homogeneous, single-style group who really "spoke the language." Each investigator feels that his own community has been corrupted from this normal model in some way—by contact with other languages, by the effects of education and pressure of the standard language, or by taboos and the admixture of specialized dialects or jargons. But we have come to the realization in recent years that this is the *normal* situation— that heterogeneity is not only common, it is the natural result of basic linguistic factors. We argue that it is the absence of style- shifting and multilayered communication systems which would be dysfunctional (Weinreich, Labov, and Herzog 1968:101).

Once we dissolve the assumed association between structure and homogeneity, we are free to develop the formal tools needed to deal with inherent variation within the speech community. Again, we find ourselves fortunate in that the patterning within this variation is by no means obscure: it does not require the statistical analysis of hundreds of speakers' records as linguists traditionally feared (Hockett 1958:444). On the contrary, we find that the basic patterns of class stratification, for example, emerge from samples as small as 25 speakers.[14] As we saw in Ch. 2, regular arrays of stylistic and social stratification emerge even when our individual cells contain as few as five speakers and we have no more than five or ten instances of the given variable for each speaker. With this regular and reproducible data, we are in a position to specify what we mean by the "stylistic" or "social" meaning which seems so elusive when language is studied out of context.

3. *The problem of recording speech in natural settings* is a technical one: and the development of professional battery-operated tape recorders has made it possible to obtain excellent results in the field. Given a good microphone, a field worker can obtain excellent recordings under noisy conditions by minimizing mouth to microphone distance for each speaker.[15] In general, it may be said that the current problem lies primarily in the failure of linguists to respond to the invention of the magnetic tape recorder in Germany in the 1930's. There is no tradition in linguistics of solving technical or experimental problems, of assessing technological developments and responding to them; otherwise the nature of linguistic operations would have been transformed 30 years ago.

4. The fourth problem to be resolved is the *rarity of crucial grammatical forms* needed for evidence. There is no immediate solution on hand but the direction of the answer is beginning to appear. A deeper understanding of the communicative function of grammatical forms will enable us to enrich the data of ordinary

14. This conclusion is supported throughout Labov 1966a and Labov et al. 1968, but most strikingly in Shuy, Wolfram, and Riley 1967. From a very large sample of over 700 interviews, 25 were selected for analysis, and extremely regular patterns of social stratification emerged for a number of linguistic variables. See also Kučera 1961:97–98, where 19 subjects are stratified into at least four classes.

15. See Sect. 1 below for some difficult consequences of this advance.

conversation. The ideal mode of operation is for the linguist to engage in a normal conversation with an informant, and be able to elicit the informant's natural use of a given form without using it himself. Obviously there is feed-back here between abstract analysis and field methods: the ability to control the production of a given form confirms our analysis and provides contextual data on its use. We have had some success in eliciting and controlling items such as the English passive and present perfect forms in this way. Eventually, we will be in a position to assert that a speaker does not have a given form in his system because of his consistent failure to use it in a context where other members of the community do so regularly.

### Sources for the Study of Language in its Social Context

There are now in print a number of empirical studies which demonstrate convincingly that the direct study of language is a practical and fruitful procedure. The research to be discussed in this chapter and the next is relatively recent: the work of ten investigators or groups of investigators who use as their primary data accurate records of language in its normal social context. The first two are brief studies incidental to other research; the others are large-scale undertakings, specifically designed for the study of the speech community.

1. John L. Fischer's brief study of the -ing suffix used by children in a New England community (1958).
2. Henry Kučera's observations of the use of Common Czech and Literary Czech variables in the speech of 19 exiles on French radio stations (1961).
3. John Gumperz' investigations of dialect stratification and code switching in Khalapur, India and Hemnes, Norway (1964, 1967), and his study of Marathi-Kannada bilingualism in Kupwar, India (1969).
4. Lewis Levine and Harry Crockett's report on the use of post-vocalic r in their sociolinguistic survey of Hillsboro, N.C. (1966); Frank Anshen's study of four phonological variables in the black population of that city (1969).
5. Investigations of Spanish-English bilingualism in the Puerto Rican community of New York City and Jersey City by Joshua

Fishman, John Gumperz, and Roxana Ma (Fishman et al. 1968) and particularly Ma and Herasimchuk's study of Spanish and English variables.

6. Roger Shuy, Walt Wolfram, and Ralph Fasold's study of the social stratification of phonological and grammatical variables in Detroit English (Shuy, Wolfram, and Riley 1967) and Wolfram's analysis of black speech within that study (1969).

7. The sociolinguistic investigations of the French of Montreal by Gillian Sankoff, Henrietta Cedergren, and their associates (Sankoff and Cedergren 1971; Sankoff, Sarrasin, and Cedergren 1971; Sankoff 1972).

8. The investigation of the social stratification of English in Norwich, England, by Peter Trudgill (1971).

9. The study of the Spanish of Panama City by Henrietta Cedergren (1970).

10. My own study of centralization on Martha's Vineyard (Ch. 1); of the stratification of English in New York City (Chs. 3–6); and with Paul Cohen, Clarence Robins and John Lewis, of the structure and use of the Black English Vernacular (Labov 1972a; Labov et al. 1968).

In addition, I will be drawing on studies of social attitudes towards languages and dialects by Lambert and his colleagues (1967). Though these are based entirely on test reactions, they fit in and help to explain the other data cited above. There are also smaller studies carried out by students, and a number of major studies now in progress which add to our understanding of the principles involved.

We can best understand the value of this empirical research if we apply it to the kind of specific theoretical problems of linguistic structure which concern all linguists. The study of language in its social context takes up the same range of linguistic problems as other approaches to linguistic theory. We can isolate five general questions:

1. What is the form of the linguistic rule? and what constraints may be placed upon it?

2. What are the underlying forms upon which rules operate, and how can they be determined accurately in any given case?

3. How are rules combined into systems? and how are they ordered within these systems?

4. How are systems related to each other in bilingual and polysystemic situations?

5. How do rules and rule systems change? What is the mechanism of the fundamental processes of language acquisition, or how do rules change in the larger course of linguistic evolution?

Sect. 1 will present methods for gathering reliable data within the speech community; Sect. 2 will deal with the methods used for analyzing these data and show the kind of solutions to internal linguistic problems that are possible; Sect. 3 will deal with the broader sociolinguistic structures and the interaction of social and linguistic factors. The theoretical analysis and the formal approach is originally my own, based to a large extent on the studies listed under 10, above, but the convergence of findings and principles in the field is very striking indeed. Most recently, important modifications have been made to the formalization of variable rules which are reflected in the version given in the following pages. Cedergren and D. Sankoff (1972) have quantified the variable constraints as underlying probabilities, and thus raised the entire discussion to a higher level of accountability.

In all of these discussions we will make use of the facts of inherent variation to resolve abstract questions which would otherwise remain as undecided, moot possibilities. The aim here is not necessarily to provide linguistics with a new theory of language, but rather to provide a new method of work.

## 1. Methodology

In any academic course that deals with research in the speech community, there is always a great deal of interest in the first steps to be taken: "What do you say to people?" This is not a trivial question. The elementary steps of locating and contacting informants, and getting them to talk freely in a recorded interview, are formidable problems for students. It is an error for anyone to pass over these questions, for in the practices and techniques that have been worked out are embodied many important principles of linguistic and social behavior. Close examination of these methodological assumptions and findings will tell us a great deal about the nature of discourse and the functions of language.

The fundamental sociolinguistic question is posed by the need to understand why anyone says anything. There are methodological questions of sampling and recording which merely set the stage for the basic problems. It was noted above that good data require good recording, especially for the grammatical analysis of natural speech. After the crucial variables have been defined and isolated, a great deal can be done with handwritten notes. But our initial approach to the speech community is governed by the need to obtain large volumes of well-recorded natural speech.

We can isolate five methodological axioms supported by the findings of the field research projects cited which lead to a methodological paradox; the solution to this paradox is the central methodological problem.

1. *Style Shifting.* As far as we can see, there are no single-style speakers. Some informants show a much wider range of style shifting than others, but every speaker we have encountered shows a shift of some linguistic variables as the social context and topic change (Ch. 3). Some of these shifts can be detected qualitatively in the minor self-corrections of the speaker, which are almost always in a uniform direction.

2. *Attention.* There are a great many styles and stylistic dimensions that can be isolated by an analyst. But we find that *styles can be ranged along a single dimension, measured by the amount of attention paid to speech.* The most important way in which this attention is exerted is in audio-monitoring one's own speech, though other forms of monitoring also take place.[16] This axiom (really an hypothesis) receives strong support from the fact that speakers show the same level for many important linguistic variables in casual speech, when they are least involved, and excited speech, when they are deeply involved emotionally. The common factor for both styles is that the minimum attention is available for monitoring one's own speech.

3. *The Vernacular.* Not every style or point on the stylistic continuum is of equal interest to linguists. Some styles show irregular phonological and grammatical patterns, with a great deal of "hypercorrection." In other styles, we find more systematic speech, where the fundamental relations which determine the course of linguistic evolution can be seen most clearly. This is the "vernacular"—the style in which the minimum attention is given to the monitoring of speech. Observation of the vernacular gives us the most systematic data for our analysis of linguistic structure.

16. See experiments of Mahl with white noise in Ch. 3.

4. *Formality. Any systematic observation of a speaker defines a formal context in which more than the minimum attention is paid to speech.* In the main body of an interview, where information is requested and supplied, we would not expect to find the vernacular used. No matter how casual or friendly the speaker may appear to us, we can always assume that he has a more casual speech, another style in which he jokes with his friends and argues with his wife.

5. *Good Data.* No matter what other methods may be used to obtain samples of speech (group sessions, anonymous observation), the only way to obtain sufficient good data on the speech of any one person is through an individual, tape-recorded interview: that is through the most obvious kind of systematic observation.[17]

We are then left with the *Observer's Paradox*: the aim of linguistic research in the community must be to find out how people talk when they are not being systematically observed; yet we can only obtain these data by systematic observation. The problem is of course not insoluble: we must either find ways of supplementing the formal interviews with other data, or change the structure of the interview situation by one means or another. Of the various research projects mentioned above, not all have been successful in overcoming this paradox. Many investigators have completed their work with only a limited range of stylistic data, concentrated in the more formal ends of the spectrum. Systematic study of the vernacular has been accomplished primarily in Gumperz' work, in our own work in New York City and in urban ghetto areas, and in the Fishman-Gumperz-Ma project in Jersey City.

One way of overcoming the paradox is to break through the constraints of the interview situation by various devices which divert attention away from speech, and allow the vernacular to emerge. This can be done in various intervals and breaks which are so defined that the subject unconsciously assumes that he is not at that moment being interviewed (Ch. 3). We can also involve the subject in questions and topics which recreate strong emotions he has felt in the past, or involve him in other contexts. One of the most successful questions of this type is one dealing with the "Danger of Death": "Have you ever been in a situation where you were in serious

17. There are some situations where candid recording is possible and permissable, but the quality of the sound is so poor that such recordings are of confirmatory value at best.

danger of being killed?" (Ch. 3, p. 92). Narratives given in answer to this question almost always show a shift of style away from careful speech towards the vernacular.[18]

One cannot expect that such devices will always be successful in obtaining a radical shift of style. A more systematic approach uses the normal interaction of the peer-group to control speech instead of the one-to-one confrontation of subject and interviewer. In Gumperz' work in Hemnes (1966), the fundamental data was obtained through recorded sessions with natural groups. In our work in south-central Harlem, (Labov et al. 1968) we studied adolescent peer groups through long-term participant observation. Individual interviews were carried out with all members of the group, yielding the individual data we needed on each individual. A series of group sessions was held in which the speech of each member (picked up from a lavaliere microphone) was recorded on a separate track. There was no obvious constraint in these group sessions; the adolescents behaved much as usual, and most of the interaction—physical and verbal—took place between the members. As a result, the effect of systematic observation was reduced to a minimum. This is at present the only quantitative study of a self-selected, naturally formed peer group in the literature. It is hoped that other such studies will be carried out in the near future.

## Rapid and Anonymous Interviews

In the methods just described, the identity and demographic position of each subject is well known. One can also carry out systematic observation anonymously, in conversations which are not defined as interviews. In certain strategic locations, a great many subjects can be studied in a short period of time, and if their social identity is well defined by the objective situation, the findings can be very rich. The department-store survey (Ch. 2) has provided a model for such rapid and anonymous work and a number of similar projects have confirmed the reliability and practicality of this approach (for details and other possibilities see Ch. 2).

---

18. One of the most interesting aspects of this question is that it involves a yes-no answer, which we normally avoid. The mechanism seems to be that the informant is willing to commit himself to the fact of having been in such a situation, though he may be unwilling to volunteer an account. But having so committed himself, he finds it very difficult to avoid giving a full account when the interviewer asks, after some delay, "What happened?" Otherwise, he would appear to have made a false claim.

## Unsystematic Observations

The crucial question to be asked in any of these studies is whether one has indeed obtained data on the fundamental, systematic vernacular form of the language. Unsystematic and candid observation in speech at various strategic points can tell us a great deal about our success in this regard. One can record a number of constant and variable features from large numbers of people in public places such as trains, buses, lunch counters, ticket lines, zoos—wherever enough members of the speech community are gathered together so that their speech is naturally and easily heard by others. There are many biases built into such observations—loud and less educated talkers, for example, are strongly selected. But as a corrective to the bias of the interview situation, such data can be very valuable.

## Mass Media

It is also possible to obtain some systematic data from radio and television broadcasts, although here the selection and the stylistic constraints are usually very strong. In recent years, we have had a great many direct interviews at the scene of disasters, where the speakers are too strongly under the immediate influence of the event to monitor their own speech. Conversation programs and speeches at public events can give us a good cross-section of a population, but here the style is even more formal than that we would obtain in a face-to-face interview.

## The Formal End of the Stylistic Range

It is relatively easy to extend the range of styles used by the speaker towards the formal end of the spectrum, where more attention is given to speech. There are many questions which naturally evoke more careful speech (such as questions about speech itself). In most of the urban studies carried out so far, reading texts were used to study phonological variations. In general, linguistic variables show a marked shift from the most formal elicitation to the least formal reading. Traditional texts such as "Grip the Rat" are relatively artificial, designed to include as many dialect-sensitive words as possible. A text that reads well, focusing on vernacular or adolescent themes, will yield much less formal speech than these or lists of isolated words. Minimal pairs can then be embedded in such a text so that the speaker is not aware of the contrast (Ch. 3). The work of Shuy, Wolfram, and Riley (1967), Wolfram (1969), and Trudgill

(1971) utilized such texts, although the construction of special readings for particular variables has not been advanced as sharply as
the work deserves.

Levine and Crockett (1966) and Anshen (1969) used another method
to extend the stylistic range of readings. Sentences were constructed
in which the variables were embedded, and at other points in the
same sentences blanks were inserted for the subject to fill in lexical
items as he read, diverting his attention from the variables. The
pronunciation of the phonological variable (r) in this context showed
less (r-1) than in the reading of isolated words.

A number of formal tests do not require any reading on the part
of the subjects. *Perception tests* of the ABX form provide useful
information: in the case of total merger of a phonological distinction,
speakers cannot hear whether X is closer to A or B; but where
variable rules are operating, and the merger is not complete, they
will show partial success. A surprising amount of grammatical information can be obtained by *repetition tests* with older subjects.
Psycholinguists have long used such repetition tests with children
2 to 5 years old, but we found to our surprise that with speakers
of nonstandard dialects the underlying grammatical rules of much
older subjects, 10 to 17 years old, controlled the form of their repeti-
tions. Speakers of the Black English Vernacular had no difficulty in
repeating accurately long sentences within their own grammatical
system, but many sentences in standard English were given back
instantly in vernacular form (Labov et al.: 1968, 3.9).[19]

A number of formal tests have been developed to isolate social
attitudes towards language, and the social information carried by
dialect forms. One can play *family background* tests—taped sections
of "typical" speakers—and ask subjects to identify their ethnic
background, race, social class (Labov et al. 1968: 4.4; Brown 1969).
This tells us whether or not the listeners can obtain this social
information from speech, but not where the information is located—
in the speaker's grammar, phonology, intonation, or voice qualifiers.
*Subjective reaction tests* allow us to separate the linguistic variables
from personal factors. The "matched guise" technique used by
Lambert and his students (Lambert 1967) presents for the subject a

---

19. These observations have since been confirmed by larger-scale tests carried out
with school populations, where the subjects' relation to the vernacular was not as well
known (Baratz 1968; Garvey and McFarlane 1968).

series of tape-recorded sections in which voices of the same speakers are heard using different languages or dialects. The subjects are asked to make judgments of the speakers' personalities. As long as they cannot know how they have rated the same speakers before, they unconsciously translate their social attitudes towards language into differential judgments of the speaker's honesty, reliability, intelligence, etc. In our own subjective reaction tests (Ch. 6) the same speakers are heard reading sentences which differ principally by their treatment of the linguistic variable being studied. The subjects' evaluation of the social significance of this variable is registered by their differential responses to the matched sentences, on such scales as "What is the highest job the speaker could hold, talking as he does?" or "If the speaker was in a street fight, how likely would he be to come out on top?"

Speakers' attitudes towards well-established linguistic variables will also be shown in *self-evaluation tests.* When asked which of several forms are characteristic of their own speech, their answers reflect the form which they believe has prestige or is "correct," rather than the form they actually use. Here again, this kind of test data cannot be interpreted without data on the subjects' actual speech patterns. (See Labov 1966a, Ch. 12; Trudgill 1971.)

We can investigate speakers' awareness of stigmatized well-marked social variants by *classroom correction tests,* asking them to correct sentences which depart from school or classroom models (Labov et al. 1968:4.4). But it is almost impossible to obtain interpretable results on the reverse type of *vernacular correction tests,* in which the subject is asked to correct standard prestige forms to the nonstandard vernacular. The influence of the formal test situation is such that the subject cannot perceive accurately the nonstandard rules. There is some evidence that the audio-monitoring norm which governed production of the nonstandard form in childhood is replaced by the prestige norm, so that it is not possible in general for most speakers to direct their attention accurately to nonstandard rules. This result reflects an important axiom of *vernacular shifting: whenever a subordinate dialect is in contact with a superordinate dialect, answers given in any formal test situation will shift from the subordinate towards the superordinate in an irregular and unsystematic manner.* The terms "superordinate" and "subordinate" here refer to any hierarchical social dimension equivalent to "prestige" and "stigmatized." Some linguists hope that by "educating" the informant in the goals of the analysis, it will be possible to diminish this effect, and gradually obtain answers characteristic of the pure vernacular. But this is an illusion. Instead, the subject may use his knowledge of the prestige dialect to avoid giving any vernacular form which is identical or similar to the standard, and so produce stereotyped forms which are simply a collection of the "most different" or "worst" sentence types. Speakers who have had extensive contact with the superordinate form no longer have clear intuitions about their vernacular available for inspection.[20]

There is further reason to regard as suspect data on a nonstandard vernacular gathered from an "educated" informant. Usually the investigator speaks the standard superordinate dialect which is dominant in this face-to-face interviewing situation. The informant's capacity to learn languages is operating at all times, and there is evidence that his grammatical rules will be heavily influenced by the standard during this period of elicitation.[21]

Once in a great while we encounter an informant who seems almost immune to "correction" of this sort—who seems to have direct access to his intuitions, despite his knowledge of the standard dialect. An important task for psycholinguists is to identify other traits which accompany or determine this behavior, so that we will be able to search a given population for "ideal" informants. But it will always be necessary to calibrate the informant's responses against other data of the vernacular to see if he does indeed have access to his original rules. To evaluate this data, we must already know the rules of the vernacular from the direct observation of casual speech. But the procedure is not entirely circular; for if we have confidence in the introspections of "immune" informants, we may obtain crucial data on forms which are too rare to find in any body of casual speech. Whether or not we are safe in extrapolating from observed stability on common forms to unobserved stability on rare forms is an open question.

These considerations do not necessarily apply to linguists studying

20. This is obviously true in the case of children. One cannot ask young children whether a nonstandard sentence of theirs is well-formed, nor ask adults to reconstruct their childhood grammars. It is true in general that learning one series of rules closely related to the older series makes it impossible to reconstruct the earlier situation.

21. Our own field worker in south-central Harlem, John Lewis, showed a strong shift of the nonstandard variables we were investigating from the time that he was first interviewed (1965) to the time that he finished interviewing others (1967).

languages through an intermediate language which is not marked socially with regard to their object language.[22] It is normal for a linguist who approaches a language for the first time to work with bilingual informants, who may not even be good speakers of the object language. Such preliminary steps in formal elicitation are of course necessary prerequisites to the accurate study of language in its social context. Good linguists can go further than this, and draw their best data from recordings of native speakers talking to each other—parallel to the group sessions mentioned above. The study of language in its social context can only be done when the language is "known" in the sense that the investigator can understand rapid conversation. When an anthropological linguist enters into this more advanced study, then the axiom of vernacular shifting will apply, for there will inevitably be stylistic levels which he will want to distinguish.

Although one can achieve a certain amount of insight working with bilingual informants, it is doubtful if as much can be said for "bi-dialectal" informants, if indeed such speakers exist. We have not encountered any nonstandard speakers who gained good control of a standard language, and still retained control of the nonstandard vernacular. Dialect differences depend upon low-level rules which appear as minor adjustments and extensions of contextual condi-tions, etc. It appears that such conditions inevitably interact, and although the speaker may indeed appear to be speaking the vernac-ular, close examination of his speech shows that his grammar has been heavily influenced by the standard. He may succeed in con-vincing his listeners that he is speaking the vernacular, but this impression seems to depend upon a number of unsystematic and heavily marked signals.[23]

There are speakers in every community who are more aware than others of the prestige standard of speech, and whose behavior is more influenced by exterior standards of excellence. They will show

22. In his first approach to Lahu, a Lolo-Burmese language of Thailand and Burma, J. Matisoff used an English-Lahu bilingual speaker. It is his opinion that if he had used a more closely related language such as Thai, the distortion of the data would have been much greater.

23. The ways in which such speakers convince their listeners that they are speaking the vernacular is an important problem for sociolinguistic study. Educated leaders of the black community in the United States provide many examples of this phe-nomenon.

greater style shifting than those who do not recognize such a stand-ard. This trait can be measured by *linguistic insecurity tests*. For a selected list of socially marked variants, the subject is asked which of two forms is correct; and then which he actually uses himself. The total number of items where the two responses differ forms a sensitive index of linguistic insecurity (Chs. 4 and 5).

## 2. Resolving Problems of Linguistic Structure

This section will present three distinct problems of linguistic structure which have arisen in the study of the black English ver-nacular (BEV): problems concerning the internal rules and the un-derlying elements upon which the rules operate. Within the abstract study of linguistic possibilities, these problems are only partly de-cidable. Data from the study of speech in its social context, obtained by the methods outlined above, will be used to provide what seems to us decisive solutions for each of these problems.

Each of these solutions is reinforced by the convergence of data drawn from many sources. Within our own studies, we have parallel data for six different adolescent BEV peer groups, several adult populations, and many exploratory samples in other cities. On each of these problems, independent confirmation is provided by the work of Wolfram in Detroit (1969) with a completely different population and different analysts. The regular convergence of data drawn from completely different studies provides the kind of strong evidence that leads us to assert that these are correct solutions.

### 1. *Consonant Cluster Simplification and the Past Tense Suffix*

As noted above, BEV shows a marked pattern of consonant cluster simplification at the ends of words. Words which show in standard English [SE] consonant clusters ending in -*t,d*, frequently appear in BEV with only the first consonant. Thus *bold, find,* and *fist* are frequently pronounced *bol', fin' and fis'*. The question arises, is this indeed a case of cluster simplification, or are these final consonants simply absent in BEV? The existence of plurals such as *lisses* for *lists* suggests that some such words have the underlying forms with-out *t*. We can put this question sharply only after a series of prelimi-nary investigations which enable us to define the variable as we have done here. The argument presented here outlines the solution given in detail in Labov et al. 1968:3.2. Given a proper definition of the variable, any small body of speech from any BEV group or individual will provide the following evidence:

a. There are no speakers who never have these clusters: nor are there any who always preserve them: it is a case of inherent variation in BEV.
b. For every speaker and every group, the second consonant is absent more often when the following word begins with a consonant than when it begins with a vowel. This regular effect of a following vowel is a characteristic feature of other phonological rules: it also constrains the vocalization of final *r*, *l* or nasals in many dialects.
c. There is little or no hypercorrection: that is, final *-t* or *-d* are not supplied for the wrong word class, giving us *mold* for *mole* or *lipt* for *lip*.

These facts show that the full cluster is present in the underlying form of *act*, *bold*, or *find*, and that a variable rule deletes the second consonant. In our formal representation of this process, fact *c* can easily be shown by supplying the correct underlying forms in the dictionary. Fact *a* can be shown by making the deletion rule optional. But in conventional generative terms, there is no way to show formally fact *b*. If we wrote:

$$15_{\text{opt}} \qquad [-\text{cont}] \rightarrow \emptyset \; / \; [+\text{cons}] \underline{\quad\quad} \# \# \; [-\text{syl}]$$

we would be stating that a stop is optionally deleted after a consonantal segment (liquid or obstruent), at the end of a word, if the next word does not begin with a vowel.[24]

This rule provides a reasonable description of the colloquial system of many middle-class speakers, who often say *firs' thing* and *las' month*, but not *firs' of all* or *las' October*. But 15 is not at all adequate for most other dialects where some clusters are simplified a good proportion of the time when the next word begins with a

---

24. Wolfram argues that only those clusters which show homogeneous voicing should be included in the rule, thus excluding *jump*, *belt*, *bent*, etc. Certainly the first has to be excluded, but we do so by restricting the rule to apical stops *t,d*. Clusters *-sp* and *-sk* are affected by a preceding rule, along with *-st* which operates at a much higher frequency and with special constraints such as the fact that *-sps* and *-sts* are categorically simplified in many dialects. But we find that there is a high percentage of simplification of *-lt*, *-nt*, etc., in many dialects, so that if the rule is restricted to homogeneous voicing, a special rule will have to be written for these types.

vowel. For these dialects we would have to remove [−syl] from the environment:

16 opt                       $[-\text{cont}] \rightarrow \emptyset \,/\, [+\text{cons}] \,\underline{\qquad}\, \# \#$

This rule states that any final -*t,d* cluster can be simplified and that it makes no difference whether or not a vowel follows. But this is so patently false to the facts of the situation that it offers a very poor description of the language. For all speakers of English, rule 16 operates *more* often when the next word does not begin with a vowel. The existence of such phonological conditioning, as we noted above, is the most important indication of the speaker's knowledge of the underlying forms. If we are to represent these facts fairly we must somehow capture in our formal representation the existence of *variable* phonological conditioning.

The first step in developing such a formal notation is to generalize the notion of optional rule to that of a *variable rule*. We do so by assigning to every rule a quantity $\varphi$ representing the proportion of cases in which the rule applies out of all those cases in which it might do so. For a categorical, invariant rule, $\varphi = 1$, and in a variable rule, $0 < \varphi < 1$. Such a variable output is indicated by angled brackets around the element to the left of the arrow. If $\varphi$ is affected by the presence or absence of some feature in the environment, that element acts as a *variable constraint* and is placed in angled brackets in the environment to the right of the slash. Thus a following obstruent or pause in BEV favors the operation of *t,d* deletion, and constrains what would otherwise be free variation.

17                       $[-\text{cont}] \rightarrow \langle \emptyset \rangle \,/\, [+\text{cons}] \,\underline{\qquad}\, \# \# \, \langle -\text{syl} \rangle$

Informally, 17 states that a stop is variably deleted after a consonantal segment at the end of a word, more often if a vowel does not follow than if a vowel does follow.

This form of the rule is quite satisfactory for many nonstandard dialects, whose speakers do occasionally say *firs' of all*. But it applies only to clusters of the form __CC without a morpheme boundary between the two consonants; if does not apply to clusters in *passed* [pæst] or *rolled* [rold] of the abstract form __C#C where the second consonant represents the past tense. In most nonstandard dialects, such clusters are occasionally deleted—in the southern United States more often than in the North, and especially in BEV. We might allow this by inserting the boundary optionally in our rule:

18                $[-\text{cont}] \rightarrow \langle \emptyset \rangle / [+\text{cons}] (\#) \underline{\phantom{xx}} \# \# \langle -\text{syl} \rangle$

This is an odd rule, for if a consonant after $\#$ is deleted, then the entire signal of the past tense disappears for regular verbs.[25] The question arises whether the boundary $\#$ is indeed present in BEV: do speakers "know" in any linguistic sense that the [-st] cluster in *passed* represents the past tense? Grammatical searching of our group sessions, individual interviews, shows that for every individual and for every group, the following facts hold:

a. There are no speakers who always delete the *-ed* in these clusters, and no speakers who never do.
b. There is phonological conditioning for these clusters as well: a following vowel has a strong effect in preserving them.
c. In each phonological environment, past tense clusters are deleted less often than monomorphemic clusters.
d. There is no hypercorrection: the *-ed* ending is not supplied wrongly where the present tense would be expected.

For any samples of speech of even moderate length, we then find the relations holding that are expressed in Fig. 8.2.

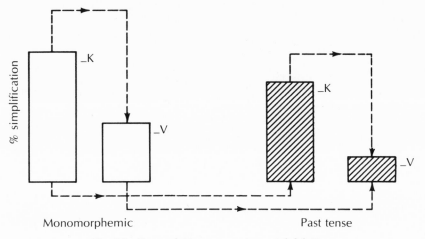

Fig. 8.2.   Four relations governing $-t,d$ deletion.

25. Whenever the consonant deleted represents a whole morpheme, then the effect of a following vowel will not allow native speakers to reconstruct the underlying form. For even if the [t] is preserved in *I passed Edith*, this does not tell us anything about whether the *-ed* signal is present in *I passed Mike*. For monomorphemic clusters in *fist*, etc., such an alternation does tell us what the underlying form of the word is.

If we divide -*t,d* clusters into these four classes, we find in every case that past tense clusters are simplified less often, and clusters before vowels less often than other clusters. These relations are remarkably uniform: they hold for every individual and every group. The constraints upon the rule then appear as

19          $[-\text{cont}] \rightarrow \langle \emptyset \rangle \, / \, [+\text{cons}] \, \langle \emptyset \rangle \underline{\quad\quad} \# \# \, \langle -\text{syl} \rangle$

Here it is the *absence* of a boundary which favors the rule. We can restate 19 informally by saying that a stop is variably deleted after a consonantal segment at the end of a word, more often if it is not a separate inflectional morpheme, and more often if it is not followed by a vowel.

The rule 19 with two variable constraints will now apply generally to a wide variety of dialects. Wherever variability exists, these constraints are binding on all speakers of English. For a particular dialect, such as BEV, we may want to establish more specific relations of order among the constraints, and weight one more heavily than the other. We can do so by the use of Greek letters to the upper left of the first angled bracket which indicates the relations of more or less. Thus 20 indicates that the phonological constraint is weighted more heavily than the grammatical constraint:

20          $[-\text{cont}] \rightarrow \langle \emptyset \rangle \, / \, [+\text{cons}] \, ^{\beta}\langle \emptyset \rangle \underline{\quad\quad} \# \# \, ^{\alpha}\langle -\text{syl} \rangle$

This representation corresponds to Fig. 8.2, where the major effect is the grammatical constraint. This is the situation for BEV among the adolescent peer groups we have studied. But as the speaker gets older, or as he talks more formally, the grammatical environment has a stronger effect, until the positions of $\alpha$ and $\beta$ are reversed. This alternation in the ordering of constraints upon rules represents one of the elementary forms of linguistic change, genetically or diachronically. It is one of the most important motivations for incorporating variable constraints into our representation of rules, for otherwise we have no formal way of registering this fundamental aspect of language development.

The existence of variation does not itself tell us that the variable element is actually present in our underlying grammar. For example, third singular -*s* also appears variably in BEV clusters, as in *He works* vs. *He work*. But in contrast with the -*t,d* situation, our grammatical searching establishes the following facts:

a. There are some speakers who show no third singular -s at all even in careful speech, and other individuals vary widely in the amount of -s they use.
b. There is no general phonological process operating on clusters ending in -s or -z, for the plural is almost completely intact in BEV.
c. A following vowel does not act to preserve third singular -s. If anything, this -s is present *less* often when a vowel follows.
d. There is a great deal of hypercorrection: the -s appears unpredictably in other persons and numbers (*We works there*) or even in nonfinite positions (*He can gets hurt*).

Evidence from formal tests confirms in many ways the analysis given here. Repetition tests, perception tests, and comprehension tests all show that the -ed suffix is easily supplied by BEV speakers of all ages, like the plural -s suffix, but that third-singular -s is very difficult for them to perceive, produce reliably, or comprehend.[26]

The independent investigation of Wolfram in Detroit provides precisely the same set of facts. Table 8.3 shows the percentages of -t,d clusters simplified in the four environments for three adult social classes and four peer groups in New York City, and four social classes in the Detroit study.[27] Here we see that for every group, the relations given in Fig. 8.2 hold. Column 1 is greater than column 2, and column 3 is greater than column 4, showing the effects of a following vowel. Column 1 is greater than column 3, and column 2 is greater than column 4, showing the effect of the past tense boundary. As with all the other sociolinguistic data to be presented here, it is obvious to the sophisticated statistician that tests of significance are irrelevant. The original data are given in a form such that statistical analysis can be carried out if desired, but it is plain that even if a

26. Recent work of Jane Torrey with younger children in south-central Harlem shows that the third singular -s can be used as a signal of the present tense, but not to distinguish singular from plural, as in *The cat splashes* vs. *The cats splash* (1972).

27. This data is given for the individual interviews in New York City and in Detroit. The relations of Fig. 8.2 are preserved in the group sessions in New York, with the grammatical constraint operating at a lower level. The Detroit figures are not exactly comparable to the New York City figures for two reasons: (1) the Detroit interviews do not distinguish casual and careful speech for any age group, while in New York the adult interviews show casual and careful styles distinct [Table 8.3 giving the latter values]; (2) final positions are included in the —K environment in the New York City studies but in —V (that is, nonconsonantal) for Detroit.

TABLE 8.3.
CONSTRAINTS ON $-t, d$
DELETION IN THE BLACK SPEECH COMMUNITY

| | % simplified | | | |
| --- | --- | --- | --- | --- |
| | Clusters in single morphemes | | Past tense clusters | |
| Speech community | ___K | ___V | ___K | ___V |
| New York City | | | | |
| Adults | | | | |
|   Middle class | 60% | 28% | 19% | 04% |
|   Upper working class | 90 | 40 | 19 | 09 |
|   Lower working class | 89 | 40 | 47 | 32 |
| Adolescents | | | | |
|   Thunderbirds (10–13) | 91 | 59 | 74 | 24 |
|   Aces (10–13) | 98 | 64 | 85 | 43 |
|   Cobras (12–17) | 97 | 76 | 73 | 15 |
|   Jets (12–17) | 90 | 49 | 44 | 09 |
| Detroit | | | | |
|   Upper middle class | 79 | 23 | 49 | 07 |
|   Lower middle class | 87 | 43 | 62 | 13 |
|   Upper working class | 94 | 65 | 73 | 24 |
|   Lower working class | 97 | 72 | 76 | 34 |

Source: Labov et al. 1968: Table 3.9, and Wolfram 1969: Figs. 7 and 9.

particular case were below the level of significance, the convergence of so many independent events carries us to a level of confidence which is unknown in most social or psychological research.

The confirmation of the New York study by the Detroit study of -t,d deletion leaves no doubt as to the existence of the underlying -ed form in BEV, and the nature of the rule which is operating. The contrast between -ed and third singular -s is also delineated clearly in the Detroit data (Wolfram 1969:161 ff.). Since Wolfram's data do not include group sessions or casual speech, we do not find the lowest levels of third singular -s, as noted under a above. But we do find b, the absence of any general phonological process affecting -s,z: not only are other inflections preserved, but the third singular -s is absent just as often after verbs ending in vowels as verbs ending in consonants. Again, c, there is no clear effect of a following vowel in preserving the -s: on the contrary, it is present in 38 percent of the cases before a consonant, and only 33 percent before a vowel.

Finally, *d*, Wolfram notes frequent but irregular hypercorrection, with the -*s* appearing in other persons and in nonfinite positions. These examples give only some indication of the precision and detail of the convergence between the New York and Detroit studies, which allows us to write both variable and categorical rules with confidence.

## Is Variation Inherent in the System?

Before proceeding, we must take into account the possibility that we have not really succeeded in isolating the basic vernacular. Even the wild and uncontrolled group sessions with adolescents may show the effect of observation, which may be responsible for some unsimplified clusters. Or perhaps children at the age of 10 have already begun to show dialect mixture with standard English in their most casual speech, and to find the pure vernacular we must look to even younger children. Two findings make this possibility seem quite unlikely. First, our work with younger children does not show us any greater homogeneity in their speech.[28] Secondly, we have already noted that the systematic character of -*t,d* deletion makes it most probable that these final consonants are present in the underlying representation. But there is a more important theoretical reason why we posit the variable rule 20 as the most accurate characterization of the basic vernacular. If the underlying rule in some "pure" system was a categorical rule which went to completion, eliminating all final -*t,d* clusters, then it would eliminate itself. There would be no basis for positing the form *bold* in the dictionary of this dialect; instead children would infer that the word was *bole* and the rule would have nothing to operate on; the same would be said for *rolled*. A categorical rule would eliminate the regular past tense inflection.[29]

It is important to note that in the course of language evolution, change does go to completion, and variable rules have become invariant. When this happens, there is inevitably some other structural change to compensate for the loss of information involved. I

28. Work done with children 4 to 7 years old by Jane Torrey in south-central Harlem shows the same patterns of variation in the -*ed* suffix and -*t, d* clusters as with older children, and similar patterns with the copula and negative concord to be discussed below.

29. This would be the case even if the categorical rule was context-restricted so that it did not operate before vowels. As noted in fn. 25 above, there is no way to reconstruct the underlying form if the morpheme disappears entirely in most positions.

would like to cite three examples of such dramatic structural change
to support this claim.

a. In a number of English-based Creoles, phonological and grammatical simplification has effectively reduced clusters so that final
inflections are typically eliminated altogether. Whereas BEV
preserves the past tense accurately with irregular verbs such as
*give—gave, keep—kep', tell—tol'*, and the *-ed* ending in *rolled*
remains embedded in a variable rule, Trinidad English and Jamaican Creole use the invariant simple forms *roll, give, keep, tell*
for the simple past. How is the past then distinguished from the
present? In Trinidad, the auxiliary *do* is used, so that now the
present tense becomes the marked form, *He does give* as opposed
to the past *He give* (Solomon 1966).
b. In the English dialects of Scotland, the simplification of *-t,d*
clusters after voiceless stops has become categorical, giving a
uniform *ac'* for *act*, and *ap'* for *apt*. The same rule would have
eliminated the past tense in *liked* and *stopped*. But a generalized
rule of epenthesis preserves these past tense morphemes so that
they do not form clusters, and we have [laɪkɪt] and [stapɪt] for
*liked* and *stopped* (Grant and Dixon 1921).
c. In the evolution of the French language, a sound change moving
down from the north eliminated final *-p, -t, -k* and *-s*. When final
*-s* was lost for most dialects the normal way of distinguishing
singular from plural in articles, adjectives, and nouns was lost
as well. Thus the singular article *la* could no longer be opposed
to the plural article *las*, except when a vowel followed. In most
cases, radical changes in the plural forms preserved the singular-
plural distinction. The *Atlas Linguistique de France* shows that
in one area of south-central France, near the southern limit for
the loss of final *-s*, another sound change was taking place: unstressed *a* was changing to *o*. Normally, this change took place
in both singular and plural forms. But in a sizeable subregion to
the northward, where *-s* was lost, this sound change was differentiated so that *a* changed to *o* only in the singular, opposing *lo*
(singular) to *la* (plural).

This recent finding of Penelope Eckert (1969) is of the greatest
importance in showing how grammatical functions can directly
modify a sound change for communicative needs. It is also relevant
for our discussion here that this compensating differentiation of the

$a \rightarrow o$ change only took place where the loss of -s had become a uniform and categorical rule. In the area of "-s disturbance," there is no compensating effect on the $a \rightarrow o$ rule. This implies that if a variable rule is regular enough, it provides language learners with enough information to preserve the basic distinctions and the underlying forms.

If a sociolinguistic study of -s were carried out in that area, we would no doubt have found a variable rule similar to 20. The deletion of final -s in France was not recorded in any detail by the dialect geographers. But a similar variable rule in Puerto Rican Spanish has been studied by Roxana Ma and Eleanor Herasimchuk (Fishman et al. 1968: 689–703). They found regular patterns of variable constraints similar to those just given for -t,d deletion: (1) a complex pattern of grammatical constraints—the plural -s on articles is retained most often, verbal -s next, and plural -s on nouns the least; (2) a phonological constraint in which deletion occurs less often before a following vowel than a following consonant; (3) a regular pattern of style shifting where increased formality disfavors the operation of the rule. There is an intermediate form [h] which complicates the rule, but the form of the Puerto Rican s $\rightarrow$ h $\rightarrow$ $\phi$ rule is probably quite similar to the French s $\rightarrow$ $\phi$.

We conclude that variation such as is shown in the deletion of -t,d clusters is not the product of irregular dialect mixture, but an inherent and regular property of the system. The status of variable rules in a grammar may be questioned on another ground: they involve a fundamental asymmetry between production and perception. We can argue that the speaker displays his knowledge of the past tense suffix by simplifying fewer -ed clusters than others (and presumably preserving -ed more often when it carries a heavy semantic load). But all that the listener has to know is whether or not the -ed is optional, since he interprets each past signal as it comes. (There is evidence that listeners can and do react to frequency, but it would be difficult to connect this capacity with the grammatical function of the 'past'; such reactions have to do with overall characterization of the speaker.) In any case, it is clear that variable rules are rules of *production*. The issue is whether or not the symmetry of production and perception is a well-founded assumption about linguistic structure, or even an attainable goal of theory construction. As attractive as this might seem, there is now solid evidence that it is an invalid assumption. In repetition tests with BEV speakers

14 to 17 years old, we find that sentences such as *I asked him if he did it* are repeated instantly as *I axed him did he do it.* The meaning of the sentence is grasped perfectly, but it is produced automatically by BEV rules—there is evidently a deep asymmetry between perception (SE and/or BEV) and production (BEV only).

Finally, one may set aside variable rules on the ground that they are rules of performance. The less said about this "wastebasket" use of the performance concept the better. For it must be noted that the great majority of our transformational and phonological rules may also be characterized as "performance" rules. Extraposition, *wh*-attraction, adverbial postposing, etc., are all means of facilitating the linearization of the phrase structure input, eliminating discontinuities and left-hand embedding, coordinating and assimilating elements to one another so as to make the "performance" of the sentence that much easier.

The ability of human beings to accept, preserve, and interpret rules with variable constraints is clearly an important aspect of their linguistic competence or *langue.* But no one is aware of this competence, and there are no intuitive judgments accessible to reveal it to us. Instead, naive perception of our own and others' behavior is usually categorical,[30] and only careful study of language in use will demonstrate the existence of this capacity to operate with variable rules.

## 2. The Deletion of the Copula in BEV

We now turn to a much more complex problem, concerning the variable appearance of the present copula and auxiliary *is* in BEV. We frequently hear in this dialect such sentences as *He wild,* and

---

30. Given a continuous range of frequency in the application of a rule, such as "dropping the g" in -*ing,* we observe listeners reacting in a discrete way. Up to a certain point they do not perceive the speaker "dropping his g's" at all; beyond a certain point, they perceive him as always doing so. This is equally true with the (th) and (dh) rules discussed below, and any other well-developed linguistic variable. The same categorical judgments appear in the perception of others' eating habits ("She eats like a bird; he never knows when to stop") or housekeeping ("She cleans night and day; the dust could be that thick . . ."). Whenever there are strong social values associated with standards of role performance, we tend to get such categorical perception. But note that even this sharp alteration of judgments requires the observer to be (unconsciously) sensitive to frequency. We can speculate that each occurrence of the marked form sets up an unconscious expectation, which becomes overt if reinforced within a given period of time, but is otherwise extinguished without effect.

*She out the game,* and *He gon' try to get up* corresponding to SE
*He is wild, She is out of the game,* and *He is going to try to get up.*
These copula-less sentences are similar to those of many languages
like Russian, Hebrew, or Hungarian, which have no present copula;
to Jamaican English or Creole which has the copula only before noun
phrases (and locatives) or to the speech of young children who say
*That a lamb,* and *Mommy busy.* The question arises whether or not
a copula is present in the deep structure or higher-level structure
of BEV; and if so, whether it is then deleted as a whole on the
morphological level or by lower-level phonological rules. These are
important questions for both theoretical and applied linguistics, for
they bear on the issue of how dialects of a language differ, and how
they are to be taught. The brief outline of the argument as presented
here is abstracted from a detailed presentation in Labov 1972a: Ch.
3 and Labov et al. 1968:3.4.

a. We first find that there are no speakers of BEV who always delete
the copula, and none who never do. so. Everyone shows some full
forms, some contracted forms, and some zero forms. The regularity of this behavior, and the pattern of the variable constraints
discussed below, show that we are dealing with a variable rule
within the BEV system.
b. There are syntactic positions where deletion never takes place:
in elliptical forms (*He is too*), after wh-attraction (*That's what
he is*). In general, we find that wherever standard English can
contract, BEV can delete the copula, and wherever SE cannot
contract, BEV cannot delete.
c. This connection between contraction and deletion makes it necessary to explore the general conditions for English contraction,
analyzing the evidence of our own intuitions within the generative
model. We find that contraction of *am, is, are, will, has, have,
had* is the removal of a lone initial schwa before a single consonant in a word which contains the tense marker. This process,
which yields *He's here, I'm coming, You're there, I'll go, He's got
it,* etc., is dependent upon rules which delete initial glides, and
upon the vowel reduction rule which reduces unstressed lax
vowels to schwa. The vowel reduction rule is in turn dependent
upon the stress assignment rules which are determined by the
syntax of the surface structure as developed by Chomsky and
Halle (1968). The rules for contraction fit in with and confirm by

independent evidence Chomsky and Halle's construction of the transformational cycle in English phonology.[31]

d. That deletion of the copula is related to contraction is also indicated by our finding that BEV does not delete forms with tense vowels which cannot be reduced to schwa: *be, ain't, can't* are preserved. That deletion is a phonological process is also shown by the fact that the *m* of *I'm* is rarely deleted: in general, final nasals are not deleted in BEV.

e. The variable rules which control contraction and deletion in BEV show a series of variable constraints according to grammatical environment. The rule is favored if the preceding noun phrase is a pronoun. The following grammatical environment constrains the rules in the order (from least favorable to most) predicate noun phrase; adjectives and locatives; verbs; and the auxiliary *gonna* before a verb. If we take the view that contraction operates first, and deletion removes the lone consonant which remains after contraction, then we see that these constraints operate in the same way on both rules, and contraction in BEV will show a pattern similar to contraction in other English dialects. The fact that there are two separate rules is indicated by the fact that the quantitative effects of these grammatical environments are intensified with deletion: the constraints have applied twice.

f. Although the same grammatical constraints operate upon contraction and deletion in BEV, the phonological effect of a preceding vowel or consonant is reversed. For contraction, the rule is favored if the subject ends in a vowel; for deletion, if it ends in a consonant. This reversal matches the phonological difference between contraction and deletion, for the former is the removal of a vowel and the latter of a consonant, and in each case the favored context leads to a CVC structure.

We thus conclude that the basic form of the contraction and deletion rules for *is* is:

31. An analysis of auxiliary reduction by Zwicky (1970) argues that there are cases of uncontractible *is* or *has* which cannot be accounted for by stress rules. In the critical cases, the *h-* of *has* is said to be deletable and the vowel reduced but not contracted: *Gerda has been to North Dakota as often as Trudi (h)as.* It is possible that these intuitive (and admittedly disputed) data are the product of contrastive stress on the second subject *Trudi.* Dependence on stress would be shown by the unreducibility of *has* in *I don't think anyone should go to North Dakota as often as Trudi has,* where there is no contrastive stress on *Trudi.*

21 Contraction

$$\mathrm{\partial} \rightarrow \langle \emptyset \rangle \,/\, \left\langle \begin{matrix} +\,\mathrm{Pro} \\ -\,\mathrm{cons} \end{matrix} \right\rangle \,\#\#\, \left[ \underline{\phantom{xx}} +\,\mathrm{Tns} \right] \mathrm{z} \,\#\#\, \left\langle \begin{matrix} +\,\mathrm{Vb} \\ +\,\mathrm{Fut} \\ -\,\mathrm{NP} \end{matrix} \right\rangle$$

22 Deletion

$$\mathrm{z} \rightarrow \langle \emptyset \rangle \,/\, \left\langle \begin{matrix} +\,\mathrm{Pro} \\ +\,\mathrm{cons} \end{matrix} \right\rangle \,\#\#\, \underline{\phantom{xxx}} \,\#\#\, \left\langle \begin{matrix} +\,\mathrm{Vb} \\ +\,\mathrm{Fut} \\ -\,\mathrm{NP} \end{matrix} \right\rangle$$

A more general form of the contraction rule shows it operating before zero or one consonant, $\underline{\phantom{x}}C_0^1$; this consonant is then generally eliminated by 22. But here we are dealing specifically with the contraction and deletion of *is*, where the variable constraints are best known. The preceding constraints show that the rule is favored by a pronoun subject (which generally ends in a vowel) or by some other noun phrase ending in a vowel or a glide. This constraint is reversed for deletion, which is favored by $\langle +\mathrm{cons} \rangle$. The following constraints shows that the rule is favored by a following verb, especially if this verb is a future form (*gonna, gon'*); if the next element is not a verb, then the rule is favored if it is not a noun phrase—that is, it is a locative or adjective. The vertical ordering of the variable constraints within the angled brackets reflects their weighting, but there is no relative weighting indicated here between the preceding and following constraints.

The full data to support 21 and 22 are given in Ch. 3 of Labov 1972a. There are some unresolved issues in the contraction rule in regard to the effect of a following noun phrase when a noun phrase precedes; in this situation, some BEV groups seem to differ from others. Otherwise, the constraints are fully independent and are replicated in each of the vernacular groups that we have studied. Table 8.4 shows a small part of the pattern: the effect of the following grammatical environment on the deletion of *is* with pronoun subjects. For each of the three New York peer groups, the frequency of deletion rises regularly across these four environments. Below these are figures derived from Wolfram's studies of black speakers in Detroit: in this case, the most comparable working-class population based on individual interviews with adults as well as adolescents. In general, these Detroit speakers follow rules 21 and 22 in

TABLE 8.4.

THE EFFECT OF FOLLOWING GRAMMATICAL ENVIRONMENT ON DELETION OF
*IS* IN *BEV* WITH PRONOUN SUBJECTS

| *Speech community* | % deletion before | | | |
|---|---|---|---|---|
| | *Noun phrase* | *Adj, Loc* | *Vb* | *gonna* |
| New York City | | | | |
| Thunderbirds | 35% | 51% | 74% | 91% |
| Cobras | 53 | 77 | 80 | 100 |
| Jets | 63 | 72 | 78 | 95 |
| Detroit | | | | |
| Working class | 37 | 46 | 50 | 79 |

Source: Labov et al. 1968:3.4, and Wolfram 1969:211.

their treatment of *is*. Table 8.4 shows that they follow the same pattern for the four grammatical environments as the New York City groups.

The contraction and deletion rules 21 and 22 are not simply summaries of the performance of particular groups. They are general constraints reflecting the linguistic system of BEV speakers in many areas. Not only do the New York and Detroit samples coincide, but we also find the same pattern in Washington, as analysis of conversations by Loman (1967) shows; in San Francisco, as Mitchell-Kernan (1969) shows in her detailed study of two adult speakers; in Los Angeles, as shown in less detail by studies of younger black children (Legum et al. 1971).

We are now in a position to look more closely at the formal character of such variable rules. In so doing, I will be following the formal interpretation developed by Cedergren and Sankoff (1972) accepting their modifications of the original semi-quantitative interpretation of Labov 1969.[32] We must first re-examine the significance of the quantity $\varphi$, which represents the proportion of cases in which a rule applies out of all those cases in which it might apply. In earlier

32. The original model presented in Labov 1969 had two related defects. Since it was additive, a postulate of geometric ordering was necessary to prevent the contributions of individual constraints from totalling more than 1. This type of ordering was not always found, so that there were cases where the two most important constraints had roughly the same effect on the rule. It would then follow that an increase in the effect of one constraint would necessarily involve a decrease in the effect of another, so that they would not be independent in their action.

discussion, $\varphi$ has been used for the output frequency of a rule for a given sample. But such frequencies cannot reasonably be seen as an aspect of the rule itself. Rather $\varphi$ must be seen as the *probability* of the rule applying for any given sample with any given configuration of relevant environments. The hypothesis made explicit in Cedergren and Sankoff's treatment is that each of the variable constraints makes an independent contribution to this probability: this hypothesis is of the greatest importance to linguistic theory, for it provides the first strong justification for the linguist's assembly of individual rules into rule schema.

There is a good empirical basis from the study of linguistic change to see most rules as tending to apply maximally—to be generalized to all environments and to go to completion in a given environment (Labov 1972a, Wang 1969, Chen and Hsieh 1971) and to be reordered to apply to the maximum number of cases (Kiparsky 1968). Within a given environment, it will be normal for $\varphi = 1$; in a variable rule there will be some factor preventing the rule from applying, so that $\varphi = 1 - k_0$. If this limiting factor $k_0 = 1$, then the rule will not apply at all. In the cases we are considering $k_0$ is limited or diminished by a series of factors which favor the rule: an input probability $p_0$, and variable constraints such as those in 21 or 22. The effect of such constraints in limiting $k_0$ may be symbolized as $v_1$, $v_2$, $v_3 \ldots v_n$. Thus the general formula for the probability of a given variable rule applying is

23          $\varphi = 1 - k_0$
24          $k_0 = (1 - p_0)(1 - v_1)(1 - v_2) \ldots (1 - v_n)$.

If a given variable constraint $\langle +\text{fea}_i \rangle$ is not present then $v_i = 0$, and the probability of the rule applying is unaffected. If the feature is present, then the factor $(1 - v_i)$ operates to diminish the limiting factor $k_0$, and so increases the probability of the rule applying in that environment.

This model of Cedergren and Sankoff is founded on the hypothesis that the variable constraints are independent, and contribute the same element $v_i$ to the probability of the rule irrespective of whatever other constraints are present. They have applied this model to establish underlying probabilities for the variable constraints on the contraction of *is* reflected in Table 6 of Labov 1969 (Labov 1972a, Ch. 3), using a slightly different form of the contraction rule from

21.[33] Through the statistical method of maximum likelihood they produced the estimates of 0.27 for the input probability $p_o$ and five other estimates for $v_i$ ranging from 0.13 to 0.90. They are then able to predict the original table with twelve cells (four following and three preceding environments) with only six parameters. The results are quite close: in eight cells, the formula predicts the original numbers of cases in the table: in four cells the prediction differs by one case.

Cedergren and Sankoff have applied their model to the quantitative investigation of a number of other variable rules in Panamanian Spanish and Montreal French. Current work of G. Sankoff, Cedergren, and their associates in Montreal is carrying the investigation of variable rules to a higher level of accountability. By the use of estimates of maximum likelihood it is possible to confirm or reject the hypothesis of independence of variable constraints in any particular instance, and thus provide crucial evidence for the validity of the basic linguistic operation of assembling rule schema.

Given a series of linguistic rules

25
$$\begin{aligned}
&\text{a. } X \rightarrow Y/A \underline{\quad} C \\
&\text{b. } X \rightarrow Y/A \underline{\quad} D \\
&\text{c. } X \rightarrow Y/B \underline{\quad} C \\
&\text{d. } X \rightarrow Y/B \underline{\quad} D \\
&\text{e. } X \rightarrow Y/ \underline{\quad} C \\
&\text{f. } X \rightarrow Y/ \underline{\quad} D
\end{aligned}$$

linguists believe that it is economical and revealing to represent all these possibilities by a single rule schema such as:

26
$$X \rightarrow Y/(\left\{\begin{matrix} A \\ B \end{matrix}\right\}) \underline{\quad} \left\{\begin{matrix} C \\ D \end{matrix}\right\}$$

The general argument of Chomsky and Halle is that the abbreviatory notations of 26 or similar ones which lead to the maximum economy give us substantive information on the formal structures available to the language learner (1968:331). However, arguments based on

33. The Cedergren and Sankoff demonstration took as variable constraints the categories under which the data were tabulated. But in terms of underlying features, several of these overlap. Thus a preceding [+Pro] ends with a vowel, so that it is also [+V] in the same way as [−Pro] noun phrases which end with a vowel like Joe. The independence of these underlying features should follow from the method, if indeed they represent the correct analysis.

simplicity have not always been convincing. In the study of linguistic change in progress we often find rules expanding to yield more complex forms (Cohen 1970), and it is possible for someone to assert that no conclusive proof through relative simplicity has yet been achieved.[34]

The demonstration of Cedergren and Sankoff now provides a crucial link in this argument. If the various subrules assembled in the schema 21 were to be dissolved into individual rules, this would be equivalent to stating that the variable constraints are not independent, and that it is impossible to arrive at estimates of $v_i$ which would predict this data. The very existence of stable contributions to the probability of a rule by variable constraints demonstrates the validity of the rule schema. The hypothesis of the independence of variable constraints is equivalent to the hypothesis that rule schemata are significant. But it is only with quantitative data that we can arrive at convincing demonstrations of this claim.

Beyond the internal evidence and reliability of the contraction and deletion rules, there is other evidence for the validity of our account. Subjects have no difficulty in repeating back the copula in imitation tests (Labov et al. 1968:3.9, Labov 1972a, Ch. 2), and they show very few problems in comprehension tests for this element. In these respects, the copula contrasts sharply with third singular -s, which does not correspond to any element in the grammatical structure of BEV.[35]

So far, we have said nothing about the input probability $p_o$. This section is concerned with problems of internal linguistic structure, but it should be evident from Table 8.3 that the Detroit speakers are

34. See the introduction to Lakoff 1971, where he argues that there has not been any successful explanation in syntax through simplicity or an internal evaluation measure.

35. Torrey's experimental approach to the comprehension of syntax used pictures which illustrated the difference between *past* and *present* or *singular* and *plural*. She tested black second-graders for their ability to use various inflections in speech and in comprehension, before and after a training period. The plural operated at a high level from the beginning, and the copula responded rapidly to practice. But in the case of third singular -s there was a sharp difference between two situations. The second-graders had no difficulty in using -s to distinguish *present* from *past* as in *The man hits the dog* vs. *The man hit the dog*. But they showed no success at all, before or after training, in using -s to distinguish singular from plural as in *The cat splashes* vs. *The cats splash*. We can conclude that they have a rule which states roughly, "Insert -s on present verbs in formal situations." (1972)

operating with a lower $p_o$, which is generally sensitive to such sociolinguistic parameters as age, group memberships, and socio-economic status. These variables operate directly upon $p_o$ in our representation and yield functions which can be isolated from the more stable internal constraints upon linguistic rules. Such socio-linguistic variables are the topic of Sect. 3 below.

## 3. Negative Concord

For the third example of the analysis of linguistic structure in its social context, I will consider the problem which revolves around the sentence:

27          It ain't no cat can't get in no coop.

This was said by Speedy, the leader of the Cobras in one of our group sessions, in a discussion about pigeon coops. Speakers of any other dialect of English besides BEV interpret 27 as meaning 'There is no cat that can't get into any coop.' They are more than a little surprised to discover from the context that Speedy was denying that cats were a problem, and that *his* meaning was 'There isn't any cat that *can* get into any coop.' At first glance, it seems that BEV speakers are behaving in an illogical, contradictory way. If dialects do not differ radically in their deep structure, as suggested above, how can it be that a negative in one is a positive in another?

First, one might ask if Speedy had simply made a mistake. This is not the case, for we have encountered a half dozen other examples of the same construction in our work in the black community. Most convincing is the example from a long epic poem of black folklore: speaking of a whore, the narrator says, *There wasn't a son of a gun who this whore couldn't shun,* meaning that she was so good that 'there wasn't any customer that could shun her'.

We noticed that the examples normally had three features in common: (a) there were two clauses, and a contradictory negative appeared in the second; (b) there was another negative in the first clause, and (c) the first clause also contained an indeterminate adverb such as *ever* or *any* (negative plus *any* = *no*). These three facts lead us to connect the phenomenon with "negative concord," the process by which negatives are attracted to indeterminates. In this investigation, we again found it necessary to develop the argument further in terms of our grammatical intuitions (as native speakers of standard English and of several nonstandard white dialects). We can begin with the generative formulation provided by Klima (1964) of the observation of Jespersen and others that in English the negative is obligatorily attracted to the first indeterminate if it precedes the verb, and optionally to the first indeterminate thereafter. Thus in place of *Anybody doesn't sit there, we have by obligatory rule, Nobody sits there. On the other hand, it is merely an optional (and stylistically somewhat formal) rule which shifts He doesn't sit anywhere to He sits nowhere. If we continued to consider only standard English, we might write a rule which takes the initial negative as a feature of the sentence and distributes it directly to the various positions with the conditions indicated. But study of a variety of English dialects leads us to the conclusion that the negative attraction rule which incorporates the negative with the first indeterminate is of a very different character from the others. It seems there are three distinct rules, all operating *after* the negative is placed in its normal preverbal position, which we can sketch in broad outline here. The first rule is the categorical one of negative attraction:

28 NEGATTRAC (obligatory for all dialects)
Indet—X-Neg
$$1 \quad 2 \quad 3 \; \rightarrow 3 + 1 \quad 2$$

Not only is this rule obligatory for all dialects, but sentences where it has not applied, such as *Anybody doesn't sit there are un-English in a very striking way; in repetition tests (Labov et al. 1968:3.9) sentences like this provoke only confusion and no one can repeat them. There are conditions which suspend the obligatory force of this rule, such as a preceding hypothetical or negative; an exact statement requires an extended discussion (see Labov 1972a, Ch. 4). But the detailed investigation of NEGATTRAC leads us to the conclusion that this rule reflects a cognitive requirement for the organization of the features of the indeterminates in relation to the negative. The general condition is that universal quantifiers may not precede a simplex negative predicate if they contain the features [+DISTRIBUTIVE] as with each and absolutely not if they also contain [−FACT] as with any.

The next two rules are of a different character:

29 Negative Postposing (optional; Standard Literary English only)

$$\text{Neg} - X - \text{Indef}$$
$$1 \quad 2 \quad 3 \; \rightarrow 2 \quad 1 + 3$$

30 NEGCONCORD (optional; for nonstandard dialects only)

$$\text{Neg} - \text{X} - \text{Indef}$$
$$1 \quad 2 \quad 3 \quad \rightarrow 1 \quad 2 \quad 1+3$$

These two rules are complementary and perform the same emphatic function. Instead of *He doesn't sit anywhere,* the first rule gives us *He sits nowhere,* and the second pleonastic rule yields *He don't sit nowhere.* Rule 30 applies without regard to clause boundaries: thus we can have *He don't like nobody that went to no prep school* = SE *He doesn't like anybody that went to any prep school.* There are also some nonstandard white dialects [WNS$_2$] which can transfer the negative back to preverbal position, so that we have *\*Anybody doesn't sit there → Nobody sits there → Nobody don't sit there.* BEV shares this property.

Careful grammatical searching of our interviews and group sessions now shows us that BEV differs surprisingly in one other way from other dialects. Rule 30 is not variable, but obligatory for BEV within the same clause. For core members of the BEV peer groups, we find that negative concord operates not at a 95 or 98 percent level, but at 100 percent, in 42 out of 42 cases, 63 out of 63, etc., whereas our corresponding white groups show inherent variation. This means that the emphatic function of negative concord is entirely lost for BEV: if the rule is obligatory, it has no stylistic or contrastive significance. This emphatic function is supplied by BEV through several extensions of the negative rules not used by Northern dialects, such as *negative inversion: Nobody can do it → Ain't nobody can do it. Nobody saw him → Didn't nobody see him.* BEV also extends rule 30 to permit transferring the negative to the preverbal position *in a following clause.* It is this emphatic usage which yields 27, *It ain't no cat can't get in no coop.*

We see finally that the apparent "contradiction" of 27 is not a difference in logical operations among dialects, but only a slight readjustment of the conditions on a transformation. We may rewrite 30 now as

30′ NEGCONCORD

$$\text{Neg} - \text{X} - \left\{ \begin{array}{l} \text{Verb} \\ \text{Indef} \end{array} \right\}$$

$$1 \quad 2 \quad 3 \rightarrow 1 \quad 2 \quad 1+3$$

and set up a table of conditions as follows. This table is in the form of values of $\varphi$, where 0 means the rule never applies, X means it is a variable rule with $0 < \varphi < 1$, and 1 means the rule is obligatory.

| 3 = | Indeterminate | | Verb | |
|---|---|---|---|---|
| 1 and 3 clause mates? | Yes | No | Yes | No |
| Dialect | | | | |
| SE | 0 | 0 | 0 | 0 |
| WNS$_1$ | x | x | 0 | 0 |
| WNS$_2$ | x | x | x | 0 |
| BEV | 1 | x | x | x |

We here make use of the distinction between a variable rule and an independent obligatory one in a new way: the variable rule has a communicative function—'stylistic', 'expressive' or 'emphatic' value in this case, while the invariant rule has none, it merely facilitates the expression of choices already made. Once again, a structural compensation appears as a variable rule becomes invariant and information is lost: BEV extends negative concord to new environments to supply this loss. BEV thus has the properties of a separate subsystem, in that changes in one part of the system seem to be inevitably accompanied with compensating changes in another to maintain the same functional operation.

### 3. Sociolinguistic Structure

We may define a *sociolinguistic variable* as one which is correlated with some nonlinguistic variable of the social context: of the speaker, the addressee, the audience, the setting, etc. Some linguistic features (which we will call *indicators*) show a regular distribution over socioeconomic, ethnic, or age groups, but are used by each individual in more or less the same way in any context. If the social contexts concerned can be ordered in some kind of hierarchy (like socio-economic or age groups), these indicators can be said to be *stratified*. More highly developed sociolinguistic variables (which we will call *markers*) not only show social distribution, but also stylistic differentiation. As noted in Sect. 1, stylistic context can be ordered along a single dimension according to the amount of attention paid to speech, so that we have *stylistic* as well as *social stratification*. Early studies such as those of Fischer (1958) or Kučera (1961) observed linguistic variables only one dimension at a time, but more recent studies (Labov 1966a; Wolfram 1969; Anshen 1969; Trudgill 1971) look at the interrelation of both dimensions.

*A Stable Sociolinguistic Marker: (th).*

One of the most general sociolinguistic markers in English is (ing): the presence or absence of a final velar for unstressed /ing/. The formal variant is always the velar, with some interesting exceptions in Southern areas.[36] There are a number of technical questions in the definition of this variable which have not always been given the attention they deserve. A naive approach focuses on the suffix -*ing* as if the variable is an alternation in the shape of this morpheme, neglecting unstressed -*ing* in *something* and *nothing*. In many Southern dialects (e.g., Atlanta) the trisyllables *anything* and *everything* are exempted from the rule and are always realized with the [ɪŋ] variant: probably the result of tertiary stress in the last syllable. On the other hand some dialects (Eastern New England) realize [ɪŋ] with tertiary stress in *workin'* [wɔ́kìn], *fishin'* [fíʃìn]. Further complications can follow as some dialects differentiate nouns from participles from progressive forms, so that inflectional and derivational boundaries, # and +, will appear as variable constraints in the rule. In the most extreme Southern treatment of this variable, all proper nouns are included as well, such as *Manning* [mɛːnɪn].

Despite these variations in the selectional process the operation of the variable itself is extraordinarily uniform. Even if we do not allow for the details noted above, we will obtain a regular pattern of stylistic and social stratification quite similar to that presented for (th) in Chs. 4 and 5. Fischer's early observations (1958) of (ing) showed that this variable reflected sensitivity to sex, formality and cultural orientation toward school. Fig. 8.3 shows the (ing) pattern of the Lower East Side study (Labov 1966a: Ch. 10). Similar patterns are obtained by other investigators for well-established sociolinguistic variables such as (ing), (th), (eh), and negative concord; these patterns share a number of common properties with Fig. 8.3:

36. A study of English in the Austin, Texas area by Stanley Legum (pers. comm.) showed an unusual reversal of the normal (ing) pattern. A number of subjects used the velar variant [ɪŋ] in the interview situation, but switched to [ɪn] in the more formal context of reading style. We seem to be dealing with a regional norm which elevates the [ɪn] variant as a symbol of local identity, recognized even by those who do not use it in their own connected speech.

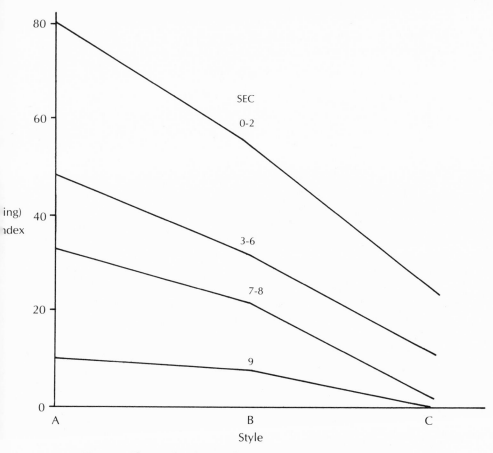

Fig. 8.3. Class and style stratification of (ing) in *working, living,* etc., for white New York City adults. Socioeconomic class scale: 0–2, 3–6, 7–8, 9. A, casual speech; B, careful speech; C, reading style.

a. In every context, members of the speech community are differentiated by their use of (ing) so that higher and lower scores for this variable are directly correlated with higher and lower positions on socioeconomic indices.

b. Yet every group is behaving in the same way, as indicated in the parallel slope of style shifting of (ing) so that higher and lower scores for this variable are directly correlated with higher and lower positions on a scale of formality of the context.

c. Since Fig. 8.3 is not visible as a whole to members, facts (a) and (b) are not part of general knowledge. The portion of Fig. 8.3 visible to any given individual is usually one vertical and one horizontal section: the range of style shifting used by his own group, and the stratified behavior of other groups in the few contexts where he interacts with them. He is not aware that others shift in the same way he does.

d. The same sociolinguistic variable is used to signal social and stylistic stratification. It may therefore be difficult to interpret any signal by itself—to distinguish, for example a casual salesman from a careful pipefitter.[37]

e. Although it is impossible to predict for any one utterance which variant a speaker will use, the striking regularity of Fig. 8.3 emerges from samples with as few as five individuals in one subgroup, and no more than five or ten utterances in a given style for each individual.

The fact that (ing) is a monotonic function of social class and contextual style is of great importance in characterizing it as a stable sociolinguistic variable. The rule which governs this variable may be stated as 31.

$$31 \qquad \begin{bmatrix} -\,\text{cont} \\ -\,\text{tense} \\ -\,\text{ant} \end{bmatrix} \rightarrow \langle \emptyset \rangle \; / \; \begin{bmatrix} +\,\text{voc} \\ -\,\text{cons} \\ -\,\text{stress} \end{bmatrix} \begin{bmatrix} +\,\text{nas} \\ +\,\text{cor} \end{bmatrix} \underline{\qquad}$$

We are not concerned here with any variable constraints which may influence this rule, but rather with the determination of the input variable $p_o$. The two major determinants of this quantity are socioeconomic class and contextual style: age, sex, and ethnic group play a minor part. For (ing) and the other stable sociolinguistic variables, the function takes this general form:

$$32 \qquad\qquad p_o = a \cdot (\text{SEC}) + b \cdot (\text{Style}) + c$$

The suggestion of 32 that this is a linear function goes beyond

37. This is one of the most striking findings of sociolinguistic research, since essays about social usage, written from "common-sense" knowledge, have tried to distinguish "functional varieties" and "cultural levels" as completely independent dimensions. But their interdependence is shown in this and every other careful empirical study to date. Though it may seem inconvenient to have one variable operate on both dimensions, it seems to be an inevitable result of the sociolinguistic processes involving attention to speech and perception of norms, as outlined below.

available data, since we cannot yet quantify the dimension of style. It may be possible to do this in future studies which develop the notion that styles are organized by the amount of attention paid to speech, but at the moment this lack of quantification is a serious limitation.

The function 32 does state concisely the basic information stated under (a) and (b) above: that stable sociolinguistic markers organize linguistic variation in a way that is directly parallel to other hier-archical indices of social status. In Ch. 9 we will see that they contrast sharply in this respect with sociolinguistic variables reflect-ing change in progress.

The five general traits a–e hold for a number of sociolinguistic markers that have been studied in the research cited above. A com-plete view of social and stylistic stratification is not available for most of these studies: some provide data only on relatively small sections of the pattern of Fig. 8.3 and its equivalents, while others cover a wider range. But all of these data can be interpreted in terms of this configuration and fitted into the pattern. Many studies have demonstrated this for (th) and (dh), among white and black popula-tions (Labov 1966a; Labov et al. 1968; Anshen 1969). Negative concord and pronominal apposition have been studied by Shuy, Wolfram, and Riley for Detroit (1967). A number of Spanish variables have been studied by Ma and Herasimchuk for Puerto Rican speakers: the most intricate and systematic variable is (S), the aspiration and deletion of syllable-final /s/, which is generally of great importance throughout the Spanish-speaking world. Ma and Herasimchuk give a good view of stylistic stratification of this variable. Cedergren studied (S) in her work on Panamanian Spanish, where she found a linear correlation with socioeconomic status. The same may be said for (R), the devoicing, fricativization, pharyngealization and deletion of syllable-final /r/ (see Ch. 9 below). Sankoff and her associates at Montreal are beginning to produce detailed reports on a number of French variables which show the pattern of Fig. 8.3, including the deletion of (l), presence or absence of (que) and many others. Trudgill (1971) has studied a number of variables in the vowel system of Norwich: again, the contrast between stable sociolinguistic variables and on-going changes is of the greatest importance. The generality and stability of the (ing) variable is reflected again in his data, drawn from an area quite remote from those where this variable was originally located. Figure 8.4 shows the linear pattern of (ing)

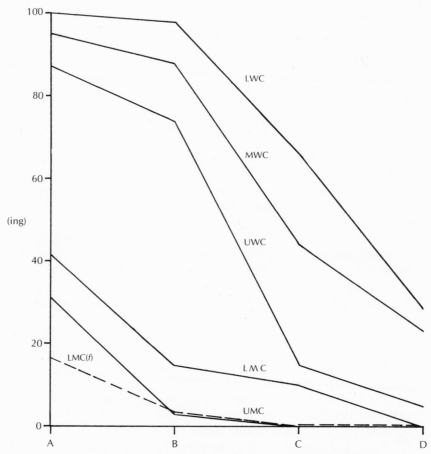

Fig. 8.4.   Class and style stratification of (ing) in Norwich (adapted
from Trudgill 1971). A, casual speech; B, careful speech; C,
reading style; D, word lists.

in Norwich, which matches all essential features of the pattern of
Fig. 8.3. The five properties a-e are preserved intact. In addition we
can see that Fig. 8.4 is a good example of *sharp stratification* as
opposed to fine stratification. In this respect Norwich (ing) is more
similar to New York City (th) in Fig. 4.1, where working-class and
middle-class groups are sharply separated. In contrast, the pattern
of New York City (r) and (ing) shows a stepwise gradient relationship
where there is no clear discontinuity between one class group and
another.

A superficial view of this regularity would lead one to conclude that further sociolinguistic studies can do no more than uncover more linear correlations. But each of these studies has led to deeper insights into the relations of internal and external determinants of language structure and change. Without a base line of stable socio-linguistic markers, there is no basis for investigating more abstract questions: the contrast between change and stability; between phonological and grammatical features, between fine and sharp stratification, or between abstract higher-level rules and low-level phonetic patterns; the role of referential function vs. expressive sociolinguistic information; the interaction of sex with social class and ethnic status; the hypercorrect pattern of the second-highest status group; and many other questions all presuppose that we have laid out the basic sociolinguistic orientation of the community with stable sociolinguistic markers.

*Men vs. Women*

There is a regular aspect of the social stratification of stable variables which is not shown on Fig. 8.3. In careful speech, women use fewer stigmatized forms than men, (Labov 1966a:288), and are more sensitive than men to the prestige pattern. They show this in a sharper slope of style shifting, especially at the more formal end of the spectrum. This observation is confirmed innumerable times, in Fischer (1958), throughout Shuy and Fasold's work in Detroit, in Levine and Crockett, and in Anshen's study of Hillsboro. The pattern is particularly marked in lower-middle-class women, who show the most extreme form of this behavior. In the example of (ing), we find the usual pattern of sex differentiation and in Trudgill's study of Norwich, women have lower values of (ing) for almost all styles and social classes. In Fig. 8.4 we have indicated this differentiation for only one social class. Here the (ing) pattern for lower-middle-class women shows a smaller use of the nonstandard form than that of the upper-middle class as a whole. Except for a small percentage of [ɪn] forms in casual speech, middle-class female speakers use the standard [ɪŋ] form exclusively. Here as elsewhere, it is clear that women are more sensitive than men to overt sociolinguistic values. Even when women use the most extreme forms of an advancing sociolinguistic variable in their casual speech (Ch. 6), they correct more sharply than men in formal contexts. Chapter 9 will examine in greater detail this pattern of sex differentiation in relation to the process of linguistic change.

*The Hypercorrect Pattern of the Lower Middle Class*

One of the most solidly established phenomena of sociolinguistic behavior is that the second-highest status group shows the most extreme style shifting, going beyond that of the highest-status group in this respect. Ch. 5 has presented the pattern in great detail, drawing upon the data of the Lower East Side study of New York City. Given this pattern, we can find parallel phenomena throughout all the literature cited above. Shuy, Wolfram, and Riley (1967) and Wolfram (1969) show many cases where the greatest style shifting is exhibited by the second-highest status group. Most of these are stable stigmatized linguistic features. The most clearcut examples of the hypercorrect pattern are to be found in on-going change from above, as with the importation of the new r-pronouncing norm throughout the previously r-less areas of the Eastern United States. Fig. 4.2 for the class stratification of (r) in New York City gave us the classic view of the crossover pattern. A striking corroboration of this pattern is supplied by Levine and Crockett's study of (r) in Hillsboro, N.C. The Hillsboro shift of (r) shown in Table 9.7 (p. 292) is a stylistic shift between sentences in which (r) is not the main focus, and word lists where it is (see above).

Here data from a completely independent study with a more limited stylistic range shows the same crossover phenomenon as in New York City. The second-highest status group—in this case, high-school graduates, shows a much greater shift towards the prestige norm in the more formal style. The significance of this pattern for the mechanism of linguistic change has been dealt with in Chs. 5 and 7 and will be considered in the more general context of Ch. 9.

The generality of our principle that "the second-highest status group" shows the most extreme style shifting is challenged by the Norwich data in Fig. 8.4, where the third-highest status group—upper working class—shows the greatest shift. Between careful speech and reading style the UWC moves from (ing)-74 to (ing)-15. However, this exception holds only for men; as far as women are concerned, it is again the lower middle class which shows the sharpest slope, and the correction shown by this group is indeed sharper than any other group. The dotted line in Fig. 8.4 shows (ing) values for lower-middle-class females who move from (ing)-67 in casual speech to (ing)-03 in careful speech. From this point on they merge with the upper middle class as far as the use of (ing) is concerned.

Granted the stability and generality of this complex pattern, it will be interesting to see if any formal simplification can be achieved. The crossover pattern may be represented abstractly as:

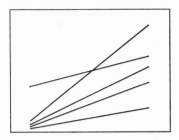

The slope of style shifting is indeed complex. The highest and lowest group have the shallowest slope; the interior groups follow behind the lead of the second-highest group, which is the steepest. How can this be formalized? The rule for the vocalization of (r) in the white community has the general form:

33        $[+\text{cen}] \rightarrow \langle -\text{cons} \rangle \,/\, [-\text{cons}] \underline{\quad\quad} [-\text{syl}]$

That is, a central segment loses its consonantal feature variably in postvocalic position if the following element is not a vowel. The problem here is to write a function for the basic constraint on the input variable $p_0$ comparable to the simple and straightforward function 32. The solution lies in an understanding of the ultimate significance of style shifting: it is governed by the recognition of an exterior standard of correctness. The strength of such behavior can be measured by the Index of Linguistic Insecurity. Table 5.1 shows us the curvilinear pattern, with the lower middle class at a maximum which we need to describe the slopes of style shifting shown above. We can then write for 33 the function

34        $p_0 = a \cdot \text{SEC} + b \cdot (\text{ILI}) \,(\text{Style}) + c$

*Problems of Sociolinguistic Structure*

As we have noted above, the most immediate problem to be solved in the attack on sociolinguistic structure is the quantification of the dimension of style. If quantitative studies of attention can be related to style shifting, we will then be able to give more precise form to rules such as 32 or 34 and specify the constants a, b, and c. Such quantification may possibly be obtained by studies of pupil dilation, or of systematic divisions of attention through mechanical and measurable tests, or by quantitatively reducing audio-monitoring through noise level.

It is also evident that many studies cited do not have enough data from the direct study of the vernacular. The methodological task is to combine surveys of individuals who give us a representative sample with longer-term studies of groups. The ideal study of a community would randomly locate individuals, and then study several groups of which that individual was a member. That is quite impossible in a normal social survey, given the numbers required, but since we have established that sociolinguistic studies require a smaller population to begin with, such a model is not beyond the realm of possibility.

A third problem lies in dealing with rules which show irregular lexical distribution. There is now good evidence that the course of linguistic change involves the temporary dissolution of word classes.[38] The most difficult problem here is that there are distributions across word classes which we would want to describe, but which are not likely to be a part of the knowledge of the native speaker. For example, only a certain proportion of English verbs with Latinate prefixes show a shift of stress when they appear as nouns like *convíct* [V]: *cónvict* [N]; others retain end stress, like *consént* [V]: *consént* [N]. It can be shown that the proportion of words in any given subclass is related to the length of the prefix, but this regularity is of no use to the native speaker since most words have a fixed accent. As another example, the tensing rule for short *a* in New York City does not normally operate in __CV environments, though there are a number of exceptions. The linguist is interested to discover that most of these exceptions have a sibilant as the medial consonant C. But in such cases, the native speaker again only needs to know in what class a given word falls. The proportion of the

38. Although Figs. 4.1 and 4.2 show word classes moving as a whole, we have encountered some rules which show a great deal of irregular lexical variation. The tensing of short a in *bad, ask*, etc., investigated in New York City by Paul Cohen (1970), shows such irregularity, while the raising rule which follows the tensing rule does not (Labov 1966a:51–52). It is the existence of a variable rule which allows the word class to be reconstituted when the change is completed, since it is defined as the class of lexical items which can vary between X and Y, as opposed to the classes which are always X or always Y. For some structural causes of such lexical variation, see Wang 1969.

original word class which has been affected by the incoming rule is of no immediate interest to him if he has no choice in the pronunciation of any given item. It may be that we will enter rules into our grammar which are *not* a part of the "knowledge" of native speakers. This particular metaphor may have lost its value at this point in our investigations.

A fourth major challenge is to enter more deeply into the study of higher level syntactic variables, such as extraposition, nominalization, placement of complementizers, negative raising, wh-attachment, or relativization. The two chief stumbling blocks to investigating these features in their social context is the low frequency of occurrence of the critical subcases, and the lack of certainty in our abstract analyses. But some beginning has been made in our recent work in urban ghetto areas, and the challenges to work with more abstract matters cannot be ignored. The study of language in its social context cannot remain at the level of such phonological variables as (ing), if it is to make a significant contribution to the problems outlined at the beginning of this chapter.

The fifth problem is to enlarge the scope of these studies beyond individual speech communities, and relate them to larger grammars of the English speech community as a whole. The discussion of negative concord in Sect. 2 indicates one way in which this might be done. The work of C. J. Bailey is most challenging here: particularly his penetrating studies of phonological rules in Southern dialects (1969a), and his broader attempts to incorporate all English phonology into a single, pandialectal set of rules (1969b). Though these studies of Bailey are not based upon the study of language in context, one must eventually hope to provide reliable data to support work of this generality and this level of abstraction.

## The Relation of Norms to Behavior

So far, in our consideration of sociolinguistic structure, we have taken into account only what people say, and only incidentally what they think they *should* say. These are the "secondary responses" to language that Bloomfield suggested that we might well observe (1944) as one part of popular lore. There is a very small vocabulary available to most people for talking about language: the same few terms recur as we hear that the other people's pronunciation has a "nasal twang," is "sing-song," is "harsh" or "guttural," "lazy" or "sloppy." Grammar is said to be "mixed-up" or "illogical."

A small number of sociolinguistic markers rise to overt social consciousness, and become *stereotypes*. There may or may not be a fixed relation between such stereotypes and actual usage. The variables (ing) and (dh) are such stereotypes in the United States: someone may be said to "drop his g's" or to be one of those "dese, dem and dose guys". Most communities have local stereotypes, such as "Brooklynese" in New York City which focuses on "thoity-thoid" for *thirty-third;* in Boston, the fronted broad *a* in "cah" and "pahk" receives a great deal of attention. Speakers of the isolated Cape Hatteras (North Carolina) dialect are known as "hoi toiders" because of the backing and rounding of the nucleus in *high, tide,* etc.

Such social stereotypes yield a sketchy and unsystematic view of linguistic structure to say the least. In general, we can assert that overt *social correction* of speech is extremely irregular, focusing on the most frequent lexical items, while the actual course of linguistic evolution, which has produced the marked form of these variables, is highly systematic. This is the basic reason why the vernacular, in which minimum attention is paid to speech, gives us the most systematic view of linguistic structure. For example, the evolution of the New York City vernacular has led to the raising of the vowel in *off, lost, shore, more,* etc. until it has merged with the vowel of *sure* and *moor*. This high vowel has been stigmatized, and is now being corrected irregularly by middle-class speakers. But the same vowel, raised simultaneously in the nucleus of *boy, toy,* etc., is never corrected.[39]

But subjective reactions to speech are not confined to the few stereotypes that have risen to social consciousness. Unconscious social judgments about language can be measured by techniques such as Lambert's "matched guise" test, and others described in Sect. 1. One basic principle emerges: that *social attitudes towards language are extremely uniform throughout a speech community*.[40]

39. We also find that the vowels of *my* and *mouth* are affected by the rotation of the long and ingliding vowels of *bad, bar, lost*. As *bar* moves to the back, *my* moves with it, and *mouth* moves in the opposite direction towards the front. But of all these systematically interrelated changes, only the raising of *bad* and *lost* shows style shifting and correction. Even for these cases, the correction is lexically irregular.

40. In fact, it seems plausible to define a speech community as a group of speakers who share a set of social attitudes towards language. In New York City, those raised out of town in their formative years show none of the regular pattern of subjective reactions characteristic of natives where a New York City variable such as the vowel of *lost* is concerned (Labov 1966a:651).

Lambert's studies show, for example, that the negative attitude towards Canadian French is not only quite uniform in the English-speaking community, but almost as unanimously held among French speakers in Quebec (1967). In our study of unconscious subjective reactions to markers such as (r), we find the most extraordinary unanimity in speaker's reactions, despite the great variation in the use of [r] just described. There is a general axiom of sociolinguistic structure which can be stated as: *the correlate of regular stratification of a sociolinguistic variable in behavior is uniform agreement in subjective reactions towards that variable.* This principle was documented in Ch. 6, where we saw in Fig. 6.2 that the development of social differentiation of (r) among younger speakers corresponded to the uniform positive evaluation of (r-1).

As we reexamine the structures shown in Figs. 4.1 and 4.2, it is apparent that the uniform slope of style shifting also reflects the uniform attitudes held in the community. But for a stable socio-linguistic marker like (ing) or (th), we can raise the question, what maintains this structure for such a long period of time? Why don't all people speak in the way that they obviously believe they should? The usual response is to cite laziness, lack of concern, or isolation from the prestige norm. But there is no foundation for the notion that stigmatized vernacular forms are easier to pronounce[41]; and there is strong evidence of concern with speech in large cities. Careful consideration of this difficult problem has led us to posit the existence of an opposing set of covert norms, which attribute positive values to the vernacular. In most formal situations in urban areas, such as an interview or a psycholinguistic test, these norms are extremely difficult to elicit. Middle-class values are so dominant in these contexts that most subjects cannot perceive any opposing values, no matter how strongly they may influence behavior in other situations. In our recent work in the black community, we have been able to uncover evidence of the existence of such opposing norms. Fig. 8.5 shows responses to the first two items on our subjective reaction test, opposing a working-class speaker to a middle-class speaker on "zero" sentences (which contain none of the variables to be tested). The upper line shows the percent of those who rated

41. Some of the extreme developments of vernacular vowel shifts in New York City, Detroit, or Chicago are tense vowels which seem to involve a great deal of muscular effort compared to the standard. Spectrographic analysis indicates that such vowels as short /a/ rising to the height of *here* are extremely fronted.

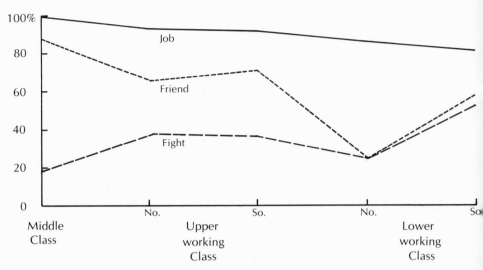

Fig. 8.5.   Percent rating middle-class speaker higher than
working-class speaker on 3 scales for 5 social groups, from
Labov et al. 1968:242.

the middle-class speaker higher on the scale of "job-suitability." It
begins very high with middle-class subjects, and falls off slightly as
we move to lower socioeconomic groups. The lower line is the
converse: this registers reactions to the "fight" or "toughness" scale:
"If the speaker was in a street fight, how likely would he be to come
out on top?" There is a simple inverse relationship here: a stereotype
that is probably reinforced by school teachers but also shows some
recognition of social reality. But the third set of reactions to the
"friendship scale" shows that there is more involved. This scale is
in response to the question "If you knew the speaker for a long time,
how likely would he be to become a good friend of yours?" For the
three upper social groups, this follows the job scale closely; but for
the lower working class, it switches abruptly, and follows the fight
scale. The same phenomenon can be observed for a whole range of
variables tested (Labov et al. 1968:3.6).

   We have therefore some empirical support in positing the opposition between two sets of values as the normative correlate of stable
sociolinguistic markers such as (th) and (ing). In this type of study,
we agree with Homans (1955) that the proper object of study should

not be behavior alone, or norms alone, but rather the extent to which (and the rules by which) people deviate from the explicit norms that they hold. It is at this level of abstraction that we can best develop linguistic and sociolinguistic theory.

### The Role of Social Factors in Linguistic Change

Although this chapter is not primarily concerned with the problems of language change, we have already introduced some data which bear on this question. In speaking of the role of social factors influencing linguistic evolution, it is important not to overestimate the amount of contact or overlap between social values and the structure of language. Linguistic and social structure are by no means coextensive. The great majority of linguistic rules are quite remote from any social value; they are part of the elaborate machinery which the speaker needs to translate his complex set of meanings or intentions into linear form. For example, the rules governing the quantifiers and negation discussed above are well below the level of social affect, and their irregular, idiosyncratic distribution in the population reflects this fact.

Variables closer to surface structure frequently are the focus of social affect. In fact, social values are attributed to linguistic rules only when there is variation. Speakers do not readily accept the fact that two different expressions actually "mean the same" and there is a strong tendency to attribute different meanings to them.[42] If a certain group of speakers uses a particular variant, then the social values attributed to that group will be transferred to that linguistic variant. Sturtevant (1947) has proposed a general model of linguistic change showing the opposition of two forms, each favored by a particular social group. When the issue is resolved, and one form becomes universal, the social value attached to it disappears.

As far as the synchronic aspect of language structure is concerned, it would be an error to put much emphasis on social factors. Gen-

---

42. When New York City *cruller* (Dutch *kroeller*) was replaced by the standard term *doughnut,* the term *cruller* was variously assigned to other forms of pastry. Similarly the local *pot cheese* (Dutch *pot kees*) was replaced by *cottage cheese* and was differentiated to indicate a drier form. The oscillation of socially marked pronunciations of *vase* led one informant to say, "These small ones are my [vezɪz] but these big ones are my [vazɪz]."

erative grammar has made great progress in working out the invariant relations within this structure, even though it wholly neglects the social context of language. But it now seems clear that one cannot make any major advance towards understanding the mechanism of linguistic change without serious study of the social factors which motivate linguistic evolution. Ch. 7 outlined a proposal for the basic mechanism by which social factors interact with internal, linguistic factors; Ch. 9 will review a much broader field and take as primary focus the range of social variables which directly influence the course of linguistic evolution.

### 4. Some Invariant Rules of Discourse Analysis

This presentation has so far concentrated almost entirely upon the variable rules of language: their use in providing decisive evidence on questions of linguistic structure, their place in sociolinguistic structure, and more briefly, their role in the evolution of language. But a very great number of linguistic rules are not variable in the least: they are categorical rules which, given the proper input, always apply. More than any other field concerned with human behavior, linguistics has succeeded in isolating the invariant structures underlying the surface phenomena, and it is upon this achievement that we have been building in the work outlined in Sects. 2 and 3. The formal representation of variable rules presented there depends upon, and interlocks with, a number of invariant rules of grammar derived from studies of language quite apart from any social context.

There are some areas of linguistic analysis in which even the first steps towards the basic, invariant rules cannot be taken unless the social context of the speech event is considered. The most striking examples are in the analysis of discourse. The fundamental problem of discourse analysis is to show how one utterance follows another in a rational, rule-governed manner—in other words, how we understand coherent discourse. We rely upon our intuitions to distinguish coherent from incoherent discourse; for example, the following is plainly not governed by any rules that we can immediately recognize (from Laffal, 1965:85).

35          A: What is your name?
            B: Well, let's say you might have thought you had some-
               thing from before, but you haven't got it any more.
            A: I'm going to call you Dean.

This is an excerpt from a conversation between a doctor and a schizophrenic patient. Our first data in dealing with such a passage will be our intuitive reactions to it, and the first challenge in discourse analysis is to account for our intuitions (as confirmed by the response of participants as in 35). The question is: how much and what kind of data do we need in order to form sound judgments and interpret sequences of utterances as the participants in the conversation do? The simplest case is that of elliptical responses, as in 36.

36          A: Are you going to work tomorrow?
            B: Yes.

Here our normal knowledge of English syntax is sufficient to allow us to derive B's utterance from *Yes, I am going to work tomorrow*. There is a simple rule of discourse of the following form:

37          If A utters a question of the form $Q\text{-}S_1$, and B responds
            with an existential E (including *yes, no, probably, maybe*,
            etc.), then B is heard as answering A with the statement
            $E\text{-}S_1$.

But now let us consider sequences of the following form:

38          A: She never helps at home.
            B: Yes.

39          A; She told you what we are interested in.
            B: Yes.

40          A: You live on 115th St.
            B: No. I live on 116th.

We encounter many such examples in our analyses of therapeutic interviews and in everyday speech. Rule 37 obviously does not apply: there is no $Q\text{-}S_1$ in the A form. Is it true that any statement can be followed with a *yes* or *no*? The following sequences seem to indicate the opposite.

41          A: I don't like the way you said that.
            B: *Yes.

42          A: I feel hot today.
            B: *No.

It is not only that 41–42 do not require or tolerate a *yes* or *no* answer, but even more strikingly that statements like 37–40 seem to *demand* such a response. We find many cases where speakers will not let the conversation continue unless a *yes* or *no* answer is given to such statements. The rule which operates here is one of the simplest invariant rules of discourse. Given two parties in a conversation, A and B, we can distinguish as "A-events" the things that A knows about but B does not; as "B-events" the things which B knows but A does not; and as "AB-events" knowledge which is shared equally by A and B. The rule then states:

43          If A makes a statement about a B-event, it is heard as a request for confirmation.

Note that in 41–42, A is making a statement about an A-event, but in 38–40 about a B-event. Anyone can immediately test this rule in an ordinary conversation and observe the force of its operation. This rule contains the social construct of "shared knowledge" which is not normally part of a linguistic rule. This is merely one of many rules of interpretation which relate "what is said"—questions, statements, imperatives—to "what is done"—requests, refusals, assertions, denials, insults, challenges, retreats, and so on. There are no simple one-to-one relations between actions and utterances; rules of interpretation (and their nearly symmetrical rules of production) are extremely complex and relate several hierarchical levels of "actions" to each other and to utterances. Sequencing rules do not operate between utterances, but between the actions performed with those utterances. In fact, there are usually no connection between successive utterances at all. The overall pattern of discourse analysis may be sketched as:

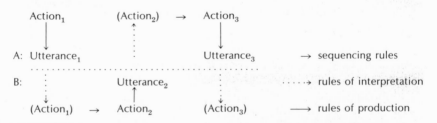

It may be helpful to consider a more difficult case, drawn from a therapeutic interview we have been investigating in some detail.[43]

---

43. From studies of therapeutic interviews being conducted by the author and David Fanshel of the Columbia School of Social Work.

44          A: Well, when do you plan to come home?
            B: Oh why-y?

There is no syntactic connection between these two questions and
no amount of abstract analysis will relate them correctly. One cannot
interpret B as Q-S$_1$: "Why do I plan to come home?" One might
interpret B as addressed to an implicit underlying form, A: [I ask
you] when do you . . . B: Why [do you ask me. . . .]? But this would
be a wrong interpretation; without detailed knowledge of the
speakers and the situation, one could not hope to arrive at the
appropriate intuitive judgments to begin analyzing. We must be
aware that A is a college student, and that B is her mother; that B
has been away for four days helping a married daughter; that A and
B both know that A wants B to come home; and that B has said many
times in the past that A cannot take care of herself, which A denies.
It is then clear that 44-A is a request for action, not for information:
A is requesting that her mother come home.

There is a general rule for interpreting any utterance as a request
for action (or command) which reads as follows:

45          If A requests B to perform an action X at a time T, A's
            utterance will be heard as a valid command only if the
            following preconditions hold: B believes that A believes
            (= it is an AB-event that)

1. X needs to be done for a purpose Y
2. B has the ability to do X
3. B has the obligation to do X
4. A has the right to tell B to do X.

Where the four preconditions do not hold in some obvious way,
we have jokes or joking insults such as: "Drop dead!" "Go jump in
the lake!" or "Get this dissertation finished by the time I get back
from lunch!"[44] These preconditions appear in almost every rule of
interpretation and production which concerns making or responding
to commands. Note that the primitive terms of 45 include *rights* and

44. Harvey Sacks has pointed out that the first decision to be made in the interpretation of any utterance is whether it is serious or not (or we might say, the degree
of seriousness involved). Appropriate reactions to jokes are limited, and almost
independent of context, but if the utterance is serious more complex rules must be
invoked. Rule 45 shows us one formal basis for this decision.

*obligations* which are plainly social constructs. Given rule 45, there is a rule of interpretation operating for B in responding to A's question in 44:

46          If A makes a request for information of B about whether an action X has been performed, or at what time TX will be performed, and the four preconditions of (45) hold, then A will be heard as making a request for action with the underlying form *B: do X!*

B's response "Oh, why?" is then aimed not at the surface request for information, but rather at the precondition 1 of the more abstract request for action: "Why are you asking me to come home?" By asking a question about precondition 1, B puts off A's request: since if any of the preconditions are not shared knowledge, the request is obviously not valid by rule 45. A's next move in this discourse is to respond to B's request for information: she explains that the housework and her studies are altogether too much for her to do. Thus the content of A's response shows that she interprets B's question as we do here.

We now find intuitively that the original request of 45 is still in force, under the operation of a further invariant rule which states generally that

47          If A has made a request, and B responds with a request for information, A reinstates the original request by supplying that information.

Since the original request is put again, B must now respond a second time. This time B puts off the request by asking another question involving precondition 2—by implying that Helen is the person who should have been asked, she indicates that she herself should not have been asked, implying that she (B) does not have the ability to comply with the request from A.

48          A: Well, things are getting just a little too much. [laugh] This is—it's just getting too hard . . .
            B: Well, why don't you tell Helen that?

It is obvious that the complexities of the situation do not end here. These illustrations of discourse rules should serve to show the form of such rules and the kind of primitive elements which they require.

Although this exposition is based upon several years of analysis of therapeutic interviews and other speech events, it is not put forward with the same confidence as the solutions to the problems of Sects. 2 and 3. On the contrary, discourse analysis is at a much more primitive stage, analogous to the earliest developments in syntax and morphology. It is a matter of some interest that the most significant advances in this field have not been made by linguists, but by sociologists. The work of Sacks (1972) and Schegloff (1968) has located many fundamental questions concerning the selection of speakers and the identification of persons, and isolated a number of sequencing rules. Linguists have been handicapped in their approach to this field by their inability to utilize essential social constructs involving the roles of speaker and listener, obligations, power relationships, membership categories, and the like.

It should be evident that the approach to the study of language in its social context outlined in Sects. 2-3 of this paper can easily accommodate the full range of elements which we need for discourse rules. The linguistic approach can contribute a number of concepts which are not well developed in anthropology or sociology. First there is the distinction between utterances and actions, and the hierarchical relations of actions whereby a question may be seen as a request for information, which is in turn interpreted as a request for action, which may appear on a higher level as a challenge. Further advancement of this field may depend upon the linguistic concept of an invariant rule, and the linguistic approach to the formalization of such rules.

Eventually, the exploration of discourse rules will reach a quantitative phase in which variable rules may be constructed and in which large bodies of data can be introduced to confirm or reject the tentative rules we have written. One area which plainly involves variable rules is in the degree of mitigation or aggravation which governs the selection of rules for making requests. We observe that in 44 the daughter *must* mitigate her request; to say to her mother "Come home right now!" would be violating a strong social constraint, although a mother can easily say this to her daughter. The exact degree of mitigation, and the way in which the request is executed involve a number of variables: age, socioeconomic class, relative status of speaker and listener, and the form of the preceding utterance. Such variable constraints will eventually appear in rules comparable to those written in Sects. 2 and 3. But our present

knowledge is too fragmentary to make such attempts fruitful.[45]
Quantitative research implies that one knows what to count, and this
knowledge is reached only through a long period of trial and approximation, and upon the basis of a solid body of theoretical
constructs. By the time the analyst knows what to count, the problem
is practically solved.

In recent years, there have been many attempts by social psychologists to characterize differences in the use of language by middle-
class and working-class speakers (Bernstein 1966; Lawton 1968).
There is little connection between the general statements made and
the quantitative data offered on the use of language. It is said that
middle-class speakers show more verbal planning, more abstract
arguments, more objective viewpoint, show more logical connections, and so on. But one does not uncover the logical complexity
of a body of speech by counting the number of subordinate clauses.
The cognitive style of a speaker has no fixed relation to the number
of unusual adjectives or conjunctions that he uses. As the example
given above shows, no useful purpose would be served by counting
the number of questions that someone asks in an interview. The
relation of argument and discourse to language is much more abstract
than this, and such superficial indices can be quite deceptive. When
we can say *what* is being done with a sentence, then we will be
able to observe how often speakers do it.

### 5. The State of Linguistics

In the introduction to this chapter, it was suggested that linguistics
was suffering from difficulty in coming to grips with the fundamental
data of language. In this respect, our field is no different from any
other social science. Linguists did take the somewhat unusual step
of redefining the field so that the everyday use of language in the
community would be placed outside of linguistics proper—to be
called *speech*, not language. Rather than worry about the difficulties
of dealing with this material, linguists found it quite unnecessary,
on theoretical grounds, to account for it; indeed, it was argued that
a linguist *should* not be concerned with the facts of speech.

Just how long such a program can continue to be productive is

---

45. The most thorough examination of a speech event which we have carried out
so far is the analysis of ritual insults in the black community (Labov 1972a: Ch. 8).
Although the discourse rules given there seem to be sound, we do not have the means
of corroboration which are available in our studies of linguistic structure.

an open question. Clearly linguistics has benefited from a restriction of its field of view. But if at this point linguistics is more advanced than any other study of social behavior, it is no doubt due to the highly structured nature of our object rather than the peculiar excellence of our strategy. In this paper, I have taken up a number of problems where progress has been blocked, where a broader field of view seems to be required to come to a decisive solution. The analysis of language out of context will undoubtedly continue as a separate pursuit; as before, we will find some linguists who spend all of their time analyzing their intuitions about language, as others will work with texts or carry out laboratory experimentation. My own view is that such activity will be increasingly valued as a necessary preliminary to the development of linguistic research. But linguistic theory can no more ignore the social behavior of speakers of a language than chemical theory can ignore the observed properties of the elements.

The penalties for ignoring data from the speech community are a growing sense of frustration, a proliferation of moot questions, and a conviction that linguistics is a game in which each theorist chooses the solution that fits his taste or intuition. I do not believe that we need at this point a new "theory of language"; rather, we need a new way of doing linguistics that will yield decisive solutions. By enlarging our view of language, we encounter the possibility of being right: of finding answers that are supported by an unlimited number of reproducible measurements, in which the inevitable bias of the observer is cancelled out by the convergence of many approaches. There are many linguists who do not believe that there is a right or wrong side to theoretical alternatives: the nature of their data does not allow convergence on any one view or a decisive confirmation of it.

I do not mean, of course, that a particular solution offered is right in any absolute sense. No one can doubt that his best effort will be criticized, modified, replaced, or perhaps re-emerge in an almost unrecognizable form. But within the framework provided in this chapter, we can say that the kind of solutions offered to problems such as consonant cluster simplification, copula deletion, and negative concord represent abstract relations of linguistic elements that are deeply embedded in the data. It is reasonable to believe that they are more than constructions of the analyst—that they are properties of language itself. The state of linguistics is indeed promising if we can assert this about any single result of our research.

# 9 | The Social Setting of Linguistic Change

THE study of language change in its social context has been described by some as a virgin field; by others, as a barren territory.[1] A brief examination of what has been written in the past on this subject shows that it is more like an abandoned back yard, overgrown with various kinds of tangled, secondary scholarship. The subject has been so badly treated with voluminous, vacuous, and misleading essays that one can sympathize with linguists who say that it is better left alone. But the consequences of avoiding the social dimension of language change are serious. We are then left with such a limited body of fact that we are condemned to repeat the arguments of our predecessors; we find ourselves disputing endlessly about bad data instead of profiting from the rich production of new linguistic change around us.

Nevertheless, historical linguists have adopted and vigorously defended a thoroughly asocial policy in the past half-century. To understand why, it will be helpful to re-examine briefly the history of the relations between linguists and society, and how they have succeeded in avoiding each other. This review will raise three questions: whether the expressive and directive functions of language are important determinants of change; whether highly abstract rules of grammar can be affected by social forces; and whether linguistic evolution is entirely dysfunctional. This chapter may be considered the diachronic correlate of Ch. 8, which was concerned almost entirely with the synchronic aspects of the first two questions. Data from recent studies of change in progress will be presented to show

1. This chapter is a revised version of the chapter on this subject prepared for *Current Trends in Linguistics,* Vol. 11, edited by Thomas Sebeok (The Hague: Mouton, to appear).

how linguistic changes may be embedded in a social context, how they are evaluated, and how change may be activated at a particular time and place. These findings will then be applied to the three questions raised above.

### The Linguistic View of Language as a Social Fact

Every linguist recognizes that language is a social fact, but not everyone puts an equal emphasis on that fact. When linguists write about language change, we find a very different degree of concern with the social context in which these changes occur. Some broaden their view to include a wide range of facts about the speakers and their extralinguistic behavior, while others constrict their view to exclude as much as possible. We can generally predict from an author's definition of language how much he will be concerned with the social factors in linguistic change. Furthermore, those who focus upon the communication of cognitive or referential information will deal more with the individual, those who become involved with affective and phatic uses of language, with social matters.

It is not difficult to find 19th-century spokesmen for the importance of the social factors in linguistic change. Whitney was firmly committed:

Speech is not a personal possession, but a social; it belongs, not to the individual, but to the member of society. (1901:404)

In considering the functions of language, Whitney emphasized communicative function in a social sense, rather than the primacy of "ideas":

Man speaks, then, primarily not in order to think, but in order to impart his thought. His social needs, his social instincts, force him to expression. (p. 401)

For an opposing view, we can look to Hermann Paul, whose individualist approach is reflected in most current theories of language change (see Weinreich, Labov, and Herzog 1968). Paul saw the language of the community as a rough mixture of the well-formed speech of individuals. On this basis, he dismisses as quite transparent the problem of explaining the diversification of language:

If we start from the undeniable truth that each individual has his or her own language, and that each such language has its own history . . . the rise of variations seems a mere matter of course [*die Entstehung der Verschiedenheit scheint ja danach selbstverständlich*]. (Paul 1889:23 = 1886:37)

For Paul, the function of language was to organize "groups of ideas (*Vorstellungsgruppen*), a process which "takes a peculiar development in the case of each individual" (1889:6 = 1886:22). Sweet studied Paul, and absorbed and endorsed this point of view; he cautions that all general principles of change are subordinate "to the main function of language . . . the expression of ideas." (1900:34) We should not be surprised, then, that Sweet defines language without any reference to social context, as "the expression of thought by means of speech-sounds." (1900:1). His explanations of language change accordingly revolve about such individual traits as "laziness" or "carelessness."

The emphasis on cognitive or representational functions of language was maintained by the Prague school in their synchronic studies. Other functions were of course recognized: following Bühler and Laziczius, Troubetzkoy would set up three divisions of phonology: the expressive, appellative, and representational, or phonology proper. The net effect of this division was to free the linguist from any concern with social factors and noncognitive functions. After devoting a few pages to an anecdotal account of these matters, the linguist could proceed with the real business at hand (1957:16–17). Martinet (see below) seems by his manner of dealing with linguistic change to be a direct descendant of this tradition.

Bloomfield inherited from Paul the same individualist psychology, though he did object to its subjective character (1933). Bloomfield's S-R model shows language as the property of the individual; his model of sound change imagines a perfectly regular but unobservable process taking place within the individual's speech pattern. Larger social factors are presented as relatively vague and confused processes, under the chapter headings of "Fluctuation in the frequency of forms" and "Dialect borrowing."

Chomsky and Halle, who differ from Bloomfield and Paul on so many other points, continue the tradition of speculation on the basis of individual models of the speaker-hearer relationship. Chomsky would deliberately exclude all social variation from the subject matter of linguistics (1965:3); Halle (1962) presents a model of linguistic change in which the individual child restructures his parents' speech.

Although Paul's individualist views have been followed in the main stream of linguistics, there has been considerable opposition from many who shared Whitney's concern with the social context of language and its wider range of social functions. Witness the well-known position of Meillet:

From the fact that language is a social institution, it follows that linguistics is a social science, and the only variable to which we can turn to account for linguistic change is social change, of which linguistic variations are only consequences. (1921:16–17)

Meillet's associate Vendryes continues in the same vein, some 20 years later:

Language is thus the social fact par excellence, the result of social contact. It has become one of the strongest bonds uniting societies, and it owes its development to the existence of the social group. (1951, p. 11)

Jespersen followed Sweet on many matters, but he laid heavy emphasis upon the role of language in social interaction:

The language of a nation is the set of habits by which the members of the nation are accustomed to communicate with one another. (1946:21)

Although Jespersen was deeply involved in his "notional" theory of grammar, we find throughout his writings a concern with the expressive and directive functions of language that enters strongly into his discussions of linguistic change. Sturtevant wrote in the same tradition:

A language is a system of arbitrary vocal symbols by which members of a social group cooperate and interact. (1947:2)

Sturtevant's proposals for the mechanism of linguistic change (1947:74ff) laid a great deal of emphasis on the assignment of social and affective values.

It is clear that we shall not understand the regularity of phonetic laws until we learn how rivalry between phonemes leads to the victory of one of them. . . Before a phoneme can spread from word to word . . . it is necessary that one of the two rivals shall acquire some sort of prestige. (1947:80–81)

But Sturtevant represented a late survival of Meillet's fading notion that we might search for an explanation of the fluctuations of linguistic change in the fluctuating course of social events. The predominant trend is expressed by many eminent linguists who fiercely resist any such involvement, and insist that we must confine ourselves to purely internal, linguistic explanations. Martinet, for example, declares that it is only the *results* of outside impact that the linguist is competent to study. In his capacity *as* a linguist, he will decline to investigate "sociological" conditioning (1964:52).

Kuryłowicz takes an even harder line:

Once we leave language *sensu stricto* and appeal to extra-linguistic factors, a clear delimitation of the field of linguistic research is lost. Thus, e.g., the physiological (articulatory) aspect may be a consequence of social factors, the latter being themselves due to certain political or economic facts (conquest, migrations involving bilingualism) . . . It seems that the field of linguistic explanation in the literal sense must be circumscribed by the *linguistic* aspect of the change in question, i.e., by the actual state of the system before and after the change ("l'état momentanée des termes du système"—Saussure). (1964:11)

Kuryłowicz wishes to purify linguistic argument of all contaminating support; he renounces the use of dialect geography, phonetics, psychology, and cultural anthropology in the reconstruction of the history of a language, in order to rise to a "higher conceptual basis" (1964:30).

Thus linguists seem to fall into two major groups in this matter. Group A, the "social" group, would pay close attention to social factors in explaining change; see expressive and directive functions of language closely intertwined with the communication of referential information; study change in progress and see on-going change reflected in dialect maps; and emphasize the importance of linguistic diversity, languages in contact, and the wave model of linguistic evolution.

Linguists of Group B, the "asocial" group, focus upon purely internal—structural or psychological—factors in explaining change; segregate affective or social communication from the communication of "ideas"; believe that sound change in progress cannot be studied directly, and that community studies or dialect maps show nothing but the results of dialect borrowing; they would take the homogeneous, monolingual community as typical, working within the Stammbaum model of linguistic evolution.

It would be unfair to argue that Group B linguists would disregard social factors entirely in explaining linguistic change. Rather they define the influence of society as alien to the normal operation of language, and view the operation of social factors as dysfunctional interference with normal development (Bloomfield 1933), or as rare and unsystematic interventions. Thus Martinet develops what we may call a "catastrophic" view of the relations of social and linguistic events. He argues that extraordinary social upheavals can disturb the linguistic equilibrium at rare intervals, setting off a wave of linguistic readjustments in which purely internal factors govern the succession of changes over "years, centuries, and millennia" (1964:522). Thus the influence of Norman French on English in the 12th and 13th centuries had profound effects, still being felt today through a long series of internally linked readjustments. Within their own perspective, Chomsky and Halle (1968) share this point of view. They argue that the underlying forms of English have undergone very little change since Middle English, and that the last serious change in the system was probably the substitution of the Romance stress rule for the Germanic stress rule as a result of the Norman invasion.

Thus there are areas of general agreement about the effects of certain violent social changes upon language. No one would deny the importance of conquests, invasions, and massive immigration, with consequent extinction, superposition, or merger of whole languages. We can distinguish three subtypes, following Lehmann (1963): (1) an invasion in which the language of the conquered people all but disappears, as with Celtic in Britain; (2) a conquest in which the conquerors eventually adopt the language of the conquered, with consequent large-scale alteration in a class-stratified vocabulary, as with the Norman hegemony; (3) an invasion which results in an intimate mingling of two populations, with intimate borrowing of vocabulary and even function words, as with the Scandinavian invasions of England. It would be interesting to add if we could the conditions for each of these outcomes, but the problem seems to be an historical and political one, appropriate for the larger focus of an interdisciplinary "sociolinguistics."[2]

2. Any discussion of the history of the study of language change in its social setting must take into account the one field where there has never been any doubt about the importance of social context: the study of pidgins and Creoles. From the time of Schuchardt (1909) Creolists have found it necessary to learn as much as possible about the social conditions under which these languages were formed and reformed (see in particular Sidney Mintz, "The socio-historical background to pidginization and

The issue is therefore not the importance of social factors, but rather whether they are deeply involved in the most systematic processes of phonological and grammatical change. Are such changes sensitive to the social and stylistic stratification of speech, and the expressive information conveyed by social and stylistic variation? Do we have to take these factors into account in order to understand the observed regularities of linguistic change? On these questions, Groups A and B diverge sharply, answering "yes" and "no" respectively. Without doing too much violence to individual views, we can line up in Group A such linguists as Whitney, Schuchardt, Meillet, Vendryes, Jespersen, and Sturtevant. In Group B, we would find Paul, Sweet, Troubetzkoy, Bloomfield, Hockett, Martinet, Kuryłowicz, Chomsky, and Halle.

But so far, we have not yet placed in this dichotomy Meillet's teacher and associate Saussure. At first glance, Saussure's definition of *langue* seems to place him squarely in Group A:

la partie sociale du langage, extérieure à l'individu . . . elle n'existe qu'en vertu d'une sorte de contrat passé entre les membres de la communauté (1962:31).

Since Saussure is said to be the most influential linguist of the century, and Meillet one of the most eminent in historical linguistics, and Jespersen is currently read and cited with the greatest attention,

---

creolization" in Hymes 1971, and the Hymes volume throughout). Many of the systematic processes of language change that we would like to trace in "normal" linguistic evolution can be observed in accelerated form in Creoles. Some of the most detailed studies of systematic morphological shifting are those of Bickerton (1971a, b). He demonstrates that speakers of the English-based Creole of Guyana move through a very wide range of pronoun paradigms, copula rules, and complementizer placement rules in a regular implicational series which seem to reflect the historical process of de-Creolization which affects the community as a whole. Bickerton argues with Bailey (1970) that such regular distributions through style and social class levels are direct reflections of change in progress. The synchronic-diachronic dichotomy of Saussure would then be collapsed, and the new version of the wave model of linguistic change would show symmetrical distributions through time, space and society (1971:182). Bailey and Bickerton argue further that the Creole examples are not special cases—that the history of most languages shows parallel processes. This recent revival of Group A forces coincides with the view of Wang and his associates that grammars must be seen as extended in time and space (Wang 1969: Chen and Hsieh 1971). The call for a final abolition of the synchronic-diachronic distinction of Saussure represents a sharp opposition to the Group B policy of dividing linguistic data and activity into discrete and limited categories.

it is not at all obvious why Group A should not be the dominant element in 20th-century linguistics. In 1905, Meillet predicted that this century would be devoted to isolating the causes of language change within the social matrix in which language is embedded. But this did not happen. In fact, there were almost no empirical studies of language change in its social context in the 50 years following Meillet's pronouncement. It is clearly Group B that dominates current linguistic theory and practice; most linguists would agree with Chomsky in taking as the object of linguistic description the "ideal speaker-listener in a completely homogeneous speech community, etc." (1965:3).

Without good evidence to the contrary, the great achievements and the good authority of the linguists cited under Group B would argue for the correctness of their asocial view. We can isolate four general conditions which favor the predominance of Group B's outlook in recent decades, which have to do with the linguistic climate of thought rather than the substantive issues involved.

1. The first element in the success of Group B involves what we may call the Saussurian Paradox. Saussure argues that *langue* is a social fact, knowledge possessed by practically every member of the speech community. It follows that one can find out about *langue* by questioning any one or two speakers of the language—even oneself. On the other hand, *parole* reveals individual differences among speakers that can be examined only in the field, by a kind of sociological survey. Thus the social aspect of language can be studied in the privacy of one's own office, while the individual aspect would require social research in the heart of the speech community.

The Saussurian Paradox explains how Bloomfield could analyze the English "spoken in Chicago" from knowledge of his own speech (1933:90–92). The popularity of Saussure's *langue/parole* dichotomy was further assured when it was transformed into Chomsky's competence/performance distinction. Both treatments illustrate the way that linguists can adapt their methodology to suit their personal style of work without abandoning principle; there is no doubt that introspection is a congenial methodology for many linguists.

2. In their relations with other disciplines, linguists have traditionally leaned to the side of psychology rather than sociology. The road between language and thought is a well-traveled one; psychologists of language have always appeared prominently in the linguistic literature, from Wundt and Paul to Bühler and Jean Piaget.

On the other hand, Emile Durkheim's influence on Meillet seems to have been a matter of historical accident which has not been repeated.

Thus nothing could be more natural for linguists than to explain language change in terms of the parent-child relationship. To explain the acquisition of language, one need only consider the mother as speaker and the child as hearer; to understand linguistic change, one considers the child first as hearer, then as speaker. Many linguists like to perform "thought-experiments" in which they put themselves in the position of an imaginary child grappling with fictional data from an imaginary mother. This image follows naturally from the small amount of data that we have on children's speech—traditionally derived by parents studying their own children. More recent psycholinguistic experimentation confronts the child with the test situation; just as the linguist traditionally summons the informant to a formal elicitation session, so the psychologist of language summons the child to the laboratory to wrestle with blocks or matrices, hoping to find some meaning in answers to meaningless questions. Since no one follows the child to observe his day-to-day interaction with other members of society, it would be strange if our explanations of his linguistic behavior took such social factors into account.

3. In the latter half of the 19th century, historical linguists were quite open to the influence of dialectology. As one striking example, one can cite the impact on Osthoff and Brugmann of Winteler's monograph on the Swiss German dialect of Kerenzen (Weinreich, Labov, and Herzog 1968:115). But in the 20th century, dialectology as a discipline seems to have lost any orientation towards theoretical linguistics, and dialect geographers have generally been content to collect their materials and publish them. Bloomfield's chapter dealing with this subject is strangely disjunct from his other chapters (Malkiel 1967); as others have noted (Sommerfelt 1930), the most solid and startling results of dialectology, such as those of Gauchat (1905), could not be fitted into the framework of neo-grammarian thinking. It was not until the 1950's that the work of Martinet (1955), Moulton (1962), and Weinreich (1954) demonstrated again the theoretical force of areal linguistics.

4. The eclipse of the social group of linguists is due primarily to the limitations of their own work and writings on the social context of language. They relied almost entirely upon an intuitive explanation of a few anecdotal events drawn from their own general knowl-

edge. When we read the comments of Whitney, Meillet, Jespersen, or Sturtevant we cannot argue that any of these authors *knew* more about society's impact on language than anyone else; they were simply willing to talk about it more. Typical of Whitney's arguments about the social nature of language is one that he raises to prove that "external circumstances" are the most important factor in linguistic change:

While a Swiss Family Robinson keep up their language, and enrich it with names for the new and strange places and products with which their novel circumstances bring them in contact, a Robinson Crusoe almost loses his for lack of a companion with whom to employ it. (1901:405)

We encounter hundreds of "thought-experiments" in these writers, taking the place of actual data. Again, Whitney says:

Let two children grow up together, wholly untaught to speak, and they would inevitably devise, step by step, some means of expression for the purpose of communication; how rudimentary, of what slow growth, we cannot tell. . . (p. 404)

The "castaway" thought-experiment occurs over and over:

Suppose an illiterate English family to be cast away upon a coral islet in the Pacific and to be left there isolated through a succession of generations. How much of our language would at once begin to become useless to them! (p. 138)

We find to our dismay that Whitney lives in a world of "facts" which are obvious to him but not to us, the kind of commonsense "experience" which has never been questioned:

The fact of variation in the rate of linguistic growth is a very obvious one. (p. 137)

The mode of argument which the 20th century inherited to deal with social matters is remarkably similar. We find most often a series of anecdotes that are designed to prove ideas already accepted as true. Thus Vendryes, expounding the Saussurian notion of the uniformity of *langue,* reports that

We know what misadventure befell Theophrastus of Lesbos in the market at Athens. When he asked the price of some commodity, a woman of the people recognized him as a stranger by his speech. (1951:240)

With distressing regularity we raise the familiar desert islands, populated with the castaways of thought-experiments:

When a solitary Frenchman meets a Persian on a desert island, each will forget the differences between them and they will naturally seek to make common cause. (p. 239)

We need only look up the word "social" in the index of any of the authors cited above—in Group A or Group B—to encounter more thought-experiments and more anecdotes. Thus Bloomfield explains the diversification of language by imaginary differences in density of communication, discovered in an elaborate thought-experiment which charts every utterance of every speaker in a community (1933:46). Since the experiment cannot be performed, Bloomfield admits that he is "forced to resort to hypothesis." The hypothesis is then enriched with a further hypothesis about linguistic change—that the relative prestige of speaker and hearer determine borrowing and the fluctuation of forms. The two hypotheses—both stated without evidence—are then combined in another thought-experiment which would provide a final accounting for the direction and rate of linguistic change:

If we had a diagram with the arrows thus weighted [by gradations representing the prestige of the speaker with reference to each hearer] we could doubtless predict, to a large extent, the future frequencies of linguistic forms. (1933:403)

It is difficult to believe that Bloomfield, with his fine sense of evidence, would give much weight to such arguments—even his own. By following the traditional mode of dealing with social facts, he was also arguing that this field lies outside the domain of the linguist's competence.

Although some of our most precise linguists are still prone to thought-experiments and anecdote, they tend to limit these to fields outside their normal linguistic activity. They are certainly sensitive to such vacuity on the part of others. To understand the strong Group B position taken by Martinet, Kuryłowicz, and Chomsky, we have to know what they were reacting against. Arguments about race and climate in the earlier literature strike us today as too absurd to take seriously, but these are the kinds of "external" arguments that Martinet and Kuryłowicz were denouncing.[3]

3. Even Sweet had a favorite argument about the effect of climate on language that he returns to over and over again. He attributes the Germanic raising of I-E long ā to ō to the fact that speakers in the northern climate tried to keep the cold, damp air out of their mouths by not opening their lips and jaws as wide as Mediterranean speakers (1900).

### Three Substantive Questions on Linguistic Change

Historical and strategic considerations influenced the linguists' decision to resist being drawn into a study of the social setting of change. But there is also a solid basis for their position in the substantive issues involved. If we decide to engage in a study of the social setting of linguistic evolution, contrary to the dominant position in current linguistic practice, we must raise at least three serious questions that must eventually be resolved.

### a. The Place of Social Variation

Does the social and stylistic variation of language play an important role in linguistic change? By "social," I mean those language traits which characterize various subgroups in a heterogeneous society; and by "stylistic" the shifts by which a speaker adapts his language to the immediate context of the speech act. Both of these are included in "expressive" behavior—the way in which the speaker tells the listener something about himself and his state of mind in addition to giving representational information about the world. Social and stylistic variation presuppose the option of saying "the same thing" in several different ways: that is, the variants are identical in referential or truth value, but opposed in their social and/or stylistic significance.

Martinet takes a strong negative position on the question of social variation. Under the heading, "Communication alone shapes language," he argues:

It is therefore the communicative uses of language which must engage our attention if we wish to discover the causation of linguistic changes. What we shall establish and be able to formulate will not necessarily hold good for those linguistic utterances which do not serve the purpose of communication. But we shall be disposed to disregard these since they are modelled on communicative utterances and so offer nothing which will not be found in these. (1964b:170)

Of course the term "communication" could include all kinds of expressive communication, but a reading of the wider context makes it clear that it is intended to exclude any information about the speaker contained in the linguistic form, as well as excluding "phatic" expression. The nonrepresentational information we are considering under this question is usually delivered simultaneously with other messages, so it is a question of neglecting one aspect and allowing others.

To simplify our analysis, we shall assume that the language in process of evolution is that of a strictly monoglot community, perfectly homogeneous in the sense that observable differences represent successive stages of the same usage and not concurrent usages . . . we must disregard these [social and geographical] variations as we did above in the case of descriptive linguistics. (1964b:164)

Martinet's position allows us to specify the phrase "play an important role." If the answer to the original question *a* stated above is positive, then the Chomsky-Martinet strategy will be defective, and produce vacuous or erroneous statements about linguistic change and its causes. In the main body of this discussion, I will assemble evidence to show that this is the case.

### b. The Level of Abstraction

Can high-level, abstract rules of phonology and grammar be affected by social factors? One of the factors that has led to the decline of the Group A approach is that linguists have steadily shifted their attention away from lexicon, phonetics, and inflectional morphology to rules of abstract phonology and syntax that operate at a "higher level"—that is, they are higher up in the ordering sequence, if changed would affect the output of many other rules, and contain more abstract information. We are increasingly aware that most rules of grammar are quite remote from conscious awareness. To state that social factors bear heavily on the systematic development of a language therefore raises a major conceptual problem, since speakers are not even vaguely aware of most of the deeper relations. How are such social factors brought to bear upon the process of language learning?

Members of Group A tended to focus strongly upon the role of the word as receiving and reflecting social influences. The contention of dialect geographers that every word has its own history (Meillet 1964:29, Malkiel 1967) fits in with this orientation. At the same time, it was recognized that grammatical particles are less subject to borrowing, more stable in the face of outside impact upon language. This would seem even more true for the rules that relate surface structure to underlying forms. Even if social factors should alter profoundly the phonetics and vocabulary of a language, and possibly the surface formatives as well, we might still argue that linguistic change in higher-level rules is purely an internal readjustment, not even remotely related to the immediate social context. We will consider this question in relation to some complex phonological rules; the answer is not at all obvious, but it can be seen to be located on the side of doubt.

## c. The Function of Diversity

Is there any adaptive function to linguistic diversification? Throughout the 19th century, there were many analogies drawn between linguistic and biological evolution, not least by Darwin himself who saw the two as "curiously parallel." He observed in language and in biological species homologies of form due to community of descent, and he compared the generalization of phonetic change to correlated growth in plants and animals. Languages and species both show the reduplication of parts, the effects of long-continued use, vestigial elements, hierarchical grouping, typological vs. genetic taxonomies, dominance and extinction, hybridization, and variability (1871:465). But Darwin felt it necessary to complete the analogy by arguing for the survival of the fittest in language, quoting as his authority Max Muller:

A struggle for life is constantly going on amongst the words and grammatical forms in each language. The better, the shorter, the easier forms are constantly gaining the upper hand, and they owe their success to their own inherent virtue.

No linguist would today endorse this point of view, which runs exactly counter to our notion of the arbitrariness of the linguistic sign. Languages do not seem to be getting better and better, and we see no evidence for progress in linguistic evolution (Greenberg 1959). Except for the development of vocabulary, we cannot argue for adaptive radiation in any area of language. The diversification of languages is not immediately and obviously functional, as the diversification of species may be. We receive no immediate benefit from not being able to understand the Russians or the Gaels, and the time taken to learn their languages does not seem to help in the survival of our own. We must seriously consider the possibility that the diversification of language is dysfunctional, and that we are worse off than if we all spoke a mutually intelligible version of post-Indoeuropean.

As far as systematic phonetic change is concerned, most linguists, both Group A and B, felt that the process of diversification was entirely negative. It was only the effects of analogy, or even conscious social intervention which restored the balance.[4] The notion that sound change destroys and analogy reconstructs is so widespread that it is almost assumed by most linguists. It is true that Martinet (1955) finds some value in the symmetry produced by the hole-filling tendency, and other linguists would find value in the simplification and generalization of rules. As far as grammar is concerned, it still must be demonstrated that analogy can be systematic, or that systematic grammatical change exists (Kuryłowicz 1964).

On the whole, linguists still seem to be confronted with the principle that diversification of language is due to the systematic and destructive effects of sound change (usually laid to the principle of least effort) and the breakdown in communications between isolated groups. This finding not only destroys the parallelism between linguistic and biological evolution, but is strangely conservative as well: it projects the view that the unchanging, homogeneous speech community of Chomsky-Martinet is the ideal towards which we should be striving, and that any degree of heterogeneity subtracts from our communicative powers. Because this is an unattractive and seemingly unrealistic result, I am inclined to reject it; some of the available evidence for this point of view will be marshalled in the final section.

### 3. The Study of Sound Change in Progress: the Uniformitarian Principle

If we are to apply ourselves to solving the three questions of linguistic change outlined above, we must immediately face one grave difficulty: we have too little information on the state of society in which most linguistic changes took place. The accidents which govern historical records are not likely to yield the systematic explanations that we need. Some historical linguists have achieved remarkable and insightful results with the texts on hand; H. C. Wyld will be cited as the most brilliant example. But such efforts have never been more than moderately convincing, and one is always free to disagree on the basis of other fragmentary evidence. The only strong solutions to the problems of language change just posed are through the study of change in progress.

Group B linguists have often claimed, in defense of neo-gram-

4. In this sense, Darwin's argument was reversed. He thought that the phonetic processes which shortened words necessarily improved them, so that the fittest or shortest survived.

marian principles, and on the basis of their thought-experiments, that linguistic change is too slow, too subtle, or too elusive to be studied as it occurs around us. In the work to be cited below, there is overwhelming evidence to the contrary, that the study of on-going change is a practical strategy. This evidence will reinforce and help us interpret the results of historical investigations. To use it in this way, we necessarily have to operate under a *uniformitarian principle*.[5] We posit that the forces operating to produce linguistic change today are of the same kind and order of magnitude as those which operated in the past five or ten thousand years.

There are certainly new factors emerging, with the growth of literacy, the convergence of widespread languages, and the development of scientific vocabulary. Yet these represent minor interventions in the structure of languages. If there are relatively constant, day-to-day effects of social interaction upon grammar and phonology, the uniformitarian principle asserts that these influences continue to operate today in the same way that they have in the past. If this principle is to any extent unjustifiable, our interpretations of the past by the present may be wide of the mark; but from present indications, the principle will be as successful in linguistics as it is in geology. To quote Gauchat, the most brilliant of the earlier workers in this field:

> . . . les dialectes parlés sont les représentants vivants de phases que les langues littéraires ont parcourues dans le cours des temps. Les patois . . . pourront nous servir de guides pour arriver à une meilleure compréhension de l'histoire des langues académiques. (1905:176)

It may immediately be argued that we do not literally observe the change "in progress." In most of the studies to be reported here, the investigator observed distribution in *apparent time*—that is, the differential behavior of speakers in various age levels. We distinguish this behavior from regular and repeated age-grading by obtaining at least one measurement at some contrasting point in real time. In the case of Martha's Vineyard, we had the Linguistic Atlas records

5. A term borrowed from geology; the concept introduced into geological theory by James Hutton at the turn of the 18th century. Hutton showed that the mountains, volcanoes, beaches, and chasms we now have are the result of observable processes still taking place around us, rather than violent convulsions at some remote time in the past ("catastrophism"). The uniformitarian doctrine is one of the accepted principles of current geomorphology—perhaps its fundamental tenet.

of 30 years before. Gauchat's study of Charmey (1905) was oriented to real time 24 years later by the supplementary observations of Hermann (1929). But even if we did repeated studies of the same area every few years, it might still be argued that we were only studying discrete stages and not the change in progress.

Such an argument is based on a vision of linguistic behavior as a set of uniform, homogeneous rules which can change uniformly, much as a beam of yellow light can gradually be changed to orange; the assumption is that we could theoretically observe the change in the same way that we watch the sunset turn to various colors. But this view is based on a faulty model of the homogeneous speech community. As Gauchat demonstrated, "l'unité phonétique de Charmey . . . est nulle." We find instead differentiated behavior, in which there is a gradual change in the frequency with which certain rules are utilized in various environments (Ch. 8). The internal evolution of linguistic rules involves shifts in the ordering and prominence of certain "variable constraints"—too abstract an object to be directly observed in the ordinary sense. We can take measurements of this process at discrete points in time, but we cannot observe the rules change from one moment to another. Consider the rule which diphthongized the low back /ɑ:/ in Charmey.

$$\emptyset \to \langle \begin{bmatrix} -\text{cons} \\ -\text{voc} \\ +\text{back} \end{bmatrix} \rangle \, / \, \begin{bmatrix} +\text{tense} \\ +\text{low} \end{bmatrix} \underline{\quad \langle +\text{stress} \rangle \quad} \begin{array}{l} [+\text{cons}] \\ \langle -\text{central} \rangle \\ \langle \begin{Bmatrix} +\text{ant} \\ -\text{cor} \end{Bmatrix} \rangle \end{array}$$

This is a variable rule which states that a back glide appears variably after a low tense vowel, and that the rule applies more often to stressed (final) words, more often if the final consonant is not an /r/ (i.e., central), and as a lesser effect, more often if the final consonant is a labial. The reflexes of Lat. *porta, corpus,* were rarely diphthongized from [pwɔrtə, kwɔ] to [pwaᵒrtə, kwaᵒ].[6] When Hermann visited Charmey in 1929, he found the rule in a more advanced state: it had gone to completion in all environments except before /r/, where it was now quite common.

6. Though the vowel before r is given by Gauchat as open o [o], and the main dipthongization rule affects ɑ, these two phones can be analyzed as conditioned variants, and so we are dealing with the same rule. A later rule deletes final r.

$$\emptyset \rightarrow \left\langle \begin{bmatrix} -\operatorname{cons} \\ -\operatorname{voc} \\ +\operatorname{back} \end{bmatrix} \right\rangle / \begin{bmatrix} +\operatorname{low} \\ +\operatorname{tense} \end{bmatrix} \underline{\qquad} \begin{matrix} [+\operatorname{cons}] \\ \langle * -\operatorname{central} \rangle \end{matrix}$$

The rule now states that the vowel is diphthongized variably, but that wherever the vowel is not followed by an /r/, the rule applies without exception.[7] It is clear that we could not follow the change of this rule from one utterance to another, for a discrete period of time would have to elapse before the new ordering of the variable constraints would be evident even for an observer who never left the scene. The qualitative changes shown in the rule involve (1) the appearance of the "categorical" symbol *, for all but noncentral environments, and (2) as a consequence, the disappearance of the stress and labial constraints which are now obliterated in the general advance.

Finally, something must be said about the distinction which is often drawn between the "origin" and the "propagation" of a change (Postal 1964:284, Sturtevant 1947, Sommerfelt 1930). Speaking on behalf of those who investigate change in progress, I do not find such a distinction coherent. What is the origin of a linguistic change? Clearly not the act of some one individual whose tongue slips, or who slips into an odd habit of his own. We define language, along with other Group A linguists, as an instrument used by the members of the community to communicate with one another. Idiosyncratic habits are not a part of language so conceived, and idiosyncratic changes no more so. Therefore we can say that the language has changed only when a *group* of speakers use a different pattern to communicate with each other.

Let us assume that a certain word or pronunciation was indeed introduced by one individual. It becomes a part of the language only when it is adopted by others, i.e., when it is propagated. Therefore the origin of a change *is* its "propagation" or acceptance by others. From that point on, we only have a continuation of the same pattern. We do not rule out the possibility of independent simultaneous innovation by a number of speakers; but we do find absurd the notion that an entire community would change simultaneously without reference to each other, without a gradual transfer of the

---

7. The asterisk notation indicates a feature in a variable rule which, when present, causes the rule to apply categorically, without exception (Labov 1972a: Ch. 3).

pattern from speaker to speaker. Every empirical study, beginning with Gauchat, shows such systematic differentiation in even the most isolated and closely knit communities.

In this chapter, I will utilize data from eight of these empirical studies of speech communities:

*1. Louis Gauchat's investigation of phonetic diversity among three generations of Swiss French speakers in the village of Charmey (1905), with Hermann's following report (1929).*

The main sound changes observed in progress are summarized in Table 9.1, showing (a) the palatalization of ł → y, proceeding variably in the middle generation, completed in the youngest; (b) the monophthongization of /ao/, variable in the oldest generation, completed in the middle; (c) the diphthongization of back ɒ → a° beginning in the middle generation, completed in the youngest except before /r/; (d) the diphthongization of ε → εᴵ, beginning in the oldest generation, variable in the middle age group, and completed in the youngest generation except for the word class with underlying /r/ following the vowel.

TABLE 9.1.
FOUR SOUND CHANGES IN PROGRESS IN THE
SWISS FRENCH OF CHARMEY, 1899

|  | *I*<br>*90–60 yrs* | *II*<br>*60–30 yrs* | *III*<br>*under 30* |
|---|---|---|---|
| (ł) | ł | ł ~ y | y |
| (aw) | a° ~ (a·) | a· | a· |
| (ey) | ε ~ (εⁱ) | ε ~ εⁱ | εᴵ |
| (ɒ) | ɒ | ɒ ~ a° | a° |

Source: Gauchat 1905.

*2. Ruth Reichstein's investigation of phonemic variables among Parisian school children (1960), against the background of Martinet's World War I inquiry.*

Reichstein tested some 570 schoolgirls for phonemic contrast with nine minimal pairs, revolving about /a∼ɑ/, /ε∼ε:/, /ε̃∼œ̃/; these contrasts seemed to be disappearing rapidly, and comparison by area and class structure shows that certain interior working-class districts led the way.

*3. My own study of the centralization of* (ay) *and* (aw) *on Martha's Vineyard, compared to earlier phonetic records made by Linguistic Atlas interviewers.*

This study showed (a) progressive centralization of /ay/ in the oldest generation, with (b) a later centralization of /aw/ in the middle generation, overtaking the first process for younger speakers: see Table 9.2 (a rearrangement of Table 1.2). The Atlas data show no centralization of /aw/ in 1933. Recent spectrographic studies of the same speakers (Labov 1972c) have confirmed the original view of the mechanism, and added considerable detail.

TABLE 9.2.
CENTRALIZATION OF (ay) AND (aw)
IN 3 GENERATIONS OF ENGLISH
SPEAKERS: MARTHA'S VINEYARD,
MASS.

| Generation | (ay) | (aw) |
|---|---|---|
| Ia  (over 75 yrs) | 25 | 22 |
| Ib  (61–75 yrs) | 35 | 37 |
| IIa  (46–60 yrs) | 62 | 44 |
| IIb (31–45 yrs) | 81 | 88 |
| III  (14–30 yrs) | 37 | 46 |

*4. My own study of the evolution of New York City vowels (1966a), as confirmed and enlarged by our current instrumental studies (1972c). Relation to real time is shown by comparison with four other reports extending back to 1896.*

The New York City investigations show (a) a rise in the stratification of final and preconsonantal /r/ among speakers below 40; (b) a tensing and raising of short *a* to form the variable (eh) and raising of long open *o* to form the variable (oh), from low to high position, with accompanying merger of mid and high ingliding vowels; (c), a backing and raising of the nucleus of /ay/ and /ah/ in *guy* and *God*, with a corresponding fronting of the nucleus of /aw/. Fig. 9.1 shows four stages in the chain shift of /ahr → ohr → uhr/ relating the word classes of *lard*, *lord*, and *lured*, from the spectrographic measurements of the vowel systems of four working-class New Yorkers.

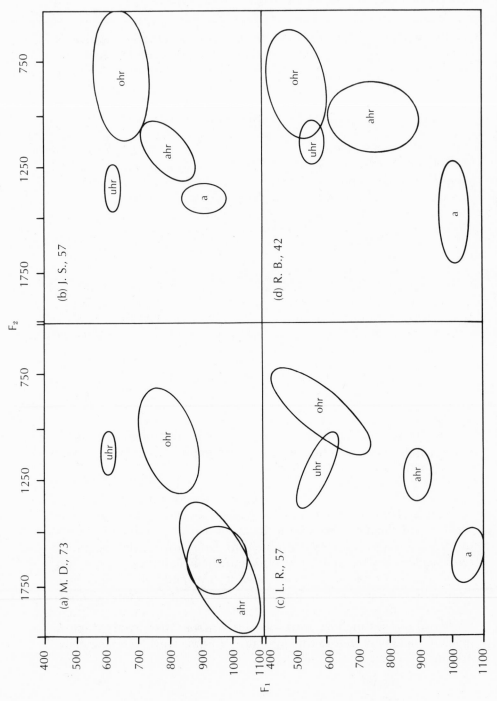

Fig. 9.1. Four stages in the New York City chain shift
ahr → ohr → uhr.

5. *The study of Hillsboro, North Carolina, carried out by Levine and Crockett, primarily through questionnaires and formal tests of pronunciation (1966); a study of the black population of the same town, using the same methods, by Anshen (1969).*

Levine and Crockett have reported so far only the pronunciation of final and preconsonantal /r/. They found a strong shift towards a new norm of r-pronunciation, parallel to 3a, but evidence for an older high-prestige norm of r-lessness surviving also.

6. *A recent investigation of the English of Salt Lake City and its environs by Stanley Cook (1969) showing an early stage in the development of an urban dialect.*

The most prominent feature in the process of change was the fronting of (aw), which was strongest among young college people, and spreading gradually outwards from Salt Lake City. Cook also studied the rural merger (and stereotype of reversal) of /ɑr/ and /ɔr/ in *far* and *for*; it was shown to be an advanced change undergoing a certain amount of overt correction. Cook was able to trace the history of the merger in a rural community, its stigmatization and reversal among younger speakers, and a tendency towards hypercorrect raising of /ɔr/ to [o˘ɚ] among younger suburban speakers. The separation of the two word classes among rural speakers is shown in Table 9.3.

TABLE 9.3.
PHONES USED FOR (ar) AND (or) IN CASUAL SPEECH: MINERSVILLE, UTAH

| Speakers | N | | ɑ | ɒ | ɔˇ | ɔˆ | Ω | o |
|----------|---|------|-----|---|-----|-----|---|---|
| Older informants | 5 | (ar) | 89 | — | 11 | — | — | — |
| (60+ yrs) | | (or) | 40 | 8 | — | 53 | — | — |
| Noncollege youth | 2 | (ar) | 100 | — | — | — | — | — |
| (ca. 17 yrs) | | (or) | 14 | — | 29 | 54 | 4 | — |
| College students | 2 | (ar) | 100 | — | — | — | — | — |
| (ca. 21 yrs) | | (or) | — | — | — | 100 | — | — |

Source: Cook 1969.

7. *An investigation of the social stratification of Spanish in Panama by Henrietta Cedergren (1970), showing five linguistic variables distributed across four socioeconomic groups.*

Cedergren found one of these variables—the retroflexion and fricativization of /č/—was in process of rapid change, while the others
showed fairly stable distributions over age levels.

*8. The study of the social stratification of language in Norwich,
England by Peter Trudgill (1971), using the same basic interview
techniques as in 4 and eliciting a range of styles from casual to word
list from a sample of 60 informants drawn from five social classes.*

Trudgill also found several linguistic variables in the process of
change, both from "above" and "below" in the social hierarchy. The
backing of short /e/ to [ʌ] before /l/ is the case we will consider
in detail, as well as Trudgill's findings on the differentiation of the
sexes in the process of change.

There are of course many studies of secondary data which give
us considerable insight into the social setting of linguistic change.
The most useful examination of historical texts, for our purposes,
is that of H. C. Wyld in *A History of Modern Colloquial English* (first
published 1921). Wyld had a strong interest in the influence of class
dialects on the history of English, and their origins in regional
dialects, because he himself was a speaker of a class dialect, "Received Pronunciation." We can profit from his close examination of
the spelling in such documents as the Cely papers, the Paston letters,
Machyn's diary, and the Verney Memoirs, by writers with a wide
range of social background.[8]

We might enlarge the list of sources indefinitely by including
qualitative and fragmentary accounts of change in progress. But
quantitative studies of actual speech communities must necessarily
take precedence. We can draw some conclusions from qualitative
observations which are framed in a three-category system: that a
given form or rule is never found, occurs variably, or is always found.
But much more profitable use can be made of linguistic variables
ranging freely from 0 to 1, so that $0 \leqslant x \leqslant 1$ where x represents the
proportion of all permitted environments in which the rule actually
applies. Here we are in a better position to detect the progress of

---

8. It has been pointed out by Asta Kihlbom (1926) that there are many serious defects
in Wyld's treatment of interpretation of this data, since he did not consult the original
manuscripts, and many of the letters are in the hands of secretaries rather than those
of the principals themselves. But Wyld's larger reconstruction of the processes involved
seems to stand.

a change or give a convincing account of how the change is correlated with social factors. A review of Tables 9.1–9.3 will show that
most of the relationships would disappear in a qualitative report.
In the case of Gauchat, we will see that the most interesting and
important findings add quantitative detail to the qualitative Table
9.1. In our most recent studies of sound change, we can move to a
higher level of precision by the use of instrumental measurements,
and this has now been done for two of the six studies outlined above
(see Labov 1972c; Labov, Yaeger, and Steiner 1972).

### 4. The Embedding of Linguistic Change in its Social Context

We can identify at least five different problems connected with
the explanation of linguistic change (Weinreich, Labov, and Herzog
1968) but not all of them are related to the social setting of the change.
The universal *constraints* upon linguistic change are by definition
independent of any given community. The question of locating the
*transition* between any two stages of a linguistic change is an internal
linguistic problem. The *embedding* problem has two aspects: the
change is seen as embedded in a matrix of other linguistic changes
(or constants), and also as embedded in a social complex, correlated
with social changes. There is also an important social component
to the *evaluation* problem—to show how members of the speech
community react to the change in progress, and discover what expressive information the variants convey. Finally, we can expect that
social factors will be deeply involved in the *actuation* problem: why
it took place at the particular time and place that it did.

It should be clear then that a full understanding of linguistic
change will require many investigations that are not closely tied to
the social setting, and other studies which plunge into the network
of social facts. Our other studies of the universal constraints on the
expansion of mergers (Herzog 1965:211), on universal principles of
vowel shifting (Labov, Yaeger, and Steiner 1972 Ch. 4), and the
internal transition of rules (ibid, Ch. 3) are concerned with the
speech community only as a source of data. In order to assemble
the data we need to answer the three questions raised in Sect. 2,
we will have to take full advantage of the available data on the
social embedding, evaluation, and actuation of the linguistic changes
under study.

Our first problem is to determine the aspects of the social context of language that are most closely connected with linguistic change. We might begin with a complete account of the immediate social setting of the speech event, following the descriptive program of Hymes (1962). We would consider all social relationships holding among speakers, addressees, audiences, and inhabitants of the social domains of the speech event (school, church, job, family . . . ). We could then ask whether changes in the language reflect changes in the relationships between these participants and settings. For example, we are now witnessing a steady series of changes in the use of second-person pronouns of respect in Spanish (Weinberg and Najt 1968), French (Lambert 1969), Serbo-Croatian, and other languages. We suspect that there is some truth to the conventional reaction of older people: that young people don't have the respect for their elders that they used to. But what independent measures of respect behavior would show us that this is more than a change in conventions or surface modes of expression? We have increasingly sophisticated means of recording and measuring linguistic behavior, relating our observations to the language used in everyday social interaction. But we do not have equally well-developed measures of authority, respect, or intimacy. We would therefore be wise to correlate our linguistic data with whatever measures of social position or behavior can be repeated reliably by others at other points in time.

It then seems reasonable to connect linguistic behavior with measures of ascribed and achieved status of the speakers. Whereas shifts of linguistic expression can register momentary changes of social attitudes, we will be more concerned with well-established ranges of linguistic expression—the way in which the individual habitually presents himself in various social settings. From one moment to another, our language gives information to answer the listener's question, "How are you feeling about me?" But the speaker's language provides general information about himself as well, answering the other's questions, "Who are you?" and "What are you?" These are matters of ascribed status—ethnic and religious membership, caste, sex, family—and achieved status—education, income, occupation, and possibly peer-group membership. Changes in language can then be correlated with changes in the position of the subgroups with which the speaker identifies himself. Current evidence shows that most incoming changes follow significant social distributions before they register any stylistic shifting (see Cook 1969 on /aw/).

## Socioeconomic Class

The social status of an individual is determined by the subjective reactions of other members of society, but it is easier for outsiders to use objective social and economic indicators to approximate the position of given individuals. In the United States, we obtain the sharpest overall stratification with various combinations of occupation, education, income, and residential area. In studying historical records, we usually judge upper-class figures by their family connections and title; less prominent individuals are easiest to classify by their occupations and habitual associations.

Henry Machyn, the Diarist, seems from his own words to have been a simple tradesman, possibly an undertaker, with a taste for pageants—especially for funerals (as was natural)—and for gossip. Of the great persons whom he mentions, he knew no more than their names and faces, scanned as they rode past him in some procession, and an occasional piece of gossip picked up, one is inclined to think from some other spectator among the crowd. (Wyld 1936:141)

Machyn's status is an important issue: he provides us with evidence for the lower-middle-class treatment of several important linguistic variables in 16th-century London English. For example, most of his -er- words are spelled as -ar-: *armyn*, 'ermine'; *hard* 'heard'; *sarmon*, 'sermon'. Wyld takes this alternation of -er and -ar- as a classic case of the correlation of social class movement and linguistic change. He raises the question: How did it come about that many words now pronounced with a mid central vowel, [ɜ], like *clergy*, *heard*, etc., were pronounced by good speakers in the 17th and 18th centuries with [aɚ]? If the [aɚ] pronunciation was "wrong," how was it adopted by the aristocracy in the first place?

Wyld collects a considerable body of data to show that the [aɚ] pronunciations entered the London dialect in the 15th century from Southeast dialects, and appear strongly in the private writings of middle-class Londoners like Machyn up to the middle of the 16th century. From this point, such spellings appear with increasing frequency in upper-class English until the end of the 18th century, when they begin to recede.

We have here a linguistic feature which found its way from a Regional dialect into Middle Class London speech, passed thence into Received Standard, only to be ousted later by a fresh wave of Middle Class influence (1936:11).

The ultimate rejection of the [ɑɚ] pronunciation by middle-class speakers in favor of the standard spelling pronunciation was a natural byproduct of upward social mobility.[9] The new bourgeoisie had no way of knowing which words spelled -er- were pronounced [ɑɚ] by elegant aristocrats, and they naturally could only adhere to the solid orthographic standard.

We see in this development three processes of social embedding: (1) the transformation of a regional dialect into an urban lower-class dialect; (2) the spread of a linguistic feature upward from a lower to an upper class; (3) the recourse to spelling pronunciation by an upwardly mobile group. We can easily find further support for Wyld's view of the matter. The [ɑɚ] pronunciation still appears in Southeast dialects today.[10] And we will see, there is ample evidence for the upward movement of lower-class innovations or importations into the standard language.

Oddly enough, a great deal of the speculative literature on dialect borrowing is based on the notion that all movement of linguistic forms is from the higher-prestige group to the lower.[11] When Group B linguists deal with this topic, they inevitably assert such a principle.

Among his occupational companions, for example, a speaker will imitate those whom he believes to have the highest "social" standing. (Bloomfield 1933:476)

This is simply a remark, with no more justification than any of the other general observations in Bloomfield's treatment of dialect borrowing. Studies of current sound changes show that a linguistic innovation can begin with any particular group and spread outward and that this is the normal development; that this one group can be the highest-status group, but not necessarily or even frequently so.

We can find two other examples in Machyn's speech of incoming changes that eventually reached the upper class. One is the high pronunciation of -ea- words from M. E. ę̄ as [i:], indicated in

9. An alternate analysis of the New York City data (Labov 1967) based on the social mobility of the speakers provides as good or better correlation with linguistic behavior than the analysis based on the speakers' socioeconomic positions.

10. As shown in data gathered by Howard Berntsen and analyzed in our current studies of sound change in progress.

11. Expressed as a general principle by Gabriel Tarde in his *Lois de l'imitation* in 1890, and since known as *Tarde's law*.

Machyn's spelling by y in prych, spyking, bryking, brykefast. Eventually, this word class was detached from the mid-vowel position of long ā words so that meat fell together with meet rather than mate. Secondly, we note in Machyn a pronounced tendency for the loss of -r- before -s, giving Woseter 'Worcester', Dasset 'Dorset', continuing a tradition which ultimately led in the 18th century to a completely r-less pronunciation for all Londoners.[12]

In more recent studies, Reichstein (1960) found that several ongoing phonemic changes she was studying were most advanced in working-class districts of Paris. Our own studies of the suburbs of Paris find the most extreme raising and backing of /ɑ/ among working-class youth, so that casser la tête can be raised to [kɔselatɛt], and j'sais pas to [špo].[13] In our other exploratory studies of the dialects of Boston, Rochester, Detroit, and Chicago, we find the most advanced forms of many vowel shifts among working-class youth. In Chicago, it is working-class youth who show the most extreme tensing and raising of short a and fronting of short o, together with the lowering of lax short vowels /i/ and /e/ to mid and low position. Fig. 9.2 shows such an extreme vowel system, that of a 17-year-old working-class girl. In her sentence, That ended that [ði:ˇətɛndɨd ði:ˇət], we observe the low vowel /æ/ raised to high position, and the mid vowel /e/ opened to low position.

Dialect studies based on the speech of college students fail to capture such remarkable transformations of vowel systems until they are already far advanced, and already being repressed.

It is not always the working class which is at the leading edge of linguistic change. Often it is a higher-status group, comparable to Machyn's. Table 9.4 gives systematic data on one of the ongoing changes in the New York City vowel system: the backing and raising of /ay/ along with the fronting of /aw/. The numbers here refer to a scale in which zero would represent a low central nucleus for either /ay/ or /aw/: [aᴵ, aᵁ], characteristic of the oldest speakers. Consistent

12. By r-less, we mean that there is a categorical rule for the vocalization of consonantal r in final and preconsonantal position: whenever not followed directly by a vowel. This style of speech was adopted in the 19th century in all those cities of the United States which looked to England as a center of cultural prestige: Boston, New York, Richmond, Charleston, and Atlanta, but not Philadelphia.

13. These data are from the field work of Bryan Simblist, of Yale University. Although the working-class Parisian youth that we have studied preserve a great phonetic distance between front and back a, the lexical distribution of this distinction is quite different from that of the standard.

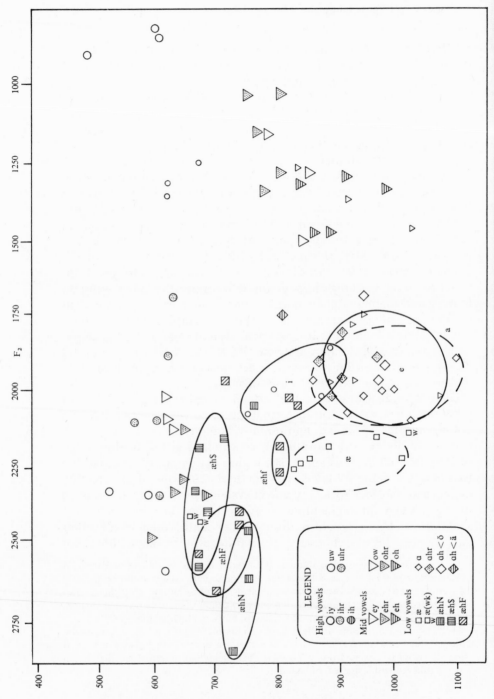

Fig. 9.2.  Vowel system of C.M., 16 years, Chicago. (Reproduced by permission of the Indiana University Press from W. Labov, "The Internal Evolution of Linguistic Rules" in R. Stockwell and R. Macaulay (eds.) *Historical Linguistics and Generative Theory*.)

TABLE 9.4.
AVERAGE (ay) AND (aw) VALUES FOR ALL
WHITE NEW YORK CITY INFORMANTS BY HALF-GENERATIONS

| | | (ay) | | | | (aw) | | | |
|---|---|---|---|---|---|---|---|---|---|
| | | Socioeconomic class | | | | Socioeconomic class | | | |
| Age | Generation | 0–2 | 3–5 | 6–8 | 9 | 0–2 | 3–5 | 6–8 | 9 |
| 5–19 | II-B | 7 | 23 | 22 | 12 | 8 | 20 | 17 | 8 |
| 20–34 | II-A | 5 | 18 | 24 | 10 | — | 7 | 10 | 4 |
| 35–49 | I-B | 8 | 17 | 18 | 20 | 4 | 7 | 8 | 1 |
| 50–64 | I-A | 5 | 10 | 10 | 15 | 2 | 7 | 5 | 5 |
| 65+ | 0 | 0 | | | | 0 | | | |

Source: Labov 1966a.

Index of (ay) and (aw) = average of phonetic ratings × 10

Phonetic scales for rating fronting of nucleus of (aw) and backing of nucleus of (ay):

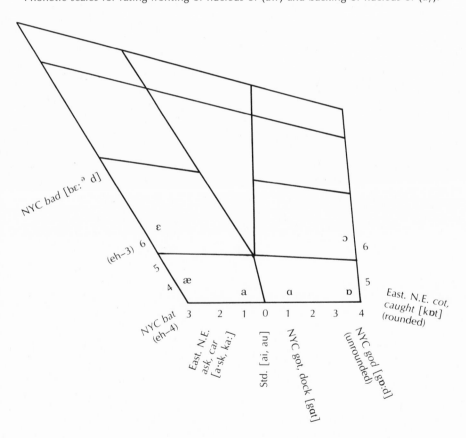

pronunciation of /ay/ as [ɒ$^I$] would yield (ay)-40, and consistent /aw/ as [æ$^U$] would also show a score of 40. Table 9.4 shows that the movement of /ay/ seems to have begun in the middle-class groups, but continued most strongly in the lower middle class, spreading gradually to the working class while upper-middle-class speakers avoided it. The fronting of /aw/ is strongest in the lower middle class, but is gradually expanding in this generation to affect the other groups.

Innovation by the highest-status group is normally a form of borrowing from outside sources, more or less conscious; with some exceptions, these will be prestige forms.[14] The original spread of r-less pronunciation in the United States was modelled on the London patterns of the early 1800's—a "change from above" spreading outwards from the centers of Anglophile influence.[15] The present reversal of this trend throughout the eastern United States can be seen in Boston and the South (Levine and Crockett 1966) as well as New York (Labov 1966a). This is another form of change from above, reversing the prestige relations. There is a sharp differentiation between older speakers, who still reflect the earlier Anglophile norms, and the younger speakers who have adopted the new broadcast norm of "general American" r-pronunciation. Change from above can be quite regular; it can affect each subgroup in proportion to its distance from the center of prestige, and the formality of the speech situation. A linguist who is interviewing subjects will observe these importations from above more clearly in reading texts than connected speech; in the unattended speech of everyday life, we observe more dramatically the effects of change from below, as in the movements of (ay) and (aw) cited above.[16] Table 9.5 shows the average indexes of r-pronunciation in casual style for New Yorkers: it is plainly an upper-middle-class phenomenon which has not affected the natural speech of other groups. Table 9.6 shows the way

14. In The Pickwick Papers, Dickens marks Sam Weller and his father with the stigmatized v ∼ w confusion; he also ridicules a foppish young lord with a stereotyped labialization of prevocalic r, all printed as w's in the text.

15. This expansion reached a radius of approximately 150 miles from Boston, Richmond, and Charleston, but was confined to the immediate vicinity of New York City.

16. In the early stages of a linguistic change, a consistent pattern can be observed in formal styles as well as casual speech. This is the case with most New Yorkers' pronunciation of front /aw/ and back /ay/. It is not until the more advanced stages of the change that formal styles show correction and irregular distribution.

TABLE 9.5.
(r) IN CASUAL SPEECH BY AGE AND CLASS

| Age | Socioeconomic classification | | | |
|-----|-----|-----|-----|-----|
| | 0-1 | 2-5 | 6-8 | 9 |
| 8-19 | 00 | 01 | 00 | 48 |
| 20-29 | 00 | 00 | 00 | 35 |
| 30-39 | 00 | 00 | 00 | 32 |
| 40-49 | 00 | 06 | 10 | 18 |
| 50- | 00 | 08 | 00 | 05 |

$N$

| | | | |
|---|---|---|---|
| 4 | 11 | 4 | 4 |
| 3 | 5 | 5 | 3 |
| — | 2 | 4 | 3 |
| 5 | 18 | 7 | 3 |
| 5 | 7 | 1 | 3 |

TABLE 9.6.
PERCENT OF (r)-00 SPEAKERS IN WORD
LISTS (STYLE D) BY AGE AND CLASS

| Age | Socioeconomic class | | | |
|-----|-----|-----|-----|-----|
| | 0-1 | 2-5 | 6-8 | 9 |
| 8-19 | 50 | 50 | 50 | 25 |
| 20-39 | 67 | 75 | 00 | 20 |
| 40-49 | 20 | 18 | 00 | 25 |
| 50- | 64 | 27 | 00 | 33 |

$N$

| | | | |
|---|---|---|---|
| 2 | 8 | 2 | 4 |
| 5 | 17 | 9 | 4 |
| 3 | 7 | 1 | 3 |
| 11 | 11 | 1 | 3 |

Source: Labov 1966a.

in which this prestige form affects speakers in the most formal style: the percentage who use the completely r-less norm in reading word lists. The second-highest status group—the lower middle class—is most affected; no adult speaker stayed with the older norm. This is one of the many indications of the strong pattern of "hypercorrect" behavior on the part of the second status group, an important element in the mechanism of linguistic change (see Ch. 5). A parallel example of this hypercorrect pattern appears in the quantitative study of r-pronunciation of Hillsboro; as Table 9.7 shows, the greatest shift from "sentence style" to word list style was on the part of the high-school educated group, rather than the college group. In the first case, subjects read sentences with blanks; their attention was drawn to the problem of filling these with a lexical item, rather than to the words of the text that contained /r/. In the word list, attention was focused directly on the variable, and the second-highest status group responded more sharply to this difference than any of the others. Returning to the age relationships in Table 9.6, we find that

TABLE 9.7.
FREQUENCY OF FINAL AND PRECONSONANTAL [r] FOR WHITE SPEAKERS:
IN HILLSBORO, N.C.

|                        | Sentence-list | Word-list | Net increase |
|------------------------|---------------|-----------|--------------|
| Age                    |               |           |              |
| 21–39 yrs              | 56.6          | 65.1      | 8.5          |
| 40–59 yrs              | 54.2          | 60.3      | 6.1          |
| 60 yrs and over        | 44.5          | 49.3      | 4.8          |
| Education              |               |           |              |
| Any college            | 52.7          | 58.9      | 6.2          |
| High school graduate   | 54.6          | 65.6      | 11.0         |
| Some high school       | 50.0          | 57.0      | 7.0          |
| Grade school or none   | 52.6          | 57.3      | 4.7          |
| Sex                    |               |           |              |
| Male                   | 52.3          | 57.4      | 5.1          |
| Female                 | 52.9          | 61.1      | 8.2          |

Source: Levine and Crockett 1966:223.

in the working-class groups, the older speakers tend to hold to the earlier norms, and the younger speakers as well; it is only among the middle-aged groups that the new prestige norms are adopted. As we will see below, overt correction tends to be rather unsystematic when it occurs late in life, and it focuses on individual words rather than on general rules.[17] We might ask: can the highest-status group ever innovate unconsciously?

In so far as any habit of speech is associated with a high-prestige group, it is apt to be remarked. Conservative critics will quickly call attention to it, as Gill ridiculed a fashionable 17th-century pronunciation which raised long ā to [iː], giving [kiːpn] for *capon* (Wyld 1936).

Not every linguistic change is attached to a particular social group. The raising of M.E. ē to [iː] seems to have been "common to the speech of all areas and classes in London" (Wyld 1936:207). In areas of the United States, the merger of short open o and long open o seems to affect everyone in certain areas.[18] But here I am speaking

17. Speakers who have acquired the norm of formal r-pronunciation late in life show regular and predictable patterns of shifting, but do not achieve consistency. The word classes containing /r/ are fairly well defined, yet there is a fair amount of hypercorrection, in *idear, lawr* and *order* and occasionally *Gard* for *God*.

18. There are exceptions to the uniformity of this merger of *hock* and *hawk, don* and *dawn*. In Phoenix, for example, it appears to be more characteristic of the Anglo population than blacks or Spanish-Americans.

from general impressions; it cannot be denied that in every case that has been studied closely, one social group or another has been found to lead strongly in the development of a linguistic change.

The difference between a change in progress and an advanced change may sometimes be seen clearly in the pattern of social distribution. A change may begin first in a social group located anywhere in the social hierarchy. As long as it is developing and spreading outward, one can still see the pyramidal pattern through various age levels, with the highest values in the youngest speakers of the original group. But when the change reaches an advanced state, and all social classes are affected, it is often stigmatized, and the social correction of formal speech begins to obscure the original pattern. In this case we get a linear distribution, with the highest social class showing the least amount of the stigmatized feature in ordinary conversation. We can see this clearly in Cedergren's study of the Spanish of Panama City (1970). Table 9.8 shows Cedergren's findings on the social stratification of five variables in Panamanian Spanish across four social classes.

TABLE 9.8.
SOCIAL STRATIFICATION OF FIVE
SPANISH VARIABLES IN PANAMA

| | Social groups | | | |
|---|---|---|---|---|
| Variable | I | II | III | IV |
| (R) | 1.62 | 1.88 | 2.29 | 2.29 |
| (PARA) | 1.11 | 1.37 | 1.39 | 1.69 |
| (ESTA) | 1.26 | 1.56 | 1.62 | 1.71 |
| (S) | 2.03 | 2.24 | 2.31 | 2.36 |
| (CH) | 1.88 | 2.24 | 2.13 | 2.00 |

Source: Cedergren 1970.

The linguistic variables in Table 9.8 may be defined briefly as follows:

(R):      the devoicing, fricativization, pharyngealization, and deletion of syllable-final /r/, with values ranging from 1 to 6 in the direction of these processes.

(PARA): the alternation of the full form of the preposition *para* with *pa*, with values of 1 and 2 respectively.

(ESTA): alternation of the full form *esta* with *ta*, assigned values of 1 and 2 respectively.

(S):        the syllable-final alternation of [s], [h] and [∅], with values
            of 1, 2 and 3 respectively.
(CH):       palatal vs. retroflex and reduced stop onset of /č/, with
            values of 1 and 2 respectively.

The figures in Table 9.8 are the arithmetical means of the values
of the variables. The social classes range from the highest (I) to the
lowest (IV), with the first four variables showing a linear distribution
with lowest scores for the highest social class. But the (CH) variable
shows a curvilinear pattern which suggests that the change originates
in the second-highest status group II. That (CH) represents an on-
going change in progress is clearly shown by Table 9.9, which gives
the distribution of scores by age groups for the same five variables.
We can see that (CH) is the only variable with a unidirectional linear
progression across age groups, with a dramatic advance in the
youngest groups quite comparable to the values shown for change
in progress in Martha's Vineyard and New York City.

TABLE 9.9.
DEVELOPMENT OF FIVE SPANISH VARIABLES BY AGE GROUPS

| Variable | Age | | | | |
|---|---|---|---|---|---|
|  | 11–20 | 21–30 | 31–40 | 41–50 | 61–70 |
| (R) | 2.28 | 1.90 | 1.95 | 2.23 | 1.46 |
| (PARA) | 1.31 | 1.34 | 1.48 | 1.33 | 1.39 |
| (ESTA) | 1.64 | 1.50 | 1.67 | 1.57 | 1.41 |
| (S) | 2.34 | 2.22 | 2.15 | 2.18 | 2.19 |
| (CH) | 2.15 | 2.29 | 2.05 | 1.81 | 1.31 |

Source: Cedergen 1970.

The situation in Panama City would not in itself justify the principle that a curvilinear pattern of social stratification corresponds to
early stages of a change in progress. But in New York City we also
find that, of five major variables studied, two show a curvilinear
distribution: the raising of (eh) in *bad, ask, dance,* is most advanced
among upper-working-class speakers, and the raising of (oh) in *off,
all, water* is most advanced in the lower middle class. Distribution
in apparent time clearly shows that these two variables are still
developing among the oldest speakers; the raising is found chiefly
in the social class which now shows the most extreme forms. Trudgill's study of the sociolinguistic structure of Norwich (1971) con-

siders a number of phonological variables which show linear social stratification—matching the hierarchical distribution of social classes. But one variable shows a curvilinear distribution—the backing of /e/ to [ʌ] before /l/ in *belt, held,* etc. Trudgill shows that the distribution of this variable in apparent time clearly indicates change in progress, with upper-working-class speakers in the lead.

An understanding of this principle demands an appreciation of the difference between the regular progress of change from below in the early stages of a sound change, and the later correction from above which occurs when the changing feature comes to the attention of those who set social norms. If the new linguistic element is associated with a lower social group, it will usually be stigmatized, and eventually its use will be inversely related to social status. The later stages of a change may then show a linear distribution, although the leading edge was originally in an interior group. If the linguistic innovation spreads upward from the very lowest social group, it will be aligned with the social hierarchy from the beginning, but this seldom happens. It does sometimes happen that a feature will be introduced by the highest class in the social system, though as a rule this is not an innovating group.

We have thus documented in some detail the embedding of linguistic change in one type of social structure: the socioeconomic system of class differentials. Change does not occur without regard to class patterns; instead, the incoming pattern enters like a wedge with one group or another acting as the spearhead. The feature is rarely confined to a particular class (unless it is stigmatized and recedes—see Sect. 5 below). It is therefore difficult to see how Martinet or Chomsky would handle this situation. Would the homogeneous society posited by the abstract linguist contain the new form or not? If not, at what point would the abstractor make the decision to include it in his homogeneous system and for what reason?

I can imagine two directions in which the abstract linguist might go. He might simply abstract from social class, and allow the incoming form to be optional for everyone. He would then argue that its association with a particular class of people is below the level of linguistic significance. In that case, the new option would appear suddenly as a blind fact, without direction or interpretation. Our discussion of the evaluation of such well-developed linguistic changes will illustrate how much significance the option can have in fact.

A second alternative would be to abandon the notion of writing a description of *langue* as a community property, and simply describe the speech of one class. If the community is differentiated according to class, we could then seize the homogeneous groups which do exist, and describe their language. As a first step this might be practical, but complications ensue when we discover that there are other social structures such as caste or ethnic group which intersect with socioeconomic class.

### Ethnic Group and Caste

The beginning of the current interest in sociolinguistic studies can be seen in the 1960 publication of Ferguson and Gumperz, *Linguistic Diversity in South Asia*. Some of the papers concern literary-colloquial oppositions, but others describe caste differences: in Kannada (Bright and McCormack), Tamil (Pillai), Bengali (Dimock and Chowdhury), and Hindi (Gumperz and Naim). Bright was primarily concerned with the effect of caste differences on linguistic change. Though his comparisons of two dialects of Kannada are based on only two informants—college students—his conclusions are of the greatest interest. The non-Brahmin dialect (NB) accepted foreign words and foreign phonemic patterns (English and Sanskrit) less readily than the Brahmin dialect (B); B was more resistant to grammatical change and phonological change from within.

For example, B has imported /f, z, ɔ/ from English, where NB has substituted native /p, j, ā/, so that B kɔfi 'coffee' = NB kāpi, and B has Sanskrit /š/ in šānti, 'peace', while NB has sānti. On the other hand, B shows original /ē/ in words where NB has differentiated to /yā/ if a mid or low vowel occurs in the next syllable: B pēṭe, NB pyāṭe.

A later secondary study of Tamil and Tulu showed the same general pattern.

The Tulu evidence shows the Brahmins as chief innovators in the more conscious varieties of change—semantic shift, lexical borrowing, and phonological borrowing. In the less conscious processes of phonological and morphological change involving native materials, both B and NB dialects innovate. (Bright and Ramanujan 1964)

Bright and Ramanujan conclude that upper- and lower-class dialects innovate independently; the more conscious importations are regularly the mark of the upper class, while the less conscious changes affect both classes. They then point out that the Brahmins can show overt correction of these changes, as in Kannada and Tamil. These findings from South Asia fit in well with the general principles of change which emerge from our New York City studies, contrasting the behavior of the highest-status group with the others.[19]

In the development of the New York City vowel system, we find that ethnic identity plays an important role—more important than socioeconomic class, for some items. The ethnic differentiation of the tensing and raising of short *a* in *bad, ask, dance*—the (eh) variable—is shown in Table 9.10. The numbers represent the average degree of openness of the vowel. Consistent pronunciation of *bad* with [æ·] at the level of unraised *bat* would show a value of (eh)-40. If the nucleus of all such short *a* words that were tensed were then raised to the level of [e:], the index would show (eh)-20, and for the level of [i:], (eh)-10. Although all groups show a gradual decrease in the openness of the vowel with age, New Yorkers of Italian background show the greatest decrease for each age level. This ethnic differentiation shows up in all but the lowest social group, which has not been drawn into this process.

TABLE 9.10.
DISTRIBUTION OF (eh) BY AGE AND
ETHNIC GROUP IN NEW YORK CITY

| Age | Jews | Italians | Blacks |
|---|---|---|---|
| 8–19 | 22 | 20 | 24 |
| 20–39 | 23 | 19 | 28 |
| 40–49 | 27 | 18 | 33 |
| 50–59 | 29 | | |

Source: Labov 1966a:357.

When we speak of ethnic identity as a part of the social context of a linguistic change, it immediately raises the question of a substratum. Is the underlying parent language the cause of this differentiation? The Martinet view would lean toward this explanation, since we are considering outside impact as reflected in "the pressure of another language." But the language-contact explanation fails by

19. Current studies of Maxine Berntsen in Phaltan are designed to examine the social distribution of nonstandard features of Marathi, using many of the same techniques as in the New York City studies. Berntsen's preliminary findings show that education is now a more important determinant of linguistic behavior than caste membership.

itself. Italian has no [æ], and first-generation Italian-Americans tend to use their native Italian low vowel [a] for the class of English short *a* words. It would then appear that the second-generation Italian tendency to raise short *a* is not the response that a structural version of contact theory would predict: it reverses the direct influence of Italian. Yiddish has no [æ] either, but first-generation Yiddish speakers tend to raise English short *a* to [ɛ]. Second-generation Jewish speakers of English have somewhat less tendency to raise this vowel than the Italians. This result can be interpreted in the light of other sociolinguistic data on second-generation speakers, who reach for native status by removing themselves as far as possible from the low-prestige pattern of their parents. This is another version of the "hypercorrect" or reverse influence that appears to play a major role in linguistic change.

We now see that linguistic change may also be differentiated by its association with a particular ethnic or caste group, and that various ethnic groups may treat the same variable in different ways. An abstract treatment of these data might still decide to ignore the association with caste and ethnic group as beneath linguistic notice. The second approach—contracting one's focus to homogeneous groups—is now somewhat more difficult. A group of working-class men will no longer do; we must be sure to insist on working-class *Italian* men.

## Local Identity

In addition to the crossclassifying assignments of class and caste status, communities often develop more concrete categories by which individuals are placed. In rural communities (or in urban villages), local identity is an extremely important category of membership—one which is often impossible to claim and difficult to achieve. In many small towns of New England, there is a large subcategory of "summer people." Then there are "incomers" or "outsiders," people who have moved into the town permanently but who are shouldered aside for many decades before they are accepted. There are immigrant groups, like the "damn Portagees," Indians, blacks, and other ethnic groups who are not immediately accepted into the main stream. The eighth- or tenth-generation Yankees form the core of the local population, but members of other groups may gradually assume local identity.

On the island of Martha's Vineyard (Ch. 1), it was this network of social categories which was most closely correlated with the linguistic change in progress—more important than occupation, geography, education, or sex. In the final analysis, the sound change being studied was associated with the assertion "I'm a Vineyarder." The Martha's Vineyard study focused on the relation of social factors to linguistic change; it demonstrated that the direction and development of this change could not be understood without relating it to the basic çategories of local identity.

### The Transformation of Regional Dialects into Urban Class Dialects

Wyld observed that a regular pattern in the development of English was the transformation of rural, regional dialects into class dialects in the cities. This process often involves the movement of rural speakers into low-prestige urban occupations, and into rapidly growing ghettos.

When the rural speaker arrives in the city, he usually finds that his country talk is ridiculed. Even if it was a marker of local identity, and a source of prestige at home, he may already have been conscious of the provincial character of his speech before he came to the city. As a result, we often see a rapid transformation of the more salient features of the rural dialects as speakers enter the city.

In the United States, the movement of the southern black population into the northern cities has brought about the creation of a uniform caste dialect—the black English vernacular of Harlem and other inner cities. Black speakers in smaller communities, unaffected by this process of dialect swamping, tend to participate in the linguistic changes taking place around them. But in the larger ghetto areas, we find black speakers participating in a very different set of changes bearing no direct relation to the characteristic pattern of the white community (Labov et al. 1968).

First we find the extreme rural forms stigmatized: lexical items such as *tote,* verbal auxiliaries such as *done* or *liketo* (= 'almost') are used less often. The characteristic vowel patterns of the regional southern dialects are modified. These differences are so extreme that the sound [dæ] can mean 'die' in Alabama but 'deer' in South Carolina. But such radical sound shifts are levelled out in the northern cities: The /ay/ of *die* is pulled back to [daᵉ], [da:ˤ ᵋ] or [dæ' :], and *deer* is [dɪ:ᵊ] or [de:ᵊ]. The basic phonological patterns which intersect with grammar—consonant cluster simplification, r and l vocalization, copula deletion—remain remarkably constant throughout the northern ghetto areas. Inflectional morphemes which are absent in the original southern black English, like third singular -s, remain absent. Syntactic patterns of southern colloquial speech are maintained or extended, as with negative concord and inversion (*Ain't nobody see that*). The end result is the black English vernacular—a consistent caste dialect, relatively constant for speakers from 6 to 20 years old, with remarkable geographic uniformity and resistance to standard English importations in the school system. Speakers in Boston, Newark, Cleveland, Detroit, Chicago, New Orleans, St. Louis, Houston, San Francisco, and Los Angeles show these grammatical patterns with startling regularity.

Similar processes appear to be operating in other languages, wherever large capital cities are developing at the expense of the hinterland. In the traditional literature described in Sect. 1, the social setting of language change is discussed in terms of the spread of the prestige patterns of urban capitals such as London and Paris. The creation of low-prestige working-class dialects is a pattern of equal linguistic interest; it embodies two major linguistic trends of the past several centuries: the decline of local dialects and the growth of vertical stratification in language.

This rapid language mixing seems to follow a kind of classic structural reductionism, and it would not be difficult to argue that it is a subtype of the same process that produces contact languages. As the history of various Creoles shows, the rapid result of sudden contact of two dissimilar structures is frequently the lowest common denominator of both, with a strong push towards inflectional simplification (see Hymes 1971 for various views on pidgin genesis and Bickerton 1971 for an opposing position). One of the universal constraints on change seem to be operating here—that in contact situations, mergers expand at the expense of distinctions (Herzog 1965:211). Yet if we are to apply our linguistic insight to predict such mergers, we must first recognize the existence of heterogeneous dialects, as the common, even normal form of language system. Not every linguist is willing to do this. Wyld and Kökeritz tried to explain the realignment of the -ea- words as the result of the upward movement of a regional dialect within the London system. But Halle preferred to abstract from any social evidence on this point (1962) and argue the history of *mate, meat,* and *meet* as if they were elements in the homogeneous speech community constructed by Chomsky and Martinet.

## The Role of Women

Gauchat's elegant and convincing study established the variability of Charmey patois, the existence of change in progress, and the role of women in furthering linguistic change. In case after case, Gauchat discovered that women used more of the newer linguistic forms than men did (1905:205, 209, 211, 218, 219, 224–26).

1. The palatalization of ł → y was found variably among speakers 30 to 40 years old, and regularly for those under 30. Above 40 years old, only women showed this trait.[20]
2. θ → h variably for postverbal pronouns so that for *veux-tu* [vuθo → vuho] among the youngest generation, under 30, "especially women."
3. a° → ā is variable in the oldest generation, and women apply the rule more than the men. Laurent Rime, 59, pronounced *douce* as [da°θə]; his wife Brigide, 63, said [dāθə].
4. ɒ → a°, variably in the middle generation, regularly in the youngest. "As always, women take this route more readily . . . than men."

Gauchat reinforced his finding by citing other examples from the history of French in which the women of Paris were portrayed as initiators of linguistic changes. We can point to similar behavior in the evolution of New York City English, and here the pattern of sex differences is even richer. In case after case, we find that women use the most advanced forms in their own casual speech, and correct more sharply to the other extreme in their formal speech. Table 9.11 compares men and women in the raising of tense short *a*, (eh), in three styles. In casual speech, women use more of the high vowels around (eh)-10 = [iˇːə], and show a modal value around (eh)-20, or [eːˇə]. But in reading lists of words with (eh) items, women shift to the opposite extreme, with a modal value around (eh)-40, = [æː]. Men, on the other hand, shift their modal value only one notch, from (eh)-22-26 to (eh)-27-32. Our instrumental studies confirm these impressionistic tables: women are almost a whole generation further along in the raising of (eh) than the men (Labov, Yaeger, and Steiner 1972; Ch. 3).

We find the same pattern in Detroit, where women clearly lead in the more extreme raising of this vowel, and in Chicago as well.

20. Gauchat reports that one woman, 63 years old, pronounced her list of ł words regularly with y: *viyo* (veclu), *Pyāre* (plorat), *byātse* (blanca) etc.

TABLE 9.11.
COMPARISON OF MEN AND WOMEN FOR (eh) AND (oh)
IN NEW YORK CITY

| | Style* | | | | | |
| | A | | B | | C | |
| Variable | Men | Women | Men | Women | Men | Women |
|---|---|---|---|---|---|---|
| (eh) 10–13 | — | 1 | — | — | — | — |
| 14–18 | 1 | 4 | — | 2 | 1 | — |
| 19–21 | 3 | 10 | 3 | 9 | 1 | 2 |
| 22–26 | 4 | 6 | 7 | 9 | — | 5 |
| 27–32 | 3 | 4 | 11 | 12 | 8 | 9 |
| 33–39 | 4 | 4 | 3 | 5 | 4 | 14 |
| 40–42 | 1 | 2 | — | 6 | 4 | 16 |
| | 16 | 33 | 24 | 43 | 18 | 46 |
| (oh) 10–13 | 3 | 4 | — | 1 | — | 3 |
| 14–18 | 3 | 10 | 4 | 10 | 2 | 5 |
| 19–21 | 4 | 14 | 7 | 7 | 5 | 13 |
| 22–26 | 3 | 5 | 8 | 16 | 5 | 4 |
| 27–32 | 3 | 4 | 5 | 10 | 5 | 8 |
| 33–40 | 1 | 1 | — | 2 | 1 | 10 |
| | 17 | 38 | 24 | 46 | 18 | 43 |

Source: Labov 1966a:313.
*Contextual styles: A Casual speech, B Careful speech, D Reading word lists

Fig. 9.2 shows the extreme rotation of the vowel system in Chicago which we cited as an example of young working-class speakers; again it is the women in this group who show the more extreme forms. Throughout Shuy's studies of Detroit speech (Shuy, Wolfram, and Riley 1967), we find the same pattern—that women show more shifting than men. Shuy's original report showed a greater shift towards prestige forms in formal style, and our current spectrographic studies confirm the advanced position of women on the vernacular raising of /æ/ and fronting of /a/.

Why do women do this? It cannot be only their sensitivity to prestige forms, since that explains only half of the pattern. We can say that they are more sensitive to prestige patterns, but why do they move forward faster in the first place? Our answers at the moment are not better than speculations, but it is obvious that this behavior of women must play an important part in the mechanism of linguistic change. To the extent that parents influence children's early language, women do so even more; certainly women talk to young children more than men do, and have a more direct influence during the years when children are forming linguistic rules with the greatest speed and efficiency. It seems likely that the rate of advance and direction of a linguistic change owes a great deal to the special sensitivity of women to the whole process.

It would be a serious error to construct a general principle that women always lead in the course of linguistic change. The centralization of /ay/ and /aw/ on Martha's Vineyard was found primarily in male speakers; women showed a much weaker tendency here. Trudgill (1971) shows in Norwich that women are more influenced by standard forms than men, but that men are in the lead in the use of new vernacular forms in casual speech. This seems to be generally true for a number of sound changes taking place in English cities. The correct generalization then is not that women lead in linguistic change, but rather that the sexual differentiation of speech often plays a major role in the mechanism of linguistic evolution.

We are now faced with data that pose even greater difficulties for those who claim that language change is independent of social variation. The sexual differentiation we are dealing with clearly depends upon patterns of social interaction in everyday life. The differentiation of men and women cannot depend upon weaknesses in communication networks as Bloomfield would have it, or the law of least effort as Sweet would argue. In the communities we have been studying there is no barrier to men and women talking to each other, and no reason to think that women are lazier than men. If anything, they put more effort into speech, as we observe from the extreme fronting in women's vowel systems in current spectrographic work. We are dealing with some positive factor here, operating upon a subtle set of conventional social values. There are of course physical differences between the vocal tracts of men and women to be taken into account, and the shorter length of women's vocal tracts does predict higher formant positions. But I. Mattingly demonstrated that there must also be conventional, social factors involved in the differentiation of men's and women's speech. A review of Peterson and Barney's data on vowel identification showed a relatively low correlation of these formant differences from one vowel to another: a purely physical explanation would produce comparable shifts in all vowels (1952). Our spectrographic studies show that in many dialects the difference is much more than an upward shift: women use a wider range of formant positions, over-lapping men's formants in all directions, with much greater distances between vowel locations. The sexual differentiation of speakers is therefore not a product of physical factors alone, or of different amounts of referential information supplied by speakers, but rather an expressive posture which is socially more appropriate for one sex or the other. On Martha's Vineyard, men are more "close-mouthed" than women, and use more contracted areas of phono-logical space; conversely, women in New York City and Philadelphia use wider ranges of phonological space than men with more extreme lip-spreading, lip-rounding, for vowels, more blade-affrication and palatalization of consonants.

## Restructuring of Early Patterns under Peer-Group Influence

Most models and studies of the acquisition of language take the mother-child interaction as the social context of language learning (Brown and Bellugi 1964; Bloom 1971). The influence of other chil-dren and peers outside of the family is usually not considered. Thus we do not know who Adam and Eve played with in Brown's studies, and when Adam suddenly turns up with negative concord to both indefinites and verbs at the age of four, it is interpreted as a purely internal development since these forms are not heard within his family. Halle's model of linguistic change is built entirely upon parent-child interaction: the parent adds new rules to his grammar later in life, and the child forms a new grammar which incorporates this more complex structure into a simpler one (1962).

The difficulty with this model is that children do not speak like their parents. In the great majority of cases that we have studied or encountered, children follow the pattern of their peers. I can cite a great many examples from my own observation, and so can every linguist who has looked into the matter. The evidence of dialectology is strong on this point. Though on principle dialectologists prefer third-generation residents in a given area, it is rare to find a second-generation speaker showing the effect of his parents' alien rules. In the study of the Lower East Side (Labov 1966a) the great majority of informants were second-generation New Yorkers, but the regular evolution of the New York City vowel system appeared in their speech in the same way as with third- and fourth-generation subjects. The critical cases were those who had moved into New York at an early age. If we consider the formative period for a native speaker to be roughly 4–13 years, it is reasonable to assume that a person had to spend at least half of those years in New York to acquire the New York City pattern. This proved to be the case: those who entered the United States after the age of 8 stood out as exceptional cases in any table or graph. For those who moved into New York City from another dialect area in the United States, the critical cut-off period appeared to be at 10 years.

*Restructuring* is an oddly unspecified notion. Are the early rules learned from parents simply abandoned, unlearned, rewritten? Or are they set aside but remain as potential rules of the grammar? It is also possible that restructuring never takes place within the native language itself: that no one unlearns vernacular rules, but simply adds new ones. It may be that the dialects learned from peers are only those rules that were not specified in the grammars learned from parents. A detailed empirical study of this process of restructuring is therefore required to resolve such questions if we are to understand how the basic vernacular changes.

A strategic research site for such a study is a community with many families moving in from other dialect areas of equal or higher prestige. Here we would be able to observe the gradual restructuring or additional development in the dialect patterns of children who enter the community with a dialect already formed to a certain extent. One such pilot study was carried out in the fifth grade in Radnor township, a suburb of Philadelphia in which roughly half of the parents come from other dialect areas. I have studied the phonological patterns of several self-selected peer-groups of 11-year-old boys; the relevant linguistic patterns of one such group are shown in Table 9.12. Jim and Charlie have local parents and were raised in Radnor; Ken came from Worcester, Mass., at the age of 8; Tim came from Cleveland at the age of 7. Ken and Tim are two of the most popular and prominent members of the class—Tim is class president—and Charlie too is among the best at a number of sports.

Table 9.12 shows that Ken and Tim have learned the specific Philadelphia rules for fronting /uw/ and /ow/; they show the Philadelphia area's sharp difference between the central allophones used for most vowels and the back vowels before /l/, which are not fronted. Furthermore, Tim has acquired the backed and centralized allophone of /ay/ before voiceless obstruents, with the sharp contrast between this and the somewhat fronted nucleus when final. On the other hand, neither Ken nor Tim has picked up the complex

TABLE 9.12.
ACQUISITION OF PHILADELPHIA PHONOLOGY
BY FOUR PREADOLESCENT BOYS

| | Jim W. | Charlie C. | Tim M. | Ken A. |
|---|---|---|---|---|
| Age | 11 | 11 | 11 | 11 |
| Born in | Radnor, Pa. | Radnor, Pa. | Cleveland, O. | Spring-field, O. |
| Moved to Radnor at the age of | — | — | 7 | 8 |
| Tensing and raising of short a: before | | | | |
|   voiceless fricatives (anterior) | 11/12 | 4/7 | 0/7* | 1/5 |
|   nasals (anterior) | 19/19 | 4/4 | 3/3 | 6/6 |
|   voiceless stops | 0/9 | 1/7 | 0/2 | 0/2 |
| Centralization of /ay/ before: | | | | |
|   voiceless consonants | 19/19 | 11/11 | 12/12 | 0/2 |
|   voiced and final | 0/22 | 3/9 | 0/4 | 0/2 |
| Distinction of low back vowels | | | | |
|   short open /ǫ/ phones | aˤ, a | aˤ, a | a | ɒ |
|   long open /ǭ/ phones | ɔˇ, oˇ | ɔˇ, oˇ | ɔ | ɒ |
| Fronting of high back vowels | | | | |
|   /ow/ nuclei | ə | ə | ə | ə |
|   /owl/nuclei | o | o | o | o |
|   /uw/ nuclei | ʉ | ʉ | ʉ | ʉ |
|   /uwl/ nuclei | u | u | u | u |

*Underlined items show original dialect pattern preserved and different from Philadelphia

conditions for the tensing of short a in Philadelphia. They do not tense a before front nasals, voiceless fricatives, and *mad-bad-glad* before /d/, excluding function words and irregular verbs with due regard to following morpheme boundaries, as good Philadelphians do, but follow much simpler patterns characteristic of their original areas: tensing and raising before nasals, without regard to function vs. lexical words, closed or open syllables, or any of the other deep-seated apparatus of the Philadelphia rule. Furthermore, Ken has not reversed the eastern New England merger of short and long open o in *hock* and *hawk,* even after three years. The higher-level rules seem to remain fixed, while the lower-level conditions seem to have shifted to the Philadelphia pattern. The merger of *hock* and *hawk* is quite general in its application, and not dependent on any prior rules; when it is complete, there is wholesale restructuring in the lexicon which is not easily unlearned. The tensing rule for short *a* is relatively abstract, and is followed by a number of rules, including the raising rule, the formation of interdental flaps, and the deletion of grammatical boundaries.

When children move to a new dialect area at the age of 3 or 4, they seem to adopt the basic patterns of the new area. But we do not have any systematic studies on this point, and there are many open questions. For the Radnor fifth-graders, there is no evidence for restructuring. It is possible that when a younger child falls under the influence of his peer group, he has not yet formed most of the rules which differ from one dialect to another, and that he merely adds the rules that do not conflict with his own. But it is also possible that 6-year-old children will actually abandon one set of rules for another. This is certainly a critical area for further research.

A case where family influence outweighs the peer group has been cited by Kostas Kazazis from personal experience (1969). It involves Athens-born middle-class teenagers whose parents or grandparents came from Istanbul. The Istanbul dialect differs prominently from Athenian Greek: one salient point is the use of the accusative for indirect objects, rather than the genitive. Though the Istanbul adolescents mixed freely with the others, and were under considerable pressure to change their speech, they did not do so. The strength and prestige of Istanbul family ties and the value of Istanbul identification seem to have been great enough to resist such pressures.

Yet the forces pressing for uniformity are apparently quite general. The survival of distinct dialects in neighboring Swiss German villages is an interesting case in point. Enderlin (1913) reported from Kesswil that up to 40 percent of the wives came from other villages, and thus spoke a different dialect. They were sharply ridiculed for their outlandish speech, and soon adopted most of the features of the Kesswil dialect. Here the remarkable heterogeneity of the area as a whole is supported by pressures for homogeneity within the village.

We must recognize, in any case, that there are many kinds of prestige and many kinds of support for minority dialects. Numbers alone do not account for the direction of linguistic change, nor does mere frequency of interaction.

## 5. The Evaluation Problem:
## Subjective Reactions to Linguistic Change

In our study of the embedding of linguistic change in its social matrix, we have seen many examples of the new form being advanced most rapidly in a particular class of speakers, often a lower-status group, and spreading outward in a wavelike fashion from that center. If we consider that the other groups are "borrowing" the new form from the originating group, we must question Tarde's law (1913) that borrowing always takes place from higher to lower prestige groups. If Bloomfield was right, the solution to the evaluation problem would be simplistic: people would simply imitate behavior associated with their superiors. They do not; in fact, the primary sociolinguistic problem was posed for me by an upper-middle-class woman who said, "Why do I say [ʋᴵ] when I don't want to?"

Even the notion of "borrowing" falls short when we consider two other major factors in linguistic change. We have seen in a number of areas that women adopt the newer forms more readily than men, and noted the strong effect of preadolescent peer groups in changing the language of its members. These objective correlations strongly argue that some machinery of social interaction is at work that cannot be the product of simple structural pressures or simple imitation. It seems that social variation does play a systematic role in linguistic change; to see how, we must see what social information is communicated by these variations. The notion of "prestige" must be defined in terms of the people using it and the situation in which it is used; that is, brought out of the area of speculation and made the focus of empirical investigation. Other dimensions of expressive social information carried by incoming linguistic forms must be explored as well.

Not every linguistic change receives overt social evaluation or even recognition. Some seem to lie far below the level of overt social reactions, as with the changes studied by Gauchat. The speakers of Charmey were unwilling to believe in these differences even when they were confronted with them: "Nous parlons tous la même chose!" (1905:202)

The same can be said of the response of Vineyarders who were confronted with changes in their pronunciation of /ay/ and /aw/. When the islanders talk about language, they concentrate on special marine jargon ("talking salty") rather than systematic rules of pronunciation.[21] It is more difficult for grammatical changes to escape public notice, but that is the case with the midwestern development of the positive *anymore,* meaning 'nowadays', in "That's the way it is with airplanes anymore." This regional feature is strongly entrenched throughout the Midland area, but most speakers are quite unconscious of it. I can record the following typical exchange from Cleveland:

> W. L.: Around here, can you say, "We go to the movies anymore?"
>
> Salesgirl: No, we say "show" or "flick."

As striking as this extension of the indefinite may seem to a linguist, it is being accomplished without public notice. A story caption in a 1969 issue of *Life* read, "What it Takes to be a Lady Author Anymore." But I could capture no spontaneous reaction to this from any readers I met.

There are a number of systematic changes taking place in the English of the western United States that have no evident social significance. In most areas, the unconditioned merger of the low back vowels in *hock* and *hawk,* which affects two very large word classes, proceeds without notice or comment. Cook shows that the fronting of (aw) in Salt Lake City is of little social concern, and shows almost no stylistic shifting (1969). In our own recent studies in Utah, we have observed an on-going merger of a number of vowels before final /l/, so that *fool = full, feel = fill,* and further pairs merged in some working-class areas. But these mergers are not reported by anyone and seem to make no impact on social consciousness.

To sum up, incoming linguistic changes rarely rise to the level of social comment in their initial stages, and not all changes become the focus of conscious attention even in their advanced stages. But there is much more to social evaluation than the overt responses that native speakers can summon up. The problem as posed so far is governed by the superficiality of the observations. The traditional literature on social evaluation is limited, on the one hand, to anec-

21. There is some indication of a social awareness of Vineyard styles of pronunciation. One of the strongest examples of centralization of /ay/ and /aw/ is a young man who went to college and returned to develop several businesses by the docks of Chilmark. His mother remarked that he only started to talk like the men on the docks when he came back, but she wasn't able to point to any particular feature of his pronunciation (See p. 31).

dotal evidence of overt reactions to gross stereotypes, and on the other, to speculation by linguists as to efficiency or economy. In the past two decades, however, considerable progress has been made in measuring unconscious social reactions to language through the *"matched guise"* technique.

The work of Lambert, Tucker, and their associates at McGill University has provided us with a firm methodology and a number of empirical principles for the study of subjective reactions (Lambert 1967). The basic technique consists of exposing listeners to a series of tape-recorded excerpts which include bilingual speakers recurring in "matched guises." These guises contrast English and Canadian French (Lambert et al. 1960), Canadian French and continental French (Preston 1963), Arabic and Hebrew (Lambert, Anisfeld, and Yeni-Komshian 1965), network English, southern black and southern white English (Tucker and Lambert 1969), and so on. The listeners record their judgments of the speakers in terms of a series of personality traits: intelligence, honesty, reliability, ambition, sincerity, kindness, sociability, sense of humor, and so on. The differential rating of the same speaker in his matched guises gives us a measure of the listener's unconscious social evaluation of the two dialects or languages, and a few central factors can be isolated from the many attributes tested.

From the work of Lambert and his associates we can derive several important principles:

1. Subjective evaluations of social dialects are remarkably uniform throughout the speech community. Canadian French speakers agree with English speakers in rating their own language lower on most of these personality traits: in the French guise the speaker was heard as less intelligent, less reliable, etc.
2. Evaluations of language are usually not available to conscious elicitation, but are readily and consistently expressed in terms of personality judgments about different speakers (Lambert, Anisfeld, and Yeni-Komshian 1965). Thus a study carried out in Texas of several well-established sociolinguistic variables failed to record any significant reactions because all of the 16 dialect variations constructed were recorded by the same speaker (Baird 1969).
3. All subjects acquire these norms in early adolescence, but upper-middle-class children show a stronger and more permanent

reaction. Brown extended the matched-guise technique to socio-economic differences in Canadian French (1969), concentrating on teenage judges. His findings give "strong support to the idea that speech is expressive of motives and values." Judges from all backgrounds favored upper-class speakers over working-class speakers of French, and English over French, on a general factor of "competence." Boys from high-prestige schools showed ratings closer to adult judges than other boys, indicating that adult norms are acquired earlier among upper-middle-class youth.[22]

Lambert is primarily concerned with the effect of underlying social values upon the bilingual child, the language learner, and the bilingual community. These matched-guise tests do not contrast individual features of language, but record undifferentiated responses to the language or dialect as a whole. A comparable series of subjective reaction tests carried out in New York City differed in two respects. The speakers recurred in the test series with sentences which were the same referentially, and in their own dialect: but with different values of one linguistic variable. Second, the scales used for measuring reactions were drawn from situations which commonly arise in everyday social interaction: "What is the highest job this person could hold, speaking as he does?"

The New York City studies (Ch. 6; Labov et al. 1968) gave full confirmation to the three principles which emerged from Lambert's work. One further principle appeared:

4. Speakers who use the highest degree of a stigmatized feature in their own natural speech show the greatest tendency to stigmatize others for their use of this form.

We can see this principle operating in regard to the raising of short a, the (eh) variable, and long open o, the (oh) variable. As noted above, the Italians show a greater tendency to raise the front vowel, while the Jews favor the back vowel. In subjective reaction tests, Italians stigmatize a speaker in his high (eh) guise (saying [be:ᵊd] for bad, etc.), and downgrade this feature more consistently than other groups. Since New Yorkers show a high level of agreement on this point, the differences are small, but Table 9.13 shows that Italians

22. On the other hand, French speakers were scored higher on a number of attributes which can be analyzed as containing the factor of "benevolence".

are somewhat more consistent than the Jews.[23] The socioeconomic differentiation of judges in subjective reaction tests follows the same principle. Whereas working-class and lower-middle-class speakers show the greatest tendency to raise the vowel of *bad, ask, dance,* etc., they are also most consistent in stigmatizing this behavior, as shown in Table 9.14. In both Table 9.13 and Table 9.14 we see that younger speakers show a definite increase in sensitivity to this well-established linguistic variable, just as they show a greater tendency to use the stigmatized form (see Table 9.10).

TABLE 9.13.
PERCENT STIGMATIZING
RAISED (eh) IN SUBJECTIVE
REACTION TESTS BY AGE
AND ETHNIC GROUP

| Age Level | Jews | Italians | | $N$ | |
|-----------|------|----------|---|-----|---|
| 20–39 | 86% | 100% | | | |
| 40– | 81 | 88 | | 14 | 6 |
| All ages | 82 | 91 | | 28 | 15 |

TABLE 9.14.
PERCENT STIGMATIZING RAISED (eh) IN
SUBJECTIVE REACTION TESTS BY AGE AND
SOCIOECONOMIC CLASS

| | Socioeconomic class | | | | | $N$ | | | |
|------|------|------|------|------|---|------|------|------|------|
| Age | 0–2 | 3–5 | 6–8 | 9 | | | | | |
| 8–15 | 100% | 75% | 100% | (100)% | | 7 | 8 | 6 | 1 |
| 16–19 | 86 | 100 | 100 | 75 | | 7 | 12 | 4 | 4 |
| 20–39 | 75 | 90 | 100 | 80 | | 4 | 10 | 11 | 5 |
| 40– | 75 | 80 | 70 | 71 | | 16 | 15 | 10 | 7 |

The most dramatic shift in subjective reactions which we have recorded is in response to an incoming prestige feature: the pronunciation of final and preconsonantal /r/ in New York City. Fig. 6.2 (p. 152) showed the pronunciation of /r/ by New Yorkers in casual

23. There is an interaction here between class and ethnic group. The Jewish subgroup shows greater upward mobility, with a heavier concentration of lower-middle-class speakers, while the Italian sample shows a greater concentration of working-class subjects. Ethnic membership appears to be the predominant influence, however, in the tendency to favor the raising of (eh) or (oh).

speech (the same data as Table 9.5) as compared to their subjective reactions to this variable in the speech of others. In casual speech, those over 40 show a sprinkling of r's without any particular direction; those under 40 show a sudden increase in stratification, with the highest-status group using [r]. In the subjective reaction tests, we see a shift from random response over 40 years old to 100 percent agreement for those under 40: they all unconsciously rate the same speaker higher on the job scale when [r] is pronounced than when it is not.

The subjective reaction tests cited so far have been reactions to a single job suitability scale, operating strictly within the dominant middle-class set of values. This brings us back to the original question: why don't people behave in a way consistent with the normative values that they express? There are four possible answers that we might consider:

1. They are too lazy or careless to use the norms that they recognize.
2. Differences in communication patterns mean that lower-class speakers would not be aware of the subjective norms of upper-class speakers.
3. Even if lower-class speakers do learn the norms, they do not do so until it is too late for them to acquire consistent productive control of the prestige forms.
4. Lower-class speakers do not want to adopt the norms of the upper class; although they do endorse the dominant norms in the test situation, there are opposing sets of values that support the vernacular forms, and that do not appear in subjective reaction tests.

We can reject (1) as a product of class bias; there is no reason to think that any one class has a monopoly on laziness. The evidence cited above disqualifies (2). There seems to be some support for (3) in the differential age at which speakers acquire subjective norms, and the differential clarity or strength (Brown 1969, Labov 1966a). We find strong support for (4) in our recent work on subjective reaction tests in Harlem, where we introduced two other rating scales: "fight" and "friend" (see Ch. 8, especially Fig. 8.3).

Granted that the social setting of linguistic change is a hierarchical, stratified society, not all prestige forms sweep through the community, and not all change from above succeeds. The best general formulation of this opposition of values is still that of Ferguson and Gumperz (1960):

1. Any group of speakers of language X which regards itself as a close social unit will tend to express its group solidarity by favoring those linguistic innovations which set it apart from other speakers who are not part of the group.
2. Other things being equal, if two speakers A and B of a language X communicate in language X and if A regards B as having more prestige than himself and aspires to equal B's status, then the variety of X spoken by A will tend towards identity with that spoken by B.

### Indicators, Markers, and Stereotypes

We can classify the various elements involved in linguistic change according to the kind of social evaluation that they receive. *Indicators* are linguistic features which are embedded in a social matrix, showing social differentiation by age or social group, but which show no pattern of style shifting and appear to have little evaluative force. The merger of *hock* and *hawk*, the extension of *anymore*, may be taken as cases in point. *Markers* such as (eh) or (r) do show stylistic stratification as well as social stratification. Though they may lie below the level of conscious awareness, they will produce regular responses on subjective reaction tests. *Stereotypes* are socially marked forms, prominently labelled by society. In the following subsection, we will consider the linguistic changes brought about by such labelling.

### The Social Stigmatization of Linguistic Forms (Stereotyping)

A social stereotype is a social fact, part of the general knowledge of adult members of the society; this is true even if the stereotype does not conform to any set of objective facts. Stereotypes are referred to and talked about by members of the speech community; they may have a general label, and a characteristic phrase which serves equally well to identify them.

1. "Brooklynese." A stereotype which is based on earlier forms of working-class New York City speech, without regard to geography. A characteristic label is *toity-toid street,* based on the older form of the preconsonantal mid central vowel with a palatal upglide, [əɪ].
2. "Deses, dems, and doses." General characteristic of working-class speech in the United States, based on the use of interdental stops for interdental fricatives.

3. "Bostonian", often labelled as "Pahk your cah in the Hahvahd Yahd", based on the r-less Boston pattern with fronted low central vowel [aː].
4. "Broad a" pronunciation, particularly for the words *aunt* [ɑnt] and *bath* [bɑθ] sometimes caricatured as "Fahncy that" [fɑnsi ðat] attributed to upper crust British and New England speakers.
5. "Southern drawl," based on various imitations of southern monophthongs, long and ingliding vowels, and in particular the word *Y'all* [jɒːl].
6. "Outer Banks" of North Carolina, known regionally as "Hoi Toiders;" based on the pronunciation of *high tide* as [hɔᴵ tɔᴵd], and the general raising and backing of /ay/.
7. "Put the harse in the born," a standard way of referring to the stigmatized stereotype of rural Utah speakers, alleged to reverse *horse* and *barn* and other /ahr/ and /ohr/ words.
8. "Parigot," working-class Parisian speech, based on such features as the absence of *ne*, backing of /ɑ/, and often characterized with *j'saispas* [šepɔ] or [špɔ].

This list of examples shows the variety of relations to fact and the variety of social values associated with stereotypes. Some stereotyped features are heavily stigmatized, but remarkably resistant and enduring, like *dese* and *dose*.[24] Others have varying prestige, positive to some people and negative to others, like Bostonian or southern drawl.

Social stigma applied to some of these stereotypes has led to rapid linguistic change, with almost total extinction. A good example is the [əᴵ] pronunciation in New York City. Table 9.15 shows how systematically and how thoroughly this feature is being extinguished in New York. For those born before World War I, it is a regular feature for all but middle-class speakers. For those born after World War II, it is found only among lower-class speakers.

In the last stages of the decline of a stigmatized variable, it may appear as a form of ritual humor. One example of this process that we can document over a long stretch of time is the Cockney confu-

---

24. In the United States, all native speakers show the ability to discriminate the word classes of /d/ and /ð/, and to pronounce the fricative in isolated words. But the strong Gaelic substratum of Ireland produces a different result. Witness the story cited to me by Jerry Crowley of Cork: the school teacher who says, "Now today we're going to study English pronunciation. And we're not going to say *dese*, and *dem*, and *dose!* We're going to say *dese*, and *dem*, and *dose!!*"

TABLE 9.15.
PROPORTION USING ANY [əɪ] IN INTERVIEWS
BY AGE AND SEC CLASS IN NEW YORK CITY

| Age | 0-1 | 2-3 | 4-5 | 6-8 | 9 | 0-9 | |
|---|---|---|---|---|---|---|---|
| 8-19 | 2/7 | 0/11 | 0/12 | 0/16 | 0/5 | 2/51 | 04 |
| 20-39 | 3/4 | 3/7 | 3/10 | 1/11 | 0/7 | 10/39 | 24 |
| 40-49 | 1/3 | 5/14 | 4/8 | 4/13 | 0/4 | 14/42 | 33 |
| 50-59 | 3/3 | 2/4 | 3/3 | 2/4 | 0/3 | 10/17 | 59 |
| 60- | 7/7 | 5/5 | 1/1 | | | 13/13 | 100 |
| 8-60 | 16/24 | 15/41 | 11/34 | 7/44 | 0/19 | 49/162 | |
| % | 67 | 38 | 32 | 16 | 00 | | |

sion of /v/ and /w/. Most Americans know this social variable only through Dickens' 1837 version of the speech of Sam Weller and his father. It is evident that the v/w alternation was already a stereotype, since Dickens was using it as heavily as possible to characterize the Wellers, exchanging almost every /v/ and /w/.[25]

This here money . . . he's anxious to put somevers, vere he knows it'll be safe, and I'm wery anxious too, for if he keeps it, he'll go a lendin' it to somebody, or inwestin' property in horses, or droppin' his pocket book down a airy, or makin' a Egyptian mummy of hisself in some vay or another. —*Pickwick Papers, p. 800.*

The spelling used by Henry Machyn three centuries earlier showed that this variable was then a regular characteristic of the respectable middle class: *wacabondes* 'vagabonds', *waluw* 'value', *wue* 'view', *welvet, woyce, voman, veyver* 'weaver'; *Volsake* 'Woolsack', *Vetyngton* 'Whittington', *Vosseter* 'Worcester' (Wyld 1936:143). The /v∼w/ merger was apparently well-stigmatized in the 18th century; Walker says that it is a "blemish of the first magnitude" that occurs among Londoners, "not those always of the low order". Eighty years later it was dead in London. Wyld notes that he never heard it actually used in the 1870's, but he did hear middle-aged people use

25. The confusion of *oil* and *Earl* in New York City ("Brooklynese") forms a stereotype quite parallel to the v∼w confusion cited here. Though there are speakers who use [ɔɪl] for the *Earl* class, it was more common to use a central vowel [əɪl] for both, or to keep the two classes apart by preserving a rounded vowel in the *oil* class. But to outsiders, the effect of a merger is that *oil* sounds like *Earl* and *Earl* sounds like *oil*. If there is free variation, no one notices those variants that are the same as the standard; it is the pronunciations which differ from the standard pattern which are noticed and remembered.

the ritual joke of saying *weal* for 'veal' and *vich* for 'which'; a joke that he never understood until he read Dickens. Long after it is actually extinct in speech, a linguistic variable can survive as a stereotyped use of certain words, then as a standard joke, and finally as a fossil form whose meaning has been entirely forgotten.

### 6. The Actuation Problem

Though we have assembled a fair amount of data in response to the embedding and evaluation problems, there is comparatively little that can be said about the particular social or linguistic events that trigger a particular change. We can point to some general circumstances that are not irrelevant to the temporal location of some linguistic changes discussed above. For instance, the reversal of New York City attitudes towards r-pronunciation can be seen as merely one prominent feature of a general shift away from British and New England models in favor of a general American broadcast standard.

At some point in time, the older prestige dialect was redefined; instead of an "international standard" it became a "regional peculiarity". This event seems to coincide with the period of World War II, and one might argue that the experience of men in the service was somehow involved. It would be difficult to prove; all we can do at this time is to point to the war as the most prominent social disturbance which coincided with the period of the linguistic change.

In examining the alternations of the New York City vowel development, we cannot help being struck by the differentiation of the Jewish and Italian ethnic groups in the raising of (eh) and (oh). The raw materials for this process seem to have been present before 1890, but the arrival of these two large immigrant groups about that time may well have put new energy into the raising process. It appears that the Jews defined the raising of (oh) in *coffee, lost,* and *all* as the basic change, and the following shift of (ah) → (oh) → was accordingly emphasized by Jewish speakers as a part of a chain shift. Italian New Yorkers focused on the front vowel, continuing the earlier tradition of treating this as the primary variable involved.

We can see a parallel tendency on Martha's Vineyard. The earlier of the two raising processes affected (ay) in the speech of the Yankees, at a time when the Portuguese population was hardly considered to be a part of the community. After 1930, Portuguese more and more took the place of the Yankees as merchants and politicians. The Portuguese then began to use centralization in their own English, but they raised (aw) to [ʌ¹] more prominently than they shifted (ay) to [e¹]. Their emphasis on the raising of (ay) would lead us to expect further generalization, with the back vowel now pulling the front one after it.

These are the kinds of fluctuations which Meillet referred to when he characterized society as

an element, in which circumstances induce continual variation, sometimes rapid, sometimes slow, but never completely suspended. (1905:16)

Observing the impact of the Jewish and Italian immigrations into New York, we might look backwards at the entry of the Irish and Germans in the 1860's; that movement might well have affected the evolution of the city's dialect by reemphasizing elements already in flux. At present, we are witnessing the rise of two new entering groups, blacks and Puerto Ricans, who do not seem to participate in or directly influence the rotations of the vowel system just described. But it is possible that the influence of the black speech pattern is acting to check or reverse the raising of the tense vowels among white speakers.

As a basis for comparison in our studies of black youth in Harlem, we selected two white (Irish) working-class groups at the northern tip of Manhattan, in Inwood, a fairly solid white residential area where considerable hostility towards blacks was expressed. We could not easily find a white working-class group in Manhattan with less direct black or Puerto Rican influence (Labov et al. 1968).[26] The intricate tensing rule for short *a* words, which selects vowels before voiced stops and voiceless fricatives, front nasals, etc., is fairly intact among members of the Inwood groups. For the general population the tensing rule is followed by a raising of [æ:] to mid and then high position, involving the successive mergers of /æh/ with /ehr/ and then with /ihr/. That is, *bad* merges with *bared* in the early stages, and then both *bad* and *bared* with *beard*. But the /æh/ of the Inwood group is not much higher than [æ:] and it has not merged with /ehr/.

---

26. The fact that a group expresses hostility towards another group does not preclude the likelihood of linguistic influence. We have observed many cases of the contrary effect: that white groups surrounded by blacks, and engaged in hostile combat with them, acquire many linguistic features from them. Such a phenomenon can be observed on the Lower East Side of New York City, or in Highland Park in Detroit.

The merger of /ehr/ and /ihr/ in *bared* and *beard, bear* and *beer,* is complete. This second merger is widespread among black speakers, reflecting the coastal South Carolina pattern, but in BEV the raising of /æh/ is quite limited.[27] We must therefore consider the high probability of black influence in the disturbance of the New York City pattern for the Inwood group. Examples such as these give weight to Meillet's contention that explanations for the irregular course of linguistic change are to be found in the fluctuating social composition of the speech community.

### 7. The Place of Social Variation in the Life History of a Linguistic Change

In the three preceding sections, we have assembled enough data to give an answer to the first of the three substantive questions raised in this chapter: does social variation play an important role in linguistic change? A review of the asymmetrical history and evolution of most linguistic changes, and of their remarkably uniform evaluation by society, shows that an asocial account would be incoherent. The histories that I have outlined would not exist if social differences were abstracted from the grammars involved, for the accounts of change would then be vacuous. The overall view is best expressed by outlining a typical life history of a sound change.

The change first appears as a characteristic feature of a specific subgroup, attracting no particular notice from anyone. As it progresses within the group, it may then spread outwards in a wave, affecting first those social groups closest to the originating group. Inevitably, the linguistic feature is associated with the expressive characteristics of the originating group, with whatever prestige or whatever social values are associated with that group by other members of the speech community (Sturtevant 1947). Whether such association is sufficient to explain the outward movement is difficult to say. We do know that the growth of the affected area may be checked by linguistic factors (Herzog 1965) or by social factors or historical discontinuities (Bloomfield 1933:344), or by the negative prestige of the group as a whole (as in the case of New York City).[28]

27. In our studies of adolescent groups in south-central Harlem, we find that about half show the merger of (ihr) and (ehr) in *beer* and *bear, cheer* and *chair*, etc. (Labov et al. 1968).

28. For the negative prestige of New York City, see Labov 1966a, Ch. 13. The severely limited scope of the New York City dialect area has been noted above.

At this point, the linguistic feature may be an *indicator* of age and social distance from the originating group.

As the linguistic feature develops within the original group of speakers, it becomes generalized in several senses. Over the course of time (three or four decades) a wider range of conditioned sub-classes may be involved, and more extreme (less favored) environments. Furthermore, the structural symmetry of the system leads to generalization to other vowels or consonants, or members of the same natural class, which begin to move in the same (or opposing) direction. In the meantime, new social groups enter the community, and through historical accident or the influence of their original dialect, reinterpret the on-going change to reemphasize other elements in this complex system.

This discussion has not focused on the internal processes involved (see Ch. 7, Labov 1972c), but it is important to note that structural generalization in linguistic systems is far from instantaneous. It is a slow process, with considerable time lag, and between the movement of one item and the associated movement of another, several decades with their accompanying social changes may have passed (Chen 1971).

As the original change acquires greater complexity, scope, and range, it comes to acquire more systematic social value, and is restrained or corrected in formal speech (a *marker*). Eventually, it may be labeled as a *stereotype,* discussed and remarked by everyone. The future prospects of this stereotype depend upon the fortunes of the group it is associated with. If the group moves into the mainstream of society, and is given respect and prominence, then the new rule may not be corrected but incorporated into the dominant dialect at the expense of the older form. If the group is excluded from the mainstream of society, or its prestige declines, the linguistic form or rule will be stigmatized, corrected, and even extinguished.

But such correction does not have the regular character of the change itself. Instead, correction focuses irregularly on certain prominent sounds or words, with consequent disturbances in the regularity of the linguistic system. Although the New York City tense back vowel is corrected and lowered in *lost, coffee, water,* and *chocolate,* it is never noticed or corrected when it occurs as the first part of the diphthong in *boy* or *Lloyd.*

The irregularity of this secondary social correction, compared with the regularity of the original change, may provide part of the expla-

nation for the massive irregularity and word-class splitting documented by Wang, Chen, and Hsieh in the history of Chinese dialects
(Cheng and Wang 1971; Chen and Hsieh 1971; Chen 1971). It is quite
probable that the original movements were more regular than the
final result indicates, if they were at all similar to the sound changes
in progress which we are now studying by instrumental means. But
at the same time we cannot neglect the effect of competing and
overlapping sound changes pointed out by Wang (1969) as an explanation for such irregularities; and even without such competition,
there is evidence for lexical irregularity in these on-going changes
which is inconsistent with the neo-grammarian hypothesis and yet
free of any social affect.

### 8. Doubts on the Level of Abstraction
### Affected by Social Factors

We can now return to the second of the three general questions
raised: can social factors affect abstract rules of grammar and phonology? First of all, it is clear that members of the speech community
do not develop social reactions to abstract rules of phonology such
as the tensing rule for æ. The highly marked social feature is
the second rule—the raising of the vowels that have been tensed.
For the first rule, we find considerable individual variation in New
York City in the treatment of words ending in voiced fricatives (*razz,
jazz*); or of weak words ending in nasals (*am, can,* and *and* variable
as against *has, as, had* which are always lax). There is a great deal
of variation in the treatment of words like *passage,* or *Abbie,* which
may be analyzed with a derivational boundary /. . æC+V . ./ as
opposed to the consistent tensing of words like *passing* or *stabbing*
with inflectional boundaries /. . æC#V . ./ or consistent lax treatment of *castle* or *cabbage* with no such boundary at all: /. . æCV . ./.
This variation is idiosyncratic; it fails to show any regular social
distribution, no matter how carefully we study the data (Cohen 1970).
Husbands and wives, brothers and sisters may differ on these points,
but unpredictably, and neither will notice the difference.[29] In general,
we find that social affect is not attached to such variations in abstract
rules, but rather to individual words (cf. Whitney 1901) or to low-

29. In a recent interview in New York City, a husband read *Abbie* with a tense,
raised vowel, while his wife used a lax, unraised vowel in the same word. They were
both from the same dialect background and showed no other systematic differences
in their vowel systems.

level rules of phonetic behavior that involve very frequent items.

Certainly there are important grammatical and phonological consequences of sociolinguistic variables. Consonant cluster simplification is a typical social variable, showing both stylistic and social stratification. One of the constraints on the rule is the existence of a morpheme boundary before the final consonant, signalling that it is a separate morpheme. If there is no such boundary, the rule will apply more often:

$$[-\text{cont}] \rightarrow \langle \emptyset \rangle \ / \ [+\text{cons}] \ \langle \emptyset \rangle \ \underline{\hspace{1cm}} \ \# \# \ \langle -\text{syl} \rangle$$

The variable constraint indicated by $\langle \emptyset \rangle$ in the environment registers the fact that without a morpheme boundary, the cluster in *last* is simplified more often than the one in *pass#d,* the cluster in *old* more than the one in *roll#d.* The rule in this form may have no immediate effect upon grammar, for it indicates that the past tense morpheme *#d* is indeed preserved and recognized. But when such sociolinguistic rules are extended and become obligatory, we find compensating and dramatic changes in the grammar. Thus when final clusters *-pt* and *-kt* were obligatorily simplified in Scots, the rule of epenthesis apparently changed to yield *slippit and workit* instead of *slip'* and *work',* allowing the regular past to be expressed. (For more detailed discussion and other examples, see Ch. 8.)

We can look back at the phonetic processes in late Old English which led to the loss of final inflections: reduction of unstressed vowels, deletion of final nasals, and loss of final schwa. All of these appear to have been optional sociolinguistic variables for some time in the history of English. Before the inflections were entirely lost, we can hazard the guess that some of the compensating changes in word order had already occurred. But this is still a speculative area, for we have not yet been able to study any such systematic grammatical change in progress.

On the whole, our evidence then points to a negative answer for our second question, but suggests that the connection between social variation and the higher-level change may be fairly rapid as the variable rule develops into a categorical one. It is important to note that social significance depends on variability. In that sense, social meaning is parasitic upon language: it is confined to those areas of variation, usually on the leading edge of a generalizing linguistic change, where there exist alternative ways of saying "the same thing."

We can observe the results of a process of syntactic generalization in the black English treatment of negative concord (Labov 1972a, Ch. 4). This is an expressive optional rule for white dialects, giving a choice between emphatic *Nobody gave him nothing* and unmarked *Nobody gave him anything*. Some white dialects optionally reduplicate the negative particle after an indeterminate subject—but only within the same clause; thus *Nobody didn't give him nothing* is a way of saying the same thing as the two preceding sentences. Black speakers have the additional option of extending this subrule across clause boundaries, as in *It ain't nobody didn't give him nothing,* meaning the same as *Nobody gave him anything*. This extension of the expressive negative concord rule coincides with the extension of normal negative concord to all indeterminates within the clause, now obligatory in most BEV; the new subrule adds the expressive feature which the old one has lost.

These last two examples are discussed after the fact, and must be taken as speculative reconstructions of an historical process which we have not yet observed in progress. Only when we have the good fortune to seize such a syntactic change as it is occurring will we be able to give a good solution to the transition problem, and provide a sound basis for other arguments about the evaluation and actuation of change.

### 9. Is There An Adaptive Function to Linguistic Diversity?

It is plain to most linguists that the "destroy and rebuild" theory of linguistic evolution is equivalent to claiming that the whole process is dysfunctional. For the systematic part is the destructive one, and the analogical reshaping seems to be making the best of a bad job. And if the principle of least effort is the evil genius behind the destruction, we can only look at language change as a kind of massive testimony to original sin.

Gauchat made it clear that the principle of least effort had been overpromoted. He pointed out (1905) that the diphthongization of ā showed every sign of being an increase in effort, not a decrease. We can say the same for the tensing and raising rules which have played such a large part in this discussion. The stigmatized phones are longer, more peripheral, with greater intensity than the older forms, and develop an offglide as well: contrasting [bæ·ˆd] with be:ˤ ᵊd]. These developments give one a sense of the strong motivating force behind sound change, one that is almost the opposite of the economy or least effort argument. We observe sound change lengthening vowels, rotating systems, merging word classes, destroying distinctions, overriding structural constraints. Why?

A classic confrontation on the issue of progress in the evolution of language may be seen in the papers of Greenberg (1959) and Hymes (1961). Greenberg takes the position that there is evolution only in the sense of diversification, but no progress in the sense of increase of complexity or adaptive radiation. Hymes points to the development of complex layers of vocabulary, scientific vocabulary, metalanguages, and other attributes of world languages as evidence in favor of continuing development. Since this chapter has been concerned with the central core of grammar and phonology, rather than lexicon, it would seem to favor Greenberg's position—that there is only diversification.

But what if this diversification were itself an important element in cultural evolution? Inevitably, we are drawn back to the third question: does diversification have an adaptive function, or is it the product of multiple local failures in the communication network? My own studies of on-going linguistic changes indicate that dialect diversification is continuing in the face of saturation by the mass media, and in spite of close contact among the social groups involved. The fact that diversity is not automatically connected with isolation suggests that it may also be connected with the normal processes of face-to-face communication.

Most linguists who work with small, diverse groups must recognize in themselves a natural prejudice in favor of the survival of their subjects. The anthropological or comparative linguist will intuitively fight for the existence of his group, and he resists the notion that the cost of bilingualism is too great to be borne. He refuses to weigh the value of a language or a dialect in terms of its attractiveness to printers, the size of its literary output, or how well it prepares children to fit into a European school system. Linguists must recognize that they are interested parties in this argument.

With this precaution, I am inclined to believe that the development of linguistic differences has positive value in human cultural evolution—and that cultural pluralism may even be a necessary element in the human extension of biological evolution.

If we are to risk speculation about the general character of human evolution, it will be helpful to have a point of comparison with other species that have developed communication systems. My thinking on this point has been stimulated by a recent overview of work on the development of bird song by Nottebohm (1970). Much of Nottebohm's work has involved the vocal learning of chaffinches; they are one of several species that differ from most birds in that their songs are not stereotyped and genetically controlled in any simple sense. Chaffinches pass through a critical period of ten months during which they learn their songs from other birds of their species. If they are deafened early in this period, they produce degenerate and extremely abnormal songs; if deafened after ten months, they continue to produce normal song. It is of immediate interest to linguists that birds like the chaffinch and the white-crowned sparrow have developed dialects. Nottebohm suggests that the shift from "self-centered" to "environmentally dependent" song production may have accompanied the rapid expansion of the birds into differentiated habitats. The examples he gives of the behavior of the white-crowned sparrows suggest that dialects may play a role in the mating system by providing a relative degree of genetic isolation but without any "necessary irrevocable commitment to actual speciation."

Whereas genetic isolation of small populations may lead to high rates of extinction and even possibly to excessive inbreeding, differences in vocalizations are probably rarely insuperable barriers to breeding, and thus the microevolutionary process is kept more flexible and open. (1970:955)

Nottebohm himself raises the possibility that human dialects may have an evolutionary function, and may have influenced the emergence of "local physiological adaptations." It is also possible that the "linguistic puberty" through which we pass, seriously reducing our language-learning ability, may itself be the product of evolutionary selection. A language-learning "block" in human development would have the same general function as in birds, encouraging diversity of dialect patterns.

In speculating about these possibilities, I would prefer to look forward rather than backward, and focus on the connection with cultural diversity rather than physiological adaptation. The value of Nottebohm's contribution is not in setting forth a theory or an hypothesis that we can test immediately, but rather suggesting an alternate view to broaden our thinking about linguistic evolution. It is an interesting point to consider that language diversity may have value for humans other than linguists, providing relative cultural isolation and maintaining cultural pluralism. And linguists themselves may be encouraged to look more deeply into the mechanisms which differentiate languages as well as the limiting conditions which form the content of a universal grammar.

# BIBLIOGRAPHY

Allen, P. 1968. /r/ variable in the speech of New Yorkers in department stores. Unpublished research paper SUNY, Stony Brook.

Anshen, F. 1969. Speech variation among Negroes in a small Southern community. Unpublished dissertation, New York University.

Avis, W. 1961. The New England short 'o': a recessive phoneme. *Language* 37:544–58.

Babbitt, E. H. 1896. The English of the lower classes in New York City and vicinity. *Dialect Notes* 1:457–64.

Bailey, C.-J. N. 1969a. The integration of linguistic theory: internal reconstruction and the comparative method in descriptive linguistics, with an appendix of 107 pan-dialectal ordered rules. Paper given before Conference on Historical Linguistics in the Light of Generative Theory, Los Angeles. Printed in part in R. Stockwell and R. Macaulay (eds.), *Historical Linguistics and Generative Theory*. Bloomington, Ind.: Indiana University Press, 1972.

———. 1969b. *Introduction to Southern states phonetics*. University of Hawaii Working Papers in Linguistics 4–5.

Baird, S. J. 1969. Employment interview speech: a social dialect study in Austin, Texas. Unpublished dissertation, University of Texas.

Barber, Bernard. 1957. *Social stratification*. New York: Harcourt, Brace.

Bernstein, B. 1964. Elaborated and restricted codes. *In* Gumperz and Hymes 1964.

Bickerton, D. 1971. On the nature of the Creole continuum. Mimeo.

Bloch, B. 1948. A set of postulates for phonemic analysis. *Language* 24:3-46.

Bloomfield, L. 1933. *Language*. New York: Henry Holt.

———. 1944. Secondary and tertiary responses to language. *Language* 20:45–55.

Bright, W., ed. 1966. *Sociolinguistics*. The Hague: Mouton.

———, and A. K. Ramanujan. 1964. Socio-linguistic variation and language change. *In* H. G. Lunt, ed., *Proceedings of the Ninth International Congress of Linguists*. The Hague: Mouton.

Bronstein, A. 1962. Let's take another look at New York City speech. *American Speech* 37:13–26.

Brown, L. 1969. The social psychology of variations in French Canadian speech. Unpublished dissertation, McGill University.

Brown, R., and U. Bellugi. 1964. Three processes in the child's acquisition of syntax. *Harvard Educational Review* 34:133–51.

Carden, G. 1970. On post-determiner quantifiers. *Linguistic Inquiry* 1(4):415–28.

Cedergren, H. 1970. Patterns of free variation: the language variable. Mimeo.

———, and D. Sankoff. 1972. Variable rules: performance as a statistical reflection of competence. To appear in *Language*.

Chen, M. 1971. *The time dimension: contribution toward a theory of sound change*. Berkeley, Cal.: University of California Project on Linguistic Analysis Reports, Vol. 2, No. 14.

———, and Hsin-I Hsieh. 1971. The time variable in phonological change. *Journal of Linguistics* 7:1–13.

Cheng, C.-C., and W. S.-Y. Wang. 1970. *Phonological change of middle Chinese initials*. Berkeley, Cal.: University of California Project on Linguistic Analysis Reports, Vol. 2, No. 10.

Chomsky, N. 1957. *Syntactic structures*. The Hague: Mouton.

———. 1964. Current issues in linguistic theory. *In* Fodor and Katz 1964.

———. 1965. *Aspects of the theory of syntax*. Cambridge, Mass.: MIT Press.

———. 1966. Topics in the theory of generative grammar. *In* T. Sebeok, ed., *Current trends in linguistics 3: linguistic theory*. Bloomington, Ind.: Indiana University Press.

———, and M. Halle. 1968. *The sound pattern of English*. New York: Harper & Row.

Cohen, P. 1970. The tensing and raising of short *a* in the metropolitan area of New York City. Unpublished Master's essay. Columbia University.

Cook, S. 1969. Language change and the emergence of an urban dialect in Utah. Unpublished dissertation, University of Utah.

Eckert, P. 1969. Grammatical constraints in phonological change: the unstressed vowels of Southern France. Unpublished Master's essay,
Columbia University.

Elliot, D., S. Legum, and S. Thompson. 1969. Syntactic variation as linguistic
data. In R. Binnick et al. (eds.), *Papers from The Fifth Chicago
Regional Meeting.* Chicago: University of Chicago Department of
Linguistics.

Enderlin, D. 1913. Die Mundart von Kesswil im Oberthurgau. *In* A. Bachman,
ed., *Beiträge zur Schweizer-Deutschen Grammatik.* Frauenfeld:
Huber and Co.

Ervin-Tripp, S. 1967. *Sociolinguistics.* Working paper No. 3, Language Behavior Research Laboratory, Berkeley, Cal.

Ferguson, C. A., and J. J. Gumperz. 1960. *Linguistic diversity in South Asia.*
Publication of the Research Center in Anthropology, Folklore, and
Linguistics, No. 13. Bloomington: Indiana University Press.

Fischer, J. L. 1958. Social influences on the choice of a linguistic variant.
*Word* 14:47–56.

Fishman, J., ed. 1968. *Readings in the sociology of language.* The Hague:
Mouton.

————. 1969. Sociolinguistics. *In* K. W. Back, ed., *Social psychology.* New
York: Wiley.

————, R. L. Cooper, R. Ma, et al. 1968. *Bilingualism in the barrio.* Final
report on OECD-1-7-062817. Washington, D.C.: Office of Education.

Fodor, J., and J. Katz, eds. 1964. *The structure of language.* Englewood Cliffs,
N.J.: Prentice-Hall.

Frank, Y. A. 1948. The speech of New York City. Unpublished dissertation,
University of Michigan, Ann Arbor.

Garfinckel, H. 1967. *Studies in ethnomethodology.* Englewood Cliffs, N.J.:
Prentice-Hall.

Garvin, P., and M. Mathiot. 1960. The urbanization of the Guarani language.
*In* A. F. C. Wallace, ed., *Men and cultures.* Philadelphia: University
of Pennsylvania Press.

Gauchat, L. 1905. L'Unité phonetique dans le patois d'une commune, In *Aus
Romanischen Sprachen und Literaturen: Festschrift Heinrich Mort,*
pp. 175–232. Halle: Max Niemeyer.

————, J. Jeanjaquet, and E. Tappolet. 1925. *Tableaux phonétiques des
patois suisses romands.* Neuchâtel: Paul Attinger.

Grant, W., and J. Dixon. 1921. *Manual of modern Scots*. London; Cambridge University Press.

Greenberg, J. H. 1959. Language and evolution. *In Evolution and anthropology: a centennial appraisal*. Washington, D.C.: The Anthropological Society of Washington.

———, ed. 1963. *Universals of language*. Cambridge, Mass: MIT Press.

Grimshaw, A. D. 1968. Sociolinguistics. *In* W. Schramm et al., eds., *Handbook of communication*. New York: Rand McNally.

Grinder, I., and P. Postal. 1971. Missing antecedents. *Linguistic Inquiry* 2:209–312.

Gumperz, J. J. 1964. Linguistic and social interaction in two communities. *In* Gumperz and Hymes 1964.

———. 1967. On the linguistic markers of bilingual communication. In Macnamara 1967.

———. 1971. Language contact or pidginization. *In* Hymes 1971.

———, and D. Hymes. 1964. *The ethnography of communication*. Special issue of *American Anthropologist* 66(6.2).

Hafner, E. M., and S. Presswood. 1965. Strong inference and weak interactions. *Science* 149:503–9.

Halle, M. 1962. Phonology in generative grammar. *Word* 18:67–72.

Harris, Z. 1951. *Structural linguistics*. Chicago: University of Chicago Press.

Hermann, M. E. 1929. Lautveränderungen in der Individualsprache einer Mundart. *Nachrichten der Gesellschaft der Wissenschaften zu Göttingen, Philosophisch-historische Klasse* 11:195–214.

Herzog, M. I. 1965. *The Yiddish language in Northern Poland: its geography and history*. Publication of the Research Center in Anthropology, Folklore, and Linguistics, No. 37. Bloomington: Indiana University Press.

Hockett, C. F. 1950. Age-grading and linguistic continuity. *Language* 26:449–57.

———. 1958. *A course in modern linguistics*. New York: Macmillan.

Hoenigswald, H. 1963. Are there universals in linguistic change? *In* Greenberg 1963.

Homans, G. C. 1955. *The human group*. New York: Harcourt, Brace.

Hubbell, A. F. 1950. *The pronunciation of English in New York City.* New York: Columbia University Press.

Hymes, D. 1961. Functions of speech: an evolutionary approach. *In* F. C. Gruber, ed., *Anthropology and education.* Philadelphia: University of Pennsylvania Press.

———. 1962. The ethnography of speaking. *In* T. Gladwin and W. C. Sturtevant, eds., *Anthropology and human behavior.* Washington, D.C. Anthropological Society of Washington.

———. 1964. Introduction. *In* Gumperz and Hymes 1964.

———, ed. 1971. *Pidginization and creolization of languages.* London: Cambridge University Press.

Jespersen, O. 1927. *A modern English grammar on historical principles,* I. London: George Allen.

———. 1946. *Mankind, nation, and individual from a linguistic point of view.* Bloomington: Indiana University Press.

Joos, M. 1959. The isolation of styles. *Georgetown University Monograph Series on Languages and Linguistics* 12:107–13.

Kazazis, K. 1969. The relative importance of parents and peers in first-language learning. Paper given before the Linguistic Society of America, San Francisco, December.

Kihlbom, A. 1926. *A contribution to the study of fifteenth-century English.* Uppsala: Lundequistska.

Kiparsky, P. 1968. How abstract is phonology? Mimeo. Bloomington, Ind.: Indiana University Linguistics Club.

Klima, E. S. 1964. Negation in English. *In* Fodor and Katz 1964.

Kökeritz, H. 1953. *Shakespeare's pronunciation.* New Haven: Yale University Press.

Kučera, H. 1961. *The phonology of Czech.* The Hague: Mouton.

Kurath, H. 1939. *Handbook of the linguistic geography of New England.* Providence, R. I.: American Council of Learned Societies.

———. 1949. *A word geography of the eastern United States.* Ann Arbor: University of Michigan Press.

———, et al. 1941. *Linguistic atlas of New England.* Providence, R.I.: American Council of Learned Societies.

————, and R. McDavid. 1951. *The pronunciation of English in the Atlantic states.* Ann Arbor: University of Michigan Press.

Kuryłowicz, J. 1964. On the methods of internal reconstruction. *In* H. G. Lunt, ed., *Proceedings of the Ninth International Congress of Linguistics.* The Hague: Mouton.

Labov, W. 1964a. Phonological indices to social stratification. *In* Gumperz and Hymes 1964.

————. 1964b. The linguistic variable as a structural unit. Paper given before the Linguistics Club of Washington, D.C., October. *Washington Linguistics Review* 3:4–22 (1966).

————. 1966a. *The social stratification of English in New York City.* Washington, D.C.: Center for Applied Linguistics.

————. 1966b. On the grammaticality of everyday speech. Paper given before the Linguistic Society of America, New York City.

————. 1969. Contraction, deletion, and inherent variability of the English copula. *Language* 45:715–62.

————. 1972a. *Language in the inner city: studies in the black English vernacular.* Philadelphia: University of Pennsylvania Press.

————. 1972b. The recent history of some dialect markers on the island of Martha's Vineyard. *In* L. Davis, ed., *Studies presented to Raven McDavid.* University, Ala.: University of Alabama Press.

————. 1972c. The internal evolution of linguistic rules. *In* R. Stockwell and R. Macaulay, eds., *Historical linguistics and generative theory.* Bloomington: Indiana University Press.

————, P. Cohen, C. Robins, and J. Lewis. 1968. A study of the non-standard English of Negro and Puerto Rican speakers in New York City. Final report, Cooperative Research Project 3288. 2 vols. Philadelphia, Pa.: U.S. Regional Survey, 204 N. 35th St., Philadelphia 19104.

————, and P. Pedraza. 1971. *A study of the Puerto Rican speech community in New York City.* Report to the Urban Center of Columbia University.

————, and B. Wald. 1969. Some general principles of vowel shifting. Paper given before the Linguistic Society of America, San Francisco, December.

————, M. Yaeger, and R. Steiner. 1972. *A quantitative study of sound change in progress.* Final report on National Science Foundation contract NSF-GS-3287. Philadelphia, Pa.: U.S. Regional Survey, 204 N. 35th St., Philadelphia 19104.

Laffal, J. 1965. *Pathological and normal language.* New York: Atherton Press.

Lakoff, R. 1971. Language in context. Mimeo.

Lambert, W. E. 1967. A social psychology of bilingualism. *In* Macnamara 1967.

————. 1969. Some current psycholinguistic research: the Tu-Vous and Le-La studies. *In* Puhvel, J., ed., *Substance and structure of language.* Berkeley: University of California Press.

————, M. Anisfeld, and G. Yeni-Komshian. 1965. Evaluational reactions of Jewish and Arab adolescents to dialect and language variations. *Journal of Personality and Social Psychology* 3:313–20.

————, et al. 1960. Evaluation reactions to spoken languages. *Journal of Abnormal and Social Psychology* 60:44–51.

Lawton, D. 1968. *Social class, language, and education.* London: Routledge and Kegan Paul.

Legum, S., C. Pfaff, G. Tinnie, and M. Nicholas. 1971. *The speech of young black children in Los Angeles.* Technical Report No. 33. Los Angeles: Southwestern Regional Laboratory.

Lehmann, W. P. 1963. *Historical linguistics: an introduction.* New York: Holt, Rinehart and Winston.

————, and Y. Malkiel, eds. 1968. *Directions for historical linguistics.* Austin: University of Texas Press.

Levine, L., and H. J. Crockett, Jr. 1966. Speech variation in a piedmont community: postvocalic r. *In* Lieberson 1966.

Lévi-Strauss, C. 1963. *Structural anthropology.* Tr. C. Jacobson and B. Schoepf. New York: Basic Books.

Lieberson, S., ed. 1966. *Explorations in sociolinguistics.* Special issue of *Sociological Inquiry* 36(2).

Loman, B. 1967. *Conversations in a Negro American dialect.* Washington, D.C.: Center for Applied Linguistics.

Lyons, J. 1968. *Introduction to theoretical linguistics.* London: Cambridge University Press.

Macnamara, J. 1967. *Problems of bilingualism.* Special issue of *The Journal of Social Issues* 23(2).

Mahl, G. 1972. People talking when they can't hear their voices. *In* A. Siegman and B. Pope, eds., *Studies in dyadic communication.* New York: Pergamon Press.

Malkiel, Y. 1967. Each word has a history of its own. *Glossa* 1:2.

Martinet, A. 1955. *Economie des changements phonétiques.* Berne: Francke.

―――. 1964a. *Elements of general linguistics.* Tr. S. Palmer. Chicago: University of Chicago Press.

―――. 1964b. Structural variation in language. *In* H. G. Lunt, ed., *Proceedings of the Ninth International Congress of Linguistics.* The Hague: Mouton.

Meillet, A. 1921. *Linguistique historique et linguistique générale.* Paris: La Société linguistique de Paris.

Mitchell-Kernan, C. 1969. *Language behavior in a black urban community.* Working paper No. 23, Language Behavior Research Laboratory, Berkeley, Cal.

Moulton, W. G. 1962. Dialect geography and the concept of phonological space. *Word* 18:23–32.

Norman, R. 1971. An ear to New York. Unpublished manuscript.

Nottebohm, F. 1970. Vocal imitation and individual recognition of finch calls. *Science* 168:480–82.

Paul, H. 1889. *Principles of the history of language.* Tr. H. A. Strong. New York: Macmillan.

Peterson, G. E., and H. L. Barney. 1952. Control methods used in a study of the vowels. *Journal of the Acoustical Society of America* 24:175–84.

Pilch, H. 1955. The rise of the American English vowel pattern. *Word* 11:57–63.

Postal, P. 1964. Constituent structure: a study of contemporary models of syntactic description. *Internal Journal of American Linguistics,* Publication 30.

Postal, P. 1971. Cross-over phenomenon. In *Specification and utilization of a transformational grammar.* Scientific report No. 3. Yorktown Heights, N.Y.: IBM (published by Holt, Rinehart, and Winston, New York).

Preston, M. S. 1963. Evaluational reactions to English, Canadian French and European French voices. Unpublished Master's thesis, McGill University.

Quirk, R. 1966. Acceptability in language. *Proceedings of the University of Newcastle upon Tyne Philosophical Society* 1:79–92.

Reich, P. 1969. On the finiteness of natural language. *Language* 45.

Reichstein, R. 1960. Study of social and geographic variation of linguistic behavior. *Word* 16:55.

Sacks, H. 1972. An initial investigation of the usability of conversational data for doing sociology. In Sudnow 1972.

Sankoff, G. 1972. A quantitative paradigm for the study of communicative competence. Paper given at Conference on the Ethnography of Speaking, Austin, Tex.

————, and H. Cedergren. 1971. Some results of a sociolinguistic study of Montreal French. In R. Darnell, ed., *Linguistic diversity in Canadian society*. Champaign, Ill.: Linguistic Research, Inc.

————, R. Sarrasin, and H. Cedergren. 1971. Quelques considérations sur la distribution sociolinguistique de la variable QUE dans le français de Montréal. Paper given at the 39th Congress, Association canadienne-française pour l'avancement des sciences.

Saussure, F. de. 1962. *Cours de linguistique générale*. Paris: Payot.

Schegloff, E. 1968. Sequencing in conversational openings. *American Anthropologist* 70:1075-95.

Shewmake, E. F. 1927. *English pronunciation in Virginia*. Davidson, N.C.

Shuy, R., W. Wolfram, and W. K. Riley. 1967. *A study of social dialects in Detroit*. Final report, Project 6-1347. Washington, D.C.: Office of Education.

Solomon, D. 1966. The system of predication in the speech of Trinidad. Unpublished Master's essay, Columbia University.

Sommerfelt, Alf. 1930. Sur la propagation de changements phonétiques. *Norsk Tidsskrift for Sprogvidenskap* 4:76-128.

Sturtevant, E. 1947. *An introduction to linguistic science*. New Haven: Yale University Press.

Sudnow, D., ed. 1972. *Studies in social interaction*. New York: Macmillan.

Sweet, Henry. 1900. *The history of language*. London: J. M. Dent.

Tarde, Gabriel. 1873. *Les lois d'imitation*.

Trager, G. L. 1930. The pronunciation of 'short *a*' in American Standard English. *American Speech* 5:396-400.

————. 1934. What conditions limit variants of a phoneme? *American Speech* 9:313-15.

————. 1940. One phonemic entity becomes two: the case of 'short *a*'. *American Speech* 15:255-58.

Troubetzkoy, N. 1957. *Principes de phonologie*. Tr. J. Cantineau. 2nd ed. Paris: Klincksieck.

Trudgill, P. J. 1971. The social differentiation of English in Norwich. Unpublished dissertation, Edinburgh University.

Tucker, G. R., and W. E. Lambert. 1966. White and Negro listeners' reactions to various American English dialects. Mimeo.

Vendryes, J. 1951. *Language: a linguistic introduction to history*. Tr. Paul Raden. New York: Barnes & Noble.

Vygotsky, L. S. 1962. *Thought and language*. Tr. E. Hanfmann and G. Vakar. Cambridge, Mass.: MIT Press.

Walker, John. 1791. *Principles of English pronunciation*.

Wang, W. S.-Y. 1969. Competing changes as a cause of residue. *Language* 45:9–25.

Watson, J. D. 1969. *The double helix*. New York: New American Library.

Webb, Eugene J., et al. *Unobtrusive measures: non-reactive research in the social sciences*. Chicago: Rand McNally.

Weinberg, M., and M. Najt. 1968. Los pronombres de tratamiento en el espanol de Bahia Blanca. *In Actas de la Quinta Asemblea Interuniversitaria de Filologia y Literaturas Hispanicas*.

Weinreich, U. 1954. Is a structural dialectology possible? *Word* 10:388–400.

————. 1959. Review of Hockett, *Modern Linguistics*. *Romance Philology* 13:329–39.

————, W. Labov, and M. Herzog. 1968. Empirical foundations for a theory of language change. *In* Lehmann and Malkiel 1968.

Whitney, W. D. 1901. *Language and the study of language*. New York: Scribner's.

Whorf, B. L. 1943. Phonemic analysis of the English of eastern Massachusetts. *Studies in Linguistics* 2:21–40.

Wolfram, W. 1969. Linguistic correlates of social stratification in the speech of Detroit Negroes. Unpublished thesis, Hartford Seminary Foundation.

Wyld, H. C. 1920. *A history of modern colloquial English*. Oxford: Basil Blackwell.

Zwicky, A. 1970. Auxiliary reduction in English. *Linguistic Inquiry* 1:323–36.

# INDEX

Abraham G.: stylistic array for, 102
Accountability principle, 72
Adolescence: crucial period for language development, 138–39. See also Child; Peer group
Age: and pronunciation, 17, 57, 59–60, 64–65, 105, 106, 116; and centralization on Martha's Vineyard, 21, 24, 30, 166–67; and linguistic change, 134–36, 178, 291–92; and lower middle class speech patterns, 117; and acquisition of community speech norms, 138–40; in subjective reaction tests, 150–56; concept of apparent time, 163; and socio-linguistic variables, 240
*ah*: and (oh) in New York City, 175
American English: Martha's Vineyard a relic area, 6–7; centralized diphthongs in, 10–11; (r)-pronunciation, 141, 145, 287n, 290–92; *o*-pronunciation, 292; changes in western US, 309; speech stereotypes, 314–15. See also Black English vernacular; Broadcasting media; Martha's Vineyard; New York City; Southern speech patterns
American Language Survey, 80n
Analogy: in language, 1, 274
Anecdote, 268, 270
*anymore,* 309
Arrays: for stylistic variation, 99–107
Articulation, 23, 40, 164, 165
Audio-monitoring, 138, 179, 208, 213, 246
Austin, Texas, 68n, 238n
(aw): history of, 1, 10–11; Martha's Vineyard form, 9; parallelism with (ay), 24–25; example of change from below, 180; in Salt Lake City, 281, 309; in New York City, 287–90; mentioned, 279. See also Centralization; Diphthongs, centralized; Martha's Vineyard
(ay): history of, 1, 10–11; Martha's Vineyard form, 9; parallelism with (aw), 24–25; in New York City, 287–90; men-

tioned, 279. See also Centralization; Diphthongs, centralized; Martha's Vineyard

*belly-gut,* 7
Bengali, 296
Bennie N.: stylistic array for, 106
Bilingualism: Spanish-English, 205–6; in study of languages, 214–215; French-English, 310–11; mentioned, 324
Biological evolution, and language. See Evolution, biological
Bird song: evolutionary analogy, 324–25
Black English vernacular: characterized, 189–90; 223, 299; repetition tests, 212; consonant cluster simplification, 216–26; sources used in study, 216; deletion of copula, 226–30; negative concord, 234–37; 323
Blacks: and Indians on Martha's Vineyard, 35; and New York City speech patterns, 54, 118–19; 157, 318–19; and process of sound change, 172n
Bloomfield, L.: on linguistic change, xiv, 22, 262, 266
Borrowing, 1, 23, 308
Boston: speech stereotypes, 248
Breathing: as channel cue, 95
Broadcasting media: pronunciation of (r), 138, 290; effect on American English, 180n, 317; as source of linguistic data, 211

Canadian English, 10n
Canadian French, 206, 232, 241, 249, 310, 311
Cape Cod, 10
Cape Hatteras, 248
Celtic, 265
Centralization: of diphthongs on Martha's Vineyard, 9–26, 39–42, 165–71. See also Diphthongs, centralized

337